Professional
Python® Frameworks
Web 2.0 Programming with Django®
and TurboGears™

Professional
Python® Frameworks
Web 2.0 Programming with
Django® and TurboGears™

Professional
Python® Frameworks
Web 2.0 Programming with Django®
and TurboGears™

Dana Moore

Raymond Budd

William Wright

Wiley Publishing, Inc.

Professional Python® Frameworks: Web 2.0 Programming Django® and TurboGears™

Published by
Wiley Publishing, Inc.
10475 Crosspoint Boulevard
Indianapolis, IN 46256
www.wiley.com

Published simultaneously in Canada

ISBN-13: 978-0-470-13809-0

Manufactured in the United States of America

10 9 8 7 6 5 4 3 2 1

Library of Congress Cataloging-in-Publication Data

Moore, Dana, 1947-
  Professional Python frameworks : Web 2.0 programming with Django and Turbogears / Dana Moore,
Raymond Budd, William Wright.
       p. cm.
  Includes index.
  ISBN 978-0-470-13809-0 (pbk.)
  1. Web site development. 2. Python (Computer program language) I. Budd, Raymond, 1976- II. Wright, William,
1964- III. Title.
  TK5105.888.M663 2007
  006.7'6—dc22

                                                                                        2007032138

For Jane, who, in our 35 years of love, has encouraged in me the belief that I can reach for and attain higher goals than I could ever imagine. And for my cherished daughter Caitlin, who is for me both luminous and a conductor of light; both possessing genius and having the power to stimulate it in others.

—DM

For Leah. You continually amaze me with your thoughtfulness, unwavering support, and above all your remarkable ability to make me laugh and smile. Also for my sisters, who have helped me out so many different times in so many different ways.

—RB

For my two favorite girls, Karan and Annette. Your encouragement and inspiration make all things seem possible.

—WW

About the Authors

Dana Moore is a division scientist with BBN Technologies and is an acknowledged expert in the fields of peer-to-peer and collaborative computing, software agent frameworks, and assistive environments. Prior to joining BBN, Dana was chief scientist for Roku Technologies and a distinguished member of technical staff at Bell Laboratories. Dana is a popular conference speaker and a university lecturer. He has written articles for numerous computing publications and coauthored the books *Peer-to-Peer: Building Secure, Scalable, and Manageable Networks*; *Jabber Developer's Handbook*; and *Rich Internet Applications*. Dana holds a Master of Science degree from the University of Maryland and a Bachelor of Science degree in industrial design, also from the University of Maryland.

Raymond Budd is a software engineer with BBN Technologies. He has designed, developed, and supported a variety of web applications and other distributed systems in Java, Ruby, and Python. He has been published in several conference proceedings such as the *Eighteenth National Conference on Artificial Intelligence* and journals including *Applied Intelligence*. Additional areas of interest include knowledge representations, knowledge engineering, and distributed planning and scheduling. He received a Bachelor of Science degree in computer science from the University of Pittsburgh.

William Wright is a senior principal investigator with SPARTA, where he develops networking software for systems distributed across the globe. His interests include real-time embedded systems, software architecture for reuse, and software agent frameworks. A frequent conference speaker, William has also written for *Dr. Dobb's Journal*, *Java Developer's Journal*, and *Embedded Systems Programming*, among others. He coauthored the books *Jabber Developer's Handbook* and *Beginning Java Networking*. William holds a Master of Science degree in computer science from George Mason University and a Bachelor of Music degree in education from Indiana University.

Credits

Acquisitions Editor
Jenny Watson

Development Editor
Maureen Spears

Production Editor
Elizabeth Ginns Britten

Copy Editor
Kathryn Duggan

Editorial Manager
Mary Beth Wakefield

Production Manager
Tim Tate

Vice President and Executive Group Publisher
Richard Swadley

Vice President and Executive Publisher
Joseph B. Wikert

Project Coordinator
Adrienne Martinez

Proofreader
Candace English

Indexer
Jack Lewis

Anniversary Logo Design
Richard Pacifico

Acknowledgments

The authors wish to thank the industry leaders who shared their thoughts with us in interviews. We thank Kevin Dangoor, creator of TurboGears, for sharing his insights on the design and development of Web 2.0 applications and the evolution of web application tools. We also appreciate the insights of Adrian Holovaty, leader of the Django project, whose thoughts on high-level languages for web applications show where we've been and where we're going.

We express our thanks to Edward Benson for his help managing the source code for this book. Thanks also to Patrick Pinkowski for his assistance with the cover photo. We are especially grateful for the efforts of Maureen Spears, our development editor at Wiley. Her combination of high standards and encouragement made the development of this book a joy.

Finally, and most importantly, we thank our friends, families, and significant others for their forbearance. Writing is a solitary activity that tends to exclude others, even those most important to us, and we appreciate all their support and promise to somehow make up for the lost time and opportunities.

Contents

Contents

Contents

Contents

Contents

Introduction

We Python developers have always been a proud lot, able to create desktop solutions with a variety of user experience libraries, ranging from GTK to PythonCard to WxPython. We Pythonists have always prided ourselves in being the best example of an end-to-end, batteries-included delivery system that could create anything imaginable for the desktop user. Even in the early days of the Web, Pythonistas led the way with Zope, and later Twisted.

Imagine the surprise of many of us when Ruby on Rails appeared suddenly and seemed to suck all the air out of the room when the topic of Web 2.0 frameworks was discussed. Python's rarely challenged position of agile-language king of the desktop hardly mattered anymore.

Most Python developers had become accustomed to having a common set of rich client APIs for Windows, MAC OS X, and Linux. Thus, many Pythonists, although familiar with the Rich Client Platform (RCP) model, were suddenly in the uncomfortable and unfamiliar position of having fallen behind in the emerging Web 2.0 world.

Now this status quo has changed, and there are two strong end-to-end frameworks (Django and Turbo-Gears) available for the Python Web 2.0 developer. Even if you haven't had exposure to the buzzwords or development model for Web 2.0 applications, this book will help you along that path. AJAX (Asynchronous JavaScript and XML), for example, is a hugely important element of the Web 2.0 interaction model, and it is well covered and explained in examining both Django and TurboGears.

In addition, there's now growing recognition, even in the most stolid of enterprises, of an important shift in customer demand that promises to change the very foundations of how we develop and deploy applications. Customers are now specifying Web 2.0 capabilities in new applications development and even in retrofitting current applications to this new model, and the Web itself is undergoing a shift from a collection of news articles, static forms, and bulletin boards to a virtual application-hosting platform in and of itself.

This book is right at the front of this trend for Python developers. Together, we will explore the elements of this change in browser-based applications—from greater dynamism and responsiveness to faster development cycles to greater embrace of social networking. In this book, the objective is to prepare both the corporate and the independent developer to take advantage of this new emerging landscape. As the world of shrink-wrapped boxes of client-side software begins to wane, a new ecology of Rich Internet Applications (RIAs) is emerging to bring both developers and end users new benefits that take full advantage of today's connected world. Python developers who can reap the benefits of this new ecology will prosper and stay at the front of their professional ranks.

Who Is This Book For?

This book is for people who are (or want to be) professional web application developers. In this book, you'll see how to take advantage of the latest technology to create compelling web applications, and create them *fast*. All of the techniques and technologies you'll see in this book are designed to help you get a professional website up quickly, without creating an unmaintainable pile of spaghetti code.

We do assume that you know at least a little Python. If you're not already on the Python bandwagon, maybe the tools and techniques in this book can convince you to hop on. Python is a very readable language and there are tons of good tutorials and references in print and on the Web to help you get up to speed.

What Is This Book's Focus?

Like our readers, the authors are all professional corporate software developers who use agile languages such as Python and Ruby with Web 2.0 techniques to deliver network-based applications to real customers, both commercial and government. We know that the quickest road to understanding code and APIs is to review working code examples, but often books consist of a stream of simple didactic examples. Although this approach may reveal important points of a topic, it ultimately leaves you unfulfilled because the examples don't build anything more compelling outside the context of the point the author is trying to make. This book builds an interesting and feature-complete application in each of three paradigms (Django, TurboGears, and Flash/Flex2-fronting TurboGears) as a unifying theme holding the book together and to give you points of comparison for multiple Python-based solutions to the same problem.

Leveraging the Rest of the Book: The Roadmap

As mentioned back at the beginning of this introduction, this book was written by and for developers. We developers (you included) are a simple tribe. Give us some fun examples to work with and we'll figure out everything we need for working through them. So that's the goal for the book—to cover the important topics in Web 2.0 and show you how to achieve results using a combination of Python and modern frameworks.

Part I: Introduction to Python Frameworks

In Chapter 1, "Web 2.0, Python, and Frameworks," you'll have a whirlwind history lesson about application development from the desktop to the Web 2.0 era. You'll see how the need for web frameworks evolved and how some of the early responses (think J2EE) failed for most developers. You'll have a brief introduction to the set of tools used later in the book, including AJAX, domain-specific languages (DSLs), Python, TurboGears, Django, JavaScript, and so on. At the end of this chapter, you'll understand how they are not just the new thing, but a fundamentally different and better thing.

In Chapter 2, "Web 2.0 with Traditional Python," you'll see an example of Web 2.0 created without using any frameworks at all. That will help to reinforce the notion that you can use normal Python libraries to write perfectly good Web 2.0 applications. This chapter offers a tutorial web application that demonstrates this point. All the hallmark features of a modern Web 2.0 application, including AJAX interaction and XMLHttpRequest (XHR) handling using a combination of Python CGI scripting on the server and JavaScript on the browser, will be shown. From the example application, you'll be able to understand that the skills you already have can produce Web 2.0 applications that are as compelling as those produced by advanced frameworks.

However, after you finish Chapter 3, "Introducing the Frameworks," chances are good you will never want to return to writing modern RIAs the painful old-school way. You'll be introduced to an easier way to combine Python with frameworks to write Web 2.0 applications, and get initial exposure to both frameworks covered by the book. After this chapter, you will have a much greater appreciation of why frameworks are important, why they are likely to save major time and frustration in the development cycle, and what characterizes a framework. The differences in creating an application using only the techniques explained in Chapter 2 versus using the frameworks approach should be much clearer by the end of this chapter. The chapter ends with an engaging interview with Kevin Dangoor, creator of TurboGears, who has clarity of vision and appreciation for the Zen of Python that all Pythonistas will appreciate.

Part II: TurboGears

Chapter 4 ("Introduction to TurboGears") begins Part II, which features the in-depth exploration of TurboGears, perhaps the most complete development tool suite available to the Python developer. This chapter shows a sophisticated and complete (yet accessible) application delivered in TurboGears. The chapter also introduces the concept of HTML templates and template engines, as well as client-side AJAX scripting and data model handling on the server side.

In Chapter 5 ("User Identity and Visitor Tracking"), you learn about the crucial issues surrounding user-level security and other user-management issues and the TurboGears library support for user management. This chapter also examines how you can use the visitor tracking components of TurboGears to capture statistics about the logged-in and anonymous users that visit your site.

In Chapter 6 ("Widgets") you explore the details of TurboGears widgets as you implement your own widget and use it throughout an example application. A widget is a key component in TurboGears that bundles HTML, JavaScript, and Cascading Style Sheets (CSS) to provide all aspects of a single slice of functionality.

Chapter 7 ("Advanced TurboGears Topics") covers important TurboGears functionality that hasn't been covered in the previous chapters. This chapter is dedicated to presenting all the *other things* you need to know when working with TurboGears—the things that you encounter quickly after departing the familiar terrain of pages and single-table models.

Part III: Django

Chapter 8 ("Dblog: A Blog Implemented in Django") begins the in-depth coverage of Django by revisiting the familiar ground of Chapter 4, except this time in Django instead of TurboGears. This chapter shows you how Django automates the production of common web development tasks so that you (the developer) can concentrate on higher-level application issues instead of low-level handling of data. Specifically, you'll see how Django supports MVC separation of concerns in a way that's different than TurboGears.

Chapter 9 ("Django Views and Users") again covers familiar ground but also points out the differences in implementation detail. In this chapter, you'll see how to leverage Django's generic views to make common tasks simple. You'll also see how Django's built-in user management functions can help you manage user permissions and identities.

Chapter 10 ("Advanced Django Topics: AJAX, RSS, and More") shows you some of Django's unique strengths with its roots in content management. You'll see how to serve RSS feeds and AJAX-enabled applications, too. As a bonus, this chapter includes an interview with Adrian Holovaty, the original lead developer of Django.

Part IV: Advanced Client-Side Topics

JavaScript is a necessary evil in most AJAX applications, but in Chapter 11 ("MochiKit—Pythonic JavaScripting") you'll see how to use the most Pythonic JavaScript toolkit to make the process less painful.

Chapter 12 ("Flash-Based Interfaces and TurboGears") presents an exciting pairing of technologies, TurboGears and Macromedia's Flash SDK. Although Flex is not *itself* open source, all modern browsers build in the capability to host Flash, and a large number of widget sets have been developed that do not require a developer investment in Macromedia's integrated development environments (IDEs). Using Flash opens an additional layer of possibilities for professional developers. This chapter covers two open source strategies that enable developers to roll out Flash-based applications. The Flex2 platform is not open source, but it is free for development and deployment, and is at the core of many new applications. ActionScript is an open source wrapper class library that provides a full set of desktop-style widgets rivaling those provided in client operating systems.

What You Need to Run the Examples

Don't get out your checkbook—all of the software you need to run the examples in this book is open source or free. The specific instructions for downloading, installing, and configuring each tool are in Appendix A. As you move into a production environment, you may want to incorporate commercial software as your database or web server, but you don't need any commercial software to run the code in this book. You can find the latest copy of the code on Wiley Publishing's Wrox site (www.wrox.com).

Conventions

To help you get the most from the text and keep track of what's happening, we've used a number of conventions throughout the book.

Code has several styles. If we're talking about code within the text (such as helloForm), it appears in this font.

In code examples we highlight new and important code with a gray background.

The gray highlighting is not used for code that's less important in the present context, or has been shown before.

Note that most long blocks of code include listing numbers and titles, as shown in the following example. Most of these listings contain code that have numbered lines so that the authors can more easily refer to specific lines and listings during the discussions that generally follow the code block.

Listing 2-1: Simple XML Example

```
 1   <?xml version='1.0' encoding='ISO-8859-1'?>
 2   <top>
 3     Text within the "top" element.
 4     <sub1 attrib="anAttribute">
 5       Text within the first "sub1" element.
 6     </sub1>
 7     <sub1 another_attrib="secondAttribute">
 8       Text within the second "sub1" element.
 9       <subsub1>
10         Text in < brackets >
11       </subsub1>
12     </sub1>
13     <sub2/>
14   </top>
```

Sometimes you see a mixture of styles. For example, if certain sections of code are changed and are being discussed, they are presented in bold as shown in the following example.

Listing 2-10: PetOwner.py

```
1    ####################################################
2    # A simple class to hold a petowner's name and
3    # a list of pets
4    ####################################################
5    class PetOwner:
6        def __init__(self, firstname, lastname, pets):
7            self.firstname = firstname
8            self.lastname = lastname
9            self.pets = pets
10
11       def __str__(self):
12           ret = self.firstname+" "+self.lastname+\
13                            " has %d pets named"%len(self.pets)
14           for p in self.pets:
15               ret = ret + " " + p
16
17           return ret
```

Here are some other styles used in the text:

❑   New terms and important words are *italicized* when first introduced.

❑   Command, class, object, module, path, directory, file, and view names within text are formatted in `this font`. Example URLs also use `this font`.

❑   URLs for active sites are formatted in `this font`.

❑   A break in a line of code is indicated with the ↩ symbol.

Source Code

As you work through the examples in this book, you may choose either to type in all the code manually or to use the source code files that accompany the book. All of the source code used in this book is available for download at `www.wrox.com`. When you get to the site, simply locate the book's title (either by using the Search box or by using one of the title lists) and click the Download Code link on the book's detail page to obtain all the source code for the book.

> *Because many books have similar titles, you may find it easiest to search by ISBN. This book's ISBN is 978-0-40-13809-0.*

Once you download the code, just decompress it with your favorite compression tool. Alternately, you can go to the main Wrox code download page at `www.wrox.com/dynamic/books/download.aspx` to see the code available for this book and all other Wrox books.

Errata

We make every effort to ensure that there are no errors in the text or in the code. However, no one is perfect, and mistakes do occur. If you find an error in one of our books, like a spelling mistake or faulty piece of code, we would be very grateful for your feedback. By sending in errata, you may save another reader hours of frustration and, at the same time, you will be helping us provide even higher-quality information.

To find the errata page for this book, go to www.wrox.com and locate the title using the Search box or one of the title lists. Then, on the book details page, click the Book Errata link. On this page, you can view all errata that has been submitted for this book and posted by Wrox editors. A complete book list, including links to each book's errata, is also available at www.wrox.com/misc-pages/booklist.shtml.

If you don't spot your error on the Book Errata page, go to www.wrox.com/contact/techsupport .shtml and complete the form there to send us the error you have found. We'll check the information and, if appropriate, post a message to the book's errata page and fix the problem in subsequent editions of the book.

p2p.wrox.com

For author and peer discussion, join the P2P forums at p2p.wrox.com. The forums are a web-based system for you to post messages relating to Wrox books and related technologies and interact with other readers and technology users. The forums offer a subscription feature to e-mail you topics of interest of your choosing when new posts are made to the forums. Wrox authors, editors, other industry experts, and your fellow readers are present on these forums.

At p2p.wrox.com, you will find a number of different forums that will help you not only as you read this book, but also as you develop your own applications. To join the forums, just follow these steps:

1. Go to p2p.wrox.com and click the Register link.

2. Read the terms of use and click Agree.

3. Complete the required information to join as well as any optional information you wish to provide, and click Submit.

4. You will receive an e-mail with information describing how to verify your account and complete the joining process.

You can read messages in the forums without joining P2P, but in order to post your own messages, you must join.

Once you join, you can post new messages and respond to messages other users post. You can read messages at any time on the Web. If you would like to have new messages from a particular forum e-mailed to you, click the Subscribe to this Forum icon by the forum name in the forum listing.

For more information about how to use the Wrox P2P, be sure to read the P2P FAQs for answers to questions about how the forum software works as well as many common questions specific to P2P and Wrox books. To read the FAQs, click the FAQ link on any P2P page.

Let Us Know What You Think

We hope you find the material in this book as useful as we do. We believe that the power of Python for web frameworks is revolutionizing web development. We've tried to put together examples and explanations that make this clear and engaging. Please let us know if we've succeeded.

Dana Moore (dana.virtual@gmail.com)

Raymond Budd (ray.budd@gmail.com)

William Wright (billwright1234@gmail.com)

Professional
Python® Frameworks
Web 2.0 Programming with
Django® and TurboGears™

Part I
Introduction to Python Frameworks

Web 2.0, Python, and Frameworks

You had me at "Hello."

—**Renée Zellweger in** *Jerry Maguire*

The authors know you. Or at least they know a few things about you. If you've grabbed this book from your favorite online (or even brick-and-mortar) bookseller, chances are that you're an accomplished Python developer, or you're on your way to becoming one. You may well have created web content using your Python skills, or perhaps you've written your share of web services backed by Python code as a Common Gateway Interface (CGI) script. You may have just heard the term "Web 2.0" or "AJAX," or you may already be an accomplished user of one or many Web 2.0 sites and are wondering how to plug into the action as a developer. You may be aware of web frameworks in other languages, such as Ruby on Rails (also referred to simply as Rails) or Google Widget Toolkit (GWT), and you may even have experimented with one or more them. If you've been unable to embrace any of these other frameworks, it may be because they have one annoying aspect — they're not Python. Actually, if you've worked with other frameworks, the fact that they don't follow the Python philosophy (they're not *Pythonic*) may be the least of your negative impressions.

The good news is that now you don't have to abandon the language that you love to get the (admittedly significant) benefits of a comprehensive framework. The Python-based frameworks covered in the chapters that follow are every bit as capable and fun to use as any other, and it might be argued, perhaps even better in some ways. The Rails language, for example, demands a certain adherence to convention that sometimes gets in the way of a coder's freedom of expression. GWT is essentially a Java-based page-element composer that enables you to bypass writing ECMAScript directly, but lacks the design center for dynamic partial page replacement for which the Python Turbogears framework is becoming renowned.

The Starting Line

The goal of this book is to help you discover a new methodology for designing, coding, testing, and deploying rich applications that reside primarily in the network cloud, rather than primarily on the desktop. This application style is at the heart of so many modern tools and sites that even if you haven't had experience in developing using the model, you have certainly experienced many sites built this way.

The problem with learning an entirely new way to create applications is, as always, where to start. The authors, being developers rather like you, have always believed that one well-worked example is worth hundreds of words of prose. You'll find those in profusion in this book, but it's important to have an understanding of why Web 2.0 is important to you as a developer or entrepreneur and how the frameworks covered will allow you to leverage your Python skills in different and powerful new ways. Thus, that's the starting point for the book, and even though this chapter is short on code, it's long on ideas, so it will be worth your time to at least skim it. To understand why web frameworks were even designed in the first place, you should understand a little about the whole Web 2.0 revolution.

What's Web 2.0?

Skeptics claim that *Web 2.0* is little more than a marketer's buzzword. Mystically inclined types say that, "To know what it means, you have to *know what it means*. Like art or smut, you'll know it when you see it." Pragmatists explain that, "Google Maps *is* Web 2.0. Yahoo! Mail (old style) *is not*." The more curmudgeonly types, such as industry pundit John C. Dvorak, decry the whole meme by saying, "How can you have a Web 2.0 when we can't even explain what 1.0 was?" Finally, others in the *avant garde* claim that "We're already on version 3.0!"

Whatever the characterization, most nondevelopers agree that the phrase is very handy for encapsulating a whole aggregation of cool, modern stuff that's going on. As a developer, though, you can begin at a much different starting line, because you have a far deeper understanding of design mechanisms and implementations than nontechnical types. Web 2.0 begins with understanding the difference between the traditional Rich Client Platform (RCP) model and the emerging Rich Internet Application (RIA) model.

The History of Application Design for Content Creation (In One Easy Dose)

As the title of Neal Stephenson's famous article explains it, "In the Beginning was the Command Line." However, the capsule history in this section begins after the advent of windowed graphical user interfaces (GUIs), and the emergence of powerful operating systems on expensive compute platforms.

The Desktop Era — No Web

You're certainly familiar with the RCP model, even if you know it by another nomenclature, such as *the desktop application model*. Almost every application you've written, used, managed, or deployed over the last three decades on microcomputers adheres to RCP capabilities and limitations. When you think in the mode of an RCP developer, you take for granted that the operating system, data access and storage, and the user's experience of the application are tightly bound to the desktop, operating in general ignorance of the larger networked world. When you think like an RCP end user, you often feel trapped by your tools in the sense that if you lose the use of them, or if you lose your disk drive, you also lose your data in a most profound way. For example, it will be hard to read your next great novel written in Enormicorp PerfectWord if you don't have Enormicorp PerfectWord.

One effect of the isolation of both the user and the application is that designers and developers of traditional (RCP) applications never considered it desirable to enable the easy sharing of content created by a specific proprietary tool, except through arrangements like OLE or OpenDoc, which open up data sharing on the operating system or on proprietary tools made by the same vendor. Additionally, they never considered building significant community or social aspects into traditional software.

As discussed in the "Design Patterns for Web 2.0" sidebar later in the chapter, community aspects such as user-created content, tagging, and commentary (common in Web 2.0 applications such as YouTube and Wikipedia) would not have made sense in the era of one user executing one application on one computer. User isolation was a condition of life — an application and the content the end user produced existed on a solitary plane.

Sharing and dissemination of data was done by ad hoc means — for example, by attaching it to e-mail. The intended recipient could share in the data only if they bought and supported the correct version of the proprietary tool. This was true during the first couple of decades of modern computing. The gap between the end users' need to create, publish, and share their creations and the ability of pre-Web–era software design to deliver even a modicum of capability in that regard was filled by what was called *desktop publishing* or *DTP*. DTP was King: the big important designs and design ideas were all about putting words, numbers, and static images onto something that looks like a page, and then printing these pages for sharing. Python was an early response to the needs of system administrators and scientific programmers.

And Then the Web (1.0) Happened

Eventually, people began to wonder why they needed to produce paper at all, and thus when the World Wide Web (the Web) sprang into existence, DTP morphed almost overnight into *Web publishing* or WP. Almost overnight, WP became the new King, efficiently producing HTML to drive applications and represent words, numbers, and multiple media types such as still and moving images. When the Web (1.0) came along, agile languages such as Python began to make inroads into areas very unlike the original class of applications written mostly to enable a higher level of scripting. With the emergence of Twisted Python as a networked-applications engine some years ago, a mimetic light bulb lit. People began to think in terms of *frameworks*, and the notion of code that writes code began to circulate. Python, Perl, and PHP developers in particular began to get a sense of empowerment, while puzzling out the reason for all the manufactured buzz over expensive tools being developed by the same proprietary vendors who dominated the RCP and DTP era. Wasn't everything really just an elaboration of a snippet of code that could write a page in response to a URL invocation of a `cgi-bin` script, such as the Python snippet in Listing 1-1 shows?

Listing 1-1: Simple Python HTML page generator

```
print("Content-type: text/html")
page = """
<html>
 <head>
  <title>Hello World Page!</title>
 </head>
 <body>
 <p>Hello World</p>
 </body>
</html>
"""
print page
```

The answer was both yes and no. In the abstract sense, what every website was striving to do was to generate HTML code (initially) to present material as a substitute for the printed page, and then (later) as a substitute for earlier form-based styles that mimicked human interaction. However, there was also an emerging need to create and maintain transactions for a new style of commerce in which the vendor side of the equation was entirely autonomous and could support a variety of free-form interactions. For that, designers had to evolve a style of architecture that clearly separated the manipulation of the underlying model from the management of the user experience, and from the business logic behind the form. This led to the rediscovery of the *model-view-controller* (MVC) design center (discussed in more detail in Chapter 3) just in time for the emergence of Web 2.0.

Web 2.0, the Next Generation

The problem with creating applications and tools based on the first set of technologies underlying the Web was that the user interaction model was really rather wretched. Creating a word-processing tool, such as Google Documents, would have been difficult, if not impossible. Consider the capabilities that a typical Web 2.0 word processor exhibits:

❑   Every keystroke and input is reflected on the screen as soon as it happens.

❑   Document modifications are silently persisted into the model, which is online and secured from the possibility of loss from the failure of an individual PC.

❑   The tool must support a reasonable number of formatting capabilities and enable the insertion of structured content such as tables or images.

In short, such a tool must be largely indistinguishable from the earlier generation's RCP equivalent.

The responsiveness that an interactive user needs in such a case could have been partially mimicked in HTML using HTTP in the Web 1.0 era, but because a write-back to the model could have been accomplished only with a synchronous HTTP request, which also would have resulted in a full page refresh, the experience would have been disorienting for the end user. The result certainly wouldn't have looked or performed like a typical RCP. As Figure 1-1 depicts, every outbound call results in a complete page refresh.

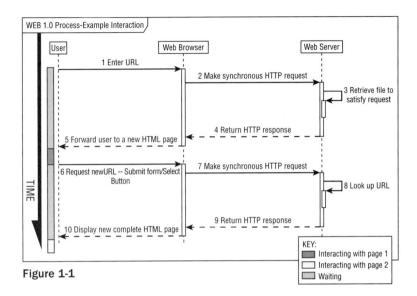

Figure 1-1

What changed the landscape forever was embedding a capability in the browser that enabled it to make an asynchronous call to the server for rendering the web page, and the supporting JavaScript capability to accept the returned data and update a portion of the page (a `<DIV/>` or `<SPAN/>` element of the page) without refreshing the entire page (an idea that Microsoft Internet Explorer 5 initially advanced). This was nothing short of revolutionary and morphed quickly into a realization by developers that the browser could now host applications that mimicked and in some aspects (scalability, robustness, accessibility, and collaboration) improved on the older RCP applications' capabilities.

Thus, the term *Rich Internet Application (RIA)* was born, ushering in the Web 2.0 era of tools and sites based on the simple idea that the Internet was becoming a hosting environment, not just for static pages and forms, but also for applications that once were restricted to the desktop.

Applications for such tasks as word processing, photo image manipulation, personal information management — which had been a stronghold for a tiny group of vendors, and were exorbitantly priced with restrictive usage covenants (the infamous and seldom comprehensible *end user license agreement* or *EULA*) — were suddenly left in the dust by browser-based versions that were not only free but consumed no private disk space. All because Web 2.0 applications are designed according to a ubiquitous standard (MVC) and use an asynchronous HTTP request with data returned in XML or *Javascript Object Notation (JSON)*. The request-and-return path is called an *XMLHttpRequest* or *XHR*, and the technique works in all modern browsers.

Suddenly, word processors, spreadsheets, and calendar management are woven directly into the fabric of the Internet, are executed entirely within the confines of the web browser, and are no longer the private preserve of a specific vendor. What's more, the Web 2.0 design doesn't stop at desktop tool replacements, important as that category is. New classes of applications, such as Base Camp, Flickr, YouTube, and Picasa are useful specifically *because of* their networked context — they wouldn't make much sense as desktop-only applications. In contrast to Figure 1-1, Figure 1-2 illustrates that asynchronous outbound calls may result in a portion of the page being refreshed without a complete browser reload.

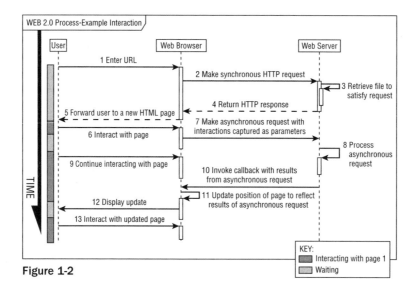

Figure 1-2

This is not to say that there are no problems for designers and developers to solve (yes, we will all still have jobs come the revolution). Even though RIAs usually have several advantages over applications that run on the client, they're not without some limitations. For example, compare an RIA e-mail client like Google Mail (GMail) to a client application like Mozilla Thunderbird. GMail has the advantage of centralized virus scanning, whereas Thunderbird relies on operating-system scanners. On the other hand, when you upload an attachment into an e-mail message, Thunderbird allows you to drag and drop files from any file window into the message, whereas GMail requires you to type in a full file path and name, or use a less convenient file chooser dialog box. Overall, though, these represent browser limitations or operating system limitations, rather than defects in the RIA model itself.

The following table illustrates some of the capabilities you get for free, just by writing to the Web 2.0 specification.

Web 2.0 Capability	Description
Plasticity and flexible recombination	Web 2.0 applications (RIAs) can be remixed into new applications in ways the original designer and developer may never have considered. Because they implement MVC, RIAs expose their server-side invocation syntax to the curious and return their data in a common format (XML or JSON) that any arbitrary process can parse (although there are ways to prevent users from invoking your service, such as requiring private API keys to be passed with the XHR). Overall, this means that your clever server-side logic can be leveraged more widely, gaining you fame, perhaps fortune, and the undying gratitude of your peers.
Invisibility and applications as services	Applications woven into the Web are no longer software — they are services that people take for granted. This is a better thing in the RIA world than it is in the relationship world, because, in the case of your well-written RIA, it may get you the kind of notice that changes your career and lifestyle. Just ask the creators of YouTube what being taken for granted is worth (in their case it was over $1.6 billion).
Ubiquity of access	For almost all Web 2.0 applications, if you have a web browser on a computer somewhere and a broadband connection (both of which are attainable in most of the First World), you can get to the content you have created whether it's the original manuscript for a book or your vacation pictures.
Low switching cost, lower total cost of ownership (TCO)	End users are switching from desktop applications to web-based applications primarily because of the virtues mentioned previously. The cost of switching from the use of tools that shackle the user to services to those that just offer access to their content is actually pretty low. Further, without having to act as an ad hoc system administrator, the cost of using a software capability is lower for the user, and without integrating with a specific operating system, the cost of production is lowered for you, the software developer. In general, Web 2.0 applications eliminate application installation, maintenance, update, and configuration management.
Zero footprint and zero configuration	Although some may argue that a browser is hardly zero footprint, the point is that for the cost of installing and maintaining a modern browser, the end user receives a magic box, from which all manner of applications can spring forth, none of which leaves a footprint on the desktop. The developer (you) receives the gift of a unifying API and development strategy, which is also enabled because of the next point.
Leveraging industry-wide data transport API (HTTP)	This means that the applications you write have worldwide reach.

Table continued on following page

9

Web 2.0 Capability	Description
Leveraging industry-wide display standards (HTML, Flex, and JavaScript)	This means that you can erase phrases such as *Windows Foundation Classes* (*WFCs*), *Cocoa*, and *Abstract Window Toolkit* (*AWT*) from your memory.
Leveraging a common data format (XML or JSON)	This means that data sharing among applications is straight-forward.
Leveraging high-speed networking	This makes running Web 2.0 applications generally as seamless as running desktop applications.
Platform-independent development	Writing to a standard that is above the platform level means that you can develop applications without having to worry about which operating systems, browsers, and so on they will run on (with caveats).

The Role of AJAX in Web 2.0

The ability to make an asynchronous call to a URL and have the data return handled by code within the browser is key to creating the RIA experience for the user. Without *AJAX* (*Asynchronous JavaScript and XML*), browser-resident RIAs would not be feasible for the reasons discussed previously. Additionally, not only can AJAX make asynchronous *external* method calls (out from the browser), but it can also make *internal* method calls (within the browser). The latter capability is the basis for providing changes in visual elements within the RIA, including special effects like growing and shrinking areas, tabbed pages, and drag and drop.

As good and as useful as AJAX is in this regard, the fact is that AJAX must be implemented in JavaScript, and that is the source of a good deal of pain for the developer. Although JavaScript has only recently been taken seriously as a development language, its idiosyncrasies and tendency to be broken in differ-ent ways in different browsers is a constant source of consternation to developers and end users alike. Even in a nonbroken world though, it's great to have a level of abstraction sitting atop JavaScript. Fortunately, MochiKit and other libraries are there to help.

> *MochiKit is covered specifically in Chapter 11, but you will find code snippets and explanations of its use in other chapters in this book.*

Leveraging the Power of DSLs

Domain-specific languages (*DSLs*) are limited computer languages designed for a specific class of problem. However, using a special-purpose language that's really good at creating solutions in a specific problem domain is not a brand-new idea. Developers have been creating special syntaxes in languages since way back when, especially in the bygone heyday of early work in Lisp (list processing) and artifi-cial intelligence. In Python and one or two other languages classified as *scripting* languages, creating a special syntax on top of the basic language becomes a highly tractable problem.

This is often called *metaprogramming*, which refers to programming structures that operate on other programming structures. Another way to think of the Python frameworks covered in the following chapters is that they are code that writes code, or even self-modifying code.

As a Python programmer, you may have come across one or two such structures in Python, even if you aren't a master of metaprogramming. The addition of decorators in Python 2.4, which are lines of code preceded by an @ (at sign), make metaprogramming much less of a mystery and really easy to use. A *decorator* is a function that takes a method as an argument and returns a method (or method-like) object. The Python interpreter generally ignores decorators, but the signs are meaningful to TurboGears, which has over a dozen of them and uses them as part of its controller structure. (Django doesn't use this approach.)

When you mention self-modifying code to most developers, you may evoke a shiver and some whispered words of deprecation, but if it's used correctly and in the right places (as with the frameworks covered in subsequent chapters), such code can lead to some very clean programming, or at least, from your standpoint, very clean-looking code. But don't forget that Python presents broader capabilities to write this type of code than almost any other mainstream language in use today. Long before TurboGears, you could dynamically modify any Python object by adding a new attribute to an instance of an object, or dynamically acquire new methods and add those to an instance.

In contrast to Ruby on Rails, which is almost another language than Ruby, both Python frameworks covered in this book require you to make minimal changes in coding style versus writing normal Python methods. For example, a TurboGears controller method has an expose decorator right before the function, which designates the template to be used and returns a Python dictionary filled with the values to be plugged into the template — everything other than that looks just like normal Python code.

You'll find a similar method at work in the Kid templating language, which uses a mixture of standard HTML and some special constructs as a Pythonic control language within the template. Another place you'll see special syntactic constructs at work is in MochiKit, which although implemented atop JavaScript, has method calls and other constructs that look remarkably (and by design) like Python code.

In Chapter 12 you'll see the ultimate pairing of DSLs. That chapter explores the mating of Flash (Adobe's DSL for creating compelling user experiences) with TurboGears. By the end of the book, you will become very familiar and comfortable with the general idea of DSLs as a way to make simple things easy and hard things possible.

Leveraging the Power of TurboGears

By the definition, TurboGears can arguably be called a domain-specific language. What makes its use compelling is that TurboGears is one of a new generation of Web 2.0 frameworks. In this context, the term *framework* means software that enables you to write full-scope software. When people talk about *full scope*, they mean that all aspects of a rich Internet application are addressed, from the user experience, through the controller logic, to the underlying data model.

So why use a framework at all — why not just write dynamic HTML, server logic, and a database handler in straight Python, or Java, or [*insert name of favorite language here*]? The answer to that is the same as it's always been. For every level of abstraction you can move up in software development, you gain an ability to encompass greater complexity.

TurboGears accomplishes the few important goals that matter:

❑ It enables separation of concerns, which makes maintenance, revision, and the addition of features easier.

❑ It is excellent in the role of a DSL layer that acts as the binding force for well-crafted Pythonic components at every level:

  ❑ SQLObject handles the model translation from a relational form (from a SQLite or MySQL database) to a Python object form (and back).

  ❑ The Kid templating engine, which can be used standalone at design time as well as in the deployed RIA, is filled in by the TurboGears layer with data from the model. The advantage to running standalone at design time without the backing model or controller logic having been fully developed is that it enables application developers and UI designers to work independently, in parallel, and then converge somewhere along the development path.

  ❑ Within the browser, JavaScript logic is organized through MochiKit, which has the avowed aim to "make JavaScript suck less." Put in more polite language, MochiKit collects a wide array of loosely related JavaScript functions into a single library, and offers a very Pythonic-looking API for method invocation. Chapter 11 covers MochiKit in greater detail.

  ❑ CherryPy creates the web server layer and the control path for transmitting the business logic to the Python code — at least for the development phase. It is likely that for deployment, especially if you use a commercial-grade ISP, you will have to deploy primarily on a web service engine such as Apache.

Leveraging the Power of Django

Django's design center is rooted in the specific domain of content management systems. As such, it's somewhat more focused than TurboGear, which as suggested in the previous section, is much more of a general tool for producing Web 2.0 applications. Thus, where TurboGears is widely focused, Django tends to feel more narrowly focused. Django was created to facilitate creating a daily online newspaper with dynamically generated columns and pages. As you work with both of these frameworks, you will come to appreciate the differences and, more importantly, why the application spaces of interest to different designers forced specific design decisions.

Leveraging the Power of Python

There is probably very little you don't know about Python unless you're new both to Web 2.0 development and to agile languages. But at the risk of telling you things you may already know, there are a few important things that ought to be said of Python as an undercarriage for Web 2.0 frameworks. If you program in Python, you already have experienced some of the attributes that make it a very suitable base.

First of all, Python is an agile, high-level, and interpreted language. For Web 2.0 development, this means that you can write a little, test a little, and deploy a little. This is a perfect quality for iterative development, and is especially perfect for creating the experimental, fast-changing applications in the Web 2.0 space. Applications change quickly here during development and testing, because they are generally driven by the passion of small teams rather than large companies seeking to implement a service-oriented architecture with many moving parts and several months or years to achieve results.

Thus, a language that writes compact, dynamically typed code at a high level of abstraction is a big plus. Additionally, Web 2.0 frameworks need to be able to create specific syntaxes that will speed RIA development without getting in the way. As mentioned in the section "Leveraging the Power of DSLs," a language that enables dynamic self-modification through code that writes code is another important feature, and Python is among the few modern languages that excel in this regard.

Additonally, there are the attributes that you may already cherish. Python is often said to be a solid, *batteries included* (in other words, *complete*) language. Here's why:

- ❑   It is solidly supported by a large and passionate community led by a pragmatic, benevolent dictator.

- ❑   It is solidly designed to provide functional programming, object-oriented programming (OOP), and metaprogramming.

- ❑   It is solidly deployed in countless contexts, from system administration to scientific programming.

Finally, Python's ability to integrate other libraries and components makes it an excellent gap-filling language. It is perfect for automating the many tedious parts of Web 2.0 MVC applications. You should have to write only the parts of your RIA that make it different and compelling, and not all the scaffolding that every RIA must have. Those you will always prefer to delegate to a capable framework. Python helps create the frameworks that make that possible.

Comparing the Frameworks

No parent ever wants to compare their children by saying that Caitlin is better than Sean (they're *both* better, just in different ways) and in this case the same is true. The Django and TurboGears frameworks are each the best at certain things.

Both the Django and TurboGears frameworks implement a strict MVC design center and depend on AJAX within the browser to invoke a server-side controller. Because they are both implemented in Python, they both promote an agile development style. To choose the best one for your needs, consider the differences presented in the following sections.

The Historical Perspective

Both the Django and TurboGears frameworks were motivated by observing that the component parts of specific application implementations were good enough to make them generic. This opened them to the possibility of reusability in other ongoing projects that were quite different from the original. Some of you may recall that Python itself had a similar genesis. TurboGears sprang from an RCP RSS newsreader client. TurboGears tends to be a little more dependent on the momentum of the open source community than Django, simply because of the number of open source components that constitute its moving parts (SQLObject, Kid, and CherryPy). Django originated in response to the need to produce a highly scalable and dynamic online newspaper, one that gets millions of page hits per day.

As a result of the differing design centers, the Django team tends to focus on content management. That's a fancy way of saying that their concern is rooted in the need to create developer methodology that enables content-based applications to be constructed quickly. The TurboGears team has focused on the RIA space as a whole and has created a highly pluggable architecture. What this means in a practical sense is that even though there are reasonable default choices for supporting componentry, substitutions may easily be made (such as using SQLite instead of MySQL for model representation, or Cheetah instead of Kid for templating).

Controller Invocation

As suggested by Figure 1-2, a URL address in the TurboGears framework results in a server-side call to a method (whose name is a part of the URL) in a file called `controller.py`. As you will discover when you start adding methods to the controller, the method becomes instantly available. You don't have a recompile step nor do you have to restart a virtual machine (VM) or the web server layer. TurboGears provides instant developer gratification.

In Ruby on Rails, there's a lot of chatter about favoring convention over configuration. Django takes the opposite approach because it uses a mapping file to map URLs to the controller code. This strategy decouples the URL path composition from the actual underlying implementation, which in turn enables Django-hosted applications to maximize code reuse and controller deployment.

JavaScript

Much as Prototype is the preferred JavaScript and AJAX library implementation in Rails, TurboGears uses MochiKit to create some very useful binding capabilities for form and effects handling. Django doesn't really have a demonstrated preference for a JavaScript library nor even a loose binding to one in particular. As you'll see demonstrated later in the book, where a project using TurboGears and Flex is shown, there are no real limits to how the user experience or the asynchronous call-and-response system is handled.

Licensing

Licensing is always a critical deployment issue. It's important to know whether you can deploy your creation unencumbered before setting out to build it in the first place. We (the authors of this book) both contribute to and strongly advocate the use of open source. Here are some guidelines to help you do the same:

- ❑ Because TurboGears is a composition layer sitting atop other frameworks, it can't be considered independent of its moving parts. Kid, the default templating engine, is licensed under the MIT License (www.opensource.org/licenses/mit-license.php), which supports full transitivity with respect to derived works. This means that, basically, you can use it without worry.

- ❑ MochiKit is dual-licensed under the terms of the MIT License, or under the Academic Free License (AFL), which is a very tolerant license with respect to the rights to use, deploy, sublicense, and distribute derivative works. SQLObject, the object-relational mapping (ORM) layer, is protected by the Lesser General Public License (LGPL), which is a bit more restrictive. If you modify the source of the SQLObject library itself, you'll have to make those changes available to all. Of course, that doesn't mean that your derived works are in jeopardy. You can create and sell them or give them away without concern.

- ❑ Django, because it was created from whole cloth, is under a single open source license (the BSD license). This is very generous with respect to improvements in Django itself and makes no demands on derived works.

Design Patterns for Web 2.0

In the book *Rich Internet Applications: AJAX and Beyond* (Wiley Publishing, 2007), the authors present seven crucial high-level design patterns for Web 2.0 developers. They are repeated here in slightly altered form for your consideration. These are important aspects that create the design center for most of the applications you'll write in this new, highly net-centric paradigm.

Design Pattern 1: Expose (at Least Some of) the Remote API

RIA developers should create content in such a way that mediating applications which other developers or end users might dream up can interact with it, display it, or repurpose its content. User-level content repurposing is extremely common in the Web 2.0 era in the form of *mashups*. Mashups and remixes occur when new applications (originally unintended) are constructed from data and services originally intended for some other purpose.

Design Pattern 2: Use a Common Data Format

A different (but similar) pattern suggests that RIA developers create data models underlying the service-based applications, so that they or another developer can leverage them. No matter what format the back-end server uses to store the data model (regardless of whether it's a SQLite relational database, an NFS-mounted, flat-file system, or an XML data store), the output to the user view should be expressed as something that any number of readers or parsers can handle.

Design Pattern 3: The Browser Creates the User Experience

In most commercially available browsers, application capabilities are limited only by the stability, extensibility, and support for JavaScript. You, the developer, can deal with this limitation because, as a trade-off, it's a lot better than the tall stack of entry limitations and barriers that drove you crazy during the previous software epoch. If you need visual sophistication beyond the capability of the modern browser, you can use other browser-pluggable alternatives, such as Adobe Flash (and write code in Python on the server side and Flex on the browser side).

Design Pattern 4: Applications Are Always Services

Although this was already mentioned briefly, it's a sufficiently important design pattern to bear repetition. RIAs are part of a service-oriented architecture (SOA) in which applications are services, created from scratch or as artifacts from recombining other application facets. Subject to limitations (such as the availability of some other service on which your application may depend), SOA creates the software equivalent of evolutionary adaptation. Remarkably, no protocol stack by a committee of desktop vendors was required to create this pattern. Unlike the UDDI or WDSL stack, the Web 2.0 SOA is simple and almost intuitive.

Design Pattern 5: Enable User Agnosticism

RIAs won't force the user to worry about operating systems or browsers. As long as the browser supports scripting, applications can unobtrusively just do their work. Developers could choose to take advantage of secret handshakes or other backend implementations that assure vendor or OS lockdown (and you can probably think of one browser and one OS vendor that does this), but the downside of making such a devil's

(continued)

bargain is that ultimately you, as a developer, will wind up expending more cycles when, after getting some user traction on a specific platform, you find that your best interests are served by extending your application to every other platform. It's better not to support vendors with their own back-end implementation agenda, and to design from the start to avoid the slippery slope that leads to the trap of relying on vendor- or browser-specific APIs. Thus, it's best if your design steers clear of OS and native library dependencies. That way, you can safely ignore much of the annoying Byzantine detail of writing applications, and specifically the parts that tend to make applications most brittle. Instead, you can concentrate on the logic of what it is that you're trying to accomplish for the user.

Design Pattern 6: The Network Is the Computer

Originally a Sun Microsystems marketing slogan from the 1980s, this bromide goes in and out of vogue. In the 1980s, Java applets exemplified it with the X11/Motif distributed models; in the 1990s, both models ultimately failed, on infrastructural weaknesses. X11 failed because it exacted a huge performance cost on the expensive workstation CPUs of the era, and because its network model couldn't extend beyond the LAN (with the broadband era still a decade or so away). Java applets failed because of their size (long load time) and sluggish performance (again, broadband was a few years away). Today, broadband is near ubiquitous in much of the cyber landscape. In addition, because the current RIA user experience is small and fits comfortably in the memory footprint of the modern browser, failure seems far less likely. Thus, the operating system for this new generation of applications is not a single specific OS at all, but rather the Internet as a whole. Accordingly, you can develop to the separation of concerns afforded by the MVC paradigm, while ignoring (for the most part) the network in the middle of the application. There are still some real concerns about the network in the middle, and given this reality, you do need to code to protect the user experience.

Design Pattern 7: Web 2.0 Is a Cultural Phenomenon

Except for the earliest days of personal computing, when the almost exclusively male Homebrew Computer Club (which gave birth to the first Apple) defined the culture of hackerdom, the PC desktop has never been a cultural phenomenon. In contrast, Web 2.0 has *always* been about the culture. Community is everywhere in the culture of Web 2.0, and end users rally around affinity content. Craigslist, Digg, and Slashdot exist as aggregation points for user commentary. Narrow-focus podcasts have become the preferred alternative to broadcast TV and radio for many; and blogging has become a popular alternative to other publishing mass-distribution formats. Remixing and mashups are enabled by the fact that data models, normally closed or proprietary, are exposed by service APIs, but they also wouldn't exist without end users' passion and sweat equity. Some enterprising developers (such as Ning at www.ning.com) have even managed to monetize this culture, offering a framework for creative hobbyists who create social applications based on existing APIs. When you create an application, you should consider the social culture that may arise to embrace your application. You can likely build in collaborative and social capabilities (such as co-editing and social tagging) pretty easily. If there's a downside to having an application exist only "in the cloud," the best upside is that a networked application also obeys the power law of networks: The application's value increases as a log function for the number of users. Most RIAs in the wild have many or all of these characteristics.

Consider the elder statesman of content-sharing applications, the blog, and its close relative, the wiki. Many blogs approach or exceed print journalism in their reader penetration, and wikis are far more flexible than their power-hungry desktop predecessors (such as Microsoft Office Groove) in supporting multi-user coordination and collaboration.

Summary

In a relatively short span of time, Python developers have seen the Web move from active to interactive to transactive. In the same span, the role of Python has evolved from page generator, to server-side control software, to the basis of exciting and capable frameworks that reduce developer burden while enabling a new class of Rich Internet Applications (RIAs). LAMP (Linux servers running Apache as Web server, backed by a MySQL Relational database, and mediated by Python, Perl, or PHP) has evolved into Web 2.0 and now developers can benefit from making the transition by using the tools and techniques described in this book. It's going to be an exciting and fun ride, so ladies and gentlemen, start your engines.

2

Web 2.0 with Traditional Python

Each success only buys an admission ticket to a more difficult problem.

—Henry Kissinger

All of the frameworks and tools shown in this book rely on some fairly simple underlying technologies, like JavaScript, Python, CGI, HTML, and HTTP, which have been used since the dawn of Web 1.0. In this chapter, you'll see how you can build Web 2.0 applications using just those old-school technologies. Even if you decide to use higher-level frameworks and tools (and you will), you'll still benefit from seeing how the nuts and bolts work together at the ground level. The example at the end of this chapter illustrates how you can build a simple Web 2.0 application using just these traditional tools. The rest of this book shows how you can use frameworks to make the job easier, more efficient, and more fun.

Old-School Web Technologies

First, this section reviews the technologies that have been used in web applications for a long time and continue to be the foundation for Web 2.0.

XML

The eXtensible Markup Language (XML) is a text document format that specifies the content and structure of a document. However, in general, it says nothing about how the document should be displayed. It is a hierarchical document format in which elements are delineated by tags like this: `<tag>`. Listing 2-1 shows an example of a simple XML document.

Listing 2-1: Simple XML Example

```
1   <?xml version='1.0' encoding='ISO-8859-1'?>
2   <top>
3     Text within the "top" element.
4     <sub1 attrib="anAttribute">
5       Text within the first "sub1" element.
6     </sub1>
7     <sub1 another_attrib="secondAttribute">
8       Text within the second "sub1" element.
9       <subsub1>
10        Text in &lt; brackets &gt;
11      </subsub1>
12    </sub1>
13    <sub2/>
14  </top>
```

If you load this XML file into Firefox, it displays the document tree shown in Figure 2-1.

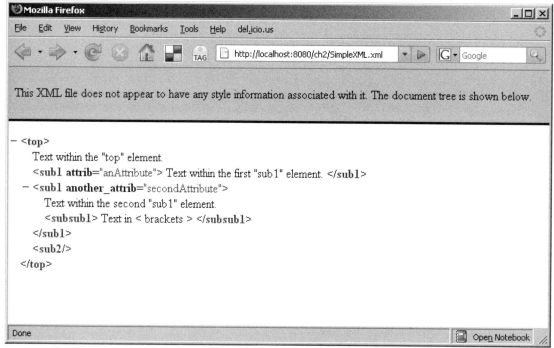

Figure 2-1

Here's a breakdown of what's happening in the example code:

❑   Line 1 identifies the version and text encoding standard of this document. In this example, you're using version 1.0 XML and encoding text per the ISO 8859-1 standard. This is boilerplate text that is rarely changed unless you need to support multibyte characters.

❑ Line 2 begins the meat of the document with the open tag for the top-level document element called `<top>`. Each opening tag requires a matching closing tag and the closing tag for this one is at the end of the document at line 14 (`</top>`). In between these tags are three subelements called `<sub1>` (at lines 4–6), `<sub1>` (at lines 7–12), and `<sub2>` (at line 13). Notice that the names of the enclosed elements don't have to be unique. As you'll see in the examples that follow later in this chapter, this property is useful for making unordered lists of subelements. The second `<sub1>` element has its own subelement called `<subsub1>` starting at line 9. The nesting of elements can be as deep as needed.

❑ Line 4 shows an example of an element attribute — in this case, `attrib` has the value `"anAttribute"`. Attributes can be handy for attaching metadata to document elements.

❑ Line 10 shows how you can use escape codes to allow the less than (<) and greater than (>) characters to appear in text. Here you use `&lt;` to represent < and `&gt;` to represent >.

❑ If an element is empty, you can open and close it with one tag, as shown in line 12.

XML can be as simple or as complicated as you like. For more details about XML, check out the World Wide Web Consortium (W3C) standard at www.w3.org/XML/.

HTML

HyperText Markup Language (HTML) is the formatting language used by web page authors to control the content of their pages. It contains the header and body information for a page. Within the header and body sections, HTML also includes directives for page layout as well as the page content itself. It's called *Hyper-Text* Markup Language because HTML documents can also include hypertext links to other documents.

Early versions of HTML parsers were pretty loose about the document-formatting requirements. This was considered a *feature* and not a bug because who wants to get all worked up about details like closing tags? Unfortunately, this laxity led to problems with web pages that would display correctly in one vendor's browser but not another. Most people these days use XHTML — a stricter version of HTML in which the HTML document is also a valid XML document. XHTML documents usually display correctly in all browsers, although you can still write one that will break certain browsers if you work at it.

Listing 2-2 shows a simple HTML document.

Listing 2-2: Example HTML Document

```
 1 <!DOCTYPE html PUBLIC "-//W3C//DTD XHTML 1.0 Strict//EN"
"http://www.w3.org/TR/xhtml1/DTD/xhtml1-strict.dtd">
 2 <html xmlns="http://www.w3.org/1999/xhtml">
 3  <head>
 4    <meta http-equiv="Content-Type" content="text/html;
         charset=utf-8"/>
 5
 6    <title>Simple HTML Document</title>
 7    <link rel=StyleSheet href="Style.css"
         TYPE="text/css">
 8  </head>
 9  <body>
10    <div id="header">
11      <h1>Here's some H1 header text</h1>
```

(continued)

Listing 2-2 *(continued)*

```
12      <h2>
13          Here's some H2 header text
14          line breaks are not important in here
15      </h2>
16   </div>
17   <!-- You can insert comments like this -->
18   <p/>  <!-- Add some blank space -->
19
20
21    Here is some regular text....
22
23   <p>
24   <a href="somepage.html">
25     This text</a> is a link to the file "somepage.html"
26   </p>
27   <p>
28   <a href="http://www.wrox.com/">
29        This text</a> is a link to another web site.
30   </p>
31   </body>
32 </html>
```

This document looks like Figure 2-2 in a browser. Pretty simple stuff.

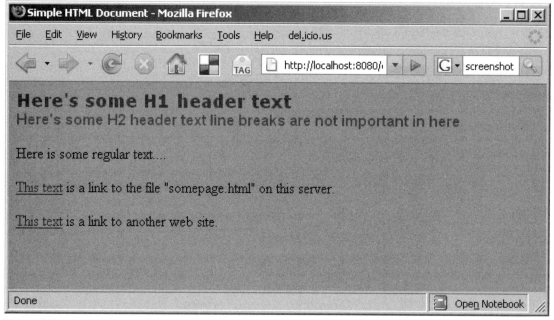

Figure 2-2

Listing 2-2 has a few highlights worth examining more closely. The first line is more boilerplate text that says this is an XHTML document of a particular version (1.0 in this case). Line 2 is the opening tag of the main element of this XHTML document, which is always <html>. The <html> element contains the following two subelements:

- ❑   <head> lines 3–8: Meta-information about the page.
- ❑   <body> lines 9–31: The content and display directives for the page.

In this example, the <head> element contains the following three subelements:

- ❑   <meta> line 4: Its attributes define the text encoding type of the document.
- ❑   <title> line 6: Includes the text that will be displayed in the title bar of the browser.
- ❑   <link> line 7: Directs the browser to load another file, which in this case is a Cascading Style Sheets (CSS) file that defines the colors and fonts for the page.

Notice that, as with the XML example, blank lines like line 5 have no effect. Line 9 starts the <body> of the document, which contains the following:

- ❑   Lines 10–16: The element at lines 10 through 16 is a <div> (division) element. The <div> allows you to give names to parts of the document (in this case, "header") so you can refer to them from other places, like CSS files and JavaScript code. By referring to document divisions by name, you can dynamically update them using JavaScript to get that dynamic page effect that is the hallmark of Web 2.0.
- ❑   Line 11 shows some text to be displayed as top-level header (h1) text, and lines 12-15 show some second-level header (h2) text. The actual display attributes (such as font and color) of these headers are in the CSS file. Notice that although the h2 text is in the HTML file as two lines, the browser displays it on one line.
- ❑   Comments in XML and HTML start with a <!-- symbol and end with a --> symbol. Line 17 shows a comment that is legal in XML or XHTML. The <p/> elements at lines 18–20 add a few blank lines before some text on line 21, which is displayed in the default text style for the page.
- ❑   Lines 23–30 show two example hyperlinks, represented as the <a> elements. The href attribute is the URL that the browser will load if the user clicks the link. The text within the <a> element is shown in a special style that identifies it as a clickable link. Line 24 shows an href that is relative to the current page. If clicked, it directs the browser to a different file on the same server. The link on line 28 directs the browser to another server on the Internet.
- ❑   Line 31 closes the <body> element that was started on line 9.

Line 32 closes the <html> element that was started on line 2.

HTTP

HyperText Transfer Protocol (HTTP) is a very simple text-based networking protocol layered on top of TCP/IP, which has become the dominant protocol for web communications. It defines a request-response protocol in which a client makes a request of a server and receives a response. There are only a few request types (called *methods* in HTTP parlance) and only a couple of them are significant to developers, as shown in the following table.

HTTP Method	Action
GET	Retrieves information from the server.
PUT	Sends information to or updates information on the server.

Consult the HTTP specification at www.w3.org/Protocols/ for details on the other methods.

HTTP also defines a number of response codes that indicate the status of a request. These include the ever-popular 404 (not found) and 500 (server error) that we all see occasionally in our everyday web surfing. Response code 200 (OK) is returned when there is no error.

SQL

Enterprise data have been stored using relational database and Structured Query Language (SQL) technologies for generations. Although most software is now object-oriented, object-oriented databases have never really caught on, so relational databases remain the dominant back-end for most web applications.

Relational databases are made up of tables with data stored in the rows and columns of those tables. Some elements in one table can be related to elements in other tables, hence the *"relational"* in relational databases.

Data are stored in and retrieved from relational databases using SQL statements like this:

```
SELECT name FROM people WHERE height > 66
```

If you run this SQL statement on the following table, it will return "Robert" and "Bobby."

Name	Height	Weight	Hair Color
Bob	66	150	Brown
Robert	67	145	Black
Bobby	68	155	Blonde

The impedance mismatch between a set of software objects with complicated interrelationships and the flat, two-dimensional tables that they must be stored in is, to put it mildly, difficult to deal with. The chore of converting back and forth between software objects and relational database tables is called *object-relational mapping (ORM)*. Later in this chapter, you'll see a simple example of manual ORM and see why automated ORM is one of the most valuable tools provided by web software frameworks.

JavaScript

Despite its name, JavaScript is not related to the Java programming language. It can be embedded in web pages and interpreted by the browser to give a page active content not possible with HTML alone. Even though this is a book about Python, you'll see lots of examples of JavaScript in this book. A good reference for JavaScript is at http://developer.mozilla.org/en/docs/About_JavaScript.

CGI and Python

In the Web 1.0 era, when a browser made a request of a web server, the server would usually just read an HTML file and send it to the client. Occasionally, the content of the page needs to be computed when requested. The Common Gateway Interface (CGI) meets this need by providing a protocol for a web server to run an external program, which computes the content of the requested page. The server then sends the content back to the client browser. Figure 2-3 shows what happens when a CGI script is invoked.

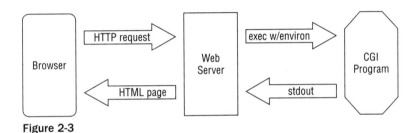

Figure 2-3

As shown on the left side of Figure 2-3, the browser makes a request of the server using standard HTTP. The server is configured to treat certain requests as CGI invocations rather than simple page retrievals. When it looks at the request, it discovers that this request is for a particular CGI script. The server takes the relevant request parameters, writes them into the execution environment for a new process, and executes the configured CGI program. Although the CGI program can be implemented in any language, you'll use Python, of course.

As shown on the right side of Figure 2-3, the CGI program reads its environment to get any request parameters, and generates the page. The CGI program just writes the HTML response to standard output using something like `print` statements in Python, `printf` in C, `System.out.writeln` in Java, and so on.

The web server reads the standard output of the CGI program and relays the output back to the client browser.

The next section provides a simple example that ties all of these technologies together into a simple web application.

A Simple Example

In this section, you look at a simple social application in which people can enter and retrieve their names and the names of their pets. We're keeping it very simple to show how these Web 2.0 technologies interact at their lowest level. Anything more complicated calls for one of the frameworks shown later in the book.

First you explore what the application does, and then you look at how it's implemented. Figure 2-4 shows the user interface for this little application.

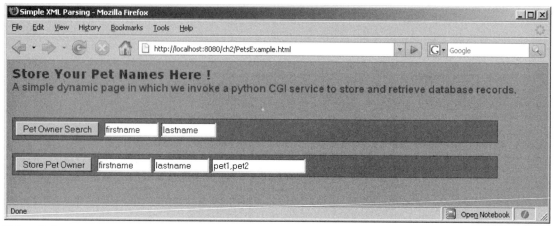

Figure 2-4

There are two buttons to store and retrieve records. When clicked, the button labeled Pet Owner Search makes a request to the server to look up the list of pets given the owner's first and last names. The button labeled Store Pet Owner sends a pet owner's names and a list of pet names to the server to be stored.

Here's how the application works:

1. The user enters the pet owner's first and last names and his pets' names, and then clicks Store Pet Owner. The page makes an asynchronous request to the server to store that information. While the server is writing the record, the page displays a banner that says "Storing ..." Notice that the page is active now, and unlike a Web 1.0 application, it is not waiting for the server to respond. Figure 2-5 shows the page while the data store is in progress.

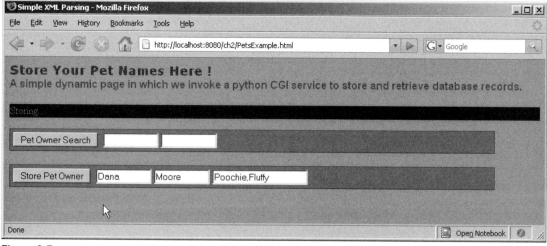

Figure 2-5

2. After the data record is stored, the developer can report the status to the user by removing the "Storing…" banner and displaying the result. The updated page is shown in Figure 2-6.

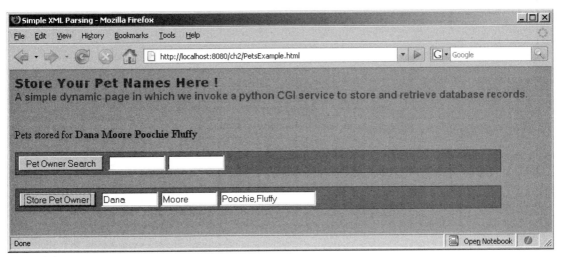

Figure 2-6

3. After the record is stored in the database, the end user can now retrieve it. Try entering the same first and last names into the Pet Owner Search area, click the button, and see what you get. Figure 2-7 shows the page while the search is in progress. The status banner now says "Loading" rather than "Storing."

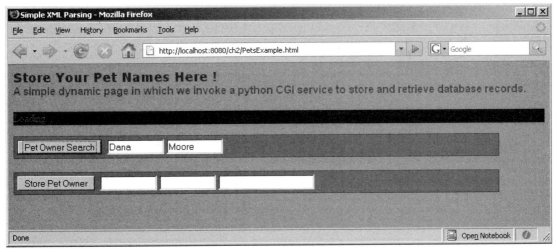

Figure 2-7

4. After the search is complete, the page is updated again to display the results. Figure 2-8 shows what you've found.

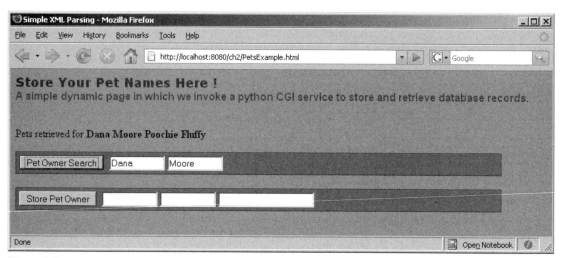

Figure 2-8

What happens if you search for a name that doesn't exist? First the page is updated to look like Figure 2-7 while the search is in progress, and then the status bar displays the word "ERROR" to indicate that the pet owner was not found (see Figure 2-9). Obviously, this is not very user-friendly. You'll want a more informative error message in a production application.

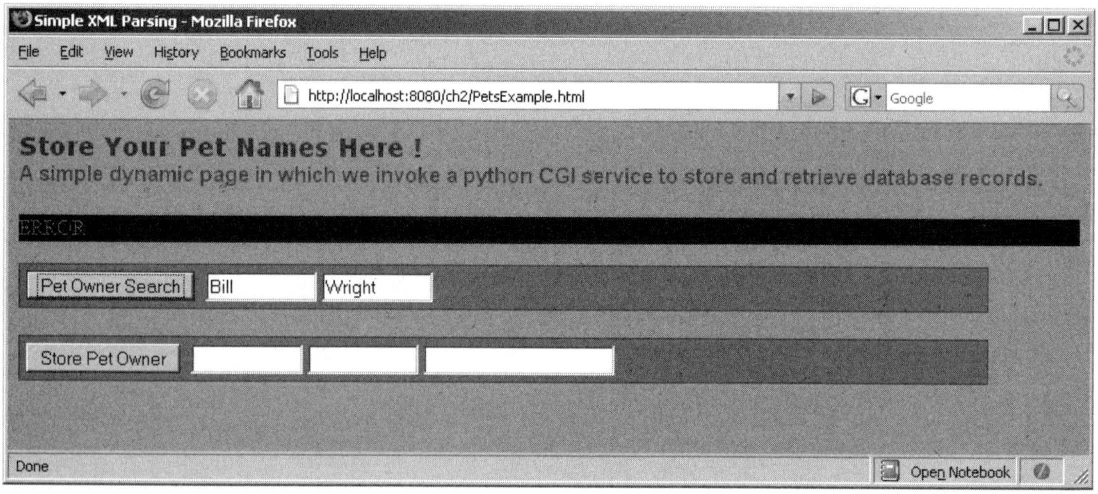

Figure 2-9

That's all there is to it. In the next section, you look at the architecture and implementation of this example application.

Architecture

The example application is made from the following four main parts:

❑   The HTML code that contains the structure of the document and the CSS file that specifies how it should be displayed

❑   The client-side JavaScript code embedded in the HTML page that controls how the page responds to button presses and interacts with the back-end server

❑   The Python CGI script that receives requests from the JavaScript code and responds with XML documents

❑   The back-end database that stores the data

Figure 2-10 shows how the parts interact. When one of the buttons is clicked, the JavaScript updates the status banner of the HTML page and makes a request of the server. The server passes that request to the Python CGI program, which queries or updates the database and responds with an XML document. The server passes that document back to the JavaScript running in the browser, which parses the XML and updates the HTML page accordingly. Sounds simple enough. The next sections examine each part in detail.

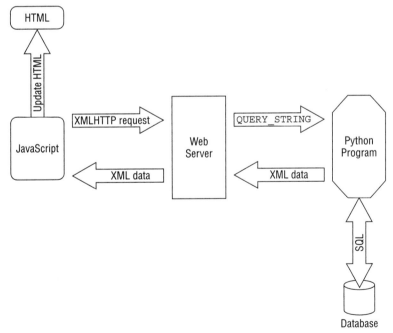

Figure 2-10

The HTML Page

The HTML page is a tree structure of document elements. The significant ones are as follows:

\<html\>: The top-level document container object

    \<head\>: Imports the JavaScript and CSS information for the page **\<body\>:** The contents of the document

        header: A document section for the static text at the top of the page.

        state: A section for the "Loading..." or "Searching..." status message that displays while a server operation is in progress.

        operation: The section in which you display information about whether the last action was a store operation or a search operation.

        firstname: This section displays the first name from the last action. It's empty when the page is first loaded.

        lastname: This section displays the last name from the last action. It's empty when the page is first loaded.

        PetsFound: This section displays the pet names stored or retrieved in the last action. It's empty when the page is first loaded.

        \<div\>: This unnamed div holds the input elements for the search function.

            unnamed button: When clicked, it calls the doQuery JavaScript function.

            searchfirstname: Text input box that holds the pet owner's first name.

            Searchlastname: Text input box that holds the pet owner's last name.

        \<div\>: This unnamed div holds the input elements for the store function.

            unnamed button: When clicked, it calls the doStore JavaScript function.

            savefirstname: Text input box that holds the pet owner's first name to be stored.

            Savelastname: Text input box that holds the pet owner's last name to be stored.

        Pets: Text input box that holds the pet names to be stored.

Listing 2-3 shows the XHTML code for the example.

Listing 2-3: PetsExample.html

```
1    <!DOCTYPE html PUBLIC "-//W3C//DTD XHTML 1.0 Strict//EN"
     "http://www.w3.org/TR/xhtml1/DTD/xhtml1-
     strict.dtd">
2    <html xmlns="http://www.w3.org/1999/xhtml">
3      <head>
4        <meta http-equiv="Content-Type" content="text/html;
             charset=utf-8"/>
5
6        <title>Simple XML Parsing</title>

7        <!-- Load our color and font preferences -->
8        <link rel=StyleSheet href="Style.css"
          TYPE="text/css">

9        <!-- Load xml processing JavaScript libraries -->
10       <script  src="xmlw3cdom.js" type="text/javascript">
         </script>
11       <script  src="xmlsax.js" type="text/javascript">
         </script>

12       <!-- Load our own JavaScript library -->
13       <script src="PetsExample.js" type="text/javascript">
         </script>
14     </head>

15   <body onload="onLoad()">
16   <!-- Static text section -->
17   <div id="header">
18     <h1>Store Your Pet Names Here !</h1>
19     <h2>
20       A simple dynamic page in which we invoke a
         python CGI
21       service to store and retrieve database records.
22     </h2>
23   </div>
24   <br/>
25
26   <!-- Display server interaction state in this section -->
27   <div class="stateelement" id="State"></div>
28   <p>

29   <!-- Display server results in these sections -->
30   <span id="operation" style="font-weight:normal">
     </span>
31   <span id="firstname" style="font-weight:bold">
     </span>
32   <span id="lastname" style="font-weight:bold">
     </span>
33   <span id="PetsFound" style="font-weight:bold">
     </span>
```

(continued)

Listing 2-3 *(continued)*

```
34      </p>
35      <!-- Button and text fields for search function -->
36      <div class="inputelement">
          <button onClick="doQuery()">
37          Pet Owner Search</button> 
38          <input id="searchfirstname"
              value="firstname" size="10"> </input>
39          <input id="searchlastname"
              value="lastname" size="10"></input>
40      </div>
41      <br />

42      <!-- Button and text fields for store function -->
43      <div class="inputelement">
          <button onClick="doStore()">
44          Store Pet Owner</button> 
45          <input id="savefirstname"
              value="firstname" size="10"> </input>
46          <input id="savelastname"
              value="lastname" size="10"> </input>
47          <input id="pets"
              value="pet1,pet2" size="20"></input>
48      </div>
49      <br />

50      </body>
51  </html>
```

Lines 1 and 2 of the HTML document contain boilerplate text that identifies this as an XHTML document.

Lines 3 through 14 are the <head> section of the document. In it, you give the page a title and import the CSS and JavaScript files necessary. Line 13 imports the custom JavaScript that implements the behavior of the page.

Lines 15 through 50 form the <body> section of the document. This section includes the various static text, input fields, and dynamic text elements referenced by the JavaScript. There are three points at which the HTML page invokes the JavaScript. The first one is at line 15:

```
15 <body onload="onLoad()">
```

The onload attribute of the <body> tag specifies a JavaScript function that should be invoked when the page is loaded. The other two JavaScript invocations are the button clicks at lines 36 and 43:

```
36 <div class="inputelement"><button onClick="doQuery()">
```

```
43 <div class="inputelement"><button onClick="doStore()">
```

The onClick element of the <button> tag specifies a JavaScript function that should be invoked when the button is clicked. You'll see these functions when you look at the JavaScript code in the next section.

The JavaScript Code

The JavaScript code is loaded when the HTML when the page is loaded or the user clicks one of the buttons. Listings 2-4 through 2-7 show the important functions in the JavaScript.

Listing 2-4: PetsExample.js Utility Functions

```
 1 var xmlhttp = false;
 2
 3 function onLoad() {
 4   if (window.XMLHttpRequest) {
 5     xmlhttp = new XMLHttpRequest();
 6     xmlhttp.overrideMimeType('text/xml');
 7   } else if (window.ActiveXObject) {
 8     xmlhttp = new
        ActiveXObject("Microsoft.XMLHTTP");
 9   }
10 }
11
12 function cleanupResponseString(response){
13   return response.slice(response.indexOf("<"),
14     response.lastIndexOf(">")+1);
15 }

16 function clearResults() {
17   document.getElementById("operation").innerHTML = '';
18   document.getElementById("PetsFound").innerHTML = '';
19   document.getElementById("firstname").innerHTML = '';
20   document.getElementById("lastname").innerHTML = '';
21 }
22
```

The first three functions in PetsExample.js are utility functions that are called from various places in the JavaScript and HTML code. The onLoad() function (lines 3–10) is called when the page is first loaded. It initializes the XMLHTTPRequest object, and the way in which it does so depends on the browser type. Lines 4 through 6 are appropriate for most browsers; lines 7 and 8 are appropriate for Microsoft browsers. As you'll see later in the book, a good framework will do this kind of thing for you.

The cleanupResponseString() function (lines 12–13) strips any leading or trailing characters from an XML document by removing everything before the first > character and everything after the last > character.

The clearResults() function (lines 16–21) removes all of the text from the four output document sections. It uses document.getElementById() to find those document sections by name.

Listing 2-5 shows the functions that get called in response to the button clicks: doQuery() and doStore().

Listing 2-5: PetsExample.js Button Handling Functions

```
 96 function doQuery() {
 97    var firstname = ↩
    document.getElementById("searchfirstname").value;
 98    var lastname = ↩
    document.getElementById("searchlastname").value;
 99    var uri = ↩
    "load&firstname="+firstname+"&lastname="+lastname;
100    clearResults()
101    queryHandler(uri, parseQueryResult, "Loading...");
102 }

103 function doStore() {
104    var firstname = ↩
    document.getElementById("savefirstname").value;
105    var lastname = ↩
    document.getElementById("savelastname").value;
106    var pets = document.getElementById("pets").value;
107    var uri = "save&firstname="+firstname+
108              "&lastname="+lastname+"&pets="+pets;
109    clearResults()
110    queryHandler(uri, parseStoreResult, "Storing...");
111 }
```

The doQuery() and doStore() functions are very similar in that they do these things:

1. Read the appropriate input text fields.

2. Build a URI query string to be parsed by the Python CGI script.

3. Clear any old results from the display using clearResults().

4. Call queryHandler() to post a request to the server.

The doQuery() function reads the first name and last name of the pet owner from the searchfirstname and searchlastname document elements. For example, if the fields contain the name "Bill Wright" it builds those into a query string that looks like this:

```
load&firstname=Bill&lastname=Wright
```

The doStore() function is similar, but it takes its input data from savefirstname, savelastname, and the pet input text fields. For example, if the owner name fields contain "Bill Wright" and the pet name field contains "Fluffy,Poochie" it builds those into a URI query string that looks like this:

```
save&firstname=Bill&lastname=Wright&pets=Fluffy,Poochie
```

Such strings are passed to the Python CGI program, where they get parsed and converted into database operations.

The doQuery() and doStore() functions both invoke the queryHandler() function. Its arguments are the URI query string, a function to be invoked when the server response is received, and a status string to be displayed while the query is in progress.

The function that handles the interactions with the server is shown in Listing 2-6.

Listing 2-6: PetsExample.js queryHandler Function

```
23 function queryHandler(target, parseFunc, status) {
24   try {
25     netscape.security.PrivilegeManager.
26       enablePrivilege("UniversalBrowserRead");
27   } catch (e) {
28   }
29   if(target !== ""){
30     var url = 'cgi-bin/backend.py?' + target;
31     xmlhttp.open('GET', url, true);
32     xmlhttp.onreadystatechange = function() {
33       if(xmlhttp.readyState == 4 &&
             xmlhttp.status == 200) {
34         var cleanXMLText =
                 cleanupResponseString(xmlhttp.responseText);
35         parseFunc(cleanXMLText);
36       } else {
37         document.getElementById('State').innerHTML =
             status;
38       }
39     };
40     xmlhttp.send(null);
41   }
42 }
```

This function creates the complete URL for the server request and makes the request. The code in lines 24 through 28 attempts to raise a security privilege that is necessary in some browsers. This is another one of those details that a good framework handles automatically. Line 30 builds the entire URL that will be invoked on the server using the base URL (cgi-bin/backend.py) and the query string target passed in by the caller. A full URL might look like this:

```
cgi-bin/backend.py?load&firstname=Bill&lastname=Wright
```

The web server will resolve cgi-bin/backend.py to the Python script and pass the rest to the script itself.

Line 31, xmlhttp.open, starts the asynchronous HTTP request, passing it your URL. The GET argument tells the request to use the GET HTTP method (rather than POST method, for example). The true argument makes this an asynchronous request, meaning the JavaScript will keep executing while the server is processing the request.

The code in lines 32 through 39 defines the function that will get called when there is a state change on the xmlhttp request. This function checks to see if the response is ready (readyState==4) and there was no HTTP error (status==200). If these two conditions are met, it cleans up the response text sent from the server and invokes the parseFunc to process the response. If not, it updates the State document element with the status text passed in by the caller of the function.

After the response XML is successfully received, one of the following two functions is called:

❑ If the request was a query, `parseQueryResult()` is called.

❑ If the request was a search, `parseSearchResult()` is called.

These two functions are very similar and could probably be combined into one function without too much trouble, but they are kept separate here for clarity. Listing 2-7 shows both functions.

Listing 2-7: PetsExample.js XML Parsing Functions

```
44 function parseQueryResult(xml) {
45   var parser = new DOMImplementation();
46   var domDoc = parser.loadXML(xml);
47   //get the root node (in this case, it is petowner)
48   var docRoot = domDoc.getDocumentElement();
49   //display the data
50   if (docRoot.getElementsByTagName("error").item(0)) {
51     document.getElementById('State').innerHTML = "ERROR";
52   } else {
53     document.getElementById("operation").innerHTML = "Pets retrieved for "
54     document.getElementById("firstname").innerHTML =
55       docRoot.getElementsByTagName("firstname").item(0).
56       getFirstChild().getNodeValue();
57     document.getElementById("lastname").innerHTML =
58       docRoot.getElementsByTagName("lastname").item(0).
59       getFirstChild().getNodeValue();
60     document.getElementById("PetsFound").innerHTML = "";
61     var i = 0;
62     for (i=0;
          pet = docRoot.getElementsByTagName("pet").item(i);
          i++) {
63       petname = pet.getFirstChild().getNodeValue();
64       document.getElementById("PetsFound").innerHTML += petname;
65       document.getElementById("PetsFound").innerHTML +=
           " ";
66     }
67     document.getElementById('State').innerHTML = "";
68   }
69 } // end function parseQueryResult
70
71 function parseStoreResult(xml) {
72   var parser = new DOMImplementation();
73   var domDoc = parser.loadXML(xml);
74   var docRoot = domDoc.getDocumentElement();
75   if (docRoot.getElementsByTagName("error").item(0)) {
76     document.getElementById('State').innerHTML = "ERROR";
77   } else {
78     document.getElementById("operation").innerHTML = "Pets stored for "
79     document.getElementById("firstname").innerHTML =
80       docRoot.getElementsByTagName("firstname").item(0).
81       getFirstChild().getNodeValue();
```

```
82      document.getElementById("lastname").innerHTML =
83        docRoot.getElementsByTagName("lastname").item(0).
84        getFirstChild().getNodeValue();
85      var i = 0;
86      document.getElementById("PetsFound").innerHTML = "";
87      for (i=0;
             pet = docRoot.getElementsByTagName("pet").item(i);
             i++) {
88        petname = pet.getFirstChild().getNodeValue();
89        document.getElementById("PetsFound").innerHTML +=
             petname;
90        document.getElementById("PetsFound").innerHTML +=
             " ";
91      }
92     document.getElementById('State').innerHTML = "";
93    }
94 } // end function parseStoreResult
95
```

It's easier to follow the XML parsing code if you know what the response XML document looks like. Listing 2-8 shows an example of an XML document that might be returned from the server.

Listing 2-8: Example XML Response

```
<?xml version='1.0' encoding='ISO-8859-1'?>
<petowner>
  <firstname>Bill</firstname>
  <lastname>Wright</lastname>
  <pet>Fluffy</pet>
  <pet>Poochie</pet>
</petowner>
```

This document contains <petowner> as its root element. Inside that element are one <firstname> element, one <lastname> element, and zero or more <pet> elements. The server returns the same document for search and save operations. Simple is good. If there is any kind of error, the document in Listing 2-9 is returned.

Listing 2-9: XML Error Response

```
<?xml version='1.0' encoding='ISO-8859-1'?>
<error/>
```

The error document has a single, empty root element. Enhancing this to include details about the error is left to the reader.

Now, let's return to Listing 2-7 to see how these documents are parsed. Line 45 instantiates a new XML parser, and line 46 loads the server response text into it. The DOMImplementation instantiated at line 45 is a DOM XML parser, so you can now reference any element by position and name. Line 46 fetches the top-level document element, which should be either <petowner> or <error>. Lines 50 and 51 check to see if this is an error response, and update the Status element if it is. Otherwise, you assume that it is a <petowner> element and extract the <firstname> and <lastname> elements at lines 54 through 59.

Line 53 updates the `operation` element to reflect that this was a query and not a store operation. This is the only difference between `parseQueryResult()` and `parseStoreResult()`. The equivalent line in `parseStoreResult` is line 78.

Lines 61 through 66 loop through all of the `<pet>` elements and append their names to the `PetsFound` HTML page section. Line 67 clears the status banner to indicate that the operation is complete.

The Database

You need some way to store the pet owner data, and a relational database is a good choice. It's easy to store data and retrieve it using SQL. You just have to handle the object-relational mapping.

The first thing you need to do is define a Python class to hold your pet owner data, as shown in Listing 2-10.

Listing 2-10: PetOwner.py

```
 1 ##################################################
 2 # A simple class to hold a pet owner's name and
 3 # a list of pets
 4 ##################################################
 5 class PetOwner:
 6     def __init__(self, firstname, lastname, pets):
 7         self.firstname = firstname
 8         self.lastname = lastname
 9         self.pets = pets
10
11     def __str__(self):
12         ret = self.firstname+" "+self.lastname+\
13             " has %d pets named"%len(self.pets)
14         for p in self.pets:
15             ret = ret + " " + p
16
17         return ret
18
19 # Test the class a little
20 if __name__ == "__main__":
21    dana = PetOwner("Dana", "Moore", \ ("Fluffy", "Poochie"))
22    ray = PetOwner("Ray", "Budd", ("Itchy", "Scratchy"))
23    bill = PetOwner("Bill", "Wright", ("Snowball1", "Snowball2"))
24
25    print dana
```

As you can see, there's not a lot to this class. There is a constructor in lines 6 through 9 that just initializes three instance variables: `firstname`, `lastname`, and `pets`. The `firstname` and `lastname` variables are intended to be strings; the `pets` variable is a list of strings.

You define the `str` function in lines 11 through 17 so you can test it easily. The class test code in lines 19 through 25 just makes three instances of `PetOwner` and prints one out.

Now you need a way to store these objects in a relational database. There are lots of ways to do this, but you can't just use one table. Tables have a fixed number of columns, but there could be an arbitrary number of pets associated with any firstname-lastname pair, so you need to define two related tables. You can define one table called people and one called pets. The CGI program will store first names and last names and references into the pets table. The pets table will store references to the people table and the pet names. Figure 2-11 shows the relationship between these two tables with some example data.

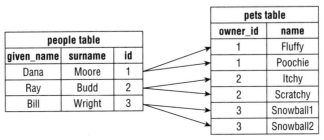

Figure 2-11

Listing 2-11 shows a little Python program that initializes the database for you. It uses pysqlite for its database, but other databases are similar. Consult the appendix for details on installing pysqlite.

Listing 2-11: mkdb.py

```
1 ####################################################
2 # A little program to initialize the two database tables
3 ####################################################
4 from pysqlite2 import dbapi2 as sqlite
5 con = sqlite.connect("petowners")
6 cursor = con.cursor()
7
8 # Delete the tables if they already exist \
9 try:
10    cursor.execute( "drop table pets")
11    cursor.execute( "drop table people")
12 except:
13    print "failed drop"
14
15 # Make the two tables
16 try:
17    cursor.execute("create table people \
18                    (given_name varchar(64), \
19                    surname varchar(64), \
20                    id integer primary key autoincrement)")
21    cursor.execute("create table pets (name varchar(64), \
22                    owner_id integer)")
23 except:
24    print "failed create"
25
26 cursor.close()
27 con.close()
```

Here's what's going on in Listing 2-11:

❑ Line 4 imports the `pysqlite` package, line 5 connects to the `petowners` database file, and line 6 creates a cursor that you'll use to query the database. First, you clear the database if it already exists by dropping (deleting) both tables in lines 10 and 11. If the tables don't exist, you'll get an exception, but no worries.

❑ Line 17 creates the `people` table. The `given_name` and `surname` columns can hold character strings up to 64 characters wide. The `id` column is an integer that you'll use to index into the `pets` table. The `primary key autoincrement` qualifiers allow you to have SQLite automatically generate a unique number for you. You'll see how that works in the next example.

❑ Line 21 creates the `pets` table. The `name` column can hold character strings up to 64 characters wide, and the `owner_id` is an integer that you'll use to reference the `people` table.

❑ Lines 26 and 27 disconnect from the database.

Now you have a Python object to represent your pet owner data and database tables to receive the data — you just need the code to convert between them. Listing 2-12 shows the Python code to store and retrieve `PetOwner` objects.

Listing 2-12: persistpetowner.py

```
 1 ######################################################
 2 # Functions to store and retrieve PetOwner objects
 3 # from the relational database
 4 ######################################################
 5 from pysqlite2 import dbapi2 as sqlite
 6 from petowner import PetOwner
 7
 8 # insert or replace an entry for this pet owner
 9 def savePetOwner(petowner, cursor):
10   q = "SELECT people.id FROM people \
11                 WHERE people.given_name = '%s' \
12                 AND people.surname = '%s'"%\
13                 (petowner.firstname, petowner.lastname)
14   cursor.execute(q)
15   data = cursor.fetchall()
16   # make a new entry if necessary
17   if (len(data) == 0):
18     cursor.execute( "INSERT INTO people VALUES \
19                 ('%s','%s', NULL)"%\
20                 (petowner.firstname, petowner.lastname))
21     cursor.execute( "select max(id) FROM people")
22     data = cursor.fetchall()
23   id = data[0][0]
24   cursor.execute( \
          "DELETE FROM pets WHERE owner_id = %d"%id)
25   for p in petowner.pets:
26     cursor.execute( \
27       "INSERT INTO pets VALUES ('%s','%d')"%(p, id))
28       # retrieve a pet owner record if one exists
29 def loadPetOwner(firstname, lastname, cursor):
```

```
30   q = "SELECT people.given_name, people.surname, pets.name " +\
31        "FROM people, pets " +\
32        "WHERE people.id=pets.owner_id "+ \
33           " AND people.given_name = '%s'"%firstname + \
34           " AND people.surname = '%s'"%lastname \
35
36   cursor.execute(q)
37   data = cursor.fetchall()
38   if (len(data) == 0):
39     return None
40   firstname = data[0][0]
41   lastname = data[0][1]
42   pets = []
43   for d in data:
44     pets.append(d[2])
45   return PetOwner(firstname, lastname, pets)
46
47 # Test the persistence code
48 if __name__ == "__main__":
49   con = sqlite.connect("ex1", isolation_level=None)
50           cursor = con.cursor()
51
52   dana = PetOwner("Dana", "Moore", \
53        ("Fluffy", "Poochie"))
54   ray = PetOwner("Ray", "Budd", ("Itchy", "Scratchy"))
55   bill = PetOwner("Bill", "Wright", \
56        ("Snowball1", "Snowball2"))
57
58   save(dana, cursor)
59   save(ray, cursor)
60   save(bill, cursor)
61
62   d = load("Dana", "Moore", cursor)
63   print d
64
65   cursor.close()
66   con.close()
```

There are two functions in this file:

❑ savePetOwner(petowner, cursor): Takes a PetOwner object and stores it in the database referenced by the cursor

❑ loadPetOwner(firstname, lastname, cursor): Queries the database referenced by the cursor for a PetOwner that matches the firstname and lastname parameters

Lines 5 and 6 import the pysqlite database code and the PetOwner object so you can convert between them.

The `savePetOwner` function starts at line 9. First, you look to see if there is already a record for this `firstname`-`lastname` pair by building the query in line 10. For example, if you're looking for a record for Dana Moore, the result will be a SQL query like this:

```
SELECT people.id FROM people WHERE people.given_name = 'Dana' AND people.surname =
    'Moore'
```

This query is executed in line 14 and the results are extracted in line 15. If there is no record matching the requested `firstname`-`lastname` pair, you insert a new record into the `people` table by building a query like the following in lines 18 through 20:

```
INSERT INTO people VALUES ('Dana', 'Moore', NULL)
```

The `NULL` for the id column tells SQLite to create a new integer key for you, which you fetch with the next query in line 21.

Now that you know the `ID` for your people table, you can insert the pet names into the `pets` table. First, you delete any existing pet records with the `DELETE` query in line 24, and then you look through the pets list, inserting each pet name at lines 25 and 26.

To retrieve the `PetOwners`, you need a `SELECT` query. This query is built in lines 30 through 34. It is a little more complicated than the other queries because it is returning data from two tables. In this case, a query for "Dana Moore" would look like the following:

```
SELECT people.given_name, people.surname, pets.name FROM
    people, pets WHERE people.id=pets.owner_id AND
    people.given_name = 'Dana' AND people.surname = 'Moore'
```

The code executes this query at line 36 and retrieves the results in line 37. If there are no results, it returns `None` at line 39. Otherwise, it fetches the `firstname` and `lastname` from the first record at lines 40 and 41. The names are going to match the queried values, so they could be omitted from the query. Lines 43 and 44 look through all of the results and build a pets list. Finally, the code calls the `PetOwner` constructor and returns the new object at line 45.

Lines 47 through 66 are test code that stores and retrieves a few objects. It's always nice to have some test code.

The Python CGI Program

Now that you've seen the browser side of our little application, we'll show you the server-side code. The request for the HTML page is handled by the web server (the Apache HTTP Server, for example) so you don't have to write any code to handle it. The interesting part starts when one of the two buttons is clicked and the JavaScript is invoked to send an asynchronous HTTP request to the server. The web server is configured to route that request to our CGI program, as shown in Listing 2-13.

Listing 2-13: backend.py

```
1     #!g:\python24\python.exe
2     ##
3     ##
4     import os
5     from pysqlite2 import dbapi2 as sqlite
6     from petowner import PetOwner
7     from persistpetowner import savePetOwner, loadPetOwner
8
9     def PetOwnerToXML(po):
10      print "<petowner>"
11      print "<firstname>%s</firstname><lastname>%s</lastname>"%\
12                    (po.firstname, po.lastname)
13      for p in po.pets:
14        print "<pet>%s</pet>"%p
15      print "</petowner>"
16
17    def EmptyResponse():
18      print "<error/>"
19
20
21    #####################################
22    # Start of main script
23    #####################################
24
25    # Print HTTP and XML headers
26    print "Content-type: text/xml; charset=iso-8859-1\n"
27    print "<?xml version='1.0' encoding='ISO-8859-1'?>"
28
29    # Separate the elements of the URL query string
30    args = os.environ.get("QUERY_STRING").rstrip('"').lstrip('"')
31    commands = args.split("&")
32
33    if len(commands) == 0:
34      exit
35
36    con = sqlite.connect("petowners", isolation_level=None)
37    cursor = con.cursor()
38
39    po = None
40
41    if commands[0] == "save":
42      firstname = None
43      lastname = None
44      pets = None
45      for cmd in commands:
46        if cmd.startswith("firstname="):
47          firstname = cmd.split('=')[1]
48        if cmd.startswith("lastname="):
49          lastname = cmd.split('=')[1]
50        if cmd.startswith("pets="):
51          pets = cmd.split('=')[1].split(',')
52      if (firstname != None) and (lastname != None) and (pets != None):
```

(continued)

43

Listing 2-13 *(continued)*

```
53              po = PetOwner(firstname, lastname, pets)
54              savePetOwner(po, cursor)
55
56          elif commands[0] == "load":
57              firstname = None
58              lastname = None
59              for cmd in commands:
60                  if cmd.startswith("firstname="):
61                      firstname = cmd.split('=')[1]
62                  if cmd.startswith("lastname="):
63                      lastname = cmd.split('=')[1]
64                  if (firstname != None) and (lastname != None):
65                      po = loadPetOwner(firstname, lastname, cursor)
66
67          else:
68              print "ERROR -- unknown command"
69
70          if po != None:
71              PetOwnerToXML(po)
72          else:
73              EmptyResponse()
74
75          cursor.close()
76          con.close()
```

This script just uses the other scripts that you've already seen. The web server or the operating system parses line 1 to find the Python interpreter for this script. Lines 4 through 7 import the scripts that you saw previously.

Lines 9 through 15 contain a Python function that prints a `PetOwner` object in the XML format expected by the JavaScript in the web page. Refer back to Listing 2-8 for an example of this format. It would be a reasonable design decision to include this as a method of `PetOwner`, too. The function `EmptyResponse` sends the error response as shown previously in Listing 2-9.

The main body of the script starts at lines 26 and 27 by printing the headers required to tell the HTTP processing that this is XML content (that's the `Content-type: text/xml` part) and printing the XML header. Line 30 cleans up any extra characters from the URL query string, and line 31 separates it using `&` as the delimiter. So if you send a query string like this:

```
save&firstname=Bill&lastname=Wright&pets=Fluffy,Poochie
```

you will get a Python list like this:

```
['save', 'firstname=Bill', 'lastname=Wright', 'pets=Fluffy,Poochie']
```

Lines 36 and 37 connect to the `petowners` database. The `isolation_level=None` in line 36 puts the connection in *autocommit* mode, which makes changes to the database effective as soon as the command completes.

Then, at line 41, you test whether this is a save operation by looking at the first element of the list. If it is a save, you loop through the other elements of the query string and split out the firstname, lastname, and pets. After the loop, if you found all three, you make a new PetOwner object at line 53 and save it to the database at line 54.

If it's not a save operation, it should be a load operation. You check for this at line 56 by looking at the first element of the list broken out of the query string to see if it matches the "load" string. If it does, then you loop through the other elements of the query string to extract the firstname and lastname strings for the database query. At line 65, you call the loadPetOwner function to execute the query on the database and return the PetOwner object (or None, if it doesn't exist).

Finally, lines 70 through 73 generate the XML content to be sent back to the client. If any function has made a PetOwner object, line 70 converts it to XML and sends it. Otherwise, line 73 sends the empty error response. The web server sends the XML back to the JavaScript client, and the interaction is complete.

Summary

You saw several technologies in this chapter that are not really new, but are being used in new ways to build Web 2.0 applications. You saw the following:

- ❑ HTML documents that include some content, but are mostly structured for dynamic updates by the embedded JavaScript

- ❑ Simple XML documents that are easily generated in Python and parsed by JavaScript

- ❑ JavaScript code that generates asynchronous requests of a back-end server, parses the results of those request, and dynamically updates the HTML document

- ❑ A simple Python class that represents the example data, and the SQL and Python code needed to carry out the object-relational mapping to store and retrieve those objects

- ❑ A Python CGI program that accepts the asynchronous requests from the JavaScript by way of the web server, queries the database, and returns the results as XML documents

Although this chapter used a very simple example, its architecture is not much different than most real-world Web 2.0 applications. It illustrates how the various client-side and server-side components interact to produce the dynamic content that makes Web 2.0 so engaging.

The rest of the book shows you how to use these concepts, along with higher-level frameworks, to build Web 2.0 applications on a scale so large they would be difficult or impossible to hand-code with the techniques shown in this chapter.

3

Introducing the Frameworks

Out of intense complexities intense simplicities emerge.

—Winston Churchill

If we wish to count lines of code, we should not regard them as lines produced but as lines spent.

—Edsger Dijkstra

At the dawn of the Internet age, web developers designed simple web pages that returned simple HTML for a simple request. Since then, the web page has grown increasingly complex. The role of a web site has evolved from the simple act of presenting a user with a view of information, to a Rich Internet Application that can provide the user with a highly interactive experience. Applications like word processors, spreadsheets, and calendars can exist exclusively online and have the capabilities commonly found in a rich client application.

Of course all of these additional capabilities don't come without a price. The technology necessary to produce complex behavior in web sites has also gotten increasingly complex. It all started with the incorporation of basic server-side PHP, and simple client-side JavaScript to make a web site more reactive to a user's actions. Now a web site may have large, sometimes unwieldy sets of objects defined in Java or Python (among a slew of other possible languages) that retrieve the data from a database for presentation. There may be complex business objects that add domain logic and process the data before it's presented. A site may also make use of increasingly complex interfaces that incorporate client-side JavaScript to create complex UI controls, manipulate the elements of a page on the fly, or make asynchronous calls to the server.

When faced with all of this complexity, it's easy to get discouraged unless you bear in mind the advantages you can leverage when faced with these issues. Consider that most applications perform the same types of operations, like generating asynchronous requests, or harder work, like maintaining data in a database. These operations also typically include a lot of boilerplate code that can be greatly condensed.

Think about the asynchronous request that you created in Chapter 2, "Web 2.0 with Traditional Python." It took 10 lines of code to instantiate the request and to ensure it would work in Internet Explorer and other browsers. Because you almost always want to create a request that works in any browser, you're relegated to spend 10 lines of code on this operation in every application.

This leads to the development and use of frameworks that can save developers from having to rewrite the complex components to manage database interactions, or map URLs to operations that the application should perform. It also saves developers from having to write and read lines of duplicate or boilerplate code. Without frameworks, a developer is relegated to needlessly reinvent (or rewrite) the wheel with every new web application.

In this chapter, you're given an introduction to the design of many web application frameworks, and you'll learn the basic capabilities that they can provide. Then you'll learn about the TurboGears and Django frameworks and get a chance to see them in action as you use them to re-implement the example from the previous chapter.

Web Application Frameworks

Recently, a lot of work has been done to develop frameworks that are intended to address and ease all aspects of web application development. The model-view-controller (MVC) pattern is commonly used as the underlying architectural pattern for the frameworks, which can be utilized to very rapidly produce a full-featured MVC web application. They do impose limitations, though, and the utility and applicability of any framework ultimately depends on the requirements of the system being developed. One significant advantage to using a framework is that you're required to write only a minimal amount of code to get up and running from scratch. The architecture of your web application also provides benefits because, by using MVC, you follow a commonly used, powerful, and well-vetted pattern.

MVC in Web Application Frameworks

The MVC pattern is an architectural pattern originally developed for Smalltalk, an object-oriented programming (OOP) language. It enables the clean separation of the presentation logic, control logic, and business objects. Architectures and frameworks incorporating aspects of the MVC concept have appeared in a multitude of applications to solve problems that require any nontrivial presentation layer. The toolkits and frameworks that are used to develop the majority of rich-client applications for Windows, Mac, Linux, and UNIX platforms incorporate the MVC concept in some way. Many common variations of the concept have been defined, and approaches to applying MVC to a variety of problems have been documented in both a language-specific and language-neutral way.

The MVC pattern defines the three main components as follows:

❑ **View:** Manages the output to the display (graphical or textual). This consists of the logic necessary to create the user interface components and use the model to load data into the components.

❑ **Controller:** Manages keyboard and mouse inputs from the user. The control examines and interprets the inputs provided. Based on the inputs, it then forwards commands to the model and/or view.

❑ **Model:** Manages domain data and processing. This includes establishing a persistence representation for the domain data, and operations that can be performed on the data.

The pattern also specifies the following constrained relationships between each of the objects:

❑ The view and controller should have a direct one-to-one correspondence. Every view should have a reference to a controller, and vice versa.

❑ The relationships between the view and model and between the controller and model are less direct. Therefore, a notification protocol should be used whereby a view or controller is registered as being interested in a set of models. When a model changes its internal state, it should notify the set of all of its interested controllers and views. A model should never directly interact with a controller or view.

Note that when you're adapting the MVC pattern to a web application, the relationships between the view and model and between the controller and model are not maintained typically. This is not a practical approach given the disconnected nature of web applications. Not only does it introduce significant additional complexity, but this type of close synchronization is not usually required in a web application. Figure 3-1 is an object model diagram of the MVC relationships when an MVC pattern is applied to a web application. Notice that the model is completely independent of the view and controller, and it can't notify them when it is updated.

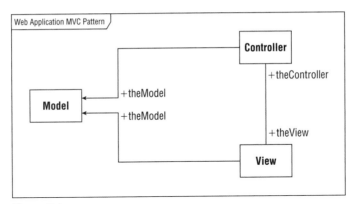

Figure 3-1

This places a responsibility on the view and controller to look for changes in the model when necessary. Depending on the requirements of the application developed, you can typically employ one of two approaches to refresh the view based on updated model data. One option, which you can frequently use when the model is unlikely to get stale, is to look for an updated model as the user interacts with the page. For example, look for updates when the user moves to a new page in the application or clicks a button on the page. The other alternative, which you generally use when the model frequently changes, is to periodically look for changes in the model with JavaScript. If you use AJAX in the web application, it is simple to make an asynchronous request to look for an updated model every time a timeout expires.

Common Web Application Framework Capabilities

Before looking at Django and TurboGears in more detail, it is useful to consider the basic types of capabilities frequently provided by a web application framework designed for Python, or any language. Although no frameworks provide everything, most provide similar capabilities to facilitate the definition of the view, controller, and model (or database) interactions, as well as a variety of project administration utilities.

View Capabilities

Common capabilities that aid a web developer when defining aspects of the view such as HTML pages or client-side JavaScript include the following:

❑   **JavaScript library:** Although not included in Django out of the box, many frameworks include a JavaScript library as an embedded or optional component. For example, TurboGears comes with MochiKit as an optional library.

❑   **Template engine:** A template engine is a component that allows you to embed a language like Python in an otherwise normal HTML page. Python code blocks can be included among standard HTML, when they are outlined with special characters. In a code block, you can use any of the capabilities of the Python language, such as assigning values to variables, or defining control flow statements like `if` or `for`.

❑   **Default templates for data access and manipulation:** Because many web applications are so datacentric, a framework usually provides a mechanism for creating templates or views to perform basic database operations. Simply defining a model, creating the database, and updating the application controller may be sufficient to let you add, edit, delete, and view the corresponding database data.

❑   **View composition:** Views frequently share the same components, such as headers and footers. Typically, the view specification language includes a mechanism that enables a composition view from a set of partial views.

❑   **Data validation framework:** Another convenience provided by a lot of frameworks is the inherent support for validating data. Whether it's done on the client, the server, or both, the validation of data specified by a user is a common issue in web applications that can be greatly simplified through the incorporation of standard validation logic.

❑   **Web server:** Traditionally, even the deployment of a web application for testing is a nontrivial activity. You may need to package a set of files, relocate to a web server deployment directory, and restart the server. Frameworks usually simplify this process by embedding a simple web server into the framework. You're usually required to execute only a single command to start the web server and deploy your test application. You don't need to restart the server as you make changes to your web application either, because servers are usually configured to automatically detect and load changes to the application.

Controller Capabilities

Similar to the capabilities for reducing the complexity of client-side development, a framework can provide the following capabilities to simplify the controller component of a web application:

❑   **Controller definition:** A fundamental aspect of most frameworks is a standard mechanism for defining controllers. This usually includes a base controller object that handles a lot of the lower-level details of HTTP requests and responses.

- ❑ **URL routing and controller-view association:** One main aspect included in most frameworks is a mechanism to ease URL routing, and the association of controllers and views. Simple conventions are frequently employed to allow URLs to be transparently translated to specific controllers or controller functions.

- ❑ **Controller routing and inheritance:** Common functions such as user login must be performed in almost all web applications. Frameworks usually simplify the specification of common controller behavior through a combination of controller inheritance and a URL routing utility.

Model and Database Capabilities

Capabilities included to ease model and database development are typically focused on providing object-relational mapping (ORM) utilities and reducing the pain of database integration. These capabilities commonly include the following:

- ❑ **Automated ORM:** Frameworks typically include a mechanism to automatically translate between model objects and database tables. The implementation may vary between frameworks, but generally the database table structure is based on the model objects or vice versa.

- ❑ **Manual ORM:** Although very powerful, the automated translation between model objects and database tables is practical only when you're starting with a new web application and don't have an existing database. Most frameworks provide a mechanism to map model objects to an existing database in case you're not starting from scratch. However, the offerings of the framework should be explored fully before a selection is made, because the level of support for and the efficiency of these tools vary greatly between frameworks.

- ❑ **Database interaction abstraction:** Any ORM component included in a framework also has the ability to abstract database interactions. A web application developer typically interacts with model objects only and isn't required to write any SQL in the web application. One huge advantage of this is that the web application isn't tied to any particular dialect of SQL or any particular database. This means that you can change from one database implementation to another without worrying about updating all the SQL in your web application.

- ❑ **Developmental database implementation:** Many frameworks include a simple database implementation that is usable with minimal or no reconfiguration out of the box. In many cases this is the SQLite relational database management system, but other implementations may be used.

- ❑ **Production database integration:** When you're ready to deploy a web application that you've developed with a framework, you will probably need a more sophisticated database implementation that can handle greater loads. This is usually accomplished by modifying a simple database configuration and rebuilding the models. Although the production database implementations supported by each framework may be different, most frameworks support the major database implementations such as MySQL, PostgreSQL, and Microsoft SQL Server.

General Capabilities

Of course, the framework must provide some general capabilities that reduce the complexity of other aspects of a web application. Typically these include the following:

- ❑ **Test framework:** The web application and software engineering community has widely adopted the practice of writing and automating unit tests, and many frameworks have been developed to support testing in a variety of languages. Most frameworks include mechanisms to aid you when developing and running unit tests.

❑ **Console:** For interpreted languages like Python, a console is usually included. When you start the console within a particular project, it is initialized to the configuration of the project. This allows you to use it as a preconfigured sandbox in which you can interactively test or otherwise interact with your new objects, the project database, and other project scripts.

❑ **Standardized project directory structure:** All projects developed with the framework conform to the same directory structure. This usually consists of locations for third-party component configuration (such as a database or web server); source code divided into model, view, and controller modules; unit test files; and so on. Utilities are commonly provided to create the shell of a project to which you can add application logic.

❑ **Community tools:** Apart from the core framework capabilities and tools, many frameworks have additional tools that you can download separately. These tools are usually developed within the user community, are freely available, and are intended to help you get the most out of a framework.

Now that you've seen the common elements frequently provided by a web application framework, you're ready to look at two Python web frameworks in more detail. You'll first be introduced to the TurboGears framework, followed by the Django framework.

Introduction to TurboGears

In this section you get a whirlwind introduction to the TurboGears framework. First you learn a little about the framework's motivation, history, and capabilities. Then you take a look at the primary Turbo-Gears components, the wealth of alternates available, and how the main components relate to the MVC architecture.

TurboGears History

Rather than being developed from the ground up as a stand-alone application, the majority of TurboGears is based on several preexisting components. The open source framework was created by Kevin Dangoor and first released in 2005. It was originally developed to be the framework behind Zesty News, a news aggregator project started by Kevin Dangoor in 2005 that has yet to be released.

Main TurboGears Components

TurboGears was created from a number of existing components. All of these components are packaged separately, and can be downloaded and used without TurboGears. The main components include the following:

❑ **MochiKit:** A JavaScript library that includes components such as logging, drag and drop, and other visual effects which are common to many libraries. The site www.mochikit.com contains documentation and downloads of the library for use without TurboGears.

❑ **Kid:** A template language that enables you to include embedded Python in an XHTML page. You can either embed Python code explicitly with a Python tag, or use an included set of attributes such as loops and conditionals to define dynamic content. You can download Kid and get detailed documentation at www.kid-templating.org.

❑ **CherryPy:** An object-oriented framework that enables you to develop web applications in Python. CherryPy includes mechanisms to do webcentric operations such as simple URL mapping, server control, and request filtering. For more information on CherryPy, or to download the standalone version, go to `http://cherrypy.org/`.

❑ **SQLObject:** A simple ORM that includes a mechanism for mapping Python objects to a relational database. It also includes a Python-based abstraction of standard SQL mechanisms that enables developers to interact with databases from a Python script or shell. For further information and downloads, go to `www.sqlobject.org/`.

TurboGears also includes a wide variety of other features and utilities, including web-based and command-line utilities to help with common project administration tasks, a project build tool, an embedded web server, a test framework, and a web-based utility for the administration of model objects, among others.

Alternate Components

TurboGears allows you to use a wide variety of alternate implementations of the various components, with the exception of CherryPy. A JavaScript library like Dojo Toolkit (`http://dojotoolkit.org/`) or script.aculo.us (`http://script.aculo.us/`) can easily be used in place of or in addition to MochiKit. In several cases, TurboGears developers have contributed add-on components that package the JavaScript as TurboGears widgets. Basically, a widget is a piece of a web site (including HTML, CSS, and/or JavaScript) that is repackaged as a reusable Python component. (You'll learn more about widgets later.)

You can also use several template engines in place of Kid, such as HtmlPy (`http://dwayneb.free.fr/turbohtmlpy/`) or Myghty (`http://www.myghty.org/`) among several others. You can even plug the Django template engine into TurboGears.

Additionally, you can use SQLAlchemy (`http://www.sqlalchemy.org/`) as an alternative to SQLObject. This very popular ORM is under development with an enthusiastic community, and may even eventually replace SQLObject as the default ORM implementation in TurboGears.

MVC Architecture in TurboGears

The TurboGears framework incorporates the MVC architecture in much the same way that most other current web application frameworks (such as Ruby on Rails) do. The TurboGears components that correspond to the MVC components are shown in the following table.

MVC Component	TurboGears Component	Description
View	Kid templates	Responsible for presenting the data selected by a controller to a user. For a given web application, all Kid templates are generally located in a `templates` directory under the project's main package.
Controller	Root controller class	In TurboGears, controller objects are located in `controller.py` in the main package of the project. Several classes may be defined in this file. The TurboGears controller contains the logic to look up database data and select a Kid template for display, given a requested URL.

Table continued on following page

MVC Component	TurboGears Component	Description
Model	SQLObjects	In TurboGears, models are maintained in `model.py` under the project's main package. Each object usually corresponds to a database table and typically includes the specification of the column details. The model specification usually determines the structure of the database.

Creating an Example Application

Now that you're a bit more familiar the components that make up TurboGears and the main capabilities it provides, you're ready to get into more detail with an example. In Chapter 2 you developed a simple web application that allows a user to store and load his name as well as the name of his pets. In this chapter you implement the same basic application using TurboGears.

Creating the Project Skeleton

The first step in developing a TurboGears project is to create a new project with the `tg-admin` tool. There is a variety of `tg-admin` subcommands (a subset is shown in the table below), but you can create a new project with the `quickstart` command, optionally providing the name of the project that you're creating. You'll be prompted for the name of the package with a default value defined, which you'll usually want to use as is. The package is simply a version of the project name that conforms to Python package formatting conventions and can be referenced in your Python code. You're also asked if you need to manage multiple users. You'll learn more about this in Part II, TurboGears, but for now say `no`.

Script	Command	Example	Description
`tg-admin`	`quickstart [project name]`	`tg-admin quickstart PetInfoStore`	Create a new project.
`tg-admin`	`shell`	`tg-admin shell`	Start a Python interactive shell initialed to your project.
`tg-admin`	`sql [command]`	`tg-admin sql create`	Manage your database defined by your SQL Object classes. The example creates a database that corresponds to your model files.
`tg-admin`	`toolbox`	`tg-admin toolbox`	Start the TurboGears web toolkit.
`start-[project name].py`	n/a	`python start-petinfostore.py`	Start the embedded web server for a project.
`setup.py`	`build`	`python setup.py build`	Build the web application.

For this example you'll create a pet-information storage project called `PetInfoStore`. To do this, open a command shell in the directory where you want to create the project, and enter the following:

```
C:\turbogears-examples>tg-admin quickstart PetInfoStore
Enter package name [petinfostore]:
Do you need Identity (usernames/passwords) in this project?
    [no]
```

This creates the base project directory `PetInfoStore` as well as a set of standard project files that include the following:

```
PetInfoStore
   + PetInfoStore.egg-info
   + petinfostore
   + config
      - app.cfg
      - log.cfg
   - controllers.py
   - json.py
   - model.py
   - release.py
   + sqlobject-history
   + static
      + css
         - style.css
      + images
      + javascript
   + templates
      - login.kid
      - master.kid
      - welcome.kid
   + tests
      - test_controllers.py
      - test_model.py
   - dev.cfg
   - sample-prod.cfg
   - setup.py
   - start-petinfostore.py
   - test.cfg
```

These files represent the fundamental components of a TurboGears application.

The base project directory also contains a few scripts and configuration files. For example, you can use `setup.py` to build your project and create distributions among several other operations as follows:

```
C:\turbogears-examples\PetInfoStore>python setup.py build
```

You can get the complete details on the `setup.py` script in the online TurboGears documentation or by passing the `--help` and `--help-message` arguments to the script, but you probably won't need to worry about building and deploying with this script as you're experimenting with basic projects.

The advantage of a framework for an interpreted language like Python makes it simple to run a web application for testing purposes. For your initial testing all you need to do is start the web application on the web server provided with TurboGears. To do this, invoke the `start-petinfostore.py` script as follows:

```
C:\turbogears-examples\PetInfoStore>python start-petinfostore.py
```

This automatically generates a test page for your web application. To see this page, open your browser and go to `http://localhost:8080/` as shown in Figure 3-2.

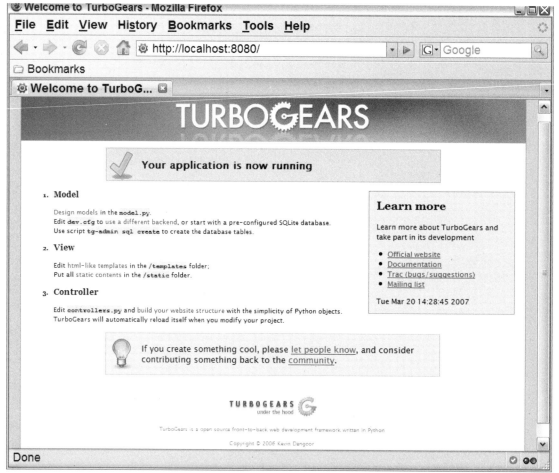

Figure 3-2

There is also a variety of configuration files in the top-level directory and the `petinfostore/config` subdirectory. You don't have to worry too much about these for now if you're using SQLLite as your database because the default development configuration works without any changes. Note, however, that the development environment configuration (`dev.cfg`) and production environment configuration (`sample-prod.cfg`) are separate.

The `petinfostore` directory shows a variety of subdirectories that you can use to define your project tests (`tests`), Kid templates (`templates`), and static web content (`static`). The most interesting files to note initially are the Python scripts at this level. The `release.py` script can be used to define some simple information about your project. Several variables are defined in this file that you may want to uncomment and tailor to your project. The main scripts in this package, however, make up the model (`model.py`) and controller (`controllers.py`) components of the MVC architecture used by the framework. The view is defined by the Kid templates.

The Model

Now that you've created the project and explored the main files in the project directory, you're ready to define a model that can store the information for a user and a pet. The database you created in Chapter 2 contained two tables: one for pets, and one for people. The `people` table maintained the given name (first name) and the surname (last name) of the pet owner, and the `pet` table included the pet name and the Identifier (ID) of the pet owner as a reference to the `people` table.

Defining the Model Classes

To define a structure in the TurboGears project that is similar to the database created in Chapter 2, open the `model.py` file and define two new classes, `Person` and `Pet`, that inherit from the base `SQLObject` class as shown in Listing 3-1. In general, any model object that you define should inherit from `SQLObject` so you can incorporate the object into the database and perform database operations such as select or update.

Listing 3-1: The TurboGears model.py file

```
 1 from turbogears.database import PackageHub
 2 from sqlobject import *
 3
 4 hub = PackageHub("petinfostore")
 5 __connection__ = hub
 6
 7 # class YourDataClass(SQLObject):
 8 #     pass
 9
10 class Person(SQLObject):
11    given_name = StringCol()
12    surname = StringCol()
13    def __str__(self):
14      return "%s %s" % (self.given_name, self.surname)
15
16 class Pet(SQLObject):
17    name = StringCol()
18    owner = ForeignKey('Person')
```

Note that the model file contains some boilerplate code on lines 1 through 6. Lines 7 and 8 include a commented-out, empty sample data object to show you where to define your models.

The `Person` class defines the `given_name` and `surname` attributes, which are database columns that contain the string objects denoted by `StringCol`. The class also establishes the string representation of the object as the given name followed by the surname on lines 13 and 14.

The `Pet` class holds the name of the pet (line 17), and a reference to a row in the `Person` table accomplished by initializing the attribute to a `ForeignKey` object and providing the name of the `Person` table as an argument (line 18).

Creating the Database

At this point you've defined the basic data elements of the pet information store. You can now create the database tables and even start playing around with them in a Python shell. To create the database, use the `tg-admin` command from the base project directory as follows:

```
C:\turbogears-examples\PetInfoStore>tg-admin sql create
```

The `sql` subcommand allows you to interact with your database and takes a variety of commands. Here are some of the most useful ones:

❑   create: You can use this command to create all the database tables for the `SQLObject` sub-classes in the project.

❑   execute: Executes an arbitrary SQL command. Simply include the SQL commands you want to execute in quotes on the command line. For example, the following uses the SQL command to select all rows in the `Person` table:

```
C:\turbogears-examples\PetInfoStore>tg-admin sql execute "select * from person;"
Using database URI sqlite:///C|\turbogears-
    examples\PetInfoStore/devdata.sqlite
id      given_name      surname
C:\turbogears-examples\PetInfoStore>
```

Although this command is quite handy if you're writing scripts to interact with the database, you probably wouldn't want to use it to interactively initialize or analyze the database. For this, you can use the shell provided by TurboGears that simplifies interactively manipulating the database.

❑   list: Generates a list of all the SQLObject classes that will be created with a `create` command.

❑   sql: Shows the SQL command that will be used to create the tables with a `create` command.

Initializing the Database with the Interactive Shell

As noted in the previous section, you could use the `execute` command to load the database from the command line, but TurboGears also provides an interactive shell that makes this much simpler. To start the shell, invoke the `tg-admin` command from the base project directory again, this time providing the `shell` subcommand as follows:

```
C:\turbogears-examples\PetInfoStore>tg-admin shell
```

This starts an interactive Python shell, initialized to the configuration of your project. It gives you access to all your model classes, as well as any other classes you've defined. Listing 3-2 shows a sample interaction with the shell that creates two new people and one pet.

Listing 3-2: An example of TurboGears Python shell interaction

```
 1 C:\turbogears-examples\PetInfoStore>tg-admin shell
 2 Python 2.4.4 (#71, Oct 18 2006, 08:34:43) [MSC ↩
v.1310 32 bit (Intel)] on win32
 3 Type "help", "copyright", "credits" or "license" for more information.
 4 (CustomShell)
 5 >>> ray = Person(given_name="Ray", surname="Budd")
 6 >>> dana = Person(given_name="Dana", surname="Moore")
 7 >>> everyone = Person.select()
 8 >>> list(everyone)
 9 [<Person 1 given_name='Ray' surname='Budd'>, ↩
<Person 2 given_name= 'Dana' surname='Moore'>]
10 >>> p = Person.select(Person.q.surname=='Budd')
11 >>> list(p)
12 [<Person 1 given_name='Ray' surname='Budd'>]
13 >>> p = Person.get(2)
14 >>> str(p)
15 'Dana Moore'
16 >>> thepets = Pet.select()
17 >>> list(thepets)
18 []
19 >>> kat = Pet(name="Herr Kat", owner=ray)
20 >>> str(kat)
21 "<Pet 1 name='Herr Kat' ownerID=1>"
22 >>> p = Pet(name="Boots", owner=2)
23 >>> list(Pet.select())
24 [<Pet 1 name='Herr Kat' ownerID=1>, <Pet 2 name='Boots' ownerID=2>]
25 >>> hub.commit()
26 >>> ^Z
27 Do you wish to commit your database changes? [yes]
28
29 C:\turbogears-examples\PetInfoStore>
```

The example interactive session in this listing shows the following useful methods to invoke when interacting with the database:

❑ To create a new row in the database, simply create a new instance of the object as shown on lines 5 and 6. The object specification includes the values to assign to the object's given_name and surname variables.

❑ The select method retrieves a list of rows as shown on line 7, and takes an optional expression as shown on line 10. Note that the expression on line 10 accesses a special object q, defined for all SQL objects, that should be used when creating select queries.

❑ To retrieve a single row when you know the identifier, use the get method with the automatically generated identifier of the row to retrieve (line 13).

❑ To insert a row with a foreign key, you can either pass a variable initialized to the foreign table entry (line 19), or reference the ID of the foreign table entry (line 22).

❑ When you exit the shell, you'll be asked whether or not you want to save the changes to the database. You can also explicitly commit your changes with the commit method (line 25).

Initializing the Database with CatWalk

Another alternative to interacting with your model objects via the interactive shell is to use CatWalk, a web-based model administration tool that can be used to manage the data in the database. You can access CatWalk using the `toolbox` subcommand of `tg-admin`, a web-based project administration tool.

First, start the TurboGears Toolbox from the base project directory as shown here:

```
C:\turbogears-examples\PetInfoStore>tg-admin toolbox
```

This displays the web page shown in Figure 3-3. It includes CatWalk and a variety of other utilities that are initialized to the settings of your project. Most notably, these utilities include WebConsole, which is a Python interpreter, ModelDesigner, which is used to design and generate code for SQLObjects, and Widget Browser, which lets you explore the widgets available for your project (discussed in Chapter 4).

Figure 3-3

Click the CatWalk link, and you're presented with the `Person` and `Pet` tables. If you select a table, you're shown all the records in the table, and through this interface you can add, delete, view, or modify all the records in the database as shown in Figure 3-4. You can even modify the columns displayed and the order of the displayed columns.

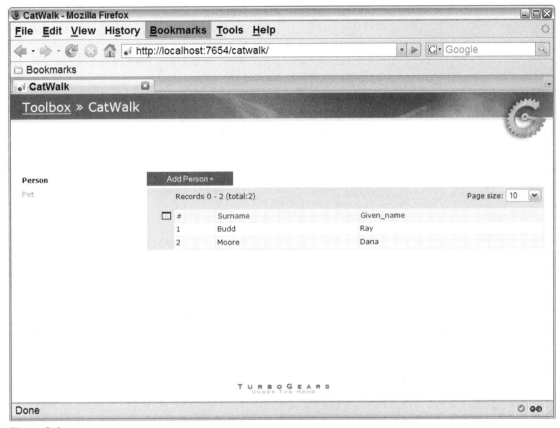

Figure 3-4

The Controller and View

At this point, you're ready to define the controller and view. In the following sections you'll see what the quick start generates for the default controller and learn a bit about how to add new pages to a web application. You'll also see several approaches to defining controllers and views that allow you to edit and view pet owner and pet data.

The Quickstart Controller

The generated project skeleton includes a default controller file, `PetInfoStore\petinfostore\controller.py`. The controller initially displays a default web page with the time and a welcome message, as shown previously in Figure 3-2. To see how this is done, look at the generated controller file:

```
 1 from turbogears import controllers, expose
 2 # from model import *
 3 # import logging
 4 # log = logging.getLogger("petinfostore.controllers")
 5
 6 class Root(controllers.RootController):
 7 @expose(template="petinfostore.templates.welcome")
 8     def index(self):
 9         import time
10         # log.debug("Happy TurboGears Controller Responding For Duty")
11         return dict(now=time.ctime())
```

This default code shows you the basics of the controller structure. Chapter 4 goes into more detail about the web application controller, but for now you can just note a few general things about this controller specification:

❑   The root controller is called `Root` and inherits from the `controllers.RootController` object. A default version of this is automatically defined for you when you create a project skeleton as shown on lines 6 through 11.

❑   The root controller gets associated with the root of the project's URI (`/`), and serves as the primary controller for the web application.

❑   You can include additional controllers by defining a reference to them in the root controller. The name of the reference automatically gets mapped to a subpath in the URL. For example, adding the following attribute between lines 6 and 7 would associate the `FooController` with the web site path `'/foo'` and cause the `FooController` to be invoked when the user enters the location `http://localhost:8080/foo` into a web browser:

```
foo = FooController()
```

You'll see an example of this when you incorporate the CatWalk controller in your web application in the section "Adding CatWalk to the Controller" later in this chapter.

❑   Each method definition maintains the logic necessary to look up any required database data and select a KID template to display the data based on the URI entered.

Incorporating a Model Object Editor

There are several ways to provide access to the pet data store and allow the user to specify and retrieve the information. Each has its own strengths and limitations. Some require modification of the controller only, and others require you to define a set of templates capable of displaying your data. In general, to provide access to a model, you can do the following:

❑   **Incorporate CatWalk into your application.** The simplest approach to allow a user to access your data objects is to simply embed the CatWalk utility in your application. All you need to do is create a CatWalk controller as an attribute of your project's root controller. This is by far the simplest approach, but it is also the least practical in a real-world application due to the fact that CatWalk provides direct access to any table and has a standard interface. Your real-world web applications would most likely have tables that you don't want to give the user direct access to, as well as customized views to manipulate the data.

❑ **Use the FastData extension.** This is an extension to TurboGears that provides a basic editor for database tables. It is similar to CatWalk in that you simply add the FastData DataController into your root controller. There has been some discussion about incorporating FastData as a base component of TurboGears, but it is still missing many features, and future support for it is unknown. Therefore, it isn't covered in detail here, but if you're adventurous you can find installation and usage information at http://docs.turbogears.org/1.0/FastData.

❑ **Use the TGCrud extension.** This is another extension to TurboGears that helps you incorporate basic SQL object manipulation functions into your web application. Rather than provide a controller and predefined templates like CatWalk or FastData, TGCrud generates controller and template code that you can tailor to provide the basic data manipulation for your project. This requires a little more work up front, but it ultimately pays off because you tailor the views to the requirements of the web application (discussed in more detail in Chapter 4).

❑ **Manually define the controller and view.** Of course, you're always free to define your own views manually. This is useful in cases where you don't want to provide basic retrieval and update logic, and would rather tailor the interaction with the model objects of the web application.

Adding CatWalk to the Controller

The easiest way to provide access to model objects is by including the CatWalk utility in your web application. All that you need to do to provide this capability is add the CatWalk controller to the root controller of your project. To do this, open the skeleton controller file, PetInfoStore\petinfostore\ controller.py, and add the code shown on lines 2 and 8 here:

```
 1 from turbogears import controllers, expose
 2 from turbogears.toolbox import catwalk
 3 # from model import *
 4 # import logging
 5 # log = logging.getLogger("petinfostore.controllers")
 6
 7 class Root(controllers.RootController):
 8     catwalk = catwalk.CatWalk()
 9     @expose(template="petinfostore.templates.welcome")
10     def index(self):
11 ...
```

Line 2 simply imports the CatWalk utility from the turbogears.toolbox package. Line 8 adds a new path called /catwalk to your web application that gets forwarded to the CatWalk controller. Note that the name of the new path is determined by the name of the attribute on line 8. For example, if the attribute were named edit, the path created would be /edit.

If you save the file at this point and the web application is already running, the web server detects the changed file and automatically reloads the web application for you. Otherwise, you can start the web application by running the `start-petinfostore.py` script, and open a browser to the web application at `http://localhost:8080/`. Notice that the index still shows the welcome template. This is due to the index mapping at line 10. However, you can get to the new path by browsing to `http://localhost:8080/catwalk`. The result is the same page that was shown previously in Figure 3-4.

Defining a Tailored View

In the real world, you'll generally want to use tailored views either generated with the TGCrud extension or manually written instead of using CatWalk. This allows a web application to create a more user-friendly and unique look and feel, as well as to more effectively control access to the components in the model. In this section you'll see how to create a simple view (a Kid template) that shows the pet information for a particular pet owner.

You can use a Kid template to embed Python code in an XHTML document. In a TurboGears project, the Kid templates for a package appear in a `templates` directory under the `package` directory. The example pet information store project includes a `PetInfoStore/petinfostore/templates` directory that already contains the following three template files:

- ❑ **login.kid:** Ignore this for now. It's used when performing multi-user management, which isn't applicable to this example pet information store application.

- ❑ **master.kid:** This is an example of a template that establishes the look and feel of all pages on the site. One advantage to using Kid templates is that common web site components like the header and footer need to be defined only once. These components are defined in a master template that gets extended by each template responsible for creating a specific view. (You'll learn more about how to define common behaviors in Kid templates in Part II.)

- ❑ **welcome.kid:** This template creates the default view presented for a new project (previously shown in Figure 3-2). Note that this template uses the master template to create a common header.

To create the tailored view, define a new Kid template, `petinfov1.kid`, under the `templates` directory as shown in Listing 3-3.

Listing 3-3: The initial version of the petinfov1.kid template

```
1 <!DOCTYPE html PUBLIC "-//W3C//DTD XHTML 1.0 Transitional//EN"
2 "http://www.w3.org/TR/xhtml1/DTD/xhtml1-transitional.dtd">
3 <html xmlns="http://www.w3.org/1999/xhtml"xmlns:py="http://purl.org/kid/ns#"
4   py:extends="'master.kid'">
5   <head>
6     <meta content="text/html; charset=utf-8"
7       http-equiv="Content-Type" py:replace="''"/>
8       <title>Welcome to the Pet Information Store</title>
9   </head>
```

```
10  <body>
11    <select id="personOption">
12      <option py:for="person in people"
13        id="${person.id}" value="${person.id}">
14        ${person.given_name} ${person.surname}
15      </option>
16    </select>
17    <div id="pets-div" name="pets-div"></div>
18  </body>
19 </html>
```

This template takes a list of `Person` model objects as input and creates a `select` element containing an entry for each `person`, as shown in Figure 3-5.

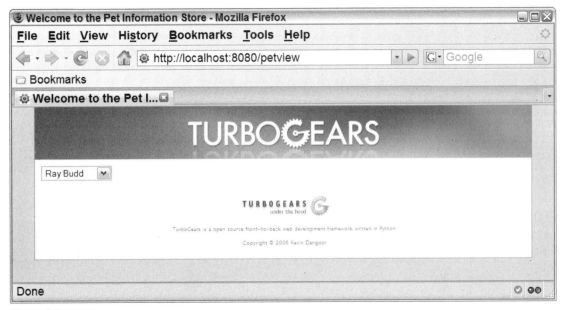

Figure 3-5

At first glance, it doesn't appear much different than a standard HTML document. A few important differences should be noted, though:

❑   The template includes an additional namespace defined by `xmlns:py="http://purl.org/kid/ns#"` on line 3. This establishes a set of attributes and elements specific to Python that can be used to incorporate Pythonic elements into an otherwise normal HTML element. Any elements or attributes that start with `py` are from this namespace.

❑ Line 4 adds the attribute `py:extends` to the HTML element, which causes the template to adopt the common look and feel of the web site as defined in `master.kid`. This removes the TurboGears header and footer, as shown in Figure 3-6.

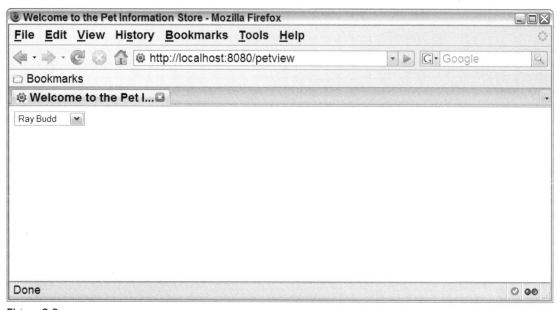

Figure 3-6

❑ On line 12, the `py:for` attribute is used to create a Python `for` loop construct. This causes an `option` element to be created for each element in the list of people.

❑ A Python expression can be embedded in the Kid template by enclosing it in braces with a leading dollar sign, as in `${<expr>}`. This is shown on line 13 where the ID and value of the option are set to the `Person` model object's `id` attribute value.

❑ Line 14 defines two expressions that retrieve the `given_name` and `surname` from the `person` model object to create the value displayed in the drop-down list.

❑ Line 17 creates an empty `div` element that will be extended later to include the pets associated with the selected person.

Calling the View from the Controller

Now that you've defined the view, you have to add a bit of plumbing to allow it to be accessed as a part of the web application. In this section, you define a new path in the root controller that goes to the new `petinfo.kid` template.

Previously, you defined a new path in the web application when you added a reference to CatWalk to the root controller. You can also add a path by defining a new method in the root controller, as shown in Listing 3-4 where the `petview` method is defined.

Listing 3-4: Defining an additional petview path in the root controller

```
 1 from turbogears import controllers, expose
 2 from turbogears.toolbox import catwalk
 3 from model import *
 4 import logging
 5 log = logging.getLogger("petinfostore.controllersv1")
 6
 7 class Root(controllers.RootController):
 8   catwalk = catwalk.CatWalk()
 9
10   @expose(template="petinfostore.templates.welcome")
11   def index(self):
12     import time
13     # log.debug("Happy TurboGears Controller Responding For Duty")
14     return dict(now=time.ctime())
15
16   @expose(template="petinfostore.templates.petinfov1")
17   def petview(self):
18     log.info("loading the pet view")
19     return dict(people=Person.select())
```

There are several interesting aspects of a controller that are exhibited in the listing:

❑ The method defined on lines 16 through 19 adds a new path, /petview, in the web application. The path name is determined by the name of the method (line 17).

❑ The Kid template must be exposed with the decorator in order to be called with an external request. The template should be specified with the full package name of the template (which in this case is petinfostore.templates) and the name of the template without the .kid extension (petinfov1).

❑ Recall that line 12 of Listing 3-3 defined a for loop that iterates over the people variable containing a list of Person model objects. The controller is responsible for defining any such variables accessed in the Kid template and returning them in a dictionary. In this case, the select method is used on line 19 to select all the Person model objects. The result of the select statement is associated with the people key in the dictionary that gets returned from the petview method.

❑ To perform logging in your controller, you can use the standard Python logging method. In Listing 3-4, this was done as follows:

  ❑ Line 4 imports the logging package.

  ❑ Line 5 creates a log variable and initializes it to the controller logger.

  ❑ Line 18 uses the standard log method info.

At this point, if you save your controller and browse to http://localhost:8080/petview, you'll see the new view in the web application (which should be similar to what was shown previously in Figure 3-5).

Extending the Template to Display the Pet Names

The next step in defining the web application is to extend the Kid template to make an asynchronous call to the server and get the list of pets associated with a given pet owner. In Chapter 2 you had to write several lines of code to correctly set up, configure, and make an asynchronous call. In this section, you'll see how to avoid writing most of the boilerplate code by using the MochiKit JavaScript library.

With MochiKit, you can define the XMLHttpRequest in a single line and associate it with a simple callback function on another line. To see how this is done, define the template file `petinfov2.kid` as shown in Listing 3-5.

Listing 3-5: The petinfov2.kid template file

```
 1  <!DOCTYPE html PUBLIC "-//W3C//DTD XHTML 1.0 Transitional//EN"
 2  "http://www.w3.org/TR/xhtml1/DTD/xhtml1-transitional.dtd">
 3  <html xmlns="http://www.w3.org/1999/xhtml"
 4    xmlns:py="http://purl.org/kid/ns#"
 5    py:extends="'master.kid'">
 6    <head>
 7      <meta content="text/html; charset=utf-8"
 8        http-equiv="Content-Type" py:replace="''"/>
 9      <title>Welcome to the Pet Information Store</title>
10      <script src="${tg.tg_js}/MochiKit.js"/>
11      <script>
12        function handleChange() {
13          var owner = $("personOption").value;
14          d = loadJSONDoc("/search", {owner: owner});
15          d.addCallback(handleCallback);
16        }
17
18        function handleCallback(result) {
19          var petDiv = $("pets-div");
20        petDiv.innerHTML = "<p>has " + result.pets.length +
21          " pets: " + result.pets + "</p>"
22        }
23      </script>
24    </head>
25    <body>
26      <select id="personOption" onchange="handleChange()">
27        <option py:for="person in people"
28          id="${person.id}" value="${person.id}">
29          ${person.given_name} ${person.surname}
30        </option>
31      </select>
32      <div id="pets-div" name="pets-div"></div>
33    </body>
34  </html>
```

This listing shows how easy it is to define an XMLHttpRequest and callback in TurboGears. Specifically:

❑   The MochiKit library must be included in the template, as is done on line 10. The `tg.tg_js` variable is automatically available to your templates and specifies the location of `MochiKit.js`. As a result, your template can use any of the MochiKit library components.

❑ The script on lines 10 through 23 defines two functions. `handleChange` gets invoked when the user changes the `personOption` element, and `handleCallback` is the function that gets invoked when the asynchronous request completes.

More specifically, the `handleChange` function does the following:

1. The selected value is retrieved on line 13 and saved in the `owner` variable. This uses a convenient `$(<id>)` function that is defined in MochiKit and is basically shorthand for a call to `getElementById`.

2. The XMLHttpRequest is created with the call to `loadJSONDoc()` on line 14. The function takes a URI, "/search", and an optional argument list contains a single key-value pair where the key is `"owner"` and the value is the ID of the selected person.

3. The function returns an instance of a `Deferred` object. This is a special class defined in MochiKit that is essentially a wrapper for asynchronous XMLHttpRequests. Don't worry too much about the details of the `Deferred` object — you learn about these in much greater detail in Part II. For now, assume you can create a variety of different types of asynchronous requests that get turned into XMLHttpRequest objects.

4. The callback is added to the `Deferred` object on line 15. This effectively tells the request to invoke the callback when the request has completed.

The `handleCallback` function displays the results of the asynchronous call as follows:

1. The `pet-div` is retrieved on line 19, again using the `$()` shorthand notation for `getElementById`.

2. After the div is retrieved, the `innerHTML` of the div is set to a snippet of HTML based on the response from the server (lines 20 and 21).

3. The value of the result variable is set to the response from the server.

❑ Line 26 defines an event handler for the `personOption` element that invokes the `handleChange` function when the user changes the selected option element.

Defining the Search View in the Controller

At this point, the view is finished. Each time the user selects a different pet owner, an asynchronous call will be made to `http://localhost:8080/search` with the selected owner ID. The only step that remains is to define the path, `/search`, and have it return the list of pets for a given owner ID. To do this, add the following new method to `controllers.py`:

```
@expose()
def search(self, owner):
    pets = [(entry.name) for entry in Pet.select(Pet.q.ownerID == owner)]
    log.info("Got the pets for owner " + owner + ": " + str(pets))
    return dict(pets=pets)
```

This method does the following:

1. It takes the ID of an `owner` as an input argument.

2. It performs a `select` operation on the `Pet` model object looking for all `Pet` objects where the `ownerID` is the same as the owner input argument. Note that the owner ID is not explicitly defined for the `Pet` model object, but is an automatic ID that generated by `SQLObject` for most model objects.

3. It loops over the selected pets, and for each pet (`entry`), itsaves the value of the `name` attribute in an array called `pets`.

4. It returns a dictionary containing a single key, `pets`, that gets set to the array of pet names.

Now if you save all the modified files and browse to `http://localhost:8080/petview`, you should get a page that looks similar to the one shown in Figure 3-7. This page displays the final version of the list of pets for a given pet owner.

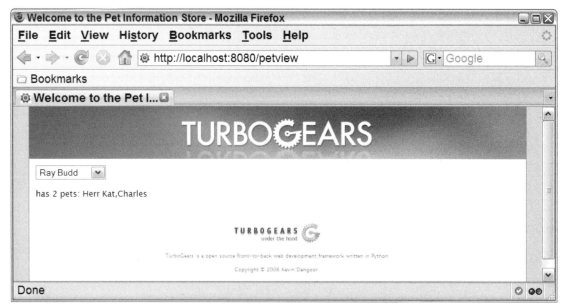

Figure 3-7

Next you'll explore Django, another popular web framework that is similar to TurboGears in many ways but is quite different in other ways. This is due to the fact that the motivation for developing Django was quite different from the motivation behind TurboGears even though both frameworks are intended to address similar needs.

Introduction to Django

Now that you've seen the basics of TurboGears, you're ready to explore Django, another similar yet very different Python web framework. Here you'll get an overview of Django's history and capabilities that the framework provides. After this introduction, you'll get into the code with another example. In this case, you'll take the example that you just implemented in TurboGears and reimplement it in Django. As you proceed, you'll see many of the similarities and differences between the two frameworks.

Django History

Looking at the history of Django helps put the capabilities that are or are not included in the framework into better perspective. Django was originally developed at World Online, a web development company for a newspaper in Lawrence, Kansas. The company maintains web sites related to the newspaper, among other sites. The group of web developers responsible for the original development of Django includes Adrian Holovaty, Jacob Kaplan-Moss, Simon Willison, and Wilson Miner. Django development was started in the fall of 2003 and open sourced in 2005. It was developed from scratch to be a framework that helps produce web sites rapidly. Given the need to frequently and quickly update the sites to post the latest news, the framework is focused on reducing the pain required to do this.

Two central principles of the Django framework (outlined as design philosophies) are to maintain loose coupling between the layers of the framework, and the Don't Repeat Yourself (DRY) philosophy. Loose coupling between the component layers ensures that undue dependencies aren't introduced into the system, and the DRY attempts to remove any redundancy such as specifying the makeup of a model object in both the database and the model class specification.

Main Django Components

The most apparent difference between TurboGears and Django is that Django was developed from the ground up, incorporating no existing components, whereas TurboGears is made up almost entirely of existing components.

Work with What You Have ... or Not

Django and TurboGears have very different design philosophies. At the most basic level, TurboGears is generally focused on integrating existing components, whereas the driving force for Django was to implement a framework from the ground up due to limitations in existing components when it was being developed.

Both projects provide an outline of the project philosophy, which gives developers an idea of where the technologies will be headed in the future. You can read the Django design philosophy at www.djangoproject.com/documentation/design_philosophies/. The TurboGears philosophy is outlined at http://docs.turbogears.org/1.0/ Philosophy, and you can garner additional insights at www.turbogears.org/about/ index.html.

The main Django components include the following:

❑ **Templates:** Django templates allow you to define control logic and embed variables in a normal HTML page similar to the way you would for Kid pages in TurboGears. The template language is intended to provide the power necessary to dynamically determine the content of a page based on changing data, while remaining simple enough for nonprogrammers to use.

❑ **Views:** The view is responsible for gathering model data and processing a template in the context of the gathered data in order to create an HTML page. A view is simply a Python function that returns the generated HTML page in an HTTP response for the given request.

❑ **URL mappings:** URL mappings are used to translate a request from a browser to an invocation of a view function. Based on regular expressions, they allow you to easily define readable URLs and translate from a request like `http://localhost:8000/petview/1` to a Django view function.

❑ **Models:** A model is the Django ORM. Model objects can be mapped automatically to and from database tables. Like SQLObjects, the base Django model object provides an abstraction of standard SQL operations. This simplifies the code required to interact with the database from a Python shell or script.

Like TurboGears, Django also includes a wide variety of other features and utilities, such as a command-line project administration tool, a powerful and highly configurable web-based administration utility, a syndication framework for generating RSS and ATOM feeds, and an embedded web server.

An important difference between TurboGears and Django is that TurboGears uses the concept of a project, whereas Django uses the concepts of both a project and an application. An application contains the specification of the models and views, and the project includes configuration details like the database configuration and URL mappings. A single project can contain multiple applications.

Alternate Components

Because it is not based on existing components like TurboGears is, Django isn't quite as focused on integration and support for alternate components. It does, however, allow you to use a different template language. You can also use a different ORM to create the model — with one significant drawback. A powerful web-based project administration utility included with Django is tightly coupled to the model classes and can't be used with alternate implementations.

MVC Architecture in Django

Although Django uses the MVC architecture, the developers have a slightly different interpretation of the MVC concept when compared to TurboGears and most other web frameworks. Unfortunately, this can cause a lot of confusion when a developer initially investigates different frameworks, but ultimately the capabilities are quite similar. In Django the distinctions between the three main components exist as they do in other frameworks, but the names and responsibilities of each component are a bit different. Basically, the main components are as follows:

❑ **Templates:** Even though these are quite similar to Kid templates in scope, they are not considered the view in Django due to the fact that they simply present the data rather than determine what data should be displayed. Templates are maintained in separate directories from the other project files, and can be shared across projects and applications.

❑ **View functions:** The view looks similar to a controller in other web frameworks, but is considered the *view* in Django because it determines what data should be displayed. Unfortunately, this may be a point of some confusion for developers when they're initially examining different frameworks. Views are defined in the `views.py` file in the application's home directory. Each view is a function that consists of the incoming HTTP request and arguments.

❑ **Django framework and URL mappings:** Django developers consider the framework, and more specifically the process of URL mapping, as the *controller* because it is though this process that a view is selected based on user input (the URL of the web request). URL mappings are defined for a project and shared across applications. The definition is in the `urls.py` file in the project home directory.

❑ **Model classes:** The *model* in Django is determined by the model classes maintained for an application. This is very similar to the approach in TurboGears and most other web frameworks. Like views, model classes are specific to an application and are maintained in a `models.py` file in the application's home directory. Much like TurboGears, each model includes the column specification and is frequently used to construct the database.

The reasoning behind this interpretation of MVC is described fully in an FAQ at www.djangoproject.com/documentation/faq/#django-appears-to-be-a-mvc-framework-but-you-call-the-controller-the-view-and-the-view-the-template-how-come-you-don-t-use-the-standard-names.

Creating an Example Application

To get a better feel for the differences and similarities between TurboGears and Django, you'll now see how to implement the same pet information store application that you implemented in TurboGears, this time using Django.

Creating the Project Skeleton

Similar to the TurboGears `tg-admin` command, Django provides two commands — `django-admin.py` and `manage.py` — that you can use to perform administrative tasks such as creating a project skeleton and creating a project database. Both command scripts take the same set of subcommands, but `django-admin.py` is project-independent, whereas `manage.py` is generated when you create a new project and should be used only when working with that project. The following table lists and describes some of the commands commonly encountered when managing a Django project.

Script	Subcommand	Example	Description
django-admin.py	startproject [project name]	python django-admin.py startproject petinfosite	Create a new project.
manage.py	startapp [application name]	python manage.py startapp petinfostore	Create a new application for a project.
manage.py	runserver	python manage.py runserver	Start the embedded web server for a project.
manage.py	syncdb	python manage.py syncdb	Create the database for a project.
manage.py	shell	python manage.py shell	Start an interactive Python shell initialized to the project settings.

To start the example application, use the following command to create a new empty project called petinfosite:

```
C:\django-examples>python django-admin.py startproject petinfosite
```

This creates a new petinfosite directory that contains the basic skeleton necessary to build a web site. It includes the following:

❑ manage.py: As mentioned previously, you can invoke this script to perform administrative tasks on your project.

❑ settings.py: This script defines a collection of settings such as the database configuration or time zone of the project.

❑ urls.py: This is a list of URLs that this project contains.

You may have noticed that the project does not have any skeletons for models, views, or controllers. This is because Django structures projects in a slightly different way than TurboGears does. A project can consist of multiple applications, each containing the models, views, and controllers necessary for the application.

Next, create a new application for your pet information store using the manage.py script as follows:

```
C:\django-examples\petinfosite>python manage.py startapp petinfostore
```

This creates a new directory called petinfostore that contains Python scripts to hold the application's models (models.py) and views (views.py).

Before getting into the details of the model definition, you need to configure the database to be used by the project. Open `settings.py` and set the database to use a SQLite database file in the project's home directory by defining the `DATABASE_ENGINE` and `DATABASE_NAME` as follows:

```
DATABASE_ENGINE = 'sqlite3'
DATABASE_NAME = 'c:/django-examples/petinfosite/site.db'
```

You also need to add your new application to the list of applications installed in the project. This is done by adding a line for the application in the `INSTALLED_APPS` setting as follows:

```
INSTALLED_APPS = (
    'django.contrib.auth',
    'django.contrib.contenttypes',
    'django.contrib.sessions',
    'django.contrib.sites',
    'petinfosite.petinfostore'
)
```

Like TurboGears, Django allows you to automatically test your web application on a web server with a single command. However, rather than including a specific script as you did in TurboGears, you start the embedded web server with the `manage.py` command as follows:

```
C:\django-examples\petinfosite>python manage.py runserver
```

Browse to `http://localhost:8000` and you'll see the welcome screen shown in Figure 3-8.

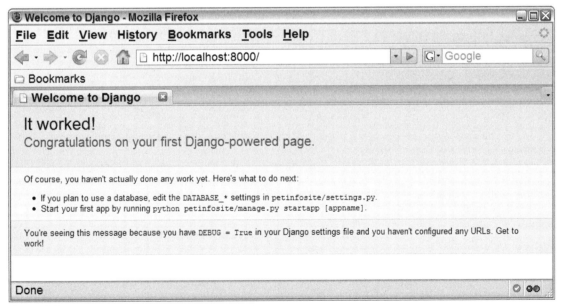

Figure 3-8

The Model

Similar to the example in Chapter 2 and the TurboGears example earlier in this chapter, the first step in defining the MVC web application is to define the model. In Django, this involves extending the application models file, `models.py`, to include the project-specific model classes that are required.

Defining the Model Classes

Like the TurboGears project, the Django model consists of two objects: `Person` and `Pet`. Define these objects by modifying the `petinfostore/models.py` file as shown in Listing 3-6.

Listing 3-6: The Django models.py file

```
 1 from django.db import models
 2
 3 # Create your models here.
 4 class Person(models.Model):
 5   given_name = models.CharField('given name', maxlength=50)
 6   surname = models.CharField(maxlength=50)
 7   def __str__(self):
 8     return "%s %s" % (self.given_name, self.surname)
 9
10 class Pet(models.Model):
11   name = models.CharField(maxlength=50)
12   owner = models.ForeignKey(Person)
13   def __str__(self):
14     return  self.name
```

The listing shows how similar the TurboGears and Django model definitions are on the surface. One difference is that Django provides its own base model class, `model.Model`, for the application model instead of using `SQLObject`. In addition, the internal implementations of the `SQLObject` and `Model` base classes are quite different. Although these classes have similar functionality, they provide very different methods and attributes for manipulating the models, as you'll see when you explore the interactive Python shell later in this chapter. The field variables are also initialized using different classes. Django uses `models.CharField` to define a character column, and it uses `model.ForeignKey` for foreign keys.

The `Person` class is defined on lines 4 through 8, and includes the given name and the surname. Note that `model.CharField` requires you to specify a `maxlength` value, and you can provide a friendlier version of the field name as an optional initial argument (line 5). The `Pet` class is defined on lines 10 through 14, and contains a pet name as well as a foreign key reference to the `Person` model object. Both classes override Python's standard string method `__str__` to ensure the object is presented in a human-readable format.

Creating the Database

After defining your model objects, you're ready to create the database. To do this, you use the `syncdb` subcommand of `manage.py` as shown in Listing 3-7. When the `syncdb` command is run the first time, it doesn't just create tables for your application's model objects (the `petinfostore_person` and `petinfostore_pet` tables). It also creates and initializes a variety of tables for the applications defined in the project's `INSTALLED_APPS` setting that manage other aspects of the project, such as the session- or user management provided by the framework. During the execution of the `syncdb` command, you are asked if you want to create a superuser. Answer `yes` to this question and define a name, e-mail address, and password for the user as shown in Listing 3-7.

Listing 3-7: Creating the database with the syncdb command

```
C:\django-examples\petinfosite>python manage.py syncdb
Creating table auth_message
Creating table auth_group
Creating table auth_user
Creating table auth_permission
Creating many-to-many tables for Group model
Creating many-to-many tables for User model
Creating table django_content_type
Creating table django_session
Creating table django_site
Creating table petinfostore_pet
Creating table petinfostore_person
You just installed Django's auth system, which means you don't have any superusers
    defined.
Would you like to create one now? (yes/no): yes
Username: root
E-mail address: root@nosite.com
Password:
Password (again):
Superuser created successfully.
Adding permission 'message | Can add message'
...
```

Initializing the Database with the Interactive Shell

Django also provides an interactive shell you can use to load or explore the database. To invoke this interactive shell, use the shell subcommand with the manage.py script as shown in Listing 3-8.

Listing 3-8: An example of a Django shell interaction

```
1 C:\django-examples\petinfosite>python manage.py shell
2 Python 2.4.4 (#71, Oct 18 2006, 08:34:43) [MSC v.1310 32 bit (Intel)] ↵
on win32
3 Type "help", "copyright", "credits" or "license" for more information.
4 (InteractiveConsole)
5 >>> from petinfosite.petinfostore.models import Pet, Person
6 >>> bill = Person(given_name="Bill", surname="Wright")
7 >>> dana = Person(given_name="Dana", surname="Moore")
8 >>> everyone = Person.objects.all()
9 >>> str(everyone)
10 '[]'
11 >>> bill.save()
12 >>> dana.save()
13 >>> everyone = Person.objects.all()
14 >>> str(everyone)
15 '[<Person: Bill Wright>, <Person: Dana Moore>]'
16 >>> Person.objects.filter(id=1)
17 [<Person: Bill Wright>]
18 >>> Person.objects.filter(id=2)
19 [<Person: Dana Moore>]
20 >>> Person.objects.filter(surname="Wright")
21 [<Person: Bill Wright>]
```

(continued)

Listing 3-8 *(continued)*

```
22 >>> max = Pet(name="Max", owner=bill)
23 >>> max.save()
24 >>> Pet.objects.all()
25 [<Pet: Max>]
26 >>> bill.pet_set.create(name='Ginger')
27 <Pet: Ginger>
28 >>> baxter = Pet(name="Baxter", owner=2)
29 Traceback (most recent call last):
30   File "<console>", line 1, in ?
31   File "c:\utilities\python-2.4\lib\site-packages\django-0.95.1- ↵
py2.4.egg\django\db\models\base.py", line 113, in __init__
32     raise TypeError, "Invalid value: %r should be a %s instance, not a ↵
%s" % (f.name, f.rel.to, type(rel_obj))
33 TypeError: Invalid value: 'owner' should be a <class ↵
'petinfosite.petinfostore.models.Person'> instance, not a <type 'int'>
34 >>> dana.pet_set.create(name='Baxter')
35 <Pet: Baxter>
36 >>> Pet.objects.all()
37 [<Pet: Max>, <Pet: Ginger>, <Pet: Baxter>]
38 >>> Pet.objects.exclude(owner=bill)
39 [<Pet: Baxter>]
40 >>> Pet.objects.filter(owner=bill).filter(name="Ginger")
41 [<Pet: Ginger>]
42 >>> Pet.objects.get(pk=2)
43 <Pet: Ginger>
44 >>> bill.pet_set.all()
45 [<Pet: Max>, <Pet: Ginger>]
46 >>> Pet.objects.get(name="Ginger")
47 <Pet: Ginger>
48 >>> Pet.objects.get(owner=bill)
49 Traceback (most recent call last):
50   File "<console>", line 1, in ?
51   File "c:\utilities\python-2.4\lib\site-packages\django-0.95.1- ↵
py2.4.egg\django\db\models\manager.py", line 67, in get
52     return self.get_query_set().get(*args, **kwargs)
53   File "c:\utilities\python-2.4\lib\site-packages\django-0.95.1- ↵
py2.4.egg\django\db\models\query.py", line 214, in get
54     assert len(obj_list) == 1, "get() returned more than one %s -- ↵
it returned %s! Lookup parameters were %s" % (self.model._meta.object_name, ↵
len(obj_list), kwargs)
55 AssertionError: get() returned more than one Pet -- it returned 2! ↵
Lookup
parameters were {'owner': <Person: Bill Wright>}
56 >>> ^Z
57
58 C:\django-examples\petinfosite>
```

This example session shows the basics of interacting with the Django model objects:

❑   Before you can use an application's model objects, they must be imported with an `import` state-ment as shown on line 5.

❑   You can create a new instance of a `Person` model object and assign it to a variable by providing the `given_name` and `surname` as shown on lines 6 and 7.

- ❑ You can select all rows in the database for a model object by using the `all` method as shown on lines 8 and line 13. Notice that the result of the `all` method on line 8 is empty because the `bill` and `dana` `Person` objects have not been saved to the database.

- ❑ Before you can create an object as a row in the database, you need to save it by invoking the `save` method (lines 11 and 12). Notice that after the `bill` and `dana` objects are saved, the result of the `all` invocation is a list of two model objects.

- ❑ You can use the `filter` method to select a list of model objects that match a given attribute, as shown on lines 16 through 21.

- ❑ You can create an object with a foreign key by referencing a variable that holds the object the foreign key refers to. For example, on line 22, a new `Pet` named `Max` is created, and the owner is defined as a `Person` named `bill`. However, as is shown on lines 28 through 33, an attempt to use the ID of the foreign key alone results in an error indicating the type does not match.

- ❑ When a foreign key (the key to the `Person` table in this example) is defined, a set is created in the foreign table (the `Person` table itself). You can also create an object using the `create` method on this set as shown on lines 26 and 34. Line 26 causes a new `Pet` to be created with the name `Ginger`, and the owner is set to the `Person` named `Bill Wright`. The object is automatically included in the `pet_set` for `Bill Wright`. Note that you don't have to save the object in this case.

- ❑ You can use the `exclude` method to select a list of model objects that do not match a given attribute (line 38).

- ❑ You can chain together `filter` and `exclude` method calls to produce simple logic for mode object selection. For example, line 40 gets all pets named Ginger who are owned by Bill Wright.

- ❑ You can use the `get` method to select a single model object (line 46), but do so with caution because it reports an error when multiple records match a single call (lines 48 through 55).

The Administration Application

The interactive shell isn't the only way to define the model objects in the database — Django provides a more user-friendly web-based approach as well. Similar to the CatWalk utility in TurboGears, Django includes an administration utility that allows you to edit and view your model objects. In the following sections, you'll see how to incorporate and tailor this utility for the pet information store, as well as the learning basics for interacting with the utility.

Incorporating the Administration Application in the Web Site

One very handy aspect of Django is that it provides a highly powerful and configurable administration utility that can be incorporated in a web application with a minimum of fuss. To include the administration utility in the pet information store, do the following:

1. Update the installed applications setting in `settings.py` to reference the administration application:

```
INSTALLED_APPS = (
    'django.contrib.auth',
    'django.contrib.contenttypes',
    'django.contrib.sessions',
    'django.contrib.sites',
    'django.contrib.admin',
  'petinfosite.petinfostore'
)
```

2. Use the `syncdb` command to rebuild the database, which adds new tables used by the administration application to it:

```
C:\django-examples\petinfosite>python manage.py syncdb
Creating table django_admin_log
Adding permission 'log entry | Can add log entry'
Adding permission 'log entry | Can change log entry'
Adding permission 'log entry | Can delete log entry'
```

3. Add the URLs used by the administration application to the list of URLs for the web site that is maintained in `petinfosite/urls.py`. Django makes this even easier by including commented-out code that can do this for you. Simply open the file and uncomment the `include` line in the file as follows:

```
# Uncomment this for admin:
  (r'^admin/', include('django.contrib.admin.urls')),
```

4. Start the web application with the `runserver` command. At this point, if you go to `http://localhost:8000/admin/` you're presented with the login screen shown in Figure 3-9.

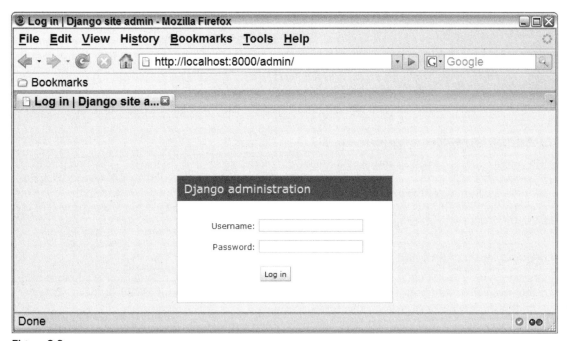

Figure 3-9

This is all that's required to get a basic administration utility for the project. You can now log in to the administration site using the username and password you defined when you ran the `syncdb` command for the first time (in Listing 3-7). After logging in, you are taken to the default administration page shown in Figure 3-10. This page allows you to manipulate the users, groups, and sites defined in the project. For now, don't worry too much about the details of this basic site administration (you'll learn more about this in Part III).

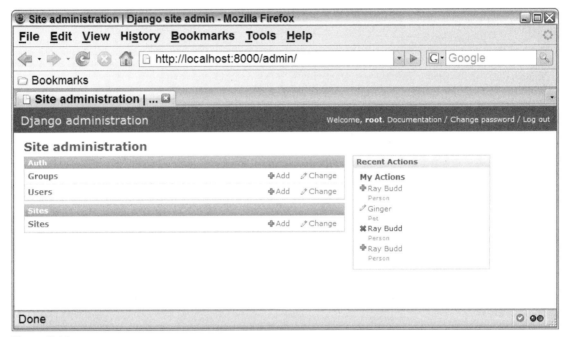

Figure 3-10

Adding Models to the Administration Application

Although the initial administration application is useful for general site management, it doesn't provide any capabilities that are specific to the pet information store application. The administrator of the pet information store should be able to view and modify the `Pet` and `Person` model objects. To provide these capabilities, you need to specify a special `Admin` inner class for each model in `petinfosite/petinfostore/models.py` that causes the model to be incorporated in the administration interface. Define this `Admin` class as follows:

```
1 from django.db import models
2
3 # Create your models here.
4 class Person(models.Model):
5   given_name = models.CharField('given name', maxlength=50)
6   surname = models.CharField(maxlength=50)
7   def __str__(self):
8     return "%s %s" % (self.given_name, self.surname)
```

(continued)

```
 9    class Admin:
10      pass
11
12 class Pet(models.Model):
13    name = models.CharField(maxlength=50)
14    owner = models.ForeignKey(Person)
15    def __str__(self):
16      return  self.name
17    class Admin:
18      pass
```

Note that the Admin class initially includes only the pass statement to indicate that the class has no methods. If you reload the main admininistration web page, you'll see that the model classes are now included in the list of site administration elements, as shown in Figure 3-11.

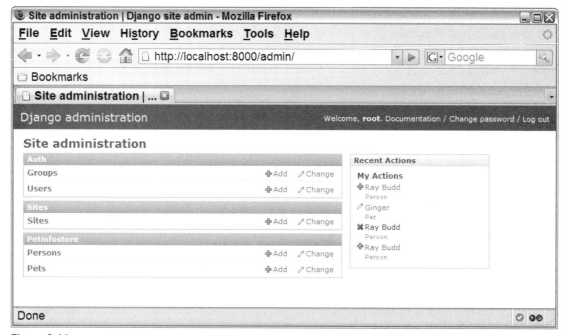

Figure 3-11

Using the Administration Application

Now that your model objects are included in the administration view, you can easily add, delete, or modify instances of the model objects as follows:

❑   On the main administration page, select either Pets or Persons object, or click the corresponding Change button. This displays the administration page for the model object, with a list of all instances of the model object from the database (see Figure 3-12). You can use the Add button on either the main administration page (previously shown in Figure 3-11) or the page for each model object (Figure 3-12) to create a new model object. Click this button and add a new user now.

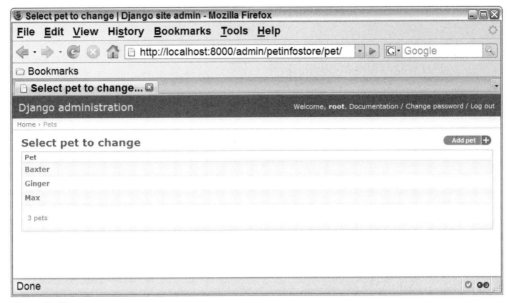

Figure 3-12

❑   Select any model object instance from the model object administration page to open the editor
     for that object. Figure 3-13 shows the pet editor. Notice that the administrator utility selects an
     appropriate form control based on the type of data maintained in the column. For example, the
     pet owner is a drop-down list populated with the list of Person objects.

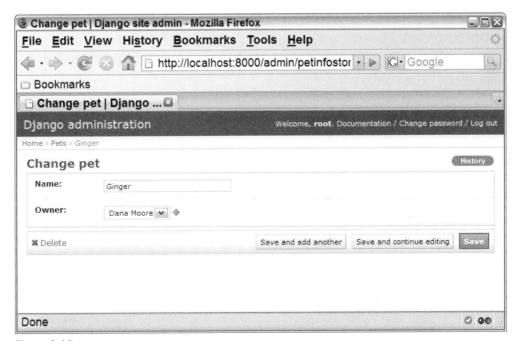

Figure 3-13

❑   The history of all model object changes made through the `administration` view are also maintained. To see the changes made to a model object, click the History button. The history of recent actions is also shown on the right side of the main administration page (as previously shown in Figure 3-11). For example, if you change Ginger's owner to Dana Moore, click the Save button, and view Ginger's history, you'll see the change in ownership as shown in Figure 3-14.

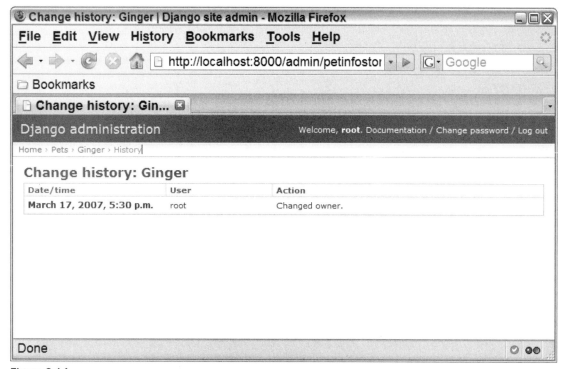

Figure 3-14

Tailoring the Administration Application

The administration application also allows you to easily tailor each view in a variety of ways. You'll learn more about this in Part III, but you can make two simple enhancements to the pet information store example now. One nice enhancement would be to show the name of the pet owner next to the name of the pet on the list of pets. You can do this by specifying a `list_display` attribute in the `Admin` inner class of `Pet` that defines the way the list of model objects is presented. By default, the string representation of the object is shown in list view, but when you add the `list_display` attribute, you can explicitly define the columns that will be included in the list view. For example, to include the name and owner of the pet in the list of pets as shown in Figure 3-15, you redefine the `Admin` class as follows:

```
class Admin:
    list_display=('name', 'owner')
```

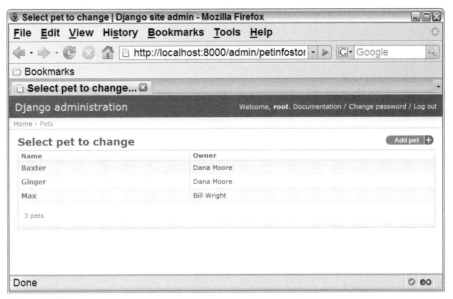

Figure 3-15

You can even add the ability to filter the displayed list of pets by adding the `list_filter` attribute as follows:

```
class Admin:
    list_display=('name', 'owner')
    list_filter=['owner']
```

With this enhancement, the list of pets displayed on the right changes when the user selects elements in the list filter on the left, as shown in Figure 3-16.

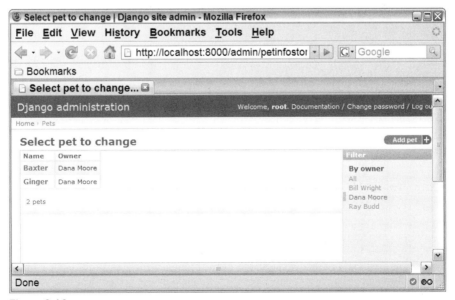

Figure 3-16

Defining a View and a Template

The administration application provides a powerful utility, but a web application generally still needs to incorporate additional tailored views for site users. In this section you'll see how to create a web page that displays the pets for a selected owner. This new page will consist of a single template that contains a drop-down list of all `people` model objects as well as an Update button, as shown in Figure 3-17. When the user selects a person and clicks the Update button, the pets owned by the selected person are displayed (see Figure 3-18).

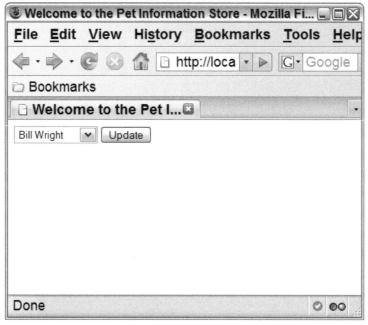

Figure 3-17

In this simple example, you'll implement a synchronous web page that completely refreshes the page with each request rather than using an asynchronous request. This is not due to any inherent limitation in the framework. A synchronous request is used here because by default Django doesn't include a JavaScript library, but leaves the developer to select and incorporate a library on his or her own. As you saw in the earlier MochiKit example, when you use a JavaScript library the creation of an asynchronous request is greatly simplified. You'll learn how to incorporate a third-party JavaScript library and make asynchronous requests in Part III.

Configuring the Project for Templates

The first step in creating the new web page is to configure the project so it can use templates. When you create a project skeleton, it doesn't automatically define a location for the project's template files. Instead, you are required to explicitly create a location for your template files and reference that location in the `TEMPLATE_DIRS` setting in `settings.py`, which accepts multiple directories. This enables you to manage your template files separately and share them among multiple projects. On the other hand, it also requires additional configuration when you're setting up a new project, and requires additional work to manage shared templates.

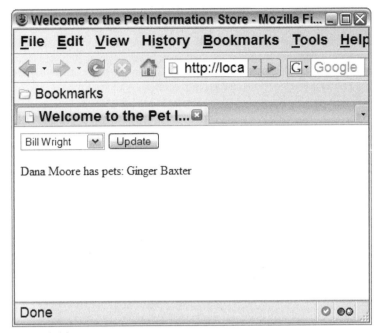

Figure 3-18

For the pet information store example, create a new empty directory called `templates` under your base project directory, `c:/django-examples/petinfosite`. Then define the new directory to the `TEMPLATE_DIRS` setting in `settings.py` as follows:

```
TEMPLATE_DIRS = (
    # Put strings here, like "/home/html/django_templates".
    # Always use forward slashes, even on Windows.
    "c:/django-examples/petinfosite/templates/"
)
```

Defining the Template

As previously discussed, a template file is a normal text file that looks a lot like an HTML file but it has some additional capabilities. A template can inherit from another template, and it contains embedded tags that define processing logic for the template as well as variables that get replaced with data when the template is processed.

There is a wide variety of tags that can be included in a template to add processing logic, such as standard flow-control tags for defining code blocks, loops, and conditionals. An embedded tag is surrounded by braces and percent signs. For example, a code block named `author` can be defined with `{% block author %}`. A variable is surrounded by double braces and contains the name of the variable. For example, the variable `foo` would be referenced with `{{ foo }}`.

Django comes with a base set of tags, including tags that you can use to define control logic, among several others. You can also define your own tags, or you can include external tag libraries for your project. You can display a complete list of tags available to your web application from the administrator utility (if it's installed for the application) by browsing to `http://localhost:8000/admin/doc/`. You can also display this information by clicking the Documentation link in the upper-right corner of the administrator utility. This link shows details about your project, including a list of the defined views and models.

After configuring the `templates` directory for the project, create a new template called `petinfo.html` under this directory and define it as shown in Listing 3-9.

Listing 3-9: The pet information template, petinfo.html

```
1    <html>
2      <head>
3        <title>Welcome to the Pet Information Store</title>
4        <script type="text/javascript">
5          function doUpdate() {
6            var owner = document.getElementById("personOption").value;
7            window.location = "/petview/" + owner;
8          }
9        </script>
10     </head>
11     <body>
12       <select id="personOption">
13         {% for person in people %}
14         <option id="{{person.id}}" value="{{person.id}}">
15           {{person.given_name}} {{person.surname}}
16         </option>
17         {% endfor %}
18       </select>
19       <button id="updateBtn" onclick="doUpdate()">Update</button>
20       {% if owner %}
21       <p>
22         {% if pets %}
23           {{owner}} has pets:
24           {% for pet in pets %}
25             {{pet.name}}
26           {% endfor %}
27         {% else %}
28           {{owner}} has no pets
29         {% endif %}
30       </p>
31       {% endif %}
32     </body>
33   </html>
```

This listing shows the basics of a template specification as follows:

❑ The template defines a basic HTML page that includes the normal base HTML elements such as the head, title, and body.

❑ The template defines a select element, `personOption`, on line 12.

❑ The `for` loop defined on lines 13 through 17 creates an `option` element for each `Person` model object in the `people` list. The template assumes that the `people` list will be provided as context data when the template is evaluated. Note that the loop is explicitly terminated with the `endfor` tag (line 17).

❑ The `ID` attribute of the `option` element is set to the `ID` of the `person` object, and the text displayed in the option defined on line 15 is the person's given name and surname.

❑ The script defined on lines 4 through 9 is called when the user clicks the Update button. This script gets the id of the currently selected person object and reloads the `petview` URL with this value appended to the end. For example, when the user selects the person object that has an id of `Bill Wright`, the URL that gets generated is `http://localhost:8000/petview/1`.

❑ Lines 20 through 31 display the person's name and a list of pets that the person owns when they are provided as context data. However, the owner's name and list of pets may not be included in every request, because no one is selected when the user visits the page for the first time.

❑ Line 20 defines an `if` statement to verify that the owner was included with the request. When no owner is included, the template doesn't display any pet information.

❑ Line 22 uses another `if` statement to verify that the person has pets. If a person doesn't have any pets, the conditional returns false, and a message is displayed as defined on line 28.

❑ If the person has pets, the message on line 23 is displayed, and a `for` loop that begins on line 24 walks over the list of pets, prints out the name of each pet, and displays a message similar to "Dana Moore has pets: Ginger Baxter" (as shown previously in Figure 3-18).

Adding the View to the List of URLs

Before defining the actual view object, you need to map a URL to the view. Django maintains the list of URLs in a `urlpatterns` variable defined in the `urls.py` file at the project root. Recall that when you added the administration utility, you uncommented a line in this file to include a set of URLs for the utility:

```
urlpatterns = patterns('',
    # Example:
    # (r'^petinfosite/', include('petinfosite.apps.foo.urls.foo')),
    # Uncomment this for admin:
    (r'^admin/', include('django.contrib.admin.urls')),
)
```

Look at this specification a bit more closely. The `urlpatterns` variable is defined by calling the `patterns` function with an initial empty string argument (you can ignore this for now) and a list of triples in the following order:

❑ The first element in the triple is a Python regular expression. For example, the regular expression `r'^admin/'` matches the string `"admin/"`. Note that the leading `'/'` is trimmed before attempting to match against the expression. Therefore, the expression `r'^/admin/'` is incorrect and would not match the URL `"http://localhost:8000/admin/"`.

❑   The second element in the triple has a few different formats, but is most commonly either an `include` statement or the name of a view function that should be invoked when the expression is matched. In the case of the `admin` utility, the element includes a set of URL patterns defined in `django.contrib.admin.urls`. If you're really curious about what's being included here, you can see the full set of administration URL patterns in `<django-home>/django/contrib/admin/urls.py`. Alternatively, you can specify the name of a view function that should be invoked when the expression matches. You'll see an example of this with the specification of the `petview` function references in the next section.

❑   The third element in the triple is optional. It is a dictionary that can contain additional arguments to the view function.

The order of this list is important because when the server needs to find a page, it walks down the list attempting to find a matching URL. When a match is found, the server invokes the associated view function. If no match is found, it returns a "page not found" error.

Returning to the pet information store example, you will define a single new `petview` in the next section that should be referenced in two different ways. This requires you to add two new entries to the `urlpatterns` variable as follows:

```
from django.conf.urls.defaults import *
urlpatterns = patterns('',
    # Example:
    # (r'^petinfosite/', include('petinfosite.apps.foo.urls.foo')),
    # Uncomment this for admin:
    (r'^admin/', include('django.contrib.admin.urls')),
    (r'^petview/$', 'petinfosite.petinfostore.views.petview'),
    (r'^petview/(?P<owner_id>\d+)/$', 'petinfosite.petinfostore.views.petview'),
)
```

The first entry matches the string `"petview/"` and simply causes the function `petview` to be invoked. The second expression is a bit more interesting because it shows you how to map a URL sub-path to an argument provided to the view function. As discussed in the previous section, when a user selects a person and clicks the Update button, JavaScript (lines 4 through 9 in Listing 3-9) creates a URL that encodes the ID of the selected person in the path. For example, if the user selects Bill Wright, the URL `http://localhost:8000/petview/1/` gets produced, and when the user selects Dana Moore, the URL is `http://localhost:8000/petview/2/`. This encoding can easily be mapped into an argument in the view function as shown in the second triple in the example code. The regular expression `r'^petview/(?P<owner_id>\d+)/$'` matches the first part of the URL, `petview/`. The second part of the expression is enclosed in parentheses, which indicates that the value is captured and passed into the view function as an argument. `?P<owner_id>` establishes that the value should be assigned to an argument named `owner_id`, and `\d+` matches against one or more numbers (which in this case is the ID of the selected person).

Defining the View

Similar to a traditional controller in a web application, a view in Django acts as the glue between the model and the templates. The view typically uses the model objects to look up data from the database, and causes the template to be evaluated in the context of this data. Specifically, the `pet information` view does the following:

1. It gathers all the context data required by the template. In this case, it creates variables for the list of people (`people`), the owner (`owner`), and a list of pets (`pets`).

2. It evaluates the template with the context data and generates an HTML page.

3. It returns the generated HTML to the user as an `HttpResponse` object.

Minimum View Requirements

A view isn't actually required to interact with model objects or evaluate a template. The only strict requirement for a view is that it must return an `HttpResponse` object. For example, you could add a trivial "hello world" view to `views.py` by defining a view class as follows:

```
# Create your views here.
from django.http import HttpResponse
def helloworld(request):
    return HttpResponse("Hello World")
```

You would also need to define a new URL mapping to reference the view in the `urlpatterns` attribute defined in `urls.py` at the base of the project directory:

```
urlpatterns = patterns('',
    . . .
        (r'^helloworld/$', 'petinfosite.petinfostore.views.
        helloworld'),
    . . .
```

After defining the view and URL pattern, you can see the resulting web page at `http://localhost:8000/helloworld`.

To define the new `pet information` view, edit the `C:\django-examples\petinfosite\petinfostore\views.py` file to include the `petview` function for the `pet information` view as shown in Listing 3-10.

Listing 3-10: views.py revised to contain a petview function

```
1 # Create your views here.
2 from django.shortcuts import render_to_response
3 from petinfosite.petinfostore.models import Person, Pet
4
5 def petview(request, owner_id=-1):
6   people = Person.objects.all()
7   if (owner_id != -1):
8     owner = Person.objects.get(id=owner_id)
9     pets = Pet.objects.filter(owner=owner_id)
10    return render_to_response('petinfo.html', {'people': people,
11 'pets': pets,
12 'owner': owner})
13   return render_to_response('petinfo.html', {'people': people})
```

This script does the following:

❑   It defines a single function called `petview` that takes an `HttpRequest` object called `request` as an argument as well as an optional `owner_id` argument with a default value of −1. The `request` object contains all of the details associated with the incoming request, including the method of the request (POST or GET) and any parameters that are part of the POST or GET operation.

❑   It retrieves a list of all `Person` objects from the database and loads them into the `people` variable on line 6.

❑   The function `render_to_response` is defined in `django.shortcuts` and is used to generate the `HttpResponse` on lines 10 through 13. This function is explored in more detail in Part III, but basically it does the following:

   1.   It defines a context that contains the `people` list, `pets` list, and `owner` object.

   2.   It evaluates the `petinfo.html` template with the generated context.

   3.   It creates a new `HttpResponse` object from the evaluated context.

❑   When no owner ID is provided and the value of `owner_id` is −1, the template is evaluated only with the list of people as context data (line 13).

❑   When an owner ID is provided:

   ❑   An `owner` variable is initialized to the `Person` object with the given ID on line 8.

   ❑   The `Pet` model object is searched for all pets that have the owner with the given owner ID defined by `owner_id` and stored in the `pets` variable.

   ❑   The three variables are defined as the context and the template is evaluated on lines 10 through 12.

Now if you visit this view at `http://localhost:8000/petview`, you should get a page like the one shown previously in Figure 3-17.

Summary

In this chapter you saw the true power of the web application framework. You learned about the use of MVC as the foundation of many frameworks, as well as the typical capabilities provided by frameworks. You were introduced to the TurboGears and Django frameworks and got your feet wet by implementing the example from the previous chapter in each framework. The next two parts of this book build on this introduction to discuss these frameworks in more detail: TurboGears in Part II and Django in Part III.

Interview with Kevin Dangoor, Industry Leader
and Creator of TurboGears

The authors drew much of their early beliefs in the capabilities of TurboGears (as well as the inspiration for this book) from watching an excellent Kevin Dangoor video, *The 20 Minute Wiki*, on `http://turbogears.org/`. Kevin is an individual of boundless energy and enthusiasm, and possesses great insight and wit. The authors sat down with him (virtually, that is) to chat in late May 2007. Here are a few of his thoughts on the "how and why" of TurboGears and some of his observations on large-scale open source projects and the future of Web 2.0.

On the Initial Motivations for TurboGears

Q: *What motivated TurboGears? What led you to recognize the need for a Python framework to support Web 2.0 developers?*

Kevin: The need grew specifically from a project I was working on. At the time, Ruby on Rails was the only full stack framework around and I needed all that same kind of functionality, but I needed it in Python because Python had a bunch of other tools that I needed. So for me, TurboGears naturally grew from that motivation. Additionally, as I looked over the library landscape, I realized that Python already had the libraries in place, things such as SQLObject, and a number of reasonable choices to implement the control layer in the MVC scheme. Finally, there were a bunch of templating languages, and I actually tried several of them out in the discovery process, and what I settled on became TurboGears.

A big motivator was that, for the web framework I was working on at the time, I needed a framework that I could use for myself.

Q: *It seems both wonderful and perhaps even a little amazing that from the collection of libraries and frameworks you wove together a real-life example of the whole being greater than the sum of its parts. This certainly seems to be a common attribute of successful mega-frameworks. In an interview with David Heinemeier Hansson for the book Rich Internet Applications (Wiley, 2007), Hansson suggested that there was a "eureka" moment when he realized that the framework he built in response to the demands of a specific problem could be the solution to the larger general class of network-centric applications. The result was Ruby on Rails. Is there a compelling reason why we are in the midst of a "golden age" of mega-frameworks? Why didn't this happen five years ago, for example?*

Kevin: There are a couple of obvious reasons. First, the problem space is better understood. Over time people have found the points of commonality — things that developers do over and over again. Further, the general complexity of web applications has increased. Everyone has a relational backing store to deal with; everyone has to deal with AJAX. So, it's this combination — a well-defined problem space and application complexity — that has acted as a forcing function. Think about it — people started working on cgi-bin scripts 10 or more years ago, and the Web was a very different thing. The tools have simply grown up around the problem space.

Q: *Thinking about the evolution of TurboGears, how did the set of "just right" components come together in your mind?*

Kevin: There are actually two disparate things; the first being how the elements emerged. I actually began by doing experimentation with a variety of tools in Python. The only thing that remained stable over time was SQLObject. Practically everything else got switched out at some point in time. MochiKit actually came out fairly late in the game. MochiKit was a great choice for me as a Python programmer because it was idiomatically consistent, and it turns out that many of MochiKit's affordances, such as iterators, are making it into JavaScript itself. Over time, I got a sense of what components seemed to work well together.

Mind you, this came about after a lot of experimentation, and it was aided by the fact that Python has such a great and varied set of resources to begin with. It's still evolving, as for example the transitions from SQLObject to SQLAlchemy and from Kid to Genshi (which is going rather smoothly). SQLAlchemy is by far the best object-relational mapper you're likely to find.

The other point is the question of there being one way to do things. When you're doing a full stack framework, you need to include all the parts of the stack and all the parts need to work well together. Of course, TurboGears is not exclusive. There are hooks provided in most places so that you can use whatever you want. For most developers, it's a question of what you get for free and how much support the framework gives you. Bear in mind that it's all pretty much standard Python, so you can certainly re-platform "to taste."

On the TurboGears Value for Developers

Q: *How do you perceive the value of TurboGears to developers?*

Kevin: To a certain extent, you can say that all programming languages are Turing complete, and therefore, there are differences without distinction. You can do anything in any language. But, I think we all know that some languages do feel more productive, and then after you get to a certain level of productivity, it becomes more a matter of taste. Looking at Ruby and Python: Although their syntaxes are, of course, different, their expressive powers are very similar. Naturally, people have preferences. TurboGears provides a large number of capabilities that are somewhat similar (perhaps superficially at least and perhaps not on a feature-by-feature basis) to things you might find in other frameworks, but many people have said that they happen to like the "feel" of TurboGears in the way that its general interaction model works — for example, in the fact that you don't need separate configuration files to handle different URLs. I personally like having a baseline that is very easy to get into, very easy to get a first application going, very easy to have things start showing up in the browser. From there, you can easily and incrementally build your way up step-by-step.

I don't like things being too "magical." It's likely to be better for a developer to have to explicitly import things from a specific and trackable source, so that if you're ever wondering what's going on under the hood, you know exactly how to find out. That helps you improve what you are able to do with the framework, and indeed, possibly also improve the framework itself.

We tend to agree. It strikes us that TurboGears seems quite a bit more straightforward than other frameworks. I claim that it's possible to teach a user TurboGears in a small fraction of the time it takes to wrap your head around Rails, for example. TurboGears may lack a few of the "Swiss Army Knife" features of Rails (such as RJS), but on the other hand, it seems to adhere to the Python dictum that there is usually one right way to accomplish something.

On TurboGears Mindshare and Market Perceptions

Q: *As the creator of TurboGears, how strongly do you think it's competing against really buzz-heavy frameworks?*

Kevin: Well, it's certainly not currently in the same league right now as, for example, Ruby on Rails. Rails is perhaps an order of magnitude larger in terms of user community. Even so, when you look at the broader spectrum of programming, most of what's going on out there right now is PHP, Java, and .NET. So in truth, those are actually the "big three." Coming up quickly behind them is Rails. But going a little deeper, the PHP community is looking for something with a little more structure; people coming from a

Java or .NET perspective are looking for something less structured, less restrictive, and certainly less tedious so they can get their jobs done quicker. Thus, coming from these perspectives, Rails has attracted enough mindshare (and certainly enough broad press), that developers have naturally started to gravitate there. However, as mindshare around agile frameworks expands generally, it doesn't take long for them to discover TurboGears, Django, and other frameworks that are available for specific languages. Thus, some portion of the community will convert out of Rails and into other frameworks. It's really a "rising tide raises all boats" situation right now. The very fact that any agile framework is drawing people away from Java and PHP is simply good for the entire collection of frameworks out there that work in a similar fashion to Ruby on Rails or TurboGears.

Q: *As TurboGears proliferates, it will naturally be compared for scalability (and on other features) to other frameworks such as J2EE …*

Kevin: Sure, it's a question that comes up frequently. First of all, application design makes a bigger difference than anything else. You have to keep the scalability requirements in mind and work with them. The Web is inherently stateless. If you create something that's designed to scale by adding more boxes, trivially, you can say it's likely to scale, because boxes are pretty cheap these days; and it probably will work. Python is one of the great languages in terms of scalability. Think of it this way: Python itself is not exceedingly fast (albeit faster than Ruby, for example, but not nearly as fast as Java). However, there are so many ways in Python to get more speed. With Python, you can measure the application hotspots and use the right tricks to optimize. If you have to, for example, you can jump down to C code — there are a lot of Python libraries that are already in C that can help you out. There are also tools like Pyrex and Psyco that can help you improve performance. There are so many things you can do to improve raw performance when you need to, but generally speaking, I am a much bigger fan of intelligent overall design decisions, such as avoiding sessions. Whenever people talk about sessions, I advise them to instead think about how to comfortably spread the application across servers. As a general rule, unless the user population is tiny and there are never going to be scalability concerns, you're much better off putting application data in a database, and using asynchronous means to access it.

Q: *Are you aware of any significant enterprise adopters of TurboGears? Our own suspicion is that the use of TurboGears in the enterprise follows the technology S curve, where most users are currently in the early-adopter community.*

Kevin: That may be correct. I have met scattered enterprise developers who are beginning to look at TurboGears for internal applications. There's likely to be a whole lot of that going on as people work on departmental applications. It's a case where they need to get things done quickly and don't have a lot of budget to do it, so TurboGears fits that application space very ably.

Q: *That and the fact that there seems to be a wholesale rush toward zero footprint, zero-install application designs going on currently, where both developers and IT people want to escape the no-win situation of having to manage rich platform applications, coordinating distribution to 5,000 desktops …*

Kevin: Enterprises tend typically to move slowly when faced with the opportunity to create revolutionary change. An enterprise in general will not be at the leading edge. Remember that there are scads of companies still creating Enterprise JavaBeans (EJBs), even though developers are sick to death of them! Even though the weight of opinion is solidly against EJB2, it's an infrastructure we'll be seeing for a long while.

On Managing Open Source Innovation

Q: *How large is the TurboGears team? How do you manage to "herd the cats"? What's the development process like?*

Kevin: At this juncture, I am no longer the "cat herder." I stepped down as benevolent dictator at the beginning of 2007. Personal commitments really had to take precedence over TurboGears (as exciting as it all is). Alberto Valverde is the current project leader. I do hang out in the background, and we bounce ideas off each other. In general, though, I can speak to how things have gone historically. Guiding a large open source project is both an interesting thing and different from an enterprise project, where you can count on having a certain level of resources to put against goals. People are often involved mainly to "scratch their own itch." They may have projects of their own where they are trying to do that, using features of TurboGears that may not be fully robust, and when they realized this, they will work on that portion of the problem only. So you really have to do whatever it takes to foster accomplishment in that environment. You have to, for example, make sure that people feel comfortable asking questions — you have to make the path from framework user, to someone who contributes patches, to framework developers as easy as possible. From the management standpoint, making sure that patches get into the release quickly is key. Over time, you find the people who are exceptionally helpful in moving the project ahead, and it's important to smooth the path for them. Unfortunately, you often find that people are able to contribute only sporadically. They may be extremely active for a time and then get moved off by something else in their work life. Happily, though, in a vibrant project, new people often come forward to take their place and so you have to be very comfortable with operating in a fluid and dynamic atmosphere. It's very different from the enterprise, where you have somewhat-known resources, timelines, and feature sets.

Something we have been discussing recently are things like how much time we can and should spend with system administration, keeping spam off of the wiki, and more mundane tasks. If there's a little funding coming in for support, it may well be useful to put that money into helping people out with this part of the mission. There is a momentum effect in which, when a project attains a certain size, it's increasingly self-sustaining, and there are more people and a more varied talent set. I actually felt great about the fact that TurboGears got large enough for me to hand over to somebody else and the project just keeps on running. It's a real success milestone.

Q: *How do people go about evangelizing TurboGears in an organization that may be hidebound or risk-averse to the point of self-injury?*

Kevin: Partially, it may come down to a *people* question — these things are sometimes emotional and don't necessarily yield to structured arguments. The best way to *win* is that the proof is in the pudding. If you can whip up a prototype of something that would take a lot longer in Java, for example, that turns out to be fairly compelling. Of course this is very hard if you are in an enterprise where you have an IT group that controls all deployment of machines, though. The more forces you have built up to protect the status quo, the harder the job becomes. Usually, you'll have to start out as a "skunk works" effort, perhaps in your spare time, or with the permission of a direct manager. Then, once others see how successful the work is, they will latch on, and say, "Aha. I need to emulate that too. It would really help out my budget!"

Of course, today, it's probably easier than it was a scant two years ago, owing again to the enormous amount of publicity that Rails has gotten. It's gotten so much attention that all the agile languages benefit directly. Suddenly, we're finding more people saying, "Perhaps J2EE is not the right approach for everything."

Q: *What drives the release priorities?*

Kevin: This being open source, it partly depends on what people have the time and inclination to work on. At times, priorities coordinate with what external projects the committers are working on. If it's something essential to an enterprise or personal project, it's likely to make it into TurboGears. The evolution of TurboGears has in part been driven by the fact that it's been built on other projects. An example is the continuing evolution of CherryPy, because TurboGears hooks into CherryPy rather deeply. So the evolution in the "feel" of TurboGears has been driven by what's going on in the major projects we use. Thus, we tend to build our releases around what people have wanted and needed to work on.

On Web 2.0 Directions

Q: *Where do you see Web 2.0 going, or to put it different way, what would Web 3.0 look like?*

Kevin: Well certainly JavaScript and standard browser technologies (as opposed, say, to Flex2) are here to stay, particularly for sites that are more page-like, where there is a lot of content that you're just really laying out for the user. Now, for sites that are more like applications, things that might traditionally have been done in a desktop client are going to move toward Flex, because it's so much easier if you don't have to worry about browser incompatibility, and frankly it's just plain faster, particularly if you're comparing it to Internet Explorer running JavaScript. There are a couple of things that might serve to mitigate an all-out migration to Flex, though — for example, if browser JavaScript engines were to get really fast and really soon, or if more standards compliance were to happen. However, for applications you're designing right now, you'd want to take a good hard look at Flex, especially with Flex becoming open source.

Part II
TurboGears

Introduction to TurboGears

Simplicity is prerequisite for reliability.

—Edsger W. Dijkstra

In Chapter 3 you were introduced to the TurboGears and the Django frameworks. Here you'll learn more about the capabilities of the TurboGears framework, common framework components, and the structure of a TurboGears project.

In this chapter you'll gain experience with TurboGears as you implement a blog. You'll start by setting up the project and defining a basic model. Then you'll see how to use TGCrud, a controller and view generator, to create a variety of views for manipulating your model objects. Finally, you'll learn about the capabilities of Kid templates as you modify the master design of the site.

TurboGears Components

Before getting into an example, it is necessary to explore some of the significant components of the TurboGears framework in a little more detail than was discussed in Chapter 3. In this section you'll learn a little more about what the models, controllers, views, and widgets are, and how they're typically used in TurboGears.

TurboGears Models (SQLObjects)

SQLObject is object-relational mapping (ORM) that enables the translation between model objects defined in Python and a relational database. Typically the model objects, defined in the model.py, inherit from the base SQLObject and include the specification of attributes that correspond to database columns. The main documentation for SQLObject is at http://sqlobject.org/SQLObject.html.

TurboGears Controllers

CherryPy is the basis for the controller framework in TurboGears. This framework is used to define the URIs available for a web application and associate those URIs with Kid templates and other Python code. The main CherryPy documentation is at www.cherrypy.org/wiki/TableOfContents.

A controller is made up of methods that establish new URIs available in the web application. A controller can even contain a reference to another controller, which establishes an additional directory that can define additional relative paths.

The Root Controller

Typically, a web application has a single root controller defined in controllers.py that inherits from a base root controller class (controllers.RootController). The root controller serves as the main entry point into the web application, and establishes any paths available from the top directory of the web application. An example root controller is shown here:

```
1 from turbogears import controllers, expose
2
3 class Root(controllers.RootController):
4     @expose(template="foo.templates.welcome")
5     def index(self):
6         import time
7         return dict(now=time.ctime())
8
9     @expose()
10    def hello(self):
11        return "Hello World"
```

This example creates two URIs, /hello and /, and shows the basic components of a controller specification as follows:

❑   Each method that is to be exposed should be preceded by the expose decorator as shown on lines 4 and 9. The decorator is a construct in Python based on the decorator pattern (see http://wiki.python.org/moin/PythonDecorators for more information). The effect of expose is to create a new URI in the web application with the same name as the method it precedes. For example, the decorator on line 9 creates a new path, /hello, in the web application.

❑   The expose decorator takes an optional template, as shown on line 4. This template is applied when generating a response.

❑   The exposed controller method can return a dict containing arguments for use in the template. The dict generated on line 7 causes a variable, now, to be passed to the template.

Creating and Using a New Controller

You can define additional controllers that generally extend the base controller class (`controllers.Controller`). Any additional controller can be included in the root controller to define an additional subdirectory in the web application. The following moves the `hello` method from the previous example into a separate controller:

```
 1 from turbogears import controllers, expose
 2
 3 class GreetingController(controllers.Controller):
 4     @expose()
 5     def hello(self):
 6         return "<H1>Hello World</H1>"
 7
 8 class Root(controllers.RootController):
 9     greeting = GreetingController()
10
11     @expose(template="foo.templates.welcome")
12     def index(self):
13         import time
14         return dict(now=time.ctime())
```

This example creates a web application with two paths, `/`and`/greeting/hello`. Note that the name of the subdirectory in the URI is determined by the attribute name of the controller (see line 9).

TurboGears Views (Kid Templates and MochiKit)

The Kid template engine is responsible for processing and creating views for a web application based on a combination of HTML and Python. Kid templates are defined for a single view, and invoked by a controller when associated with an exposed controller method as shown previously. A comprehensive reference to the Kid template language is available at `http://kid-templating.org/language.html`.

The Kid template specification provides basic constructs such as conditionals and loops for use in a template, and allows a template to extend other templates. This enables you to define common components like style sheets, headers, and footers once and share them on all pages in a site.

When generated with the `quickstart` command, a master template, `master.kid`, is created automatically. This template is responsible for establishing the layout of the web application, including any header, footer, menus, or other components. The content of each view is then defined in a separate Kid template that extends `master.kid`.

MochiKit is a client JavaScript library that provides a variety of JavaScript usability enhancements such as drag and drop, improved event handling, and a simple yet powerful asynchronous request mechanism. The MochiKit library is automatically included in Kid templates that extend the site template included in TurboGears, or it can be included explicitly as follows:

```
<script src="${tg.tg_js}/MochiKit.js"/>
```

See `http://mochikit.com/doc/html/MochiKit/index.html` for detailed MochiKit documentation.

TurboGears Widgets

The widget is another component used extensively in TurboGears. You can think of a widget as a complete and reusable piece of a web application. A widget is stateless, can take parameters, and includes any of the details necessary to create the component, like HTML, JavaScript, and Cascading Style Sheets (CSS).

TurboGears provides a set of widgets that simplify form creation and management, such as widgets that can help you create complex form elements for an AJAX-based autocomplete field. There are also widgets that aid in the presentation of data, such as the `DataGrid` widget that simplifies the display of data in a table.

As a site developer, you can even extend a set of widgets by defining your own widget classes (which you'll learn about in Chapter 6, "Widgets"). Several very useful widgets not included with TurboGears are available for download from The CogBin (`www.turbogears.org/cogbin/`), a repository of publicly developed and contributed TurboGears extensions.

The widgets available may vary depending on the TurboGears installation, and even the particular project. The TurboGears Toolbox provides a Widget Browser that shows information about the widgets available for a particular TurboGears configuration. You access the TurboGears Toolbox with the `tg-admin toolbox` command.

An Example: A Simple Blog Site

Now that you've learned a little more about the components that make up TurboGears, you're ready to implement a more complex web application. In this section, you explore the internals of TurboGears by implementing a blog application that does the following:

- ❑ Maintains a list of blog authors:
    - ❑ Allows the creation, and editing of authors
    - ❑ Displays the details for a single blog author or a list of all authors
- ❑ Maintains a list of blog entries:
    - ❑ Allows the creation and editing of a blog entry as plain text or HTML
    - ❑ Shows each blog entry formatted as an HTML document
    - ❑ Displays a list of all blog entry titles, authors, and creation dates
- ❑ Includes a main view that presents all blog entries over several pages
- ❑ Provides a tailored look and feel, rather than the default generated for a TurboGears project

Creating the Project

The first step is to create the TBlog project skeleton using the `quickstart` subcommand `tg-admin` as follows:

```
C:\turbogears-examples>tg-admin quickstart tblog
Enter package name [tblog]:
Do you need Identity (usernames/passwords) in this project? [no] yes
Selected and implied templates:
turbogears#tgbase          tg base template
...
```

As you learned in Chapter 3, you can use the tg-admin *tool to perform a variety of project administration tasks such as creating the database, starting a Python shell, and creating a new project skeleton. Refer to Chapter 3 if you need a refresher on the basics of TurboGears; also see the second table in Chapter 3 for common* tg-admin *commands.*

When you are asked if you need identity in the project, answer `yes`. You won't be making use of it in this chapter, but you'll use the generated identity elements in Chapter 5, "User Identity and Visitor Tracking," to add user management to your web application.

Defining the Model

After you create the project skeleton, you're ready to define the model the same way as you did in Chapter 3. In this case, the model needs to include a representation for a blog author and a blog entry.

Open `c:/turbogears-examples/tblog/tblog/model.py`, and add the `BlogAuthor` and `BlogEntry` classes as shown in Listing 4-1.

Listing 4-1: The initial tblog model specification, model.py

```
 1 ...
 2 # class YourDataClass(SQLObject):
 3 #      pass
 4
 5 class BlogAuthor(SQLObject):
 6     firstName = StringCol(varchar=True, length=10)
 7     lastName = StringCol()
 8     emailAddress = StringCol()
 9     def __str__(self):
10       return "%s %s" % (self.firstName, self.lastName)
11
12 class BlogEntry(SQLObject):
13   date = DateTimeCol()
14   entryText = StringCol()
15   entryTitle = StringCol()
16   author = ForeignKey("BlogAuthor")
17
18 # identity models.
19 class Visit(SQLObject):
20 ...
```

Note the following:

- ❑ The BlogAuthor class (lines 5 through10) extends the base class SQLObject and represents an author of an entry in the blog.

- ❑ The BlogEntry class (lines 12 through 16) extends SQLObject and represents an entry in the blog.

- ❑ The BlogAuthor specification includes three columns of type StringCol. The author's name is identified by the firstName (line 6) and lastName (line 7) columns, and the emailAddress column defined on line 8 holds the author's e-mail address.

- ❑ The string representation of a BlogAuthor is defined on line 9 and 10. It consists of the first and last name of the author, separated by a space.

- ❑ Each BlogEntry includes an entry date (line 13) that contains a date and time value. Text for the blog entry is defined as entryText (line 14). The title is defined as entryTitle and consists of a short string description of the blog entry (line 15). Finally, the author of the blog is represented as a foreign key from the BlogAuthor table (line 16). The value of this field is a reference to a row in the BlogAuthor table.

- ❑ The column specification shown on lines 6 through 8 and lines 13 through 16 enables you to use a variety of optional attributes, as shown on line 6. Some are common to all columns, whereas others, such as varchar, are specific to a particular column type. Attributes common to all columns are shown in the following table.

- ❑ The file initially contains several models (beginning on line 18) that are needed to represent the required data for user identity. These can be ignored for now.

Attribute	Description
dbName	The name to use for the column in the database.
default	The default value for the column.
alternateID	A Boolean value that establishes whether or not the column can be used as an alternate identifier. This should be True only when the unique attribute is True, because additional methods are generated to retrieve the object based on this column.
unique	A Boolean value that establishes whether or not the column must be unique.
notNone	A Boolean value that establishes whether or not the column will accept null values.
sqlType	The SQL type of the column, This attribute is necessary only when you're not using a column class from this table, and is used only when the SQLObject is being used to create the database tables.

The types of the columns in the model are not limited to StringCol, DateTimeCol, and ForeignKey. See the following table for a guide to some common column types for SQLObject attributes.

Column Type	Description
BLOBCol	Contains binary data.
BoolCol	Contains a Boolean value. This creates a value like 1/0 or t/f in the database depending on the implementation used.
CurrencyCol	Contains a monetary value. This is represented by a floating-point number with a precision of 2.
DateTimeCol	Contains a date and time and accepts datetime or mxDateTime objects.
DateCol	Contains a date and accepts datetime or mxDateTime objects.
TimeCol	Contains a time and accepts datetime or mxDateTime objects.
DecimalCol	Contains a number with a fixed precision. This column type establishes size and precision attributes to enable you to specify the number of digits stored and the number of digits maintained after the decimal point.
EnumCol	Contains an enumeration value. This establishes an enumValues attribute that contains a list of possible enumeration values.
FloatCol	Contains a floating-point number.
ForeignKey	Defines a reference to a key from another table.
IntCol	Contains an integer value.
PickleCol	Contains a Python object.
StringCol	Contains text data. This enables you to specify a length attribute that establishes a maximum length for the column values. When a length is provided, you can define the varchar with a Boolean value to indicate whether the column should be created as a fixed CHAR type or a VARCHAR type (if supported by the database implementation).
UnicodeCol	A text data column that is encoded as UTF-8 when it's stored.

Building the Database for the Model

After the model is defined, you need to create a database that corresponds to the model files. You can accomplish this by using the tg-admin command as follows:

```
C:\turbogears-examples\tblog>tg-admin sql create
Using database URI sqlite:///C|\turbogears-examples\tblog/devdata.sqlite
C:\turbogears-examples\tblog>
```

Note that this listing uses the sql create command to create the tables in the database. There are several other subcommands available for sql, including the following:

❑   sql: Shows the sql used to create the database

❑   drop: Drops the tables from the database

❑   `list`: Shows the list of `SQLObject` classes found for your project

❑   `help`: Shows the complete list of available subcommands

Using CatWalk

You can use the CatWalk tool to view or modify data in the database (described in detail in Chapter 3). Access CatWalk using the TurboGears Toolbox, which you can start as follows:

```
C:\turbogears-examples\tblog>tg-admin toolbox
```

Using TGCrud

Now that you've set up the database and model for the blog, you need to define views that let the blog's users create new blog-entry authors and add new blog entries. There are other alternatives outlined in Chapter 3, but when you're not defining a completely tailored view, you'll frequently want to use the TGCrud extension explored here.

TGCrud is an extension to the core TurboGears framework that enables you to quickly generate and tailor views for the basic manipulation of a data object. It generates a skeleton for views and a controller that allows the user to perform basic data manipulation operations like create, read, update, and delete (CRUD). After generating the skeleton for a model object, the application developer modifies the skeleton to define the look and feel of each operation as required for the data.

For this example, the blog entry authors use TGCrud v0.8, which includes a `crud` subcommand for `tg-admin`. The command takes the name of a model class and a package as arguments, and can be used to generate the template code for a model class.

A beta version of TGCrud 1.0 is also available. It includes support for both SQLObject and SQLAlchemy, as well as a mechanism that lets you to define your own view templates.

Generated TGCrud Code

When you run TGCrud, several files are generated that you can easily incorporate into your web application. These include `controllers.py`, at the base directory for the generated code, and several Kid templates under a `templates` subdirectory. The `controllers.py` file contains the specification of a controller class that manages all the views created by TGCrud. You can use these views to do the following:

❑   **Create a new entry.** For example, you can browse to the `new` path element at `http://localhost:8080/<controller-path>/new`. This view is defined in the Kid template `new.kid`.

❑   **Show all entries defined in the database.** The `list` path is associated with the `list.kid` Kid template and is available at `http://localhost:8080/<controller-path>/list`.

❑   **Update an existing entry.** The `edit` path element takes the identifier of a database row encoded as a part of the URL. For example, `http://localhost:8080/<controller-path>/edit/1` is the URL that will show the view for the first row in the database with `id=1`. The Kid template `edit.kid` is used to create this view.

❑ **Delete an existing entry.** Like `edit`, the `destroy` path element takes a database row identifier as a part of the URL. Browsing to `http://localhost:8080/<controller-path>/destroy/1` removes the row with `id=1` from the database. There is no Kid template associated with the `destroy` operation.

❑ **Show a single entry in the database.** The `show` path element shows another view relevant to only a single entry. Browse to `http://localhost:8080/<controller-path>/show/1` to display the row with `id=1`. This view uses the `show.kid` Kid template.

The view templates are set up to facilitate navigation between each view. For example, the `list` template includes a link next to each list entry that allows the user to show, edit, or delete the entry.

> *The generated code also includes a template called `master.kid` that is extended by each of the view's Kid templates. Note that this template is similar to the master template of the project. As you'll see in the section "Changing Your Site's Look and Feel," you'll most likely want to use a single master template for the entire site.*

The code generator further simplifies the views by using widgets to create the form used in the new and edited views. The list of widgets used in the views is, however, left up to the developer as an additional setup task. This list is defined in a class in the `controllers.py` file that extends a base `WidgetList` class.

The other bit of tailoring required is the definition of the code in the `list` and `show` views. A skeleton provided in each view reduces the amount of tailoring required and helps make the requirement obvious. For example, the `list` view includes code that walks through the list of all records selected and creates a row in a table for each entry.

The final result is that after generating the code, you (the developer) need to perform only four additional steps:

1. Include the generated controller as an additional path in the web application.

2. Define the list of widgets displayed in the forms used by `new` and `edit`.

3. Tailor the `list` view to include the details of the model object being displayed.

4. Tailor the `show` view to include the details of the model object being displayed.

Installing TGCrud

Because TGCrud is not initially included as a core component of TurboGears, you need to install it before you can use it. You can download it as a Python egg file from `http://cheeseshop.python.org/pypi/tgcrud/`, but it's easiest to install it using the `easy_install` command as follows:

```
C:\turbogears-examples\tblog>easy_install tgcrud
```

This command automatically installs the latest version of TGCrud when none is currently installed, or updates the currently installed version to be the latest available.

Creating the Blog Author Views with TGCrud

Now that you've learned about the basic capabilities and installed TGCrud, it's time to get your feet wet and use TGCrud to create the views and controller for the BlogAuthor model object.

Generating the Code

After installing TGCrud, you're ready to generate the controller and views for the BlogAuthor. To do this, run the following crud command with the name of the model object as the first argument and the package name as the second argument:

```
C:\turbogears-examples\tblog>tg-admin crud BlogAuthor BlogAuthorController
```

This creates a new subdirectory named BlogAuthorController under c:\turbogears-examples\ tblog\tblog. The BlogAuthorController directory contains all the generated files, which initially includes a controller (controllers.py) and a template subdirectory with a set of Kid files (edit.kid, list.kid, new.kid, and show.kid) that define the CRUD operation views.

> *Before getting into the details of tailoring the generated code, you may want to look over each of the generated files to get a sense of what's going on. You don't need to worry too much about the details right now — you'll learn more about each of these files as you tailor them for the BlogAuthor model object.*

Creating a New Web Application Path

The next thing you need to do is update the root controller in tblog\tblog\controllers.py to include BlogAuthorController, as follows:

```
...
# log = logging.getLogger("tblog.controllers")
from BlogAuthorController import BlogAuthorController
class Root(controllers.RootController):
    authors = BlogAuthorController()
    @expose(template="tblog.templates.welcome")
...
```

The first change imports the generated controller from the BlogAuthorController package. The second change creates a new path, http://localhost:8080/authors, in the web application. When the user browses to anything under this path, it is delegated to BlogAuthorController.

After adding the new reference, you can start the web application and see the new paths that were created. The application can be started with the following command:

```
C:\turbogears-examples\tblog>python start-tblog.py
```

The author list page is displayed by default. This page doesn't contain any entries unless you've already created blog authors with something like CatWalk. The path elements created for BlogAuthor include list, show, new, edit, and destroy for the basic operations, but you must tailor the controller and views before the new views can be used.

Defining the Widgets

Next you need to tailor the `BlogAuthorFields` class defined in the `BlogAuthorController` to include the list of widgets required to edit or define a new blog author. To do this, open `tblog/tblog/BlogAuthorController/controller.py` and edit it as shown in Listing 4-2.

Listing 4-2: The controller for BlogAuthors defined in controller.py

```
 1 class BlogAuthorFields(WidgetsList):
 2     #Replace to your Fields
 3     #name = TextField(name="name", validator=validators.NotEmpty)
 4     #url = TextField(name="url")
 5     firstNameField = TextField(name="firstName", label="First Name",
 6                                validator=validators.NotEmpty,
 7                                default="first")
 8     lastNameField = TextField(name="lastName", label="Last Name",
 9                               validator=validators.NotEmpty,
10                               default="last")
11     emailAddressField = TextField(name="emailAddress",
12                                   label = "Email Address",
13                                   validator=validators.Email(not_empty=True),
14                                   attrs=dict(size="30"))
```

❑   Notice that `TextField` widget attributes are automatically generated for the name and URL columns on lines 3 and 4. These have been commented out, and should be replaced with fields that can be used for the columns in the `BlogAuthor` model object. You must define a field for each column in your model object that doesn't have a default value. The name value of the field should correspond to the name of the model object column that the field value is stored in. For example, the value of `"firstName"` used for the `name` attribute of the `firstNameField` ensures that the data entered in the field is stored in the `firstName` attribute of the model object.

You can set a variety of attributes for a widget that determine the appearance and behavior of the field. The following table shows some common arguments that can be provided for a widget.

Attribute	Description
name	The name of the widget.
validator	The validator to check the widget against when the form is submitted. The validation logic and processing are actually performed by a third-party project called FormEncode (http://formencode.org/), which was developed by Ian Bicking.
attrs	A dictionary of HTML attributes to set for the generated HTML element.
default	The default value of the widget.
template	The Kid template to use when creating the HTML. You don't have to worry about this one too much unless you're defining your own widget.
label	(For form widgets only.) The label to be displayed next to the form field.
help_text	(For form widgets only.) Text to be displayed next to the form field. For example, defining a help_text attribute with the value "Enter an e-mail address" in the emailAddressField causes the string to be displayed next to the element.

Returning to Listing 4-2 note the following:

Lines 5 through 7 define a `firstNameField` text field attribute and associate it with for the `firstName` model object. This field uses a tailored label, cannot be empty, and has a default value of `first`.

Lines 8 through 10 define a second text field attribute, `lastNameField`, which is similar to `firstNameField`.

Lines 11 through 14 define an `emailAddressField` attribute and initialize it to a text field associated with the `emailAddress` model object attribute. This text field uses the `Email` validator, which includes a `not_empty` attribute for accepting or rejecting empty e-mail addresses. It also uses the `attrs` attribute to override the default size for the text field, setting it to `30`.

At this point, you've made all the modifications necessary to edit or create a new blog author. An example NewBlogAuthor page is shown in Figure 4-1, which you access by browsing to `http://localhost:8080/authors` and clicking the New BlogAuthor link, or by going directly to `http://localhost:8080/authors/new`.

Figure 4-1

If you add a few entries and return to the main view, it will look similar to Figure 4-2. Notice that none of the data for the authors is shown initially, which you'll deal with next. For now, note the additional Show, Edit, and Destroy links next to each row. If you click the Edit link for a row, you're presented with a view that is similar to the new view.

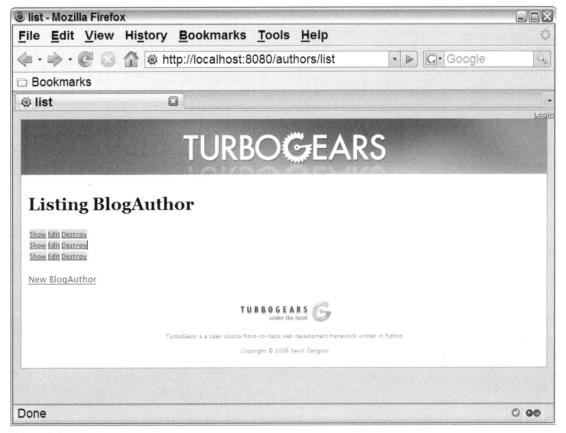

Figure 4-2

Defining the List View

The next step in tailoring the TGCrud-generated code is to tailor the `list` view so that it actually displays the data from the database. Luckily, a skeleton for this is generated for you in a Kid template called `tblog/tblog/BlogAuthorController/templates/list.kid`. Simply open this file and modify it as shown in Listing 4-3.

Listing 4-3: The BlogAuthorController list template, list.kid, updated to include blog author details

```
1  <!DOCTYPE html PUBLIC "-//W3C//DTD XHTML 1.0 Transitional//EN"
2    "http://www.w3.org/TR/xhtml1/DTD/xhtml1-transitional.dtd">
3  <html xmlns="http://www.w3.org/1999/xhtml"
4    xmlns:py="http://purl.org/kid/ns#" py:extends="'master.kid'">
5    <head>
6      <meta content="text/html; charset=utf-8"
7        http-equiv="Content-Type" py:replace="''"/>
8      <title>list</title>
9    </head>
10   <body>
11     <h1>Listing ${modelname}</h1>
12
13     <table>
14       <tr>
15         <!--th> name </th>
16         <th> url </th-->
17         <th> First Name </th>
18         <th> Last Name </th>
19         <th> Email </th>
20       </tr>
21       <tr py:for="record in records">
22         <!--td>${record.name}</td>
23         <td>${record.url}</td-->
24         <td>${record.firstName}</td>
25         <td>${record.lastName}</td>
26         <td><a href="mailto: ${record.emailAddress}">
27           ${record.emailAddress}</a></td>
28         <td><a href="show/${record.id}">Show</a></td>
29         <td><a href="edit/${record.id}">Edit</a></td>
30         <td><a href="destroy/${record.id}"
31             onclick="if (confirm('Are you sure?'))  {
32               var f = document.createElement('form');
33               this.parentNode.appendChild(f);
34               f.method = 'POST';
35               f.action = this.href;
36               f.submit();
37             };
38             return false;">
39             Destroy</a></td>
40       </tr>
41     </table>
42
43     <br/>
44     <a href="new">New ${modelname}</a>
45     <!--span py:for="page in tg.paginate.pages">
46     <a py:if="page != tg.paginate.current_page"
47       href="${tg.paginate.get_href(page)}">${page}</a>
48     <b py:if="page == tg.paginate.current_page">${page}</b>
49     </span-->
50   </body>
51 </html>
```

Notice that the majority of the code shown in this listing is automatically generated. You're required to add only the table header (lines 17 through 19) and row detail (lines 24 through 27) for the BlogAuthor model object.

The listing also shows the basics of a typical Kid file specification. You can see the complete Kid template language specification at http://kid-templating.org/language.html, but for now just take a look at how Listing 4-2 uses this specification:

- ❑ The template looks much like a normal HTML document, but must conform to the XML specification. For example, any element specification must include both the opening tag (such as <td>) and the closing tag (such as </td>) as shown on line 24, or use the shorthand (<br/>) as shown on line 43.

- ❑ A Python expression can be embedded in the Kid template by enclosing it in braces with a leading dollar sign (${<expr>}), as shown on line 24. When the template is evaluated, the expression is replaced with the expression result.

- ❑ Although this is not shown in the listing, you can also embed a Python code block in the template with the Python processing instruction. For example, you can define a function in the template for later use, as follows:

```
<?python
    def doubleX(x):
        return x*2
?>
```

- ❑ A Kid template defines a Python namespace (line 4) and includes a variety of Python-specific attributes from that namespace (such as py:extends on line 4 and py:for on line 21). The following table describes the available Python attributes.

Attribute	Description
for	This attribute is constructed like a normal for loop in Python and causes an element to be processed once for each item in a given list.
if	A conditional attribute that takes an expression. An element and its descendents are output only when the expression defined for the attribute evaluates to true.
content	An attribute that can be used to generate content dynamically. It replaces any descendants of the element with the result of the expression.
replace	This is similar to the content attribute, but it replaces the element and its descendants with the result of the expression.
strip	Similar to the if conditional attribute, this can be used to control whether or not an element is output. When the containing expression evaluates to true, the element is not output. Unlike the if conditional attribute, this has no effect on descendent elements.
attrs	Allows the dynamic creation of attributes for an element. The evaluation of the expression for this attribute should result in a dict, a list, or a comma-separated collection of key value pairs (such as k1=foo, k2=bar).

Table continued on following page

Attribute	Description
def	Takes a name and argument list, and creates a named template function. An element containing this attribute and any of its descendents is not output during normal template evaluation. It is included in the resulting HTML only when the template is invoked by another template attribute.
match	Allows you to define custom tags for use in a template. The element and its descendents are output only when the tag defined for the element appears in the document.
extends	This should appear on the root element of the document. It takes the name of a template and allows for inheritance, which causes any named template functions (defined with def) and custom tags (defined with match) in the extended template to be inherited.
layout	Like extends, this should appear only on the root element. It takes the name of a template and causes the referenced template to be used to establish the layout of a template. The named functions, custom tags, and other parameters defined in the template containing the layout attribute are used by the layout template to generate the page content.

After tailoring and saving the list template, you should see a page that looks similar to Figure 4-3 if you browse to http://localhost:8080/authors/list or http://localhost:8080/authors.

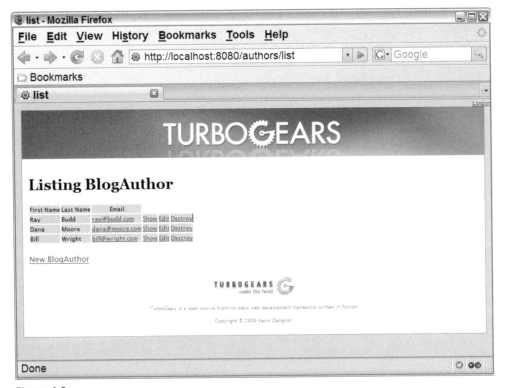

Figure 4-3

Defining the Show View

The final step in setting up the author CRUD views is to specify the show view. Similar to the list view, this view is initially empty and appears as shown in Figure 4-4.

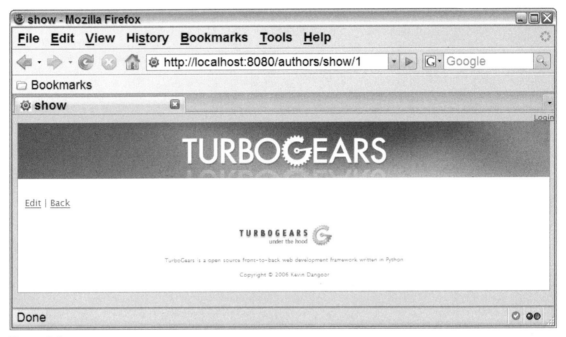

Figure 4-4

The show view is defined in the file tblog/BlogAuthorController/templates/show.kid and must be tailored as shown in Listing 4-4 so that the author detail is displayed. Note that the url and name values in the generated file are replaced with references to the firstName, lastName, and emailAddress columns of the author on lines 12 through 19.

Listing 4-4: The BlogAuthorController show template, show.kid, updated to include blog author details

```
1 <!DOCTYPE html PUBLIC "-//W3C//DTD XHTML 1.0 Transitional//EN"
2   "http://www.w3.org/TR/xhtml1/DTD/xhtml1-transitional.dtd">
3 <html xmlns="http://www.w3.org/1999/xhtml"
4   xmlns:py="http://purl.org/kid/ns#" py:extends="'master.kid'">
5   <head>
6     <meta content="text/html; charset=utf-8"
7       http-equiv="Content-Type" py:replace="''"/>
8     <title>show</title>
9   </head>
10  <body>
11    <table>
12      <tr>
13        <th>Name: </th>
```

(continued)

Listing 4-4 (continued)

```
14          <td>${record.firstName} ${record.lastName}</td>
15        </tr>
16        <tr>
17          <th>Email: </th>
18          <td>${record.emailAddress}</td>
19        </tr>
20      </table>
21      <br/>
22      <a href="../edit/${record.id}">Edit</a> |
23      <a href="../list">Back</a>
24    </body>
25 </html>
```

After tailoring this view, you can see any author in the list by clicking the Show link next to the entry. This displays a page similar to the one shown in Figure 4-5.

Figure 4-5

Creating the Blog Entry Views with TGCrud

Now that you've created the CRUD views for the author, you're ready to create a basic interface for blog entries. To do this, you use TGCrud to create a controller and views for the `BlogEntry`.

Generating the Code

First you'll need to generate the controller and views for `BlogEntry` objects. To do this, use the `crud` subcommand of `tg-admin` with `BlogEntry` as an argument, as follows:

```
C:\turbogears-examples\tblog>tg-admin crud BlogEntry BlogEntryController
```

This creates the `BlogEntryController` directory and generates the CRUD view and controller code.

Creating a New Web Application Path

Once again, you need to edit the root application controller defined in `tblog\tblog\controllers.py` to reference the new controller, as follows:

```
...
# log = logging.getLogger("tblog.controllers")
from BlogAuthorController import BlogAuthorController
from BlogEntryController import BlogEntryController
class Root(controllers.RootController):
    authors = BlogAuthorController()
    entries = BlogEntryController()

    @expose(template="tblog.templates.welcome")
...
```

This creates a new path called `entries` in the web application.

Defining the Widgets

Before you can create and edit new blog entries, you must define the set of widgets that describe a `BlogEntry`. After you tailor the blog entry fields, the new page (`http://localhost:8080/entries/new`) and edit page (`http://localhost:8080/entries/edit/<id>`) will look similar to the page shown in Figure 4-6.

Define the `BlogEntryFields` class in `tblog/BlogEntryController/controllers.py` as shown in Listing 4-5.

Listing 4-5: The BlogEntryFields class defined in controllers.py

```
 1 from tblog.model import BlogAuthor
 2
 3 class BlogEntryFields(WidgetsList):
 4     #Replace to your Fields
 5     #name = TextField(name="name", validator=validators.NotEmpty)
 6     #url = TextField(name="url")
 7     author = SingleSelectField(name="author",
 8                                    options=[(entry.id,entry.firstName + " " +
 9                                        entry.lastName) for entry in
10                                        BlogAuthor.select()])
11
12     date = CalendarDateTimePicker(name="date",
13                                    label="Entry Date",
14                                    validator=validators.DateTimeConverter())
```

(continued)

Listing 4-5 *(continued)*

```
15        entryTitle = TextField(name="entryTitle", label="Entry Title",
16                        validator=validators.NotEmpty)
17        entryText = TextArea(name="entryText", label="blog Entry",
18                        validator=validators.NotEmpty,
19                        rows=25, cols=70))
```

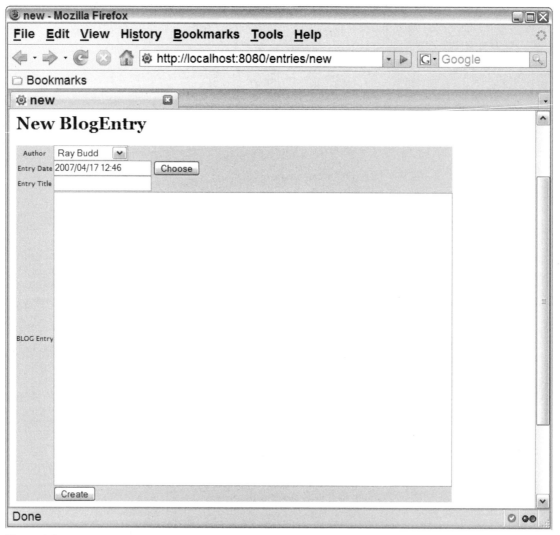

Figure 4-6

The specification in this listing is similar to the `BlogAuthorFields` specification in Listing 4-1, with the following significant similarities and differences:

❑ As in Listing 4-1, the default `name` and `url` fields are commented out on lines 5 and 6.

❑ The author does not include a `label` attribute. This causes the default label to be used, which is the name of the element with the first letter capitalized.

❑ In Listing 4-1 a variety of additional widgets are used instead of the `TextField` widget. Many different types of widgets are available for use in your project, as shown in the following table. You can find out the details of the widgets available for use in a project by starting the TurboGears Toolbox from a project home directory and examining the Widget Browser shown on the main TurboGears Toolbox site (available at `http://localhost:7654/widgets/`).

Widget	Purpose
AutoCompleteFormField	An AJAX-based text field that suggests a text field value to the user. As a user enters text in the field, a pop-up menu is populated with a set of possible values provided by the server.
Button	The standard form button.
CalendarDatePicker	A text field linked to a pop-up calendar. It includes a button that displays a calendar when the user clicks it. When the user selects a date in the pop-up calendar, the text field is populated with the selected date.
CalendarDateTimePicker	This is similar to the CalendarDatePicker, but allows the user to specify a time as well as the date in the pop-up calendar.
CheckBox	The standard form on/off check box.
CheckBoxList	A list of related check boxes.
FieldSet	A field that serves as a container for a set of related form fields.
FileField	A text field linked to a file browser. A Browse button displays a file browser when clicked. After the user selects a file, the text field is populated with the path name of the file.
HiddenField	The standard hidden form field. No field is displayed, but the parameter is included when the form data is sent to the server.
ImageButton	A button that displays an image rather than text.
Label	A read-only label to be displayed on the form.
MultipleSelectField	A list of predefined options, which allows multiple values to be selected simultaneously.
PasswordField	A text-input field that replaces each entered letter with an asterisk (*) for security purposes.
RadioButtonList	A collection of mutually exclusive buttons. Each button on the list creates an entry in the form, but only one button may be clicked at a time.

Table continued on following page

Widget	Purpose
RepeatingFieldSet	A collection of form fields that is included multiple times in the same form.
ResetButton	The standard form Reset button, which resets the form to its initial state.
SingleSelectField	A drop-down list containing a predefined set of options.
SubmitButton	The standard form Submit button, which causes the form field values to be sent to the server.
TextArea	A multiline field for text input.
TextField	A single-line field for text input.

❑ Because the author is a foreign key, a SingleSelectField widget is used. This particular widget creates a select form element populated with a list defined by the options attribute. This attribute should contain a list of key-value pairs, where the key establishes the key of the select field and the value defines the displayed value. In the case of the author select field, the list contains keys made up of author IDs, and values contain the name of the author (lines 8–10).

❑ In Listing 4-5 the BlogAuthor must be imported on line 1 to enable the select function call made on line 10.

❑ In Listing 4-5 the date of the blog entry uses the CalendarDateTimePicker widget (lines 12–14) to enable the user to specify a date and time more easily. This widget is shown in Figure 4-7.

❑ When used with the DateTimeConverter validator as specified on line 14 of Listing 4-5, the text value of the field is automatically converted into a datetime object when the entry is added or edited.

❑ Because the content of a blog entry is likely to be a large string, a TextArea widget is used in Listing 4-5 instead of the TextField widget. This allows the user to input multiple lines, and takes optional arguments rows and cols that allow the specification of the width and height of the text area.

Defining the List View

After implementing the widgets for the new and edit views, you need to define the Kid template used to create the list view. Listing 4-6 shows the updated Kid template tblog/BlogEntryController/templates/list.kid.

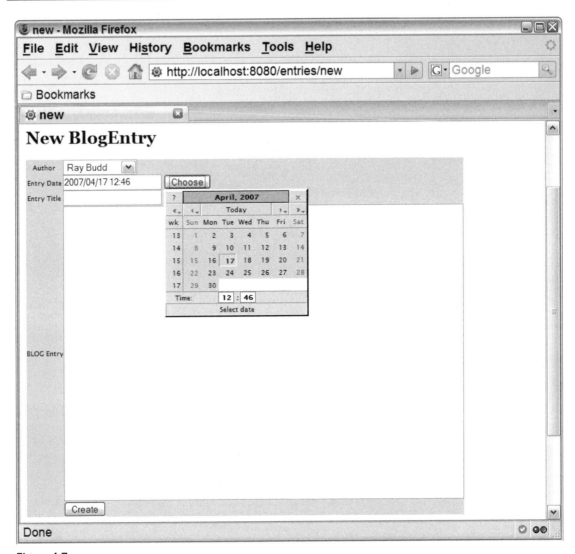

Figure 4-7

Listing 4-6: The BlogEntryController list template, list.kid, updated to include blog entry details

```
1 <!DOCTYPE html PUBLIC "-//W3C//DTD XHTML 1.0 Transitional//EN"
2   "http://www.w3.org/TR/xhtml1/DTD/xhtml1-transitional.dtd">
3 <html xmlns="http://www.w3.org/1999/xhtml"
4   xmlns:py="http://purl.org/kid/ns#" py:extends="'master.kid'">
5   <head>
6     <meta content="text/html; charset=utf-8"
7       http-equiv="Content-Type" py:replace="''"/>
8     <title>list</title>
9   </head>
```

(continued)

Listing 4-6 *(continued)*

```
10    <body>
11      <h1>Listing ${modelname}</h1>
12      <table>
13        <tr>
14          <th> Date </th>
15          <th> Blog Author </th>
16          <th> Entry Title</th>
17        </tr>
18        <tr py:for="record in records">
19          <td>${record.date}</td>
20          <td>${record.author}</td>
21          <td>${record.entryTitle}</td>
22          <td><a href="show/${record.id}">Show</a></td>
23          <td><a href="edit/${record.id}">Edit</a></td>
24          <td><a href="destroy/${record.id}"
25            onclick="if (confirm('Are you sure?')) {
26                var f = document.createElement('form');
27                this.parentNode.appendChild(f); f.method = 'POST';
28                f.action = this.href; f.submit(); };
29              return false;">Destroy</a></td>
30        </tr>
31      </table>
32      <br/>
33      <a href="new">New ${modelname}</a>
34      <!--span py:for="page in tg.paginate.pages">
35      <a py:if="page != tg.paginate.current_page"
36      href="${tg.paginate.get_href(page)}">${page}</a>
37      <b py:if="page == tg.paginate.current_page">${page}</b>
38      </span-->
39
40    </body>
41  </html>
```

As with the blog authors, the only changes you make here are to replace the url and name header and row data with the blog entry column names (lines 14 through 16) and row detail (lines 19 through 21). In this case, only the blog title is displayed to save space. After you make the changes in this listing, the new blog entry list page (http://localhost:8080/entries/list) looks like Figure 4-8.

Defining the Edit View

The final step in setting up the blog entry views is to tailor the edit view. Listing 4-7 shows the updated Kid template, tblog/BlogEntryController/templates/edit.kid.

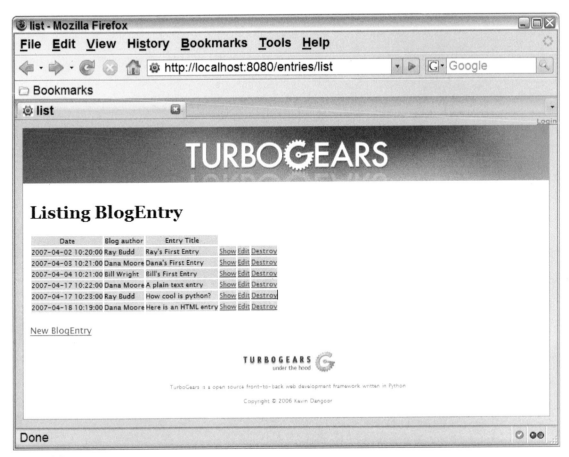

Figure 4-8

Listing 4-7: The BlogEntryController edit template, edit.kid, updated to include blog entry details

```
 1 <!DOCTYPE html PUBLIC "-//W3C//DTD XHTML 1.0 Transitional//EN"
 2 "http://www.w3.org/TR/xhtml1/DTD/xhtml1-transitional.dtd">
 3 <html xmlns="http://www.w3.org/1999/xhtml"
 4   xmlns:py="http://purl.org/kid/ns#" py:extends="'master.kid'">
 5   <head>
 6     <meta content="text/html; charset=utf-8"
 7       http-equiv="Content-Type" py:replace="''"/>
 8     <title>show</title>
 9   </head>
10   <body>
11     <table>
12       <tr>
13         <th>${record.date} ${record.author} ${record.entryTitle}</th>
14       </tr>
15       <tr>
```

(continued)

Listing 4-7 *(continued)*

```
16          <td>${XML(record.entryText)}</td>
17        </tr>
18      </table>
19      <br/>
20      <a href="../edit/${record.id}">Edit</a> | <a href="../list">Back</a>
21    </body>
22  </html>
```

In this case, the format of the view is slightly different. Specifically:

❑   The date, author, and title for the entry make up the header of the table (line 13).

❑   The text of the entry makes up the single row of content for the table (line 16) so that lengthy blog entries will be displayed correctly.

❑   The entry text is not referenced using simple expression substation as is done with the other elements like the date and author. Instead, the XML function is invoked with the entry text as an argument. This function is very useful when the value of a variable is encoded as XML or

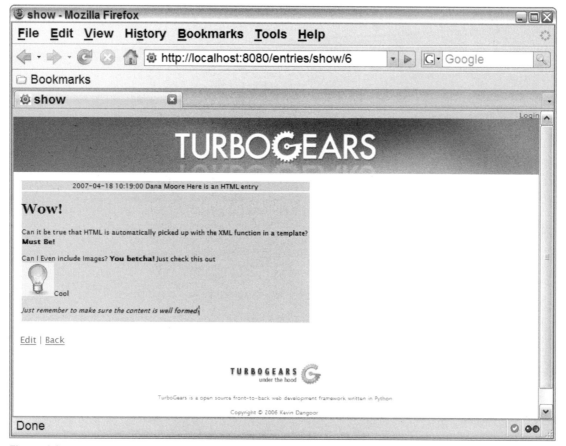

Figure 4-9

HTML, and causes the content to be included as XML rather than as a string. As a result, a blog entry that is defined using HTML can be formatted appropriately. For example, Figure 4-9 shows the page created for the following entry:

```
<h1>Wow!</h1>
<p>Can it be true that HTML is automatically picked up with the XML function in a
template?<br/>
<b>Must Be!<b></p>
<p>Can I Even include images? <b>You betcha!</b>
Just check this out <br/>
<img src="/static/images/info.png">Cool</img> </p>
<p><i>Just remember to make sure the content is well formed!</i></p>
```

When the entryText isn't passed through the XML function, the result (shown in Figure 4-10) is much less interesting.

For this feature to work correctly, the data provided must be valid XML. If it isn't, the Kid template will raise an exception.

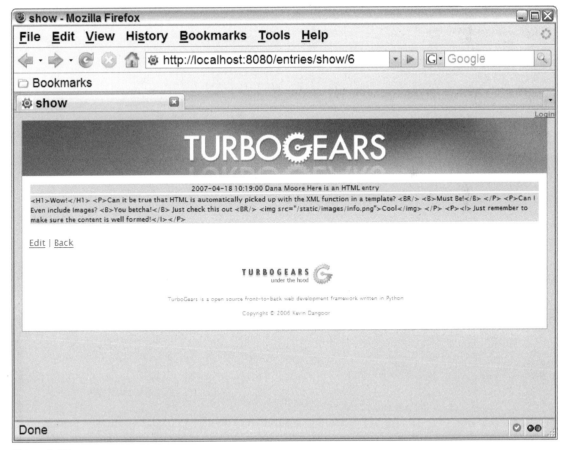

Figure 4-10

Replacing the Blog Welcome Page

At this point, the blog web application has a variety of pages that allow the specification and viewing of blog entry and author details. One very critical aspect of the site is still missing, though. The site needs a page that presents a read-only view of multiple blog entries for the blog's viewers rather than the authors. Of course, it's possible to modify the list view defined in the BlogEntryController package to present the data in a more user-friendly way, but the required view is not intended to be used in conjunction with the other blog entry operations such as entry editing. Therefore, a new view should be defined. In this section you specify the new view in the root controller and define it in the project's main template directory under tblog\tblog\templates.

Defining the Kid Template

The first step is to define a new Kid template, beView.kid. You do this in the tblog\tblog\templates directory as shown in Listing 4-8.

Listing 4-8: The new Kid template, beView.kid

```
 1 <!DOCTYPE html PUBLIC "-//W3C//DTD XHTML 1.0 Transitional//EN"
 2 "http://www.w3.org/TR/xhtml1/DTD/xhtml1-transitional.dtd">
 3 <html xmlns="http://www.w3.org/1999/xhtml"
 4   xmlns:py="http://purl.org/kid/ns#"
 5   py:extends="'master.kid'">
 6   <head>
 7     <meta content="text/html; charset=utf-8"
 8       http-equiv="Content-Type" py:replace="''"/>
 9   </head>
10   <body>
11     <div class="blogEntry" py:for="blogEntry in blogEntries">
12       <div class="beHeader">
13         <h1>${blogEntry.entryTitle}</h1>
14         <h2>${blogEntry.date}<br/>
15           ${blogEntry.author}</h2>
16       </div>
17       <p>${XML(blogEntry.entryText)}</p>
18     </div>
19     <div class="pageList">
20       Go to page:
21       <span py:for="page in tg.paginate.pages">
22         <a py:if="page != tg.paginate.current_page"
23           href="${tg.paginate.get_href(page)}">${page}</a>
24         <span py:if="page == tg.paginate.current_page">${page}</span>
25       </span>
26     </div>
27   </body>
28 </html>
```

For the most part, this view is pretty straightforward. However, it does contain some interesting differences from other views:

❑ This view expects a list of BlogEntry objects to be provided in the blogEntries parameter.

❑ A for attribute is used on line 11 to create a div for each blogEntry in the blogEntries list.

❑ Similar to the `show` view in the `BlogEntryController` package, the `BlogEntry` entry content is filtered through the XML function (line 17) to ensure that any HTML tags in the entry are used to format the entry rather than being included as string data.

❑ Lines 19 through 26 define a `div` that makes use of the paginate feature in TurboGears. This feature greatly simplifies the presentation of large sets of data across multiple pages and is necessary to ensure that all blog entries aren't shown on a single page.

You can enable the paginate feature via a `paginate` decorator when creating your new web application path (as described in the next section). This decorator ensures that several variables describing the page information are accessible from a template. For example:

❑ A list of all page numbers that are being paged over is retrieved with the `tg.paginate.pages` attribute on line 21.

❑ The current page number is retrieved with `tg.paginate.current_page`.

❑ A page number can be translated into a URI with the `tg.paginate.get_href` function, as shown on line 23.

The paginate feature is described in greater detail at `http://docs.turbogears.org/1.0/PaginateDecorator`.

Creating a New Web Application Path

After defining the new Kid template, all that remains is to modify the index path currently defined in the root controller to use the new Kid template. To do this, open `tblog\tblog\controllers.py` and edit the index function definition as shown in Listing 4-9.

Listing 4-9: The root controller, in controllers.py, extended to use the beView

```
 1 from turbogears import controllers, expose
 2 from model import *
 3 from turbogears import identity, redirect
 4 from cherrypy import request, response
 5 # from tblog import json
 6 # import logging
 7 # log = logging.getLogger("tblog.controllers")
 8 from BlogAuthorController import BlogAuthorController
 9 from BlogEntryController import BlogEntryController
10 from turbogears import paginate
11
12 class Root(controllers.RootController):
13     authors = BlogAuthorController()
14     entries = BlogEntryController()
15
16     @expose(template="tblog.templates.beView")
17     #@identity.require(identity.in_group("admin"))
18     @paginate('blogEntries', limit=5)
```

(continued)

Listing 4-9 *(continued)*

```
19    def index(self):
20        blogEntries = BlogEntry.select(orderBy=BlogEntry.q.date).reversed()
21        return dict(blogEntries = blogEntries)
22
23    @expose(template="tblog.templates.login")
24    def login(self, forward_url=None, previous_url=None, *args, **kw):
25 ...
```

Here's what's being done in this listing:

❑ The model files are imported on line 2.

❑ The `paginate` decorator is imported on line 10. Note the following:

❑ The first argument to the `paginate` decorator is the name of the select result that should be shown across multiple pages.

❑ The `limit` indicates the number of matching blog entries to include on each page.

❑ The decorator takes additional optional arguments to establish aspects of the paging, such as the column that should be used when sorting the page data.

❑ The template exposed on line 16 is changed to use the new `beView` template.

❑ The index function specification is changed as well. The `BlogEntry select` method is used on line 20 to get the list of all blog entries. The list returned is ordered by date, with the most recent entries appearing first. Several additional options are available that affect the result returned by a `select` statement:

❑ The `orderBy` argument is passed to `select` and given the name of the date column in the blog entry. Notice that the database column must be used when defining a selection limiter for the `select` statement (such as all entries before 1/1/01) or ordering the results of a selection. You do this by the accessing the column via the q attribute (`BlogEntry.q.date`), rather than directly referencing the model object attribute (`BlogEntry.date`).

❑ The `select` function takes a `distinct` argument, which you can use to remove any duplicate elements from the selection results. For example:

```
BlogEntry.select(distinct=True)
```

❑ You can specify a selection limiter. For example, you can get all entries posted before the current time with the following statement:

```
BlogEntry.select(BlogEntry.q.date < datetime.now())
```

❑ By default, when ordering by date, the `select` result includes earlier dates in earlier positions in the list. However, you can use the `reverse` function to show the most recently added blog entries at the top of the list.

❑ You can use the `count` function to return the count of matching elements. For example, use the following statement to return the number of blog entries:

```
BlogEntry.select().count()
```

After defining and saving the new controller, you'll get a page similar to the one shown in Figure 4-11 when you reload the index page at `http://localhost:8080`.

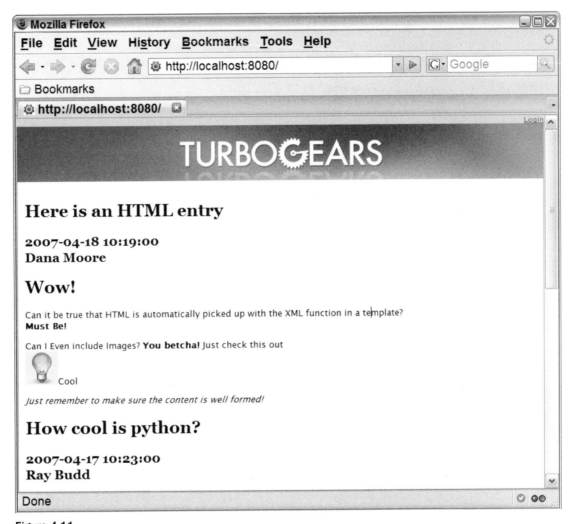

Figure 4-11

Changing Your Site's Look and Feel

At this point you have a fully functional blog. In this section you'll make some enhancements to the look and feel of the website by defining your own global template and using it in each of the views that you've created.

Thus far, you used the standard TurboGears master template, CRUD-specific master templates, and style sheets as the basis for the site's look and feel. However, the use of TurboGears labels and other standard template elements isn't practical for the majority of websites in the real world.

The look and feel of the site is typically defined in a single master template that is extended by most (if not all) views. This master template establishes standard style sheets, headers, and footers. To establish a master template for your site and create a tailored look and feel for the entire site, you need to do the following:

1. Define a master template, similar to the project's `master.kid`, that establishes the look and feel of the site.

2. Define a style sheet to be used by the master template when creating the site's look and feel.

3. Change each view to extend the new master template.

Defining the Master Template

When you create a project in TurboGears, a master template is generated and included under the project templates directory (`tblog/templates/master.kid`). If you look at this file, you can see some of the more advanced features of the Kid template system at work.

To define a new template, start with the existing master as a basis, and create a new master template named `tblog/templates/blog-master.kid`, as shown in Listing 4-10.

Listing 4-10: The master template, master.kid, tailored for TBlog

```
1  <!DOCTYPE html PUBLIC "-//W3C//DTD XHTML 1.0 Transitional//EN"
2    "http://www.w3.org/TR/xhtml1/DTD/xhtml1-transitional.dtd">
3  <?python import sitetemplate ?>
4  <html xmlns="http://www.w3.org/1999/xhtml"
5    xmlns:py="http://purl.org/kid/ns#" py:extends="sitetemplate">
6    <head py:match="item.tag=='{http://www.w3.org/1999/xhtml}head'"
7      py:attrs="item.items()">
8      <meta content="text/html; charset=UTF-8" http-equiv="content-type"
9        py:replace="''"/>
10     <title py:replace="''">TBlog: A TurboGears Blog</title>
11     <meta py:replace="item[:]"/>
12     <style type="text/css">
13       #pageLogin
14       {
15       font-size: 10px;
16       font-family: verdana;
17       text-align: right;
18       }
19     </style>
20     <style type="text/css" media="screen">
21       @import "/static/css/blog-style.css";
22     </style>
23   </head>
24   <body py:match="item.tag=='{http://www.w3.org/1999/xhtml}body'"
25     py:attrs="item.items()">
```

```
26      <div py:if="tg.config('identity.on',False) and not 'logging_in'
in locals()"
27         id="pageLogin">
28         <span py:if="tg.identity.anonymous">
29           <a href="/login">Login</a>
30         </span>
31         <span py:if="not tg.identity.anonymous">
32           Welcome ${tg.identity.user.display_name}.
33           <a href="/logout">Logout</a>
34         </span>
35      </div>
36      <div id="header">TBlog: A TurboGears Blog</div>
37      <div id="main_content">
38        <div py:if="tg_flash" class="flash"
39          py:content="tg_flash">
40        </div>
41        <div py:replace="[item.text]+item[:]"/>
42      </div>
43      <div id="footer">TBlog: A TurboGears Blog</div>
44    </body>
45  </html>
```

There are several aspects of the template that are interesting to note:

- ❑ The template imports (line 3) and extends (line 5) another template, sitetemplate, which is defined as part of the TurboGears framework.

- ❑ The template uses a standard style sheet (line 21), blog-style.css, which is defined under /static/css. (You'll learn how and where to define this in the next section.)

- ❑ The main content provided in the body of a specific view is shown in the main_content div (defined on lines 37 through 42). This is accomplished as follows:

  - ❑ The match attribute is used to match the body tag in the content-producing view (line 24).

  - ❑ When the body tag is matched, the content of the body tag (the child elements and text) defined in the content-producing template is specified as an attribute list of the master template body element with attrs (line 25).

  - ❑ The replace attribute is used to replace an empty div with the value of the new attributes (line 41).

- ❑ The relocation of any content allows the master template to define the following:

  - ❑ A default title to be shared across views (line 10)

  - ❑ A common header to be shared across views (line 36)

  - ❑ A common footer to be shared across views (line 43)

- ❑ Controls (lines 26–35) and styles (lines 12–19) to handle user management are created and shared across all views. These are retained from the original master template (discussed in more detail in Chapter 5).

Defining the Style Sheet

A new default style sheet is defined in the new master template. The new style sheet, `blog-style.css`, is shown in Listing 4-11, and should be defined under `tblog/tblog/static/css/`.

All static files appear under `tblog/tblog/static/`. *This directory serves as a location for files that do not change at runtime, and are referenced statically by Kid templates and each other. This includes subdirectories for common static elements like JavaScript (`js/`), cascading style sheets (`css/`), and images (`images/`).*

Listing 4-11: The style sheet for TBlog, blog-style.css

```
 1 #header {
 2    height: 50px;
 3    font-size: 20pt;
 4    text-align: center;
 5    border: thin solid black;
 6    background: #E1DEFE;
 7    margin: 10px auto 10px auto;
 8 }
 9
10 html, body {
11    color: #4D4B5F;
12    font-family: verdana;
13    font-size: 9pt;
14    margin: auto 10px auto 10px;
15 }
16
17 .beHeader {
18    background: #E6FDC6;
19    border: thin solid black;
20 }
21
22 .beHeader h1 {
23    margin: 2px;
24    text-align: center;
25    font-size: 12pt;
26 }
27
28 .beHeader h2 {
29    margin: 2px;
30    text-align: right;
31    font-size: 7pt;
32 }
33
34 #footer {
35    margin: 10px auto 10px auto;
36    border: 1px solid #aaa;
37    color: #999;
38    background-color: #CCC;
39    padding: 10px;
40    font-size: 80%;
41    text-align: center;
42    vertical-align: bottom;
43 }
```

```
44
45 .pageList {
46    background: #E0FFFF;
47    border: thin solid black;
48    padding: 10px;
49 }
```

Using the Master Template

Every TurboGears project gets a master template automatically generated under the project's `templates` directory as part of the project `quickstart` command. In many cases, it's sufficient to modify this template to contain the tailored look and feel of your site, but TGCrud provides a separate master Kid template for each controller package. This makes it necessary to update each of the Kid templates generated by TGCrud to use the new master template.

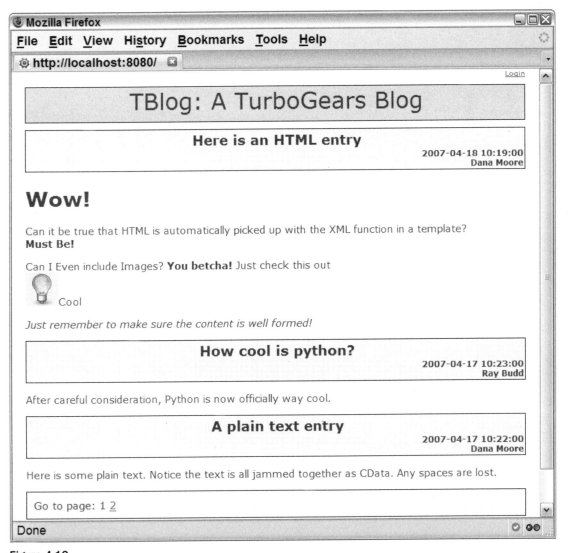

Figure 4-12

To finish the modifications required to tailor the look and feel of the `tblog` site, you need to modify the view extended by each generated view to be the new master view `tblog/templates/blog-master.kid`. The files that are affected include any Kid files defined for your project, such as those defined under `tblog/BlogAuthorController/templates` and `tblog/BlogEditorController/templates`. Replace the original `extends` attribute defined for the HTML element with one that references the new master Kid template, as follows:

```
py:extends="'../../templates/tblog-master.kid'"
```

After changing all the references and reloading the index page, you should see a page similar to the one shown in Figure 4-12.

You can now change the look and feel of the web application simply by changing the master template or the corresponding `css` file. For example, you can change the background of the header `div` for all pages by changing the value of line 6 in Listing 4-9.

Summary

In this chapter you explored some of the main components of TurboGears — controllers, widgets, and Kid templates — in detail. You also gained more hands-on experience with TurboGears by implementing an example blog application. Through this example, you learned how to do the following:

- ❑ Use controllers to separate your web application into a variety of paths and reduce the complexity of the root controller.

- ❑ Use TGCrud to create and tailor basic views for model operations.

- ❑ Define a Kid template that makes use of the paginate feature to avoid presenting the user with too much data on each page.

- ❑ Use a master template and style sheet to establish a common look and feel of a website and to define common elements in a single file.

In the next chapter you continue building your blog application and explore some of the more advanced features of TurboGears, including user management and widget definition.

5

User Identity and Visitor Tracking

How often, or on what system, the Thought Police plugged in any individual wire was guesswork. It was even conceivable that they watched everybody all the time. But at any rate, they could plug in your wire whenever they wanted to.

—George Orwell in *1984*

In the last chapter, you got a whirlwind introduction to TurboGears and created a usable blog application. In this chapter, you'll build on that foundation as you learn the ins and outs of user identity and visitor tracking. The TurboGears Visit Tracking framework creates and tracks sessions associated with the users of your web application; the TurboGears Identity framework enables you to easily identify users and add security to a web application. More specifically, in this chapter you'll learn the following:

❑   How cookies are used to track known and anonymous user visits

❑   The main components of the Identity framework:

  ❑   User identity model objects that get generated when you create a new project

  ❑   The main user identity configuration options available for a project

  ❑   The main components provided by the user identity framework

❑   The main components of the Visit Tracking framework:

  ❑   The model objects used to track visitors

  ❑   The main configuration options that modify the behavior of the visitor tracking framework

  ❑   How to write your own visitor tracking plug-ins to record and analyze site visitor behavior

You'll gain hands-on experience as you expand the TBlog application to make use of the users, groups, and security provided by the Identity framework. You'll also use the Visit Tracking framework to collect and analyze information about your site's visitors.

This chapter builds on the example constructed in Chapter 4. Ideally, you have already read that chapter and explored the example, but it's not absolutely required. If you're comfortable with the basics of Turbo-Gears and are interested in jumping right into user identity and visitor tracking, you can start with this chapter. Just be sure to download and familiarize yourself with the code from the previous chapter.

Tracking Visits through Cookies

Before getting into the details of the components provided by the Identity and Visit Tracking frameworks, you need to understand how the frameworks themselves work.

The first time someone browses to a web application that uses identity management, the Identity framework sends them a cookie. On subsequent requests from the same browser, the cookie is used to identify that the browser has already accessed the site. If the browser doesn't make any requests for some amount of time, the Identity framework assumes that the person has gone on to do something else and invalidates the cookie. At that point, if the user comes back to the application, making another request, the Identity framework creates a new cookie and sends it to the browser. See Figure 5-1 for an example interaction.

From the perspective of an identified user, the ultimate effect is that after he logs in to the site, he remains logged in until he either logs out or the session times out due to inactivity. Each time the user makes a new request, the session is extended, meaning that it could continue indefinitely as long as the user is interacting with the application.

It's important to note that the same process is used for logged-in users as well as anonymous users. This is because the cookie gets issued on the first site request before the user has the opportunity to log in. A user may have no idea that he's being tracked by the web application. He may be completely anonymous and not even have a login name for the system. What you can do with this information is discussed in more detail under the "Visitor Tracking" section.

If cookies aren't enabled on the client, the visit tracking and user identification become much less useful. The application attempts to set a cookie, but it is not accepted and therefore not included in subsequent requests from the browser. The application doesn't see a cookie with the next request, assumes that it's a new visitor, and tries to issue a new cookie. Figure 5-2 shows an example interaction with a browser that has cookies disabled.

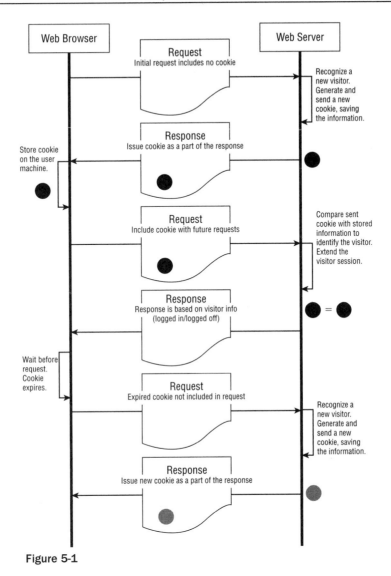

Figure 5-1

You may want to test this out as you're going through the examples later in the chapter. After completing the sections "Managing User Identity" and "Visitor Tracking," disable cookies in your browser and try visiting the site. You'll get very different behavior than when the cookies are enabled.

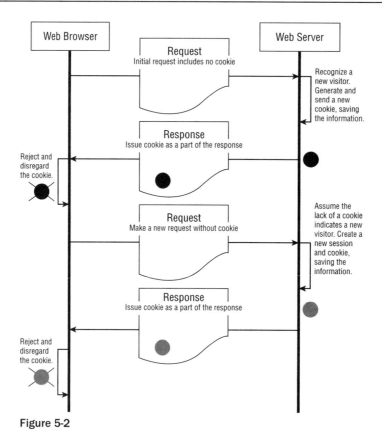

Figure 5-2

Managing User Identity

Enabling user cookies causes user sessions to be maintained, which allows you to perform the higher-level user management tasks discussed here. In this section, you'll do the following:

❑ Learn about identity model objects and see how to incorporate them into TBlog

❑ Gain more experience with CatWalk as you use it to define new users and groups

❑ Explore different ways that you can use the Identity framework for web application security and to tailor a user's experience

User Identity Model Objects

When you created the TBlog project with the `quickstart` command in the previous chapter, you indicated that the project required identity management. This option creates several model objects capable of representing and managing user identity, including objects that can be used to maintain users, groups, and permissions, as well as those that track the details of user visits. Figure 5-3 shows a class diagram of the automatically generated identity model objects.

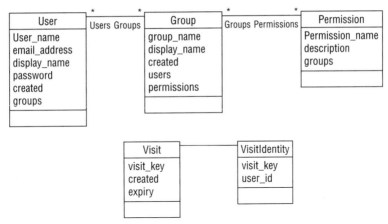

Figure 5-3

Any of these objects can be modified to include additional attributes, but by default the fields for these objects provide the basic details necessary to perform role-based security for a web application. For example, the user object could be augmented with a user's birthday, or with a set of preferences that are used to tailor the look and feel of the site based on the user's specifications.

There are two main types of objects generated for you. The User, Group, and Permission objects are used to maintain information about user login and security rights. The Visit and VisitIdentity objects are used to track known and unknown application visitors. These are discussed in more detail in the "Visitor Tracking Model Objects" section.

The User object represents a user that can log into the web application and includes the following fields:

❑ **user_name:** This represents the name that the user types in when he or she logs into the application. By default, this is a Unicode column that is limited to 16 characters, but it can be changed.

The user name is defined as an alternate identifier (alternateID). When this field is set to True, the generated table adds constraints on the column to ensure that it is unique. The field also causes creates a method that enables you to select instances of the model object by the alternate identifier (user_name in this case).

By default, the select method follows standard accessor method conventions and consists of get followed by the name of the field, with the first letter capitalized (which would be getUser_name in this case). This behavior can be overridden with the alternateMethodName argument passed into the column constructor. In the case of the user name, this is used to create a by_user_name method, which enables you to look up a user by his or her username. For example, you could use the following statement to retrieve a user named "buddy":

```
User.by_user_name("buddy");
```

❑ **email_address:** The e-mail address for the user is another Unicode column limited to 255 characters by default. This is also an alternate identifier and includes the by_email_address method, which enables you to look up a user by his or her e-mail address, as in this example:

```
User.by_email_address("buddy@foo.com")
```

141

❑ **display_name:** This is used to create a more user-friendly representation of the user's name, such as the user's first and last name. This is maintained with a 255 character Unicode column.

❑ **password:** This field contains the user's password. By default, it is a Unicode column limited to 40 characters.

❑ **created:** This field contains the date and time that the user was created.

❑ **groups:** These are the groups to which the user belongs. This field uses the `RelatedJoin` column type to create one end of a many-to-many relationship between the `Group` and `User` model objects. You'll see below that the Group model object establishes the other end of this relationship in the users column. Ultimately, this column enables you to easily access the set of the user's groups with a query, as shown in the following example shell interaction:

```
>>> User.by_user_name('bill').groups
[<Group 1 group_name=u'authors' display_name=u'Authors'
created='datetime.datetime...)'>]
```

The `Group` object establishes groups to which the user can belong. Like other file-system or application groups, you can use this to restrict the activities available to a user. `Group` fields include the following:

❑ **group_name:** This 16-character Unicode column denotes the name of the group. It is defined as an alternate identifier to guarantee name uniqueness and allow the group object to be retrieved with a `by_group_name` method as follows:

```
Group.by_group_name("admin")
```

❑ **display_name:** This is the display name of the group, defined by a 255-character Unicode column.

❑ **created:** This is the date and time that the group was created.

❑ **users:** As noted above, this field establishes the other end of the many-to-many relationship with the `User` table. Like the groups field in the `User` table, this ultimately enables you to retrieve all the users that are in a given group, as shown in the following shell interaction:

```
>>> Group.by_group_name('authors').users
[<User 1 user_name=u'ray' email_address=u'ray@foo.com' display_name=u'Ray Budd'
password=u'ray' created='datetime.datetime...)'>, <User 3 user_name=u'bill'
email_address=u'bill@foo.com' display_name=u'Bill Wright' password=u'bill'
created='datetime.datetime...)'>]
```

❑ **permissions:** This is a set of permissions associated with the group. Similar to the many-to-many relationship created between groups and users, this is used to establish one end of a many-to-many relationship with the `Permission` object. It enables you to directly access the set of permissions associated with a group.

The final object is `Permission`, which enables you to establish multiple permissions associated with a group and ascribed to users in that group. This makes it possible to concisely capture more complex relationships between user types with related responsibilities. For example, you may have two groups, `authors` and `admins`, which both have read and write permissions. The `admins` group may have an additional permission, `create_user`, which enables this group's members to create new web application users. The permission fields include the following:

❑   **permission_name:** This alternate identifier is represented with a 16-character Unicode column and enables you to retrieve a `Permission` object with the `by_permission_name` method.

❑   **description:** This 255-character Unicode column contains a description of the permission.

❑   **groups:** This field contains the groups with which the permission is associated. It is the second end of the many-to-many relationship between the `Group` and `Permission` objects.

Identity Configuration Options

The Identity framework has a variety of options, most of which are included and described in the application-level configuration file (`tblog/tblog/config/app.cfg`). These options enable you to tailor the model objects used to maintain identity as well as adjust the behavior of the Identity framework. The following table lists some of the more common configuration options and their default values. Note that several properties in the table begin with `soprovider` (such as `soprovider.model.user`). These options are specific to the Identity framework implementation in SQLObject and are ignored in SQLAlchemy projects. There are corresponding options that start with `saprovider` (such as `saprovider.model.user`), which are generated when you use the `quickstart` command to create a SQLAlchemy project.

In many cases, you need to restart the application, the TurboGears Toolbox, or the Python shell after changing configuration option values before they will take effect.

Option	Default Value	Description
on	True	Determines whether identity management is on or off. This should be `True` if your web application makes use of the `identity` module.
failure_url	/login	When a site visitor attempts to access a page that he or she doesn't have access to, the request gets forwarded to a new page determined by this property.
soprovider.model.user	\<packagename\>.model.User	Contains user identity information. This can be overridden so that you can specify your own user identity class as long as it provides the same basic capabilities.
soprovider.model.group	\<packagename\>.model.Group	Defines the class to use for `Group` data.
soprovider.model.permission	\<packagename\>.model.Permission	Establishes the class to use for `Permission` information.
soprovider.model.visit	Not specified	Determines the class to use when tracking visitors logged in to your web application (discussed in more detail later in this chapter).
soprovider.encryption_algorithm	None	Establishes the type of encryption to use when storing passwords in the database. You are required to set the password with `User.password = "value"` for the value to be encrypted. Valid values include `"None"`, `"md5"`, and `"sha1"`.

Other Identity Framework Components

The Identity framework provides several additional components that can help you use the model objects described previously to log users in and out, and to control access to parts of your web application. Specifically, when you create a project that uses the Identity framework, you have the following additional capabilities:

❑ Views to log a user in and out are automatically incorporated into the system as follows:

    ❑ The root controller (`tblog/tblog/controller.py`) has additional paths for `/login` and `/logout` that collect and validate the user login information.

    ❑ An additional Kid page (`tblog/tblog/templates/login.kid`) is provided to collect and send the user login information. (It even encrypts the password for you.)

    ❑ The base template (`tblog/tblog/templates/master.kid`) automatically creates and manages a link that the user can use to log in to and out of the system.

❑ Properties and methods that provide information about the currently logged in user (if any) are available to the application controllers. The controller can do the following:

    ❑ Use `identity.current` to access details of the currently logged-in user as a user model object.

    ❑ Use the Boolean property `identity.current.anonymous` to find out if a user is logged in or not.

❑ The template can access the `current` property with `tg.identity` (for example, `tg.identity.user` and `tg.identity.anonymous`).

❑ Controllers can easily restrict user access to parts of the application. Access can be restricted with the following:

    ❑ The `require` property, which when specified for the controller restricts access to all paths provided by the controller

    ❑ The `identity.require` decorator, which can be added to a controller method to restrict access to a specific path

You'll see examples of each of these as you enhance the TBlog application to make use of the Identity framework.

Using the Identity Model Objects

Now that you're familiar with the Identity framework's model objects, capabilities, and configuration options, you're ready to try them out with an example. In this section, you'll see how to enhance the existing TBlog application to use the Identity model objects provided by TurboGears.

To use the new `User` model object rather than the `BlogAuthor` object, you need to make a few changes to the existing controllers. In the previous chapter, you defined a controller and templates for viewing and manipulating the `BlogAuthor` records. You'll need to remove these references first.

You also defined a controller and templates in the previous chapter for viewing and modifying the blog entries. Because the blog entry structure has also changed, you'll need to make a few small adjustments to this component as well.

Updating the Model

The first step is to update the model to use the `User` SQLObject rather than `BlogAuthor`. Open `tblog/tblog/model.py` and replace the foreign key specification in the `BlogEntry` model object to reference the `User` model object as shown here:

```
class BlogEntry(SQLObject):
    date = DateTimeCol()
    entryText = StringCol()
    entryTitle = StringCol()
    author = ForeignKey("User")
```

You can also remove, or comment out, the `BlogAuthor` model object at this point too, because it will no longer be used.

After modifying the database structure, you need to re-create your database by removing the old data and tables with the `drop` command and creating the tables with the `create` command, as follows:

```
C:\turbogears-examples\tblog>tg-admin sql drop
Using database URI sqlite:///C|\turbogears-examples\tblog/devdata.sqlite
C:\turbogears-examples\tblog>tg-admin sql create
Using database URI sqlite:///C|\turbogears-examples\tblog/devdata.sqlite
```

Creating Users in CatWalk

After the database is created, you can specify a new set of users with CatWalk or the Python shell. To use CatWalk, start the TurboGears Toolbox as follows:

```
C:\turbogears-examples\tblog>tg-admin toolbox
```

Browse to CatWalk, and enter a set of users similar to the ones shown in Figure 5-4.

You also need to set up a new group to identify authors, rather than other types of users. To do this, browse to the `Group` table and add a new group with a `display_name` of `'Authors'` and a `group_name` of `'authors'`.

After creating the new group, you're ready to add some of the users you specified previously to it. Browse to the `authors` group in CatWalk and expand the `users` row. Click the Manage Relations link. This displays a table containing the list of users in the `authors` group on the left, and the list of all users in the database on the right. You can add or remove users from the group by highlighting one or more users in the table on the left or right and clicking the `add selected` or `remove selected` link. In Figure 5-5, `ray` and `bill` have been added to the group, while `dave` and `dana` are not members.

Using Password Encryption

In many cases, you'll want encrypt the user passwords stored in the database to provide more effective security. You can specify that passwords are encrypted in the database with the `encryption_algorithm` property in `tblog/tblog/config/app.cfg`. To see an example, set up TBlog to use md5 encryption by removing the comment from the original property and replacing it with the following:

```
identity.soprovider.encryption_algorithm='md5'
```

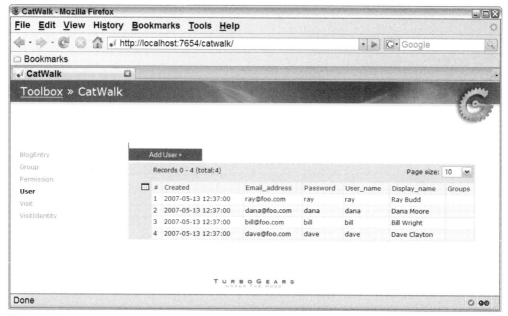

Figure 5-4

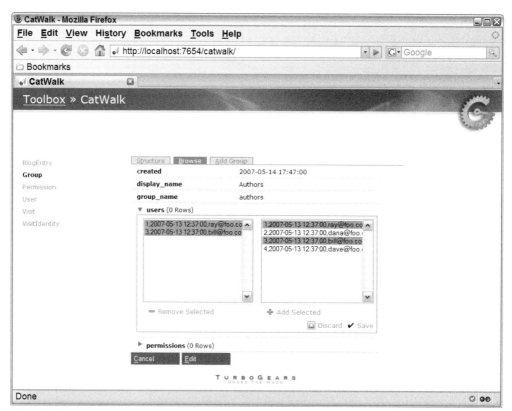

Figure 5-5

That's all that's required to enable the encryption, but you should know that whenever you change this property, existing users won't be able to log in with their passwords if they were stored with a different encryption scheme. One other caveat concerning the use of encryption is that you can't specify an encrypted user password through CatWalk. This is because CatWalk doesn't use the password field (user.password) when creating user objects or updating user passwords.

One simple option to encrypt existing passwords is to use the shell to read the old unencrypted passwords, and then write them back out again. This will encrypt them in the process. See Listing 5-1 for the shell interaction when encrypting the passwords for the users shown in Figure 5-5. Note that if you restart the TurboGears Toolbox after committing these changes, the encrypted form of the password is shown in CatWalk rather than in plain text.

Listing 5-1: Python shell interaction to encrypt user passwords

```
1 C:\turbogears-examples\tblog>tg-admin shell
2 Python 2.4.4 (#71, Oct 18 2006, 08:34:43) [MSC v.1310 32 bit (Intel)] on win32
3 Type "help", "copyright", "credits" or "license" for more information.
4 (CustomShell)
5 >>> allUsers = User.select()
6 >>> for user in allUsers:
7 ...        user.password
8 ...
9 u'ray'
10 u'dana'
11 u'bill'
12 u'dave'
13 >>> for user in allUsers:
14 ...        user.password = user.password
15 ...
16 2007-05-16 17:10:42,592 turbogears.identity.soprovider INFO Succesfully ➥
loaded "tblog.model.User"
...
32 >>> for user in allUsers:
33 ...        user.password
34 ...
35 u'070dd72385b8b2b205db53237da57200'
36 u'21cb4e4be93c09542ffa73b2b5cb95ea'
37 u'e8375d7cd983efcbf956da5937050ffc'
38 u'1610838743cc90e3e4fdda748282d9b8'
39 >>> ^Z
40 Do you wish to commit your database changes? [yes] yes
```

There are a few interesting things to note in this listing:

❑   Starting the shell from the project home makes the classes defined in the project model, such as User and Group, automatically available.

❑   In lines 9 through 12, the values for the passwords are simply retrieved and displayed (no data has changed).

❑   The only real work is performed on lines 13 and 14, where the password is copied onto itself. During this process, the password is encrypted.

❑   The encrypted form of the password is retrieved and displayed on lines 32 through 38.

Of course, you can use the shell to change any user's password if you change the value of the property for the user object. However, in most cases, you'll want to provide a component in the web application to handle user registration.

An alternative to writing your own user management capabilities is to use the registration package. This component generates a set of standard user management pages for inclusion in your project. It's documented at http://patrickhlewis.googlepages.com/registration.html and can be installed as follows:

```
easy_install registration
```

The package can be used to generate a set of user management controllers, models, templates, and widgets for a project as a part of the quickstart process. It provides a variety of capabilities for a project, such as forms for creating new users and changing user passwords, as well as an e-mail address validation component.

Removing the Blog Author Model and Controller

With the model defined and the users created, you're almost ready to incorporate them into the project, but before you get started, you need to remove some old references to the BlogAuthor model object. At this point, because the BlogAuthor model object is no longer used, it's safe to remove the BlogAuthorController. First, delete the tblog/tblog/BlogAuthorController directory, and then remove the references to BlogAuthorController in the root controller (tblog/tblog/controllers.py) as shown here:

```
...
#from BlogAuthorController import BlogAuthorController
...
class Root(controllers.RootController):
    #authors = BlogAuthorController()
    entries = BlogEntryController()
...
```

Updating the BlogEntryController

After removing the BlogAuthorController, you need to update the BlogEntryController to use the User table instead of the BlogAuthor table. Open tblog/tblog/BlogEntryController/controller.py and modify it as follows:

1. Replace the BlogAuthor import statement. Originally the BlogAuthor was imported from the model package with the following statement:

   ```
   from tblog.model import BlogAuthor
   ```

   Replace this with an import of the User and Group from the model package, as follows:

   ```
   from tblog.model import User, Group
   ```

2. Replace the `author` widget in `BlogEntryFields`. The list of widgets defined in the `BlogEntryFields` class originally created a drop-down list of author based on the values in the `BlogAuthor` table. This was accomplished with the specification of the `author` field shown here:

```
author = SingleSelectField(name="authorID",
                           label="Author",
                           options=[(entry.id,entry.firstName + " " +
                                     entry.lastName) for entry in
                                     BlogAuthor.select()])
```

In the new version, the list should be populated with the name and ID of all users in the `'author'` group. To accomplish this, replace the `author` field with the following:

```
authorGroup = Group.by_group_name('authors');
userList = [(entry.id, entry.display_name) for entry in authorGroup.users]
author = SingleSelectField(name="authorID",
                           label="Author",
                           options=userList,
                           validator=validators.NotEmpty)
```

Note the following regarding these changes:

❑ The `by_group_name` method of `Group` retrieves the group with the name `'authors'`.

❑ The `userList` is an array of user IDs, and displays names similar to the array of `BlogAuthor` IDs, first names, and last names. The `options` argument of the `SingleSelectField` is set to this value and is ultimately used to populate the drop-down list in the form.

Now run the application with `start-tblog.py`, and browse to the new blog entry page at `http://localhost:8080/entries/new`. Notice that the Author drop-down list is populated only with users in the `authors` group (Ray Budd and Bill Wright). Other users (Dana Moore and Dave Clayton) are not included.

Displaying the Author Name

There is one minor issue with the author name as it is currently implemented that should be fixed next. If you add a new entry and look at the index page or the `show` or `list` view, you'll notice that the author name displayed by default isn't very useful (see Figure 5-6).

The initial implementation in Chapter 4 displayed the first and last name of the blog author, but now it shows all the details of the `User` model object. This is because the author is a foreign key to another model object, and when a foreign key attribute is used, the string representation of the model object pointed to by the foreign key is used. By default, the string representation of a model object is a string of all model object attributes, but the `BlogAuthor` model object specification includes the following overriding string function implementation:

```
def __str__(self):
    return "%s %s" % (self.firstName, self.lastName)
```

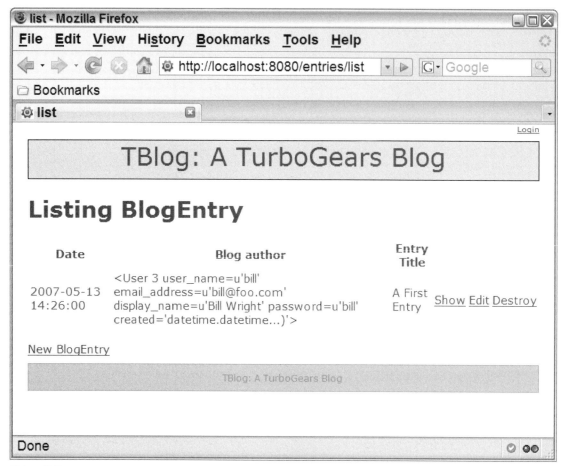

Figure 5-6

To fix the display of the author name, you simply need to add a new string method that returns the user's display name to the User model object in `tblog/tblog/model.py` as shown here:

```
def __str__(self):
    return  self.display_name
```

If you reload the list page, you get a more useful value for the author name (see Figure 5-7).

Using the Identity Module

At this point, the Identity objects have been incorporated into the project, and you're ready to use them to provide security and tailor the users' experience. With the identity module, it's easy to restrict access to a page or a path in a web application based on the logged-in user's groups or permissions. The identity module also enables you to personalize the experience of a logged-in user. For example, you can use details of the logged-in user to tailor the way information is presented, or to create elements in a Kid template based on a user's permissions or groups.

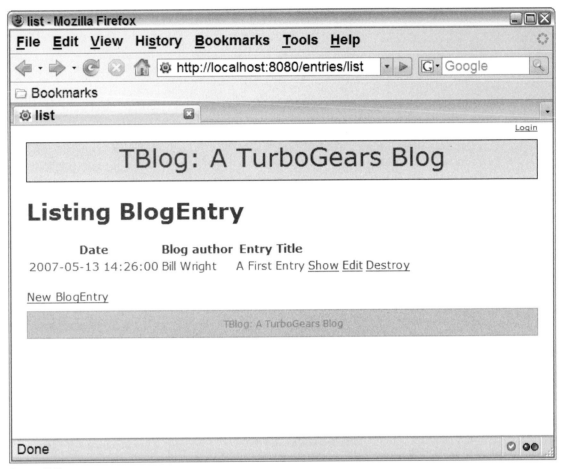

Figure 5-7

Restricting Page Access in a Controller

After defining some users and establishing the author's group, it's simple to restrict access so that only blog authors can add or modify the blog entries. All you need to do is modify `tblog/tblog/BlogEntryController/controllers.py` as follows:

1. Uncomment or add an `import` statement to the `identity` module as follows:

```
from turbogears import identity
```

2. Make `BlogEntryController` a secure resource by extending `identity.SecureResource` as follows:

```
...
class BlogEntryController(controllers.Controller,identity.SecureResource):
    """Basic model admin interface"""
...
```

3. Require the user to be in the `authors` group to have access to the controller. Do this by adding a special `require` attribute to `BlogEntryController` as shown here:

```
...
class BlogEntryController(controllers.Controller,identity.SecureResource):
  """Basic model admin interface"""
    require = identity.in_group("authors")
    modelname="BlogEntry"
...
```

This uses a predicate called `in_group`, which is defined in the `identity` module. This predicate takes the name of a group and validates that the currently logged-in user is in the group.

Note that although you simply restrict access to the entire entries path with the `in_group` function in step 3, there are many other powerful options that you can use when you're implementing identity management in a web application.

The following table shows the available identity validation predicates. Through these predicates, you can validate that a user has one or more permissions, belongs to one or more groups, or is coming from one or more hosts. You can even use `All` or `Any` as described in the table to ensure that multiple validation conditions are satisfied.

Predicate	Example	Description
`in_group(groupName)`	`identity.in_ group("authors")`	Succeeds when the logged-in user is in the `"authors"` group.
`in_any_ group(groupName, ...)`	`identity.in_any_ group("authors", "viewers")`	Succeeds when the logged-in user is in either the `"authors"` or `"viewers"` group.
`in_all_ groups(groupName, ...)`	`identity.in_all_ groups("authors")`	Succeeds when the logged-in user is in both the `"authors"` and `"viewers"` groups.
`has_pernission (permissionName)`	`identity.has_ permission("write")`	Succeeds when the logged-in user has the `"write"` permission.
`has_any_permission (permissionName, ...)`	`identity.has_any_ permission ("write", "read")`	Succeeds when the logged-in user has either the `"write"` or `"read"` permission.
`has_all_permissions (permissionName, ...)`	`identity.has_all_ permissions ("write", "read")`	Succeeds when the logged-in user has both the `"write"` and `"read"` permissions.
`from_host(ipAddress)`	`identity.from_ host("127.0.0.1")`	Succeeds when the logged-in user is looking at the page from the local host. Note that either the IP address or the hostname can be specified in the browser (http://127.0.0.1:8080/ or http://localhost:8080).

Predicate	Example	Description
`from_any_` `host(ipAddress, ...)`	`identity.from_any_host` `("127.0.0.1",` `"192.168.1.1")`	Succeeds when the logged-in user is looking at the page from either the local host or the host at `192.168.1.1`.
`All(predicate, ...)`	`identity.All (identity` `.from_host("127.0.0.1"),` `identity.in_` `group("authors")`	Succeeds when the logged-in user is in the `"authors"` group and is looking at the page from the the local host.
`Any(predicate, ...)`	`identity.All (identity` `.has_permission` `("write"), identity. in_` `group("authors")`	Succeeds when the logged-in user is in the `"authors"` group or has the `"write"` permission.

You can also restrict access to a specific path within the controller by using a `require` decorator, which takes an identity validation predicate as an argument. For example, instead of using the `require` field, you could restrict access to the new and edited pages at `http://localhost:8080/entries/new` and `http://localhost:8080/entries/show` by changing the appropriate methods in the `BlogEntryController` as follows:

```
    ...
    @expose(template='kid:tblog.BlogEntryController.templates.new')
    @identity.require(identity.in_group("authors"))
    def new(self, **kw):
        """Create new records in model"""
    ...
    @expose(template='kid:tblog.BlogEntryController.templates.edit')
    @identity.require(identity.in_group("authors"))
    def edit(self, id, **kw):
        """Edit record in model"""
    ...
```

In this case, it's cleaner to restrict access to the entire `BlogEntryController` as shown here instead of restricting each page specifically because any user without write permissions should typically access only the main blog view at `http://localhost:8080/`.

After implementing the changes described in this section, any path under `http://localhost:8080/entries` is restricted to authors. This means that if users aren't logged into the system, they are forwarded to the login page shown in Figure 5-8 if they try to access anything under the `entries` path.

A logged-in user that is not a member of the appropriate group is also denied access to the page. For example, if the user named `"dana"` tries to access the `entries` path, he is denied access and forwarded to the login screen shown in Figure 5-9 because he's not in the `"authors"` group.

Of course, the read-only view of the blog at `http://localhost:8080/` has no restrictions, and can still be seen by a user who is logged in as `dana` or `dave`, or who isn't even logged in at all.

Figure 5-8

Selecting the Author Based on the Logged-In User

Because the user is now required to be logged in before creating any blog entries, a simple and nice enhancement is to automatically determine the author's name based on the logged-in user. You can accomplish this by looking up the currently logged-in user's ID and including it as part of the request when a new blog entry is created. Just do the following:

1. Open `tblog/tblog/BlogEntryController/controllers.py`, and edit the `new` function of `BlogEntryController` to include the ID of the currently logged-in user as follows:

```
...
class BlogEntryController(controllers.Controller,identity.SecureResource):
...
    @expose(template='kid:tblog.BlogEntryController.templates.new')
    def new(self, **kw):
        """Create new records in model"""
        return dict(modelname = self.modelname,
```

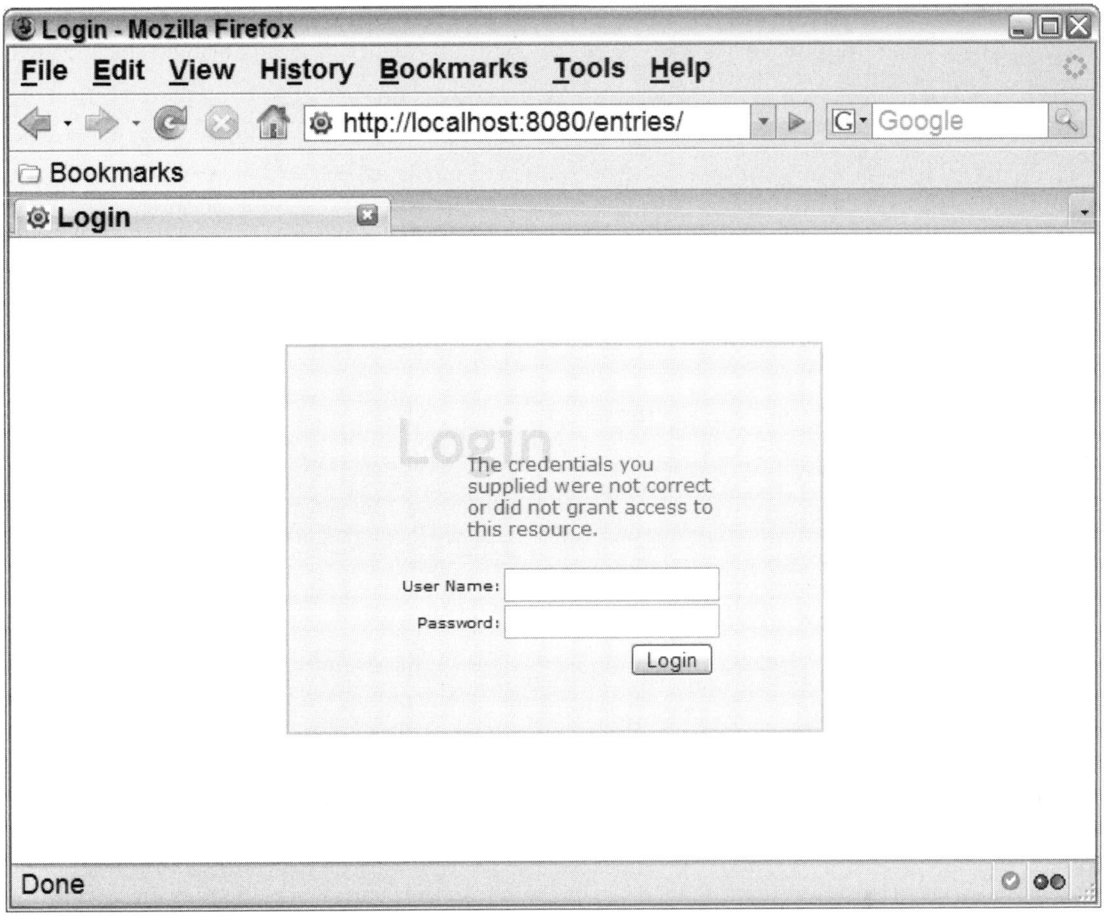

Figure 5-9

```
                    data = dict(authorID=identity.current.user.id),
                    form = model_form)
    ...
```

Note the following:

❑   The identity module is used to retrieve the currently logged-in user with the identity.current.user field. The authorID is then set to the ID of this user. A few additional useful properties are defined for identity.current, as shown in the table that follows this procedure.

❑   A dict is created and includes an entry for the authorID that is the ID of the logged-in user. You could easily establish different values for other form elements by specifying additional dict entries that have keys set to the names of other form widgets in BlogEntryField. For example, you can include a default title of "A New Entry" for all new form fields by defining dict as follows:

```
data = dict(authorID=identity.current.user.id, entryTitle="A New Entry")
```

2. Open `tblog/tblog/BlogEntryController/templates/new.kid`. Include the new data parameter as an argument to be used when the form is created; simply add a `value` attribute to the form constructor as follows:

```
${form(value=data, action='save')}
```

If you reload the page now and log in as **bill**, the author is automatically set to `"Bill Wright"` when a new blog entry is created.

property	Description
anonymous	Indicates whether or not the site visitor has logged in. This is `True` after the user has logged in, and `False` otherwise.
user_name	The name of the current user.
user	The `User` model object for the current user. This can be used to access any of attributes defined for the user, such as `email_address` or `display_name`.
groups	A list containing the name of each group to which the current user belongs.
permissions	A list containing the names of the permissions assigned to the current user.

Restricting Element Display in a Template

You can also use the `identity` module to restrict the elements that are displayed in a Kid template. To see an example of this, you can create a link to the blog entry editor from the `beView` template that serves as the application's main page (`http://localhost:8080/index`). To avoid confusion, this link should be shown only when a blog author is logged into the site. This change is as simple as adding a few elements to the `tblog/tblog/templates/beView.kid`. At the start of the `body` tag add the following:

```
...
    <body>
      <p>
        <a py:if="'authors' in tg.identity.groups" href="/entries">
          Edit Entries</a>
      </p>
      <div class="blogEntry" py:for="blogEntry in blogEntries">
...
```

This change adds an Edit Entries link to the page when the currently logged-in user is in the `"authors"` group. This is enabled via the Kid template's `tg.identity` property. `tg.identity` is similar to `identity.current` (described previously) and has access to the same properties (shown in the previous table).

After making this change, if you log in as **ray**, you'll see the index page shown in Figure 5-10. Now log off and log in again as **dana**. Note that the Edit Entries link does not appear on the page for this user (shown in Figure 5-11).

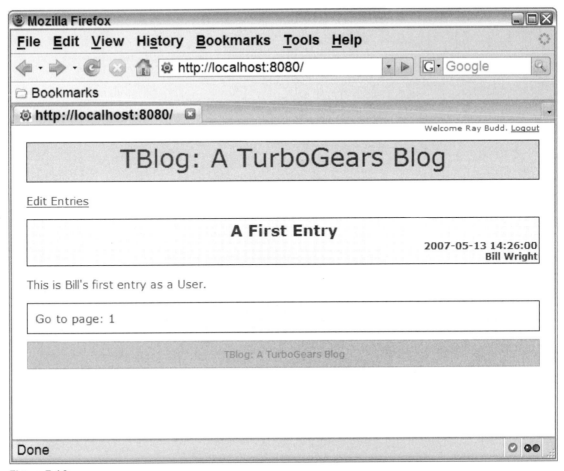

Figure 5-10

You can see another example of a tg.identity *user in* tblog/tblog/templates/ blog-master.kid. *This template is based on the* master.kid *generated by* tg-admin quickstart, *and includes a* div *that displays the Login and Logout links that appear in the upper-right corner of all the site's pages (shown previously in Figures 5-7 and 5-10).*

Adding a Return Link to the Entries List

You've finally finished all the changes that are required to secure the web application. To gain access to the blog entry views, the user must be logged in and be a member of the "authors" group. You may, however, want to make one small enhancement and add a return link from the entries list. This will allow the web author to return to the main blog page after he or she has finished editing the entries without having to manually type the URL into the browser.

Figure 5-11

To add a return link, simply open `tblog/tblog/BlogEntryController/templates/list.kid` and add the following after the link to create a new entry:

```
<br/>
<a href="new">New ${modelname}</a>
<a href="/index">Return to Blog View</a>
<!--span py:for="page in tg.paginate.pages">
```

After you save the template, browse to `http://localhost:8080/entries/list`. The new link is now displayed on the page as shown in Figure 5-12.

Figure 5-12

Visitor Tracking

Now that you've seen how to manage logged-in users and provide security, you're ready to explore tracking users that may or may not have logged in. In this section, you focus on using the Visit Tracking framework to collect statistics about your web application's users.

Because the Visit Tracking framework automatically creates cookies and tracks sessions with remote users, it's quite simple to use the framework to collect all types of information about an application's users over time. In many applications, it's highly desirable to capture as much information about a site's users as possible for a variety of reasons.

Example uses of the Visit Tracking framework include tracking the paths in a web application that are requested by the user and tracking the order in which they're requested. You can use this information to see the popular and unpopular areas of your site, or analyze when a user starts a process (such as filling out a survey or making a transaction in an online store) but ends it prematurely.

You can also use the framework to analyze a wide variety of statistics about the site's users, such as how long the average user stays on the site, how frequently the same host accesses the site, or how many visitors to the site log in with usernames versus those that remain anonymous.

In the remaining sections of the chapter, you enhance the blog example to capture some simple statistics about the site visitors. You'll see how to extend the blog to capture the IP address of each visitor, the number of times a user has visited a site, and the time of his or her most recent visit. You also create a simple template to present this information to registered blog authors.

Visitor Tracking Model Objects

To understand the visitor tracking model objects, recall the discussion and Figures 5-1 and 5-2 from the "Tracking Visits through Cookies" section at the beginning of the chapter. When a user visits the application for the first time, a cookie is generated and included in the server response. This cookie contains a key that is based on information associated with the user's initial request, such as the IP address.

When the server generates the key and the cookie, it also stores the key in a model object that maintains additional information about the session with the remote browser. On future requests from the browser, the server uses the key to look up any additional details of the session.

The `Visit` model object is used to capture the session time and key detail, and is defined in the project model file (which is `tblog/tblog/model.py`). It includes the following attributes:

❑ **visit_key:** The key that is included in the cookie sent to the user. This is an alternate ID, and can be looked up with `by_visit_key` as follows:

```
aVisit = Visit.by_visit_key("2beec2e1a1bfa7ee3023593f8fb71676058cca91")
```

   On subsequent requests, the `Visit` object is looked up based on this field.

❑ **created:** The date and time that the visit was created.

❑ **expiry:** The date and time that the visit session will expire based on user inactivity. This is initially set to 20 minutes after the visit creation time, but is updated to be 20 minutes after the current time with each request. If a user is idle for more than 20 minutes, the time is exceeded and the session is timed out.

❑ You can change the visit idle time with the `visit.timeout` property as shown later in this section. With each user request, the visit idle time is extended.

Another model object related to the Visit Tracking framework is the `VisitIdentity` table. This object is simply used to associate a `Visit` object with a logged-in user. After a user logs in, a new `VisitIdentity` instance is created with the current `visit` key and contains the ID of the newly logged-in in user. The `VisitIdentity` table includes the following two columns:

❑ **visit_key:** As in the `Visit` table, this corresponds to the key included in the cookie sent to the user. It is an alternate identifier that is retrievable with `by_visit_key` as follows:

```
anIdentity = VisitIdentity.by_visit_key("2beec2e1a1bfa7ee3023593f8fb71676058cca91")
```

❑ **user_id:** This is maintained as an `int` value, but denotes the ID of a `User` model object. This value corresponds to the ID of the user that logged in during this session.

As with all the other model objects that deal with identity and visitor tracking, this model object is used only when you set the corresponding configuration property to the project's model object. In this case, you define the property `soprovider.model.visit` in your application configuration file (`tblog/tblog/config/app.cfg`) by adding the following line:

```
identity.soprovider.model.visit="tblog.model.VisitIdentity"
```

If you're interested in seeing how visitors are tracked, add this line before you implement the example.

Also note that `VisitIdentity` entries are cleaned up when a user logs out, whereas `Visit` entries are not. This makes it possible to examine the `Visit` table periodically to track the length of user sessions or perform other types of user analysis.

Visitor Tracking Configuration Options

Like the `identity` module, the visitor tracking component has a variety of options that can be tailored to suit the requirements of each web application. These are defined and documented in the application configuration file (`tblog/tblog/config/app.cfg`) generated for a project that uses the Identity framework. The following table describes that options that are most commonly used.

Option	Default	Description
on	True	Determines whether visitors should be tracked or not.
timeout	20	How long a visitor can be idle before the visit expires. Note that this doesn't effect the life of any cookies.
cookie.name	tg-visit	The name to assign to the cookie sent to the visitor.
cookie.domain	None	The domain to set on the cookie. This should typically be None.
cookie.path	/	The path of the cookie. This can be used to restrict the scope of the cookie to a specific path in the application.
soprovider .model	\<projectname\> .model.Visit	Like the Identity model classes shown in the first table in this chapter (see the section "Identity Configuration Options"), this option specifies the model object to use when storing visit information. This can be overridden so that you can provide your own visit identity class as long as it provides the same basic capabilities.

Visitor Tracking Plug-Ins

The final component of the Visit Tracking framework is the visit plug-in. The framework follows a plug-in model and allows you to define logic to be triggered within the context of a visit. Visit plug-ins are invoked every time a browser makes a request to the server as long as visit tracking is turned on. You can define as many plug-ins as you want — the only requirements are that they include a `record_request` method and are enabled when the application starts up.

The `record_request` method takes a `Visit` object that includes a `key` corresponding to the key included with the request's cookie and maintained in the `visit_key` field of the `Visit` model object, and a Boolean `is_true` property. The `is_true` property is `True` if the request is the first request associated with a particular visitor key.

You can register a plug-in with the `enable_visit_plugin` method that is included as a part of the Visit Tracking framework. As you implement the controller in the example, you'll see how you can incorporate a plug-in by adding it to a list of functions invoked when the project starts up.

Adding Visitor Tracking

After seeing the basic components of the Visit Tracking framework, you're ready to extend the TBlog to make use of it. In the remainder of the chapter, you'll enhance TBlog to track the IP address of TBlog visitors, capture the latest visit time, and track how many repeat visits have been made from a particular IP address.

Defining the Model Object

The first step in capturing additional user statistics is to define a model object to hold the details you want to capture about your visitors. In this case, you'll want to include the visitor IP address, the number of visits, and the time of the latest visit from a particular host. In `tblog/tblog/model.py`, create a new object called `VisitorCount` to maintain this data, as follows:

```
class VisitorCount(SQLObject):
    hostname = StringCol(length=20, alternateID=True,
                         alternateMethodName="by_hostname")
    count = IntCol(default=1)
    lastVisit = DateTimeCol(default=datetime.now)
```

`VisitorCount` defines the following three properties (or columns):

❑   **hostname** is stored as a string and represents the IP address. It is a unique value that is accessible with `by_hostname`. For example, `VisitorCount.by_hostname('127.0.0.1')` returns the visitor count object that references 127.0.0.1.

❑   **count** is an integer value that corresponds be the number of times a new visitor key has been created for the IP address. Note that the default count is `1`.

❑   **lastVisit** is a `datetime` that holds the time last visit was created, which by default is the current time.

After defining the new model object and saving `model.py`, make sure that the TurboGears Toolbox and web application aren't running, and add the new table to the database with the following statement:

```
tg-admin sql create
```

Because you have only added a table and haven't changed the structure of your existing tables, this command adds the new `VisitorCount` table without corrupting any existing data in the database.

Creating the Plug-In

After the new model object is defined, you need to create a new plug-in that will populate the table based on user visits. Listing 5-2 shows the code to define and incorporate the new plug-in, `VisitorCountPlugin`. Add this code to the bottom of your controller file (`tblog/tblog/controllers.py`).

Listing 5-2: The VisitorCountPlugin class defined in controllers.py

```
 1 class VisitorCountPlugin(object):
 2     def record_request(self, visit):
 3         log.info("Got a record request call: " + request.object_path)
 4
 5         if visit.is_new:
 6             log.info("This is a new visitor: " + request.object_path)
 7             vcSelectResults = VisitorCount.select(
 8               VisitorCount.q.hostname==cherrypy.request.remoteHost)
 9
10             # Since the hostname is a unique ID there will only be one
11             # response at most. Check to ensure it was found. If so,
12             # update the count, and latest visit time.
13             if vcSelectResults.count() == 1:
14                 log.info("Found an existing visitor: " +
15                          str(vcSelectResults))
16                 theVCount = vcSelectResults[0]
17                 newCount = theVCount.count+1
18                 theVCount.set(count=newCount, lastVisit=datetime.now())
19             else:
20                 log.info("Creating a new visitor for " +
21                          cherrypy.request.remoteHost)
22                 VisitorCount(hostname=cherrypy.request.remoteHost)
23
24 def addVisitorCountPlugin():
25     visit.enable_visit_plugin(VisitorCountPlugin())
26
27 startup.call_on_startup.append(addVisitorCountPlugin)
```

You also need to add the following `import` statements and create a logger in the beginning of your controller (if it isn't already there):

```
import logging
from model import VisitorCount
from turbogears import visit, startup
from datetime import datetime
log = logging.getLogger("tblog.controllers")
```

Listing 5-2 shows the basics of plug-in specification and incorporation. The plug-in is specified on lines 1 through 22, and consists of a single method called `record_request`. This method creates a new `VisitorCount` record for new hostnames, or increments the count and visit time when the visitor count already exists, as follows:

❑ The `is_new` property of the `visit` argument is used on line 5 to ensure that the visit is tracked only when it's created. This ensures that the same visit isn't counted more than one time.

❑ If the visit is new, the `VisitorCount` table is examined to see if there is already an entry for the hostname associated with the request. Line 7 selects all `VisitorCount` objects by hostname.

❑ The IP address of the host that generated the request is retrieved with the `cherrypy.request.remoteHost` property on line 8.

❑ If a `VisitorCount` object was found for the hostname, the count of the results will be 1 (see line 13). In this case, the `VisitorCount` object will be retrieved from the `select` results (line 16), the count for this object will be incremented (line 17), and `VisitorCount` will be updated to include the new count and a new visit time set to the current time (line 18).

❑ If the IP address hasn't been encountered before, the count property of `VisitorCount` will be 0, and the `else` clause will be entered (line 19). This simply creates a new visitor count for the IP address, which is initialized to the default visit time and count.

The remaining lines (24 through 27) are used to incorporate the plug-in into the Visit Tracking framework:

❑ The `addVisitorCountPlugin` function on lines 24 and 25 creates a new visitor count plug-in and registers it with `enable_visit_plugin`.

❑ Line 27 incorporates the `addVisitorCountPlugin` method into the project startup by appending it to the list of functions to be called at startup (`turbogears.startup.call_on_startup`) with `append`.

At this point, you've done everything necessary to record user visits. Restart your project and look at the TBlog site. Then look at the `VisitorCount` table using `quickstart` or the shell, and you will see a new record that captures the visit that you just made to the site.

> *If you don't have access to two machines for testing, you can use the local host as well as your real IP address. First, point your browser to* http://localhost:8080/, *and then use your real hostname or IP address (such as* http://192.168.1.1:8080/). *This records multiple entries because one request uses the local loopback and originates from 127.0.0.1 rather than your actual IP address. After you visit both addresses, you will have two entries in your* VisitorCount *table.*

Defining the Template

Of course, it's not very practical to force authors to use CatWalk to look at the count information. In this section you'll create a new simple view in `tblog/tblog/templates/` called `statistics.kid` to show the visitor statistics in a more user-friendly way. Listing 5-3 shows the new Kid template.

Listing 5-3: A simple view of visitor statistics, statistics.kid

```
 1 <!DOCTYPE html PUBLIC "-//W3C//DTD XHTML 1.0 Transitional//EN"
 2 "http://www.w3.org/TR/xhtml1/DTD/xhtml1-transitional.dtd">
 3 <html xmlns="http://www.w3.org/1999/xhtml"
 4   xmlns:py="http://purl.org/kid/ns#"
 5   py:extends="'blog-master.kid'">
 6   <head>
 7     <meta content="text/html; charset=utf-8"
 8       http-equiv="Content-Type" py:replace="''"/>
 9   </head>
10   <body>
11     <h1>Visitor Statistics</h1>
12     <table class="statTable">
13       <tr>
14         <th>Hostname</th>
15         <th>Count</th>
16         <th>Last Visit Time</th>
17       </tr>
18       <tr py:for="entry in visitorcount">
19         <td>${entry.hostname}</td>
20         <td>${entry.count}</td>
21         <td>${entry.lastVisit}</td>
22       </tr>
23     </table>
24     <p>
25       <a href="/index">Return to Blog View</a>
26     </p>
27   </body>
28 </html>
```

Note the following aspects of statistics.kid in the listing:

❑ A single argument visitorcount is required for the template. This should contain the list of all VisitorCount objects in the database.

❑ The template extends the master template blog-master.kid (line 5) to ensure it has the standard look and feel.

❑ The template creates a single table to hold the visitor statistics (lines 12–23).

❑ Each row in the table corresponds to a different visitorcount element, and includes the hostname, count, and last visit time.

❑ Rather than use the default visual formatting for the table, the statistics table is formatted using the style sheet class statTable (line 12). You may also want update the style sheet to use a tailored appearance for each cell in the table. Listing 5-4 shows two additional classes that you should add to the bottom of the site's tblog/tblog/static/css/blog-style.css style sheet to enhance the formatting of the table.

Listing 5-4: Additions to blog-style.css to format the visitor statistics table

```
.statTable {
  border: thin solid black;
  background: #E1DEFE;
  text-align: center;
}
.statTable td {
  border: thin solid black;
  background: white;
}
```

Adding the Location to the Controller

Now that you've created the template, you need to expose it in your controller and create a new path in the web application. Open `tblog/tblog/controllers.py`, and add the following `/statistics` path to the `RootController` specification:

```
@expose(template="tblog.templates.statistics")
@identity.require(identity.in_group("authors"))
def statistics(self):
  return dict(visitorcount=VisitorCount.select())
```

This new method does the following:

❑   Uses the `expose` decorator to expose the `statistics` Kid template.

❑   Restricts this view to authors with the `identity.require` template. This decorator is similar to the `require` property you specified for the `BlogEntryController` in the earlier example, but is used to restrict access to a single path rather than all paths provided by the controller. This means that if a user is not logged in and a member of the `"authors"` group, he will be forwarded to the login screen if he attempts to access this path.

❑   Returns a `visitorcount` argument that consists of all `VisitorCount` objects.

At this point, if you save and reload you'll get a new `http://localhost:8080/statistics` path, which is available if you're a logged in as an author. Figure 5-13 shows the new `Statistics` view.

Creating the New Link

The final step is to add a link to the Statistics page that is similar to the Edit Entries link. You should add the link to the main blog view. The link is visible only when a user is logged in and is a member of the `"authors"` group. To add the link, open `tblog/tblog/templates/beView.kid` and add the following after the Edit Entries link:

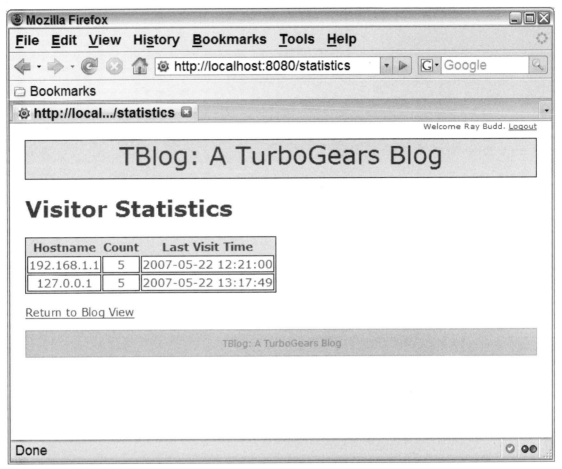

Figure 5-13

```
<body>
  <p>
    <a py:if="'authors' in tg.identity.groups" href="/entries">
      Edit Entries</a>
    <a py:if="'authors' in tg.identity.groups" href="/statistics">
      View Statistics</a>
  </p>
```

The main blog view will now have the additional View Statistics link as shown in Figure 5-14.

Figure 5-14

Summary

This chapter introduced you to the Identity and Visit Tracking frameworks that are provided by TurboGears. You learned about the frameworks' capabilities as well as the model object and configuration options that can be used to tailor the behavior for a specific project. You also got some hands-on experience with the frameworks as you enhanced the blog example from Chapter 4 to make use of the frameworks. The blog has been extended to manage your blog authors, restrict blog entry creation to logged-in users that are authors, and collect statistics about your blog viewers.

In the next chapter you'll gain a deeper understanding of the widget framework. As you extend the TBlog web application, you will see how to use existing widgets and create your own widgets by combining HTML, CSS, and JavaScript into highly portable and reusable components.

6

Widgets

Always code as if the guy who ends up maintaining your code will be a violent psychopath who knows where you live.

—**Martin Golding**

Regardless of the development language or type of application, developers should always attempt to develop well-organized and reusable code. If the organization of code is ignored for an application, the result is a tangle of duplicated code that is difficult to understand and maintain. In such systems, a capability is typically implemented, and then copied and pasted into other parts of the system as the need to reuse the capability is seen. This in turn makes it extremely difficult for you or others to maintain the code after it's written. A single change may have a ripple effect and require a series of changes to many other similar pieces of code.

Any language provides a set of programming constructs that help you write organized, maintainable code with minimal duplication. Procedural languages use procedures and functions to help alleviate this issue by grouping common operations into logical chunks. These may be collected further and organized into packages, modules, and libraries. Object-oriented languages take this a step further with object specifications that enable you to group common functions and data into a single entity. Inheritance is useful to ensure that common capabilities are specified only once in a parent class, and inherited by subclasses.

In a web application, however, it's not always possible to represent a single reusable entity with only the data and functions available in object-oriented languages. This is because a web application typically relies on a combination of three very distinct elements that may produce a reusable component only when taken together. The structure of the component is established with HTML, JavaScript is required to define client-side behaviors for the component, and finally style sheets are necessary to tailor the site's appearance.

TurboGears provides *widgets* to enable a web application developer to write reusable components that include all the elements wrapped together in a single package. The ultimate effect is a reduction in duplicate code, a more maintainable and reusable component, and a more logical organization of *all* the code that is necessary to create a component.

In Chapter 4, "Introduction to TurboGears," you were introduced to the concept of widgets when you used TGCrud to generate a simple interface to view, modify, and delete blog authors and entries. In this chapter you build on that introduction and explore the possibilities of the widget framework in more detail, including the following:

- ❑ Widget design motivations and advantages
- ❑ The Widget Browser, a tool used to catalog and document widgets
- ❑ How to use existing widgets to easily add complex capabilities to a web application
- ❑ How to implement and package your own widgets for reuse in one or more web applications

Throughout the chapter, you enhance the TBlog web application to represent, accept, and display user comments for a given blog entry. First you use existing form elements to accept new comments, and then you define your own widget that can be used to display user comments.

> *This chapter builds on the TBlog example from Chapters 4 and 5. You may want to explore those chapters before starting here, but it isn't absolutely required. Before starting off with the widget examples here, however, you should download and review the Chapter 5 version of the TBlog application from the book's site.*

TurboGears Widgets

Before jumping into the examples, it's useful to explore a bit about the intent of the widget framework. A widget is an extensible component that bundles Hypertext Markup Language (HTML), JavaScript, and Cascading Style Sheets (CSS) to provide all aspects of a single slice of functionality. HTML is used to establish the structure of the element, the behavior is provided with JavaScript, and the appearance is determined by the CSS. The self-contained nature of widgets makes them quite portable and reusable. Examples of standard widgets include an autocomplete field, or a field that allows a user to pick a date from a JavaScript calendar (such as those found on hotel or air travel search forms).

Figure 6-1 shows the elements of a widget definition, and the relationships between a widget specification, instances, and other elements of a web application. Note that each element of a widget definition can be overridden within each web application, and that widget instances are shared by all views within a particular web application.

As shown in the figure, a widget can be defined once and reused throughout the web application. This makes it possible to change only the widget, and have the change reflected in all views that use the widget. For example, consider a widget used in several places in a web application (or even in multiple web applications) to create a formatted table for a given set of data. If you need to change the format of the table, you need only to modify the widget, and all the views that contain the widget will make use of the change automatically.

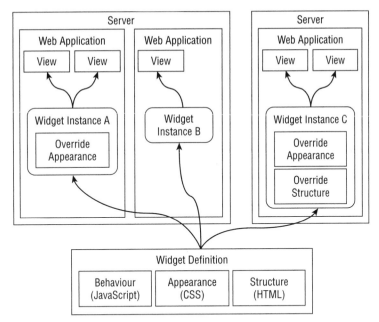

Figure 6-1

Apart from the reusability within a single web application, the all-inclusive nature of a widget makes it easy to use it across different web applications. This has led to the development and packaging of widgets and widget libraries for public use. The TurboGears distribution even includes a variety of widgets that provide several capabilities, such as simple AJAX-enabled components, and simpler form-creation and form-handling techniques (which you saw in Chapter 4). The CogBin (www.turbogears.org/cogbin/), a repository of existing TurboGears components, includes an even larger set of widgets in the core library. It is designed to emphasize reusability and is available for public use. Most widgets are installable with easy_install and are incorporated into the library of available widgets.

Another focus of the design of the widget framework is extensibility. Because widgets are normal Python objects, it is easy for a developer to override any single aspect of a predefined widget when using it in a web application. For example, if you want to change the appearance of the DataGrid widget (a widget capable of showing arbitrary model objects in a table), all you need to do is define a widget that extends DataGrid and includes a different CSS specification, or simply provide a css argument when creating the widget.

One important aspect of widgets to bear in mind is that they are inherently stateless entities. A widget doesn't maintain any detail of the state of the system internally. What this means to the widget user is that only one instance of a widget should be used across all pages in a web application. You'll see an example of this later when you use the same comment widget instance in three separate locations.

A widget instance should also be considered immutable, and should not be changed after the widget is created. This means that any detail of the widget that depends on the incoming request should be sent only when the widget is rendered, rather than when it's created. In this chapter, you learn how to pass state information in a widget parameter that gets associated with the request when it is rendered.

Using the Widget Browser

The widget framework emphasizes reusability, portability, and extensibility. This means that any given TurboGears installation may have a variety of widgets installed — some from the default installation, and others developed locally or downloaded from CogBin. The Widget Browser, available from the TurboGears toolbox, is a web-based tool to help developers know which widgets are available for a particular installation. It displays and describes the available widgets as shown in Figure 6-2.

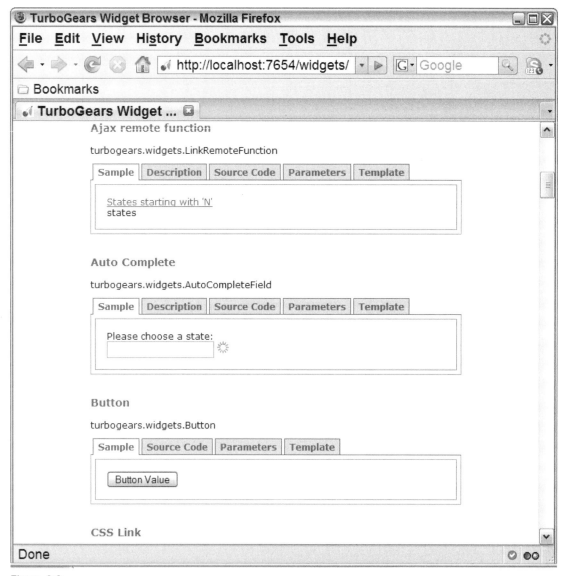

Figure 6-2

Using Existing Widgets

Now that you've learned a bit more about the concept of a widget, you're ready to explore it in more detail with an example. In Chapter 4 you defined a form with widgets when using the code generated by TGCrud. In this section you learn more about how the code generated by TGCrud works and get more exposure to the existing widgets as you use the standard form widgets to create a form from scratch and save data entered by a user. This example enhances the TBlog web application to represent user comments for a given blog entry, and adds the ability to accept user comments.

Defining the Model Object

The first step required to add comment-handling to the TBlog is to define a new model object that represents the comment. Open `tblog/tblog/model.py`, and define a new `BlogComment` model object as follows:

```
class BlogComment(SQLObject):
    date = DateTimeCol(default=datetime.now)
    commentText = StringCol()
    commenter = StringCol()
    # Setting cascade to true causes any comments
    # associated with a blog entry to be deleted when
    # the blog entry is deleted.
    entry = ForeignKey("BlogEntry", cascade=True)
```

The `BlogComment` model object includes the following four attributes:

❑   **date:** The date that the comment was left. Note that the column is initialized to the current time by default.

❑   **commentText:** A string that holds the content of the comment being left.

❑   **commenter:** The name of the person leaving the comment. Notice that value is maintained as a string rather than as a foreign key to the `User` table. This allows any viewer of the page to leave a comment, regardless of whether they have a login name or not. If you wanted to accept comments from logged-in users only, you could use a foreign key to the `User` table, similar to the `author` attribute of `BlogEntry`.

❑   **entry:** A reference to the `BlogEntry` that this comment pertains to. This is accomplished by specifying a foreign key with the name of the table (`BlogEntry`) provided as the first argument. Notice that the `cascade` argument is used here to establish how referential integrity should be maintained when a `BlogEntry` that has associated comments is deleted. In this case, `cascade` is set to `True`, which causes all `BlogComment` objects to be deleted when the associated `BlogEntry` is deleted. The possible values of the `cascade` option are shown in the following table.

Value	Behavior
None	Deleting the row referenced by the foreign key doesn't affect this row. For example, deleting a BlogEntry would not change any of the associated BlogComment objects. This is the default behavior when no cascade argument is given.
False	Deleting the row fails when you attempt to delete the row referenced by the foreign key, and raises a SQLObjectIntegrityError exception. For example, if you attempt to delete a BlogEntry that has any comments defined for it, an exception is raised.
True	Deleting the row referenced by the foreign key deletes all rows with the reference. For example, when you delete a BlogEntry, any comments associated with that BlogEntry will be deleted as well.
'null'	Deleting the row referenced by the foreign key sets the value of the column to null for any row with the reference. For example, when you delete a BlogEntry, any comments associated with the BlogEntry will remain in the database but will not reference any BlogEntry.

As with other changes to the model specification, you're required to add the new table to the database before it can be used. In this case, you don't have to drop any existing tables from the database first, because you're adding a new table and haven't changed the structure of any existing table. This enables you to retain any data that you've already defined in the database. You simply need to run the sql create command as follows:

```
C:\turbogears-examples\tblog>tg-admin sql create
Using database URI sqlite:///C|\turbogears-examples\tblog/devdata.sqlite
```

Accepting User Comments

Now that you've defined a comment model object, you could use CatWalk to add, edit, view, or delete BlogComment objects, but this isn't typically practical in a real web application. You could also use TGCrud to generate the skeleton for CRUD (create, read, update, and delete) operations as shown in Chapter 4. This would probably be overkill in this case, though, because you really only want to allow a user to add a new comment or look at existing comments for a given blog entry. In this section, you learn more about how to use form widgets by doing the following:

❑ Defining your own form widget that allows a user to create a new comment

❑ Creating a Kid template that uses the form widget

❑ Incorporating the template into the controller

❑ Writing a controller function to save the new comment

❌ Linking to the comment from the main blog view

Defining the Form Widget

The first step is to define a form widget that can capture a user comment. Typically a form widget is made up of two main parts specified as two separate classes. The fields that appear on the form are defined in a class that extends turbogears.widgets.WidgetList, and the form itself is defined in a class that inherits from turbogears.widgets.TableForm and contains an instance of the widget list. Finally, an instance of the form widget is typically instantiated. This form instance may then be used in various controller methods, as the form is passed to Kid templates for display.

> *Chapter 4 describes some common form widgets in the table under the section "Defining the Widgets," and outlines common widget attributes in table under the section "Defining the Model." You may want to reference these tables as you proceed through this example.*

In more complex web applications, you may want to specify your form widget in a separate Python file, but for this example you can simply add it to your existing controller file, tblog/tblog/controllers.py.

Because all base widget classes and form widgets are defined in turbogears.widgets, you need to import it along with some validation components and your new comment model object. Add the following to controllers.py after the last import statement:

```
from turbogears.widgets import *
from turbogears import validators, validate
from model import BlogComment
```

Now you're ready to define the widget. Do this by adding the code shown in Listing 6-1 before the root controller specification.

Listing 6-1: The CommentFields and CommentForm classes defined in controllers.py

```
 1 class CommentFields(WidgetsList):
 2     entryField = Label(name="entryTitle",
 3                         label="Blog Entry")
 4     entryId = HiddenField(name="blogEntryId")
 5     commenterField = TextField(name="commenter",
 6                                 label="Commenter Name",
 7                                 default="Anonymous",
 8                                 validator=validators.NotEmpty)
 9     commentField = TextArea(name="commentText",
10                              label="Comment",
11                              validator=validators.NotEmpty)
12
13 class CommentForm(TableForm):
14     fields = CommentFields()
15     submit_text = "Add Comment"
16     action = "/saveComment"
17     method = "POST"
18
19 comment_form = CommentForm()
20
21 class Root(controllers.RootController):
22 ...
```

The `CommentFields` object defined on lines 1 through 11 extends the `WidgetsList` (line 1) and has attributes for each element that should appear on the field.

Possible form field arguments are discussed in more detail in Chapter 4, but in this case the `name`, `label`, `default`, and `validator` are used as follows:

Attributes in the `CommentFields` object include the following:

- ❑ The `entryField` attribute (lines 2–3) is a read-only `Label` rather than a form field for input data. This serves to inform the user of the title of the blog entry to which the comment pertains.

- ❑ The `entryId` attribute (line 4) defines a hidden field that doesn't appear on the form. This field is initialized to the ID of the blog entry that the comment pertains to, and will be included in the parameter list when the comment is saved. This is used to set the blog entry foreign key when saving the comment.

- ❑ The `commenterField` attribute (lines 5–8) is a text field that captures the name of the person leaving the comment. The only requirement established with the `validator` argument is that the field cannot be empty. By default this is set to `Anonymous`.

- ❑ The `commentField` attribute (lines 9–11) is a text area that holds the actual comment. Like the `commenterField`, the only requirement is that this field cannot be empty.

The `CommentForm`, defined on lines 13 through 16, extends the `TableForm` object. It includes the following attributes:

- ❑ The `fields` attribute (line 14) is simply an instance of the `CommentFields` widget list you defined on lines 1 through 11.

- ❑ The `submit_text` attribute (line 15) is the string to display on the Submit button. When you don't specify this optional attribute, the Submit button is labeled with `Submit Query`.

- ❑ The `action` attribute (line 16) establishes the URL that should be used when the form is submitted. In this case, the form will be sent to `/saveComment`, a new web application path that you define in the section "Writing the Save Operation" later in this chapter.

- ❑ The optional `method` attribute (line 17) establishes the HTTP method that should be used when submitting the request.

Any additional attributes that should be included in the `form` tag or `table` tag can be specified with the optional `form_attrs`, and `table_attrs` fields.

`TableForm` is not the only possible base class for `CommentForm`. You could alternatively extend the `ListForm` class. The end result is quite similar — the primary difference is that the form fields are embedded in an unordered list rather than a table.

You also have the option of specifying either the form or the widget list for the form inline, rather than using two separate classes. For example, the form in Listing 6-1 could be rewritten as follows:

```
comment_form = TableForm(
  fields = [Label(name="entryTitle", label="Blog Entry"),
            HiddenField(name="blogEntryId"),
            TextField(name="commenter", label="Commenter Name",
                      validator=validators.NotEmpty),
            TextArea(name="commentText", label="Comment",
                      validator=validators.NotEmpty)],
  submit_text = "Add Comment",
  action = "/saveComment",
  method = "POST")
```

Another aspect to note about form widgets is that the widget list for a form (either specified inline or as shown in Listing 6-1) is ultimately just a list. You can perform any of the list operations after you create the form. For example, you could append a new field to the form as follows:

```
comment_form.fields.append(TextArea(name="commentText", label="Comment",
                                    validator=validators.NotEmpty))
```

You can also remove an element from the form. For example, the following statement removes the blog entry label from the form:

```
comment_form.fields.pop(0)
```

The comment_form is instantiated to a CommentForm on line 19.

Creating the Kid Template

After defining the form, you're ready to create a template that uses the form. Create a new tblog/tblog/templates/comments.kid file and define the template as shown in Listing 6-2.

Listing 6-2: The comments Kid template, comments.kid

```
1 <!DOCTYPE html PUBLIC "-//W3C//DTD XHTML 1.0 Transitional//EN"
2 "http://www.w3.org/TR/xhtml1/DTD/xhtml1-transitional.dtd">
3 <html xmlns="http://www.w3.org/1999/xhtml"
4   xmlns:py="http://purl.org/kid/ns#" py:extends="'blog-master.kid'">
5   <head>
6     <meta content="text/html; charset=utf-8"
7       http-equiv="Content-Type" py:replace="''"/>
8   </head>
9   <body>
10     <p><a href="/">Back to Blog</a></p>
11     <h1>Add Comment</h1>
12     <div py:content="form.display(formData)"></div>
13   </body>
14 </html>
```

Most of the code in this listing is boilerplate template code (see Chapter 4 for the basics of Kid templates). The most important section to note is the body defined on lines 9 through 13. This includes a link back to the main blog page on line 10, and a div that will contain the form that you defined in the controller.

As noted previously, a widget should be stateless, and any aspect of the form that depends on a specific request should be provided as an argument to the display method. Recall from the widget list specification in Listing 6-1 that the form includes a label for the title of the blog entry and a hidden field for the ID of the blog entry that the comment pertains to. These bits of state data are added to a dict named formData, passed into the display method, and included in the form.

You can also override other aspects of the form specification within the display method, depending on state data. For example, you can remove the commenter fields by adding a disabled_fields argument as follows:

```
<div py:content="form.display(formData, disabled_fields=['commenter'])"></div>
```

The possible display method arguments for a TableForm are described in the following table.

Argument	Example	Description
submit_text	submit_text='Send'	The text to include on the Submit button.
disabled_fields	disabled_fields= 'entryTitle']	A list of form fields that aren't relevant.
table_attrs	table_attrs = dict(border=1)	A dict containing additional attributes for the table element.
form_attrs	form_attrs = dict(enctype='app- lication/x-www- form-urlencoded')	A dict containing additional attributes for the form element.
action	action='/save'	The URL to use when submitting the form.
method	method='GET'	The HTTP method (either GET or POST) that should be used for the request. POST is used by default.
convert	convert=False	Specifies whether the validator should be applied to convert any existing data values when the form is being displayed. This is set to True by default.

Incorporating the Template in the Controller

Now the template has been defined, but you still need to modify the root controller to expose it to the user on a specified path in the web application. To do this, return to tblog/tblog/controllers.py, and add the new comments method as follows:

```
1 class Root(controllers.RootController):
2     entries = BlogEntryController()
3 ...
4     @expose(template='tblog.templates.comments')
5     def comments(self, entryId, **kw):
6         entryTitle = BlogEntry.get(entryId).entryTitle
7         formData = dict(entryTitle=entryTitle, blogEntryId=entryId)
```

```
 8              return dict(form=comment_form, formData=formData, **kw)
 9 ...
10 class VisitorCountPlugin(object):
```

This `comments` method uses the `@expose` decorator on line 4 to make the `comments` Kid template available. The template path (`/comments`) is derived from the method name (line 5).

Line 5 indicates that the `comments` method requires an argument, `entryId`. This argument identifies the BlogEntry that the comment pertains to. Based on the `entryId` provided, the title of the blog entry is retrieved on line 6.

A `dict` named `formData` is created, and set to contain two entries. This `dict` contains items where the key is a form field name, and the value is the initial value for that form field. In this case, the dictionary includes the blog entry title for display on the form label, and the blog entry ID as the value of the hidden form field. Note the distinction between specifying an initial value for the form field, which can make use of arguments provided in the associated request, and specifying a default value (as shown on line 7 of Listing 6-1), which cannot rely on state information.

A second dictionary containing the parameters passed to the Kid template is created on line 8. This dictionary includes an entry for the comment form, and the `formData` dictionary. Recall from Listing 6-2 that the Kid template calls the `form` parameter's display method and passes the `formData` dictionary as the set of initial values for the form fields.

The `comments` method takes an unspecified number of additional arguments with `**kw` (line 5), and forwards these as parameters passed to the Kid template (line 8).

If you save all the modified files at this point, the application will be reloaded and you will have access to the new application path `http://localhost:8080/comments`. Attempting to browse to the path without a blog entry ID will produce the following exception due to the lack of a parameter that identifies the blog entry:

```
TypeError: comments() takes at least 2 arguments (1 given)
```

If you include a parameter with the ID of an existing blog entry as shown here:

```
http://localhost:8080/comments?entryId=1
```

or use the shorthand version of the same request like this:

```
http://localhost:8080/comments/1
```

you will get a page similar to the one shown in Figure 6-3.

Because you haven't defined the `saveComment` path yet, you can't submit the form with the Add comment button. If you attempt to do this, you are forwarded to a page containing the following error:

```
404 Not Found
The path '/saveComment' was not found.
```

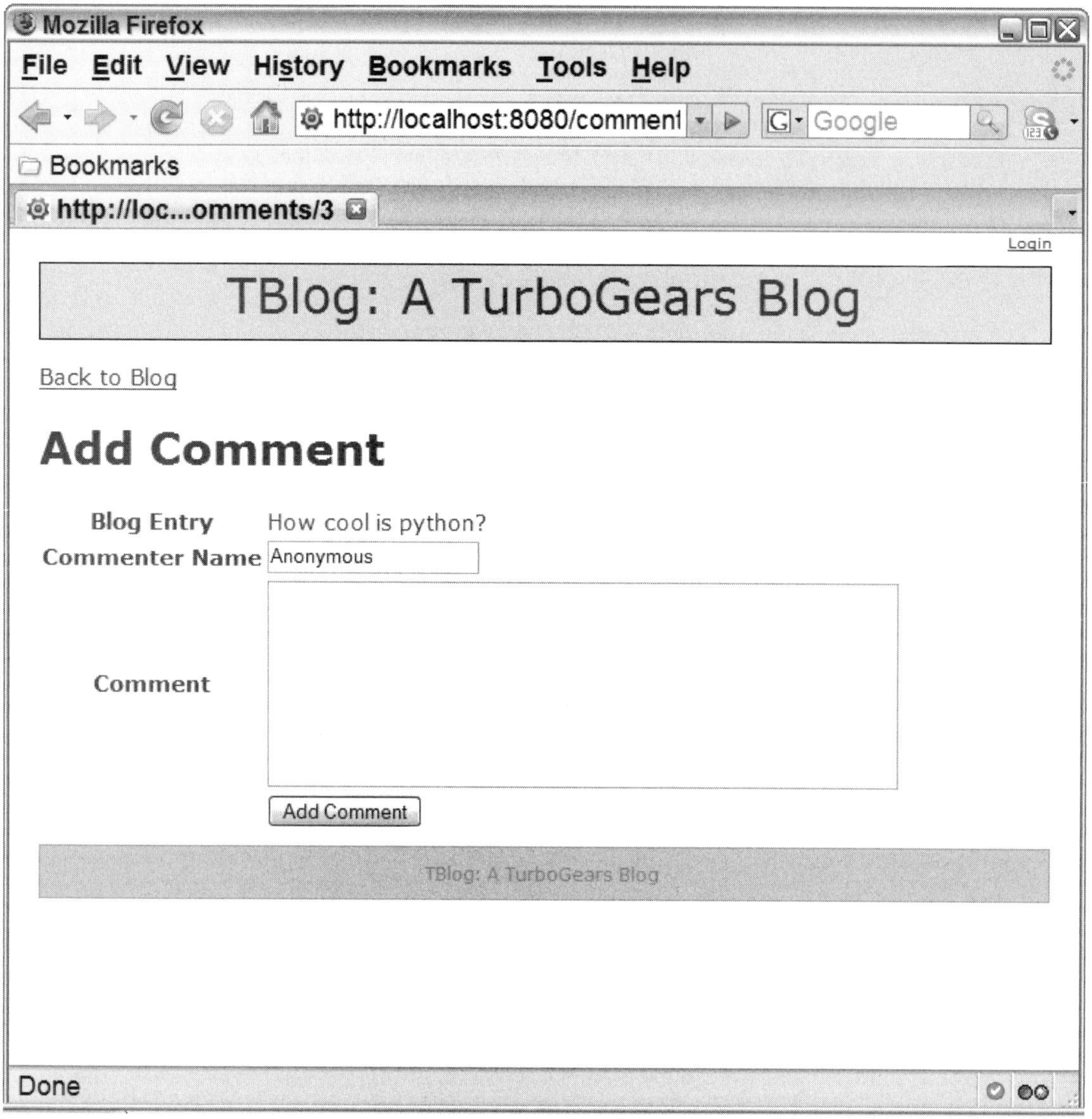

Figure 6-3

Writing the Save Operation

Now you're ready to complete the capability that allows you to add a comment by defining the save operation. To do this, you first need to import the error_handler decorator from TurboGears, as in this example:

```
from turbogears import error_handler
```

After this, all you need to do is add a couple of new methods below `comments` in the controller, as shown here:

```
1              return dict(form=comment_form, formData=formData)
2  ...
3    @expose()
4    def commentError(self, **kw):
5        raise redirect("../comments/" + kw['blogEntryId'],
6                       tg_flash="Comment contains errors!")
7
8    @expose()
9    @error_handler(commentError)
10   @validate(form=comment_form)
11   def saveComment(self, **data):
12       BlogComment(commentText=data['commentText'],
13                   commenter=data['commenter'],
14                   entry=BlogEntry.get(data['blogEntryId']))
15       raise redirect("/comments", entryId=data['blogEntryId'],
16                      tg_flash="Comment Successfully Added")
17 ...
18 class VisitorCountPlugin(object):
```

The `saveComment` function defined on lines 8 through 16 includes the following:

❑   An empty `expose` decorator (line 8). This decorator is used because the path has no corresponding Kid template, and instead redirects the view on line 15.

❑   A `validate` decorator (line 10) that causes the form to be validated before the method is invoked. The validation process applies all of the validators defined for the widget list class to the data entered on the form. If the form fails validation, an error is raised and the `error_handler` is invoked.

❑   An `error_handler` decorator (line 9). This decorator indicates that when a validation error is encountered, the view should be redirected to the `commentError` path (see lines 3 through 6). In turn, the `commentError` page redirects to the `comments` view with an associated error message encoded in `tg_flash` (see lines 5 through 6). When you use a master template based on the root template, `tg_flash` parameters are automatically displayed below the standard header. Figure 6-4 shows an example of the `comments` view after an attempt is made to insert a comment with no value.

❑   All of the form data is encoded in the `data` argument (line 11).

❑   A new blog comment added to the database (lines 12 through 14). The attributes of the comment are initialized to the corresponding form field values. Note that the entry associated with the Blog comment (line 14) is looked up based on the hidden field in the form.

❑   The use of the `tg_flash` parameter (lines 6 and 16). When a comment is created successfully or fails the site returns a `tg_flash` parameter that indicates the success or an error message. When present, the `tg_flash` parameter is automatically displayed near the top of the page as long as the page extends the autogenerated master template (which is `blog-master` in this case). Figure 6-5 shows the `comments` view after a new comment has been added. If you're curious to see how this is done, look at how the `tg_flash` parameter is used in the master template (`tblog/tblog/templates/blog-master.kid`).

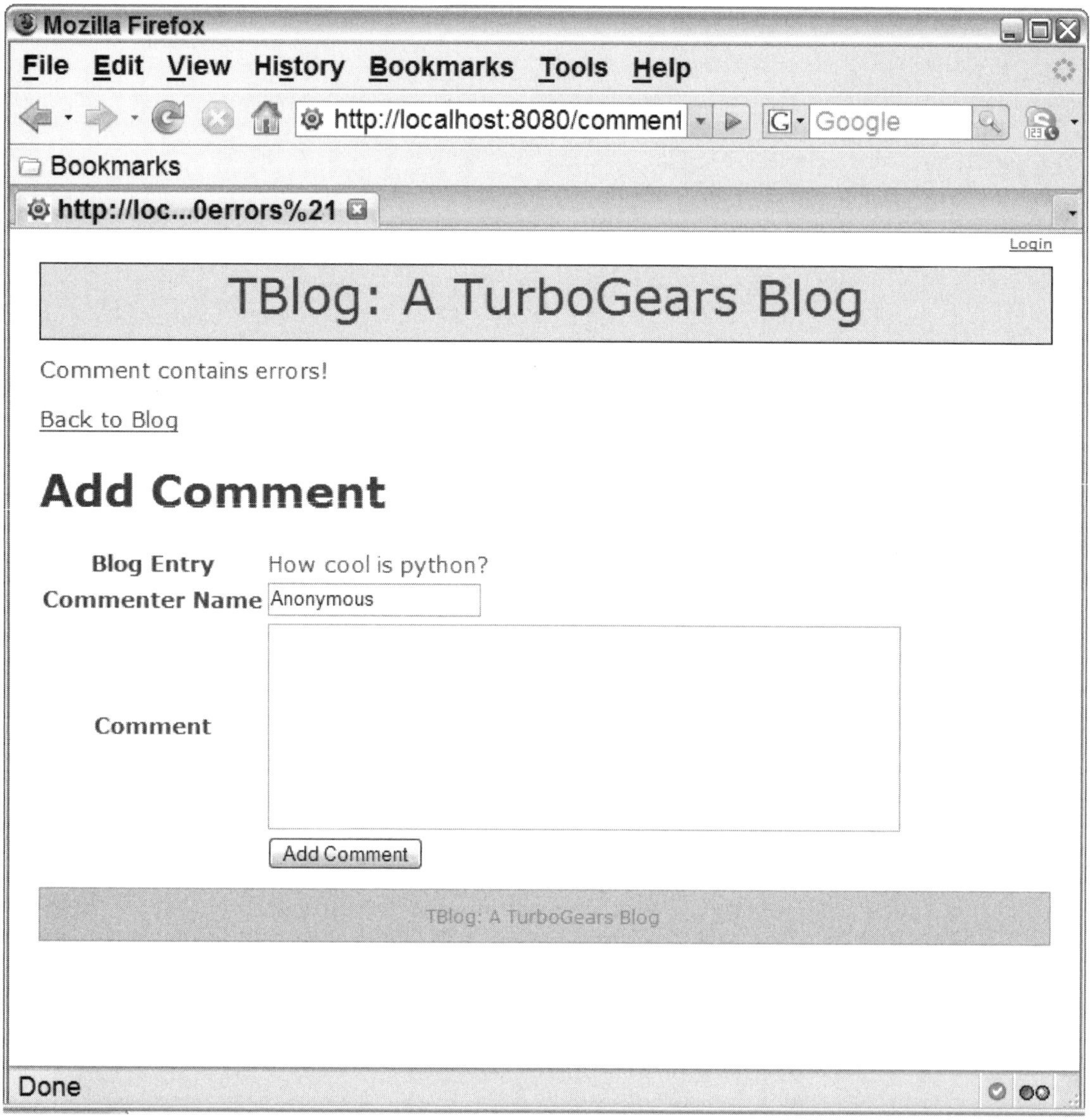

Figure 6-4

Linking to the Add Operation

The final step in accepting new user comments is to create a link to the new comments page from the main blog view. This simply requires you to open the index template, `tblog/tblog/templates/`beView.kid, and augment the code that generates the header for each blog entry. The new template should create a link to the comments for the entry as shown in the following code.

Figure 6-5

```
<div class="blogEntry" py:for="blogEntry in blogEntries">
    <div class="beHeader">
...
        <h2>${blogEntry.date}<br/>
          ${blogEntry.author}<br/>
          <a href="/comments/${blogEntry.id}">Comments</a></h2>
    </div>
...
```

Notice that this code creates a URL that includes the ID of the blog entry in the shorthand form. For example, `http://localhost:8080/comments/4` is the URL generated for a blog entry with an ID of 4. Figure 6-6 shows the new blog entry view.

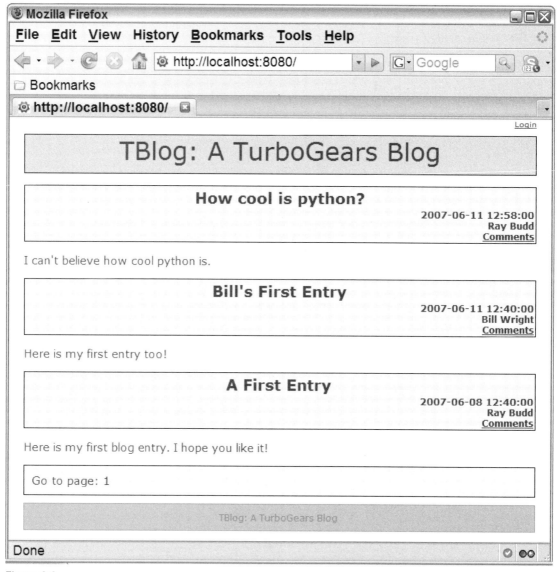

Figure 6-6

Creating New Widgets

The widgets included in the TurboGears distribution (such as the form widgets) enable you to easily incorporate and build up complex components in your web application, and can greatly simplify your code. It's important to bear in mind, however, that the capabilities of widgets aren't limited to simple reuse. As mentioned previously, one very powerful aspect of widgets is that they're easy to build and they're highly portable. The widget library was designed with an emphasis on extensibility, and widgets are inherently portable given the fact that a widget is self-contained. All the code for structure, appearance, and behavior is localized so that you can reuse it in other situations. After a widget is defined, you can use it on several pages within a web application and (with a little repackaging) make it available for use in other projects.

This section introduces you to the world of widget development. First you learn about the basic components of a widget specification as you implement a very simple widget that displays a hello message. Then you really get your hands dirty when you create a more complex widget from scratch that you can use in TBlog.

Creating a Simple Hello Widget

To understand a bit more about what a widget is made up of, take a look at a very simple example. This widget can be used to create a red `div` element that displays a personalized hello message. When the hello message is clicked, an alert pops up.

Defining the Widget

Start by creating a new Python file called `hellowidget.py` under `tblog/tblog`, and define the widget as shown in Listing 6-3.

Listing 6-3: The HelloWidget specification in hellowidget.py

```
1 from turbogears import widgets
2 from turbogears.widgets import JSSource, CSSSource
3
4 class HelloWidget(widgets.Widget):
5     template= """
6     <div class='hellodiv' onclick='handleClick("${helloname}")'>
7       Hello ${helloname}!
8     </div>
9     """
10    css=[CSSSource("""
11    .hellodiv {
12      background: #CC0000;
13      color: #FFFFFF;
14      }""")]
15
16    javascript=[JSSource("""
17    function handleClick(thename) {
18      alert(thename + ' clicked me!'); }""")]
19
20    parameters=["helloname"]
21
22 hello_widget = HelloWidget()
```

This listing shows the basic anatomy of a widget. Specifically:

❑ The majority of the code is in the `HelloWidget` class itself, which extends `widgets.Widget` (line 4).

❑ The widget contains four attributes commonly defined for a widget:

  ❑ **template (lines 5–9):** This attribute contains the widget template. In this case, there is a single `div` with a CSS class set to `hellodiv`, and an `onclick` event handler that invokes the `handleClick` JavaScript function. The content of the `div` is a hello message that references the `helloname` parameter.

  ❑ **css (lines 10–14):** This is a list of CSS resources applicable to the widget. This includes a single inline CSS resource defined with the `CSSSource` class. `CSSSource` takes a string of CSS data and an optional `media` specification. The `media` specification is `all` by default, and is included in the final page as an attribute of a style element generated to hold the CSS source. Note that this class is actually a widget itself, and is described in the Widget Browser.

  ❑ **javascript (lines 16–18):** Similar to the CSS attribute, this is a list of JavaScript resources that are required for the widget. In this case, the JavaScript is defined using the `JSSource` widget, and consists of a single function, `handleClick`, that takes a `name` argument.

  `JSSource` takes a string containing the JavaScript code, and an optional `location` argument that establishes where the JavaScript code should be embedded in the final page. The default location for this code is the head of the document, but you can place it at the top of the body using `js_location.bodytop`, or at the bottom using `js_location.bodybottom`. For example, the following statement adds a bit of code to the bottom of the body:

```
javascript=[JSSource("...", location=js_location.bodybottom)
```

  ❑ **parameters (line 20):** The parameters that can be specified when displaying or creating the widget. Here, the `helloname` parameter used by the template is the single element in the list.

The final aspect to note about the widget specification is that a global instance of the widget is created for use within the web application. This is possible because the widget is stateless and should be reused throughout the web application. Reusing the global widget saves you from having to waste time and memory to create and maintain multiple instances.

Using the Widget in a Template

After defining the widget, you need to use it within a template. Create a new Kid template called `helloWorld.kid` under `tblog/tblog/templates` as shown in Listing 6-4.

Listing 6-4: The helloWorld.kid template

```
 1 <!DOCTYPE html PUBLIC "-//W3C//DTD XHTML 1.0 Transitional//EN"
 2 "http://www.w3.org/TR/xhtml1/DTD/xhtml1-transitional.dtd">
 3 <html xmlns="http://www.w3.org/1999/xhtml"
 4    xmlns:py="http://purl.org/kid/ns#" py:extends="'blog-master.kid'">
 5   <head>
 6     <meta content="text/html; charset=utf-8"
 7       http-equiv="Content-Type" py:replace="''"/>
 8   </head>
 9   <body>
10     <div py:content="hello_widget.display(helloname=hello_name)"></div>
11   </body>
12 </html>
```

This is primarily boilerplate template code, with a couple of exceptions. Line 10 creates a `div` and invokes `display` on the `hello_widget` to generate the content. That state is passed into the template via the `helloname` parameter, which gets initialized to a `hello_name` template parameter.

Adding the Path to the Controller

The final step in setting up the `hello` widget example is to create a new path in the web application for the template, and passing the widget and `hello_name` parameter to that template when it's invoked. To do this, open `tblog/tblog/controllers.py`. Use the following statement to import the widget you created:

```
from tblog.hellowidget import hello_widget
```

Then, define the method for the new path after the `saveComment` method as follows:

```
    ...
    @expose(template='tblog.templates.helloworld')
    def sayHello(self, aname):
        return dict(hello_widget=hello_widget, hello_name=aname)
    ...
class VisitorCountPlugin(object):
```

Notice that the method assumes that a `name` parameter will be provided with the request. It forwards this `name` parameter to the Kid template as the `hello_name` argument. Also note that the widget itself is provided as a parameter to the template.

At this point, you've completed the `hello` widget and incorporated it into the controller. If you save all the modified files and browse to `http://localhost:8080/sayHello/Ray`, you'll see the page shown in Figure 6-7.

Figure 6-7

If you click anywhere in the div containing the Hello Ray! message, you'll be presented with the pop-up message shown in Figure 6-8.

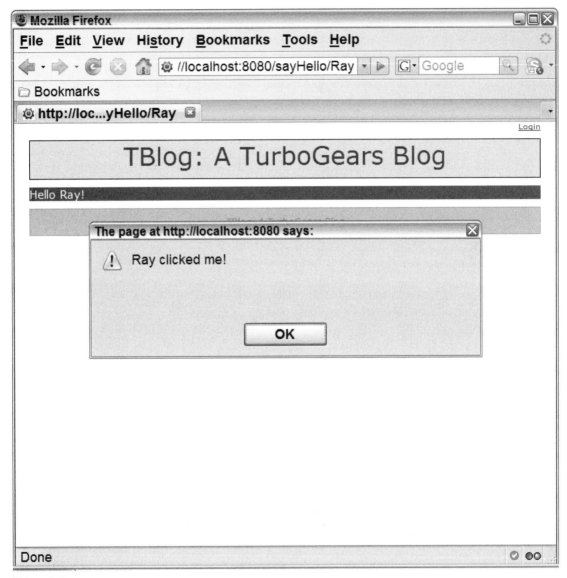

Figure 6-8

Creating a Comment Widget

Now that you've seen the basic elements of a widget, you're ready to create a component that can provide more useful functionality for the TBlog web application. In the section "Accepting User Comments" earlier in the chapter, you enabled a user to leave comments for a given TBlog entry, but you still need a mechanism to view the comments associated with a blog entry.

In this section you create and package a widget that is capable of showing the comments for a blog entry, and you reuse this widget in several places in the web application. The component includes an optional Show/Hide button that enables you to toggle the comments. When the Show Comments button is clicked, the comments associated with a blog entry are retrieved via an asynchronous request and dynamically added to the page, and the button text changes to Hide Comments. Clicking the button again removes the comments from the display and changes the button text back to Show Comments.

After creating the widget, you'll see how to incorporate it into the web application in three places. You'll add it to each blog entry in the index view, in the view shown when adding comments, and in the blog entry editor view that shows a single blog entry.

Packaging Your Widgets

Although you can specify all the elements of a widget directly in a controller Python script as you did with the `hello` widget, you will typically want to package the widget and all supporting components apart from the controller. Not only does this reduce the complexity of your controller; it also makes it easier to reuse the widget in other areas of the web application, and allows you to easily repackage the widget for use in other web applications if desired.

To reiterate, the main elements of a widget include the following:

- ❑ The widget specification itself
- ❑ Any templates required to render the widget
- ❑ Any CSS files that establish the appearance of the widget
- ❑ Any JavaScript files that are used to establish the behaviors required of the widget

You can package these components together or in any directory structure desired, but the most common approach is to mimic the structure used in a TurboGears project similar to the one shown in Listing 6-5.

Listing 6-5: The directory structure used for the comment widget

```
tblog
   + tblog
     + widgets
       - __init__.py
       - widgets.py
       + static
         + css
           - comment.css
         + javascript
           - comment.js
       + templates
         - __init__.py
         - comment.kid
```

This directory structure cleanly modularizes the widget by placing all widget-related files under the main `widgets` directory. The main widget specification is in the top-level Python file, `widgets.py`. Any Kid templates required to render the widget are maintained under `templates`. The comment includes a single template, `comment.kid`.

Any static supporting files used by the widget or Kid template appear under `static`. This may include style sheets, JavaScript files, images, and so on. In the case of the `comment` widget, it uses a single JavaScript and style sheet.

If you're curious to see some example widget specifications and typical packaging, you can find them in the core TurboGears library. Just look in the root Python directory under `site-packages` (for example, `c:/Python-2.4/Lib/site-packages/TurboGears-1.0.1-py2.4.egg/turbogears/widgets/`).

Creating a Comment Widget Class

The first step in defining the comment widget is to create the component that ties all the external files together, the `CommentWidget` class. Create the `tblog/tblog/widgets` directory and an empty `__init__.py` file. Next, define the widget in `widget.py` as shown in Listing 6-6.

Listing 6-6: The comment widget defined in widget.py

```
 1 from turbogears import widgets
 2 from turbogears.widgets.base import mochikit, CSSLink, JSLink
 3 from turbogears.widgets.base import register_static_directory
 4 import os.path
 5 import pkg_resources
 6 pkg_path = pkg_resources.resource_filename("tblog",
 7                                    os.path.join("widgets",
 8                                                     "static"))
 9 register_static_directory("tblog.widgets.static", pkg_path)
10
11 class CommentWidget(widgets.Widget):
12     template = "tblog.widgets.templates.comment"
13     params = ["entry_id", "initiallyVisible", "showLabel"]
14     css = [CSSLink("tblog.widgets.static", "css/comment.css")]
15     javascript = [mochikit, JSLink("tblog.widgets.static",
16                                     "javascript/comment.js")]
17     initiallyVisible = False
18     showLabel = True
19
20 comment_widget = CommentWidget()
```

Before jumping into a widget specification itself, note the first few lines after the `import` statement, specifically lines 6–9. By default, a web page only has access to static content located under the standard directory (`tblog/static`). Because you're attempting to serve static content such as JavaScript and CSS files from a different directory (`tblog/widgets/static`), you need register this directory so the web page can access it.

Line 6 uses `pkg_resources` to establish the fully qualified directory that contains the static files (`/projects/tblog/tblog/widgets/static`), and line 7 registers the directory under the module name `tblog.widgets.static`. This enables you to reference a resource in this directory relative to the module name, as is done on line 14.

The widget specification on lines 11 through 18 uses the same basic attributes you used to define the hello widget. In this case, however, the attributes reference external components, as follows:

❑ The template attribute (line 12) establishes that the widget should use a new Kid template, comment.kid, which you will create in the next section.

❑ The params attribute (line 13) defines the set of parameters that are relevant for the widget. The comment widget takes an entry_id that corresponds to the ID of the blog entry that the comments pertain to.

❑ The css attribute (line 14) uses a CSSLink widget to create a link to the external CSS file tblog/tblog/widgets/static/css/comment.css. A CSSLink is similar to CSSSource, but it doesn't include the code inline. Instead, it takes the module name for the CSS script followed by the relative name to use when retrieving the deployed file. Because the module points to the static directory, the relative name includes the css subdirectory in addition to the name of the script. Also similar to the CSSSource class, an optional media parameter can be included.

❑ The first item in the javascript list (line 15) is a reference to the global mochikit defined in the base widget package. This enables your JavaScript files to use the MochiKit library.

❑ The second item in the javascript list (lines 15 and 16) is similar to the css specification. The JSLink class is used to create a link to an external JavaScript file, in this case tblog/tblog/widgets/static/javascript/comment.js. Note that the parameters for the JSLink are similar to CSLink, and include the module name and the relative path of the resource.

An optional location parameter can be provided to establish the location of the JavaScript (head, top of the body, or bottom of the body) as previously described for JSSource.

As was the case with JSSource and CSSource, you can examine the JSLink and CSLink widgets in detail in the Widget Browser.

❑ The initiallyVisible and showLabel attributes (lines 17 and 18) establish default values for the parameters defined in params. If the template provides either of these parameters when displaying the widget, the override value will be used. Otherwise the defaults are used. For example, a template can display the widget with initiallyVisible set to True as follows:

```
comment_widget.display(initiallyVisible=True)
```

The final aspect of the widget script in Listing 6-6 is the creation of a global comment_widget instance on line 20. As mentioned previously, because widgets are stateless, this instance should be referenced by all components instead of having each component create its own instance.

Defining the Widget Template

Now that you've set up the widget, it's time to define all the external components that it references. The first component that you'll define is the Kid template for the widget. First create the template directory tblog/tblog/widgets/templates and an empty __init__.py. Next define the comment.kid template file as shown in Listing 6-7.

Listing 6-7: The comment widget's template file, comment.kid.

```
 1 <div xmlns:py="http://purl.org/kid/ns#" id="commentDiv">
 2   <label py:if="showLabel" id="commentlabel${entry_id}"
 3     class="commentLabel" onclick="updateCommentsDiv(${entry_id})">
 4     Show Comments</label>
 5   <div id="allComments${entry_id}"/>
 6   <br/>
 7
 8   <script py:if="initiallyVisible">
 9     updateCommentsDiv(${entry_id})
10   </script>
11 </div>
```

This is similar to most Kid files, but it doesn't include the basic elements found at the beginning and end of a typical site-wide template. This is because a widget is typically reused across several pages or applications, and will always be defined within a template. To make a widget more generic, it shouldn't inherit from a particular application's master template.

You can see an example of the differences between a widget and a typical Kid template if you compare comments.kid in Listing 6-7 with Listing 6-2. Note that the widget doesn't have doctype, html, head, or body tags. Instead, it simply starts with the div element. However, note that the widget template still defines the py namespace on line 1.

In Listing 6-7, the div (lines 1 through 11) consists of a Label with the text Show Comments that invokes a JavaScript function updateCommentsDiv when clicked. The if statement on line 2 ensures that label is created only when the showLabel parameter is set to true. Otherwise, the label is not created, and the comment display cannot be toggled.

After the Label, an initially empty div is defined on line 5. This div will be used to hold the comments when they are displayed.

The final element is a script on lines 8 through 10 that gets generated only when the initiallyVisible parameter is true. The script simply forces the comments to initially be shown by explicitly invoking the updateCommentDiv function on line 9.

You may have also noticed that the label and div elements have ID values that are based on ID of the blog entry, and that the blog entry ID is provided to the updateCommentsDiv function. As you write the JavaScript and incorporate the widget into a few of your views, you'll see that this enables you to show and process multiple comments on the same page.

Writing the Widget JavaScript

After defining the template, you're ready to write the widget's JavaScript. Create the JavaScript directory tblog/tblog/widgets/static/javascript, and define the comment.js JavaScript file, as shown in Listing 6-8.

Listing 6-8: The comment.js JavaScript file

```
 1 function updateCommentsDiv(entryId) {
 2   var allCommentsDiv = $('allComments' + entryId);
 3   if (allCommentsDiv.hasChildNodes()) {
 4     replaceChildNodes(allCommentsDiv);
 5     var label = $('commentlabel' + entryId);
 6     if (label) {
 7       label.childNodes[0].nodeValue = 'Show Comments';
 8     }
 9   } else {
10     d = loadJSONDoc('/getComments/' + entryId);
11     d.addCallback(showComments, entryId);
12   }
13 }
14
15 function showComments(entryId, result) {
16   var label = $('commentlabel' + entryId);
17   if (label) {
18     label.childNodes[0].nodeValue = 'Hide Comments';
19   }
20   var allCommentsDiv = $('allComments' + entryId);
21   replaceChildNodes(allCommentsDiv,
22                     P({'class' : 'commentInfo'},
23                       'Showing ' + result.comments.length + ' comments'));
24
25   for (i=0; i < result.comments.length; i++) {
26     var headerStr = result.comments[i].date + ' ' +
27       result.comments[i].commenter;
28
29     var commentDiv = DIV({'class' : 'comment'});
30     appendChildNodes(allCommentsDiv, commentDiv);
31     appendChildNodes(commentDiv,
32                      DIV({'class' : 'commentHeader'}, headerStr));
33     appendChildNodes(commentDiv, P({'class' : 'commentText'},
34                                    result.comments[i].commentText));
35   }
36 }
```

The JavaScript in this listing consists of two functions. The first function, updateCommentsDiv, is invoked when the user clicks the comments label. This function either displays or hides the comments depending on whether they are already displayed or hidden. When the comments are hidden, the function retrieves the comments via an asynchronous request and causes the second function, showComments, to be invoked as the request callback. When the comments are already displayed, the function removes all the displayed comments.

Looking at the updateCommentsDiv function (lines 1 through 13) in more detail shows the following:

❑ The function takes an argument for the ID of the blog entry that the comments pertain to. This is used in several places to identify which div and label should be updated, as well as to establish which set of comments should be retrieved from the server.

❑ On line 2, the `div` that contains the comments is retrieved with `$()`, which is the MochiKit shorthand for `getElementById` and takes an element ID argument.

❑ Line 3 tests the `allCommentsDiv` to see if it contains anything. This determines whether or not the comments have been retrieved.

❑ The `if` statement on lines 3 through 8 handles the situation when the comments are already displayed. Specifically:

  ❑ The MochiKit DOM function, `replaceChildNodes`, is used to remove all the nodes under `allCommentsDiv` (line 4). This function optionally takes one or more nodes to be added as children of the first node argument (as is done on lines 21 through 23). This causes all the comments to be removed from the resulting page.

  ❑ The label associated with the comment is retrieved (line 5) when defined. Recall from the template code that this is determined by the Kid template parameter `showLabel`.

  ❑ If the label exists (line 6), the text is changed to `Show Comments` (line 7).

❑ When the comments aren't currently displayed (line 9):

  ❑ An asynchronous request for `getComments` is created on line 10 with the blog entry ID provided as an argument. For example, the request when displaying the comments for the blog entry with an identifier of 1 would be `http://localhost:8080/getComments/1`.

  ❑ The `showComments` function is added as a callback that will be invoked after the request has completed (line 11).

Proceeding to the `showComments` callback on lines 15 through 36, you can see that the empty `div` is replaced with the list of comments and the label text is changed to `Hide Comments`. More specifically:

❑ The `showComments` function takes two arguments: `entryId` and `result`. The `entryId` argument is provided when the callback is registered on line 11, and the `result` argument is the server response to the `getComments` request. In this case, the result is a comments attribute that lists the `BlogComment` objects associated with the given blog entry.

❑ The label is retrieved on line 16, and when it exists, line 18 changes the text of the label to `Hide Comments`.

❑ The comment div is retrieved on line 20, and any existing children are replaced with a paragraph element (`<p>`) that indicates the number of comments being displayed (lines 21 through 23).

This is an example of a very powerful feature of the MochiKit DOM API. Rather than build up a convoluted string that creates the paragraph element and its children, the DOM element is created with `P`. This is actually an alias for the `createDOM` function that allows you to efficiently create various DOM elements. The first argument provided describes any attributes that need to be set on the DOM element, or should be `null` when there are no attributes. The second argument takes a variety of objects that typically get translated into a child DOM node. (You'll see how this can be used to concisely build up DOM structures later.) Of course, in addition to the `P` alias, there are aliases for most of the other HTML tags, like `table` or `a`, too.

❑   Beginning on line 25, a `for` loop goes through the list of comments and creates a `div` element that serves as a container for two child `div` elements that make up the actual contents of the comment. Specifically:

   ❑   A string of header information that includes the date of the comment as well as the name of the commenter is constructed on lines 26 and 27.

   ❑   A `div` element, `commentDiv`, is created on line 29 using the `DIV` alias for `createDOM`, and is established as having the `commentInfo` class. It is then appended as a child of the `allCommentsDiv` on line 30. This separate `div` serves primarily to create a border around the entire comment, including both the text and author.

   ❑   The `commentDiv` children are defined and appended to the `commentDiv` on lines 31 through 34. The first `div` has the `commentHeader` class and includes the header text. The second `div` has the `commentText` class and holds the text of the comment.

Defining the Widget's Look and Feel

The last element of the widget specification is the style sheet that defines the appearance of the widget. Create the CSS directory under the `static` directory (`tblog/tblog/widgets/static/css`), and then define a style sheet called `comment.css` as shown in Listing 6-9.

Listing 6-9: The widget stylesheet, comment.css

```
 1 .comment {
 2   border: thin solid black;
 3   color: black;
 4   font-size: 7pt;
 5   width: 80%;
 6   margin: 5px auto 5px auto;
 7 }
 8
 9 .commentHeader {
10   font-weight: bold;
11   margin: 2px;
12 }
13
14 .commentText {
15   margin: 2px;
16 }
17
18 .commentInfo {
19   margin: 2px;
20   color: black;
21   font-size: 7pt;
22 }
23
24 .commentLabel {
25   padding: 2px;
26   color: black;
27   border: thin solid black;
28   background-color: #FEED78;
29 }
```

Defining the getComments Path

Now that you've completed the widget specification, you need to create a new path in the controller that is capable of retrieving the comments associated with a blog entry. To do this, open the root controller, tblog/tblog/controllers.py, and define a new getComments method after sayHello as shown here:

```
@expose()
def getComments(self, entryId):
    comments = BlogComment.select(BlogComment.q.entryID == entryId,
                                  orderBy=BlogComment.q.date).reversed();
    return dict(comments=comments)
```

This function takes a blog entry ID, entryId, and retrieves all the BlogComment objects that match the ID. The comments are ordered by the date column and the reversed function to ensure that the most recent comments appear first.

Using the Comment Widget in the Main Blog View

At this point, you're ready to start using the widget. The first step is to add the widget to the main blog view. Start by opening the root controller, tblog/tblog/controllers.py, and adding the following import statement for the comment_widget:

```
from tblog.widgets.widgets import comment_widget
```

Next you need to change the index method to include the comment_widget as a parameter to beView as shown here:

```
@expose(template="tblog.templates.beView")
#@identity.require(identity.in_group("admin"))
@paginate('blogEntries', limit=3, allow_limit_override=True)
def index(self, **kw):
    log.info("User is logged in " + str(identity.current.anonymous));
    blogEntries = BlogEntry.select(orderBy=BlogEntry.q.date).reversed()
    return dict(comment_widget=comment_widget,
                blogEntries = blogEntries, **kw)
```

Finally, modify tblog/tblog/templates/beview.kid to display the widget after each blog entry by calling display on the comment after the blog entry text as follows:

```
<div class="blogEntry" py:for="blogEntry in blogEntries">
  <div class="beHeader">
    <h1>${blogEntry.entryTitle}</h1>
    <h2>${blogEntry.date}<br/>
      ${blogEntry.author}<br/>
      <a href="/comments/${blogEntry.id}">Comments</a></h2>
  </div>
  <p>${XML(blogEntry.entryText)}</p>
    ${comment_widget.display(entry_id=blogEntry.id)}
</div>
```

Note that as each blog entry is encountered in the for loop, the entry_id parameter associates the comment_widget with the specific blog entry.

That's all you need to do to use the widget. If you reload the web application, you should see a page like the one shown in Figure 6-9. When you click Show Comments, the comments are asynchronously retrieved and displayed under the blog entry. When you click Hide Comments, the comments are removed again.

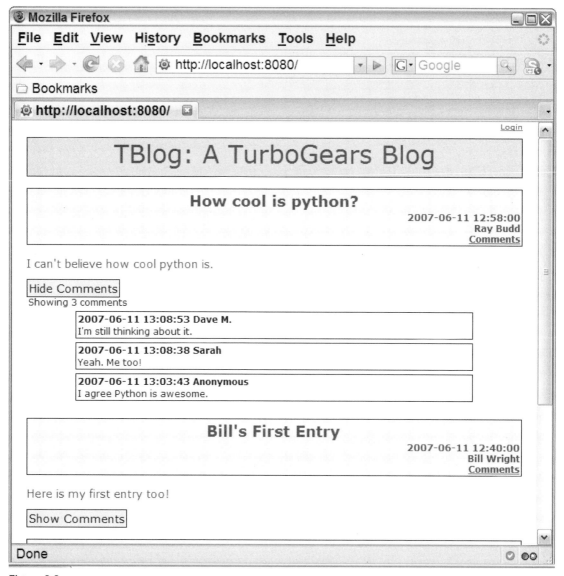

Figure 6-9

Using the Comment Widget in the Other Views

The real utility of widgets can be seen by how easily you can incorporate them into other views. To add your new widget to the comment view, simply return to controllers.py, and provide the widget as a parameter returned from the comments method as follows:

```
@expose(template='tblog.templates.comments')
def comments(self, entryId, **kw):
    entryTitle = BlogEntry.get(entryId).entryTitle
    formData = dict(entryTitle=entryTitle, blogEntryId=entryId)
    return dict(comment_widget=comment_widget, form=comment_form,
                formData=formData, **kw)
```

Then, all you need to do is update the comments.kid template to use the widget. In this case, however, you'll also make use of the parameters to tailor the way the widget is presented. Update the template as follows:

```
<body>
    <p><a href="/">Back to Blog</a></p>
    <h1>Comments</h1>
    <div py:content="comment_widget.display(entry_id=formData['blogEntryId'],
                        initiallyVisible=True, showLabel=False)"></div>
    <h1>Add Comment</h1>
```

Because this view contains only a single comment, it makes sense to automatically show the comments and remove the Show/Hide button. Calling display with the value of initiallyVisible set to True causes the comments to be displayed automatically when the widget is loaded. Setting showLabel to False removes the label from the widget. The entry_id parameter is established based on the hidden form field blogEntryId. Figure 6-10 shows the updated Add Comment view.

You can also easily show the comments in the show view of the blog entry CRUD views. Simply use the following statement to import the widget in the blog entry controller, tblog/tblog/BlogEntryController/controllers.py:

```
from tblog.widgets.widgets import comment_widget
```

Then pass the widget as an argument to the show view as follows:

```
@expose(template='kid:tblog.BlogEntryController.templates.show')
def show(self,id, **kw):
    """Show record in model"""
    record = BlogEntry.get(int(id))
    return dict(record = record, comment_widget=comment_widget)
```

And finally, update the show template to call display on the widget at the bottom of the body (tblog/tblog/BlogEntryController/templates/show.kid) as follows:

```
    <a href="../edit/${record.id}">Edit</a> | <a href="../list">Back</a>
    <h1>Comments</h1>
    <div py:content="comment_widget.display(entry_id=record.id,
                        initiallyVisible=True, showLabel=False)"></div>
    </body>
</html>
```

199

Figure 6-10

Figure 6-11 shows the updated show view.

It's just as simple to use the widget in other views as well. If you're feeling adventurous, you may want to experiment with adding the comments widget to the list view.

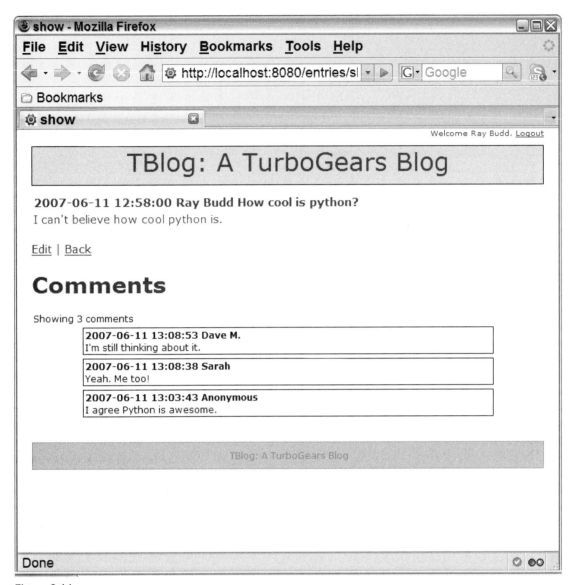

Figure 6-11

Summary

In this chapter, you learned about the using and developing widgets in depth. You were introduced to the underpinnings of the widget framework, and saw the advantages of widget development and use. You experimented with both the user and developer sides of widgets. First, as a widget user, you implemented your own form to accept blog comments. Then, as a widget implementer, you saw how to develop a widget from scratch and incorporate it into TBlog.

7

Advanced TurboGears Topics

It's not easy being green.

—Kermit the Frog

In addition to being green, there are several other things that aren't easy. This is especially true of learning to create applications with a multifaceted framework. After the first examples you encounter, the framework seems almost magical — as though achieving a working application happens almost at the speed of thought. Then you begin to hit stone walls when the next application's nuances and subtleties starts testing the limits of the framework, or at least what you think you know about the framework. In the worst-case scenario, you begin to see the imperfections and shortcomings — places where the framework's design center seems to have failed to take into account something you urgently need in your application, or alternatively, perhaps the flaw is simply in your own level of understanding of how the framework was intended to function.

This chapter is dedicated to presenting all those *other things* you need to know when working with TurboGears — those things that you encounter quickly after departing the familiar terrain of pages and single table models. Based on delving into the TurboGears forums and on the authors' own experiences in doing moderate (to hard) TurboGears projects, here are some of the questions you are bound to encounter:

- ❑ Are there helper tools that I can use to aid my thinking on the application design, or that generate code (beyond what TurboGears does for me already)?

- ❑ How do I integrate TurboGears with other web services? Does TurboGears preclude doing mashups with other application programming interfaces (APIs)?

- ❑ How do I get information from multiple parts of the model? How do I do one-to-one and one-to-many table joins?

- ❑ How do I coordinate elements of the visual model the RIA way (for example, coordinating map and table data)?

❑   How do I do nifty on-page effects that seem to be everywhere in Web 2.0 applications?

❑   How do I create those cool RSS feeds that everyone finds so useful?

Your Assignment

Let's start out with an imaginary (but realistic) application. Suppose you are charged with implementing a Rich Internet Application (RIA)-based application for your local cable company's repair scheduling. You can imagine the elements of the problem. The company has a fixed fleet of repair trucks, but their current locations could be anywhere within the confines of your operations area. There are multiple customers to be served, and their outages are reported asynchronously. The operations controller at the cable company wants to see the fleet, be alerted to the outages, assign a repair person, and have the backing model updated as assignments are made. Because you're writing a cool RIA management console, you want an uncluttered look and feel — you would like things (such as tables, forms, and maps) to appear when the operations controller wants to access them and disappear when he doesn't (aka the *nifty effects* requirement). Figure 7-1 shows the completed RIA in operation.

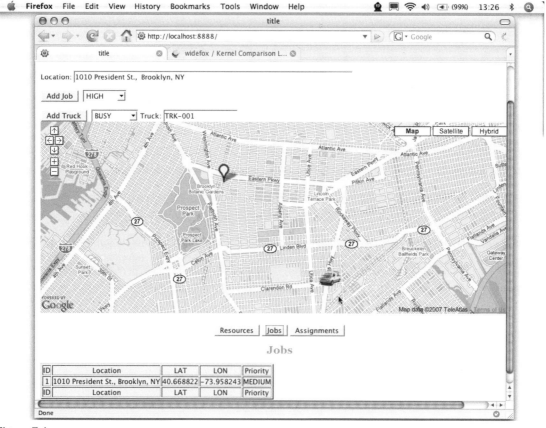

Figure 7-1

This RIA has a primarily geospatial interface. That's probably appropriate given the nature of the application. An attraction of many RIAs is that their functionality is largely self-evident and revealed by the interface itself. If creating this application were your assignment in real life, you would want the application to be useable by a range of people in roles varying from the operations controller to managers, and you would want to build on the interface to support forward growth of the particular application from analysis of how long an average job takes to perhaps providing a simple front-end to a fancy genetic algorithm scheduler back-end. In this version none of those more advanced elements are included, but the fundamental *hooks* are included in the design to illustrate that you should design with the future in mind.

The Operational Concept

Cable outages will be shown on a map of the company's operational area along with the fleet of repair trucks. When the controller wants to schedule a repair, he drags a truck to the location of an outage, and the truck becomes assigned to the repair. When the cable guy calls back to say that the repair is done, he becomes available for a new assignment. The dispatcher should be able to add a repair job by typing in a valid address and clicking a button, and it should show up on the map and be recorded in the backing data store simultaneously. Whenever someone makes a change to add or delete a job or reassign a repair truck, the change should be reflected in the backing store and the visual elements.

You can make up other constraints, but for the purposes of getting the hang of building a moderately complex application with lots of moving parts, this will be a good starting point. Along the way, the code narrative describes the design and implementation in greater detail so that you can see how your own design decisions will translate into TurboGears structures and work in conjunction with external (non-TurboGears) APIs.

With these goals in mind, the next several sections cover the thinking and implementation involved in creating an RIA that demonstrates the TurboGears approach to solving a complete, moderately challenging real-world problem. These sections present the application's model, controller, and view.

As Chapter 3 mentions, TurboGears applications are built using the model-view-controller (MVC) design pattern paradigm, which comprises the following three parts:

❑ A *model* **containing your data, as well as the methods and logic necessary to maintain that data.** In Python, this is usually expressed in the `model.py` module. An interesting feature of this application is the use of multiple, loosely connected models for supporting the various views of the data.

❑ *Controller* **logic to process user actions, handle HTTP requests, and provide responses.** In Python, this is usually expressed in the `controllers.py` module. This controller is the channel for translating user directives and inputs to the model.

❑ **One or more *views* to orchestrate what the user sees and manipulates.** In the TurboGears paradigm, views are expressed in Kid files, which contain mixed XHTML, tags with embedded Python directives, and possibly JavaScript to incorporate other elements. This application incorporates a map provided through the Google Maps API. Part of the application's challenge (and its appeal as a learning tool) is synchronizing the visual elements provided by the map with those provided by the model.

Designing the Model

Although you can begin by arbitrarily designing any aspect of the application, it's best if you first consider and then solidify the data model. It might be tempting to work from the user experience back into the model (and some very smart folks such as the creator of Ruby on Rails, David Heinemeier Hansson, advocate this outside-to-inside approach); however, beginning with the object representation enables you to make a late binding decision (and change your mind a few times along the way) about what the user will see without having to recreate the data model every time. If you get the data model right to begin with, everything else will be grounded in the vision of the data. Additionally, you'll find that Kid template development flows faster if you understand what data you need to supply to the template.

TurboGears Toolbox

This model was generated by hand, but you should know that the TurboGears Toolbox offers an attractive and reasonably robust web-based GUI model designer tool. You can invoke the Toolbox from the command line with the following statement:

```
tg-admin toolbox
```

The initial page will resemble Figure 7-2. Although the Toobox web interface supports a number of tools, you'll need only the CatWalk model browser and the ModelDesigner database design tool for this project.

Figure 7-2

ModelDesigner

From the initial TurboGears Toolbox web page, you can select the ModelDesigner tool. The ModelDesigner interface has three tab panes for working with a new or existing model: Diagram, Settings, and Generate Code.

Figure 7-3 shows the Diagram tab with the visual diagram for the model behind the cable repair assignment application.

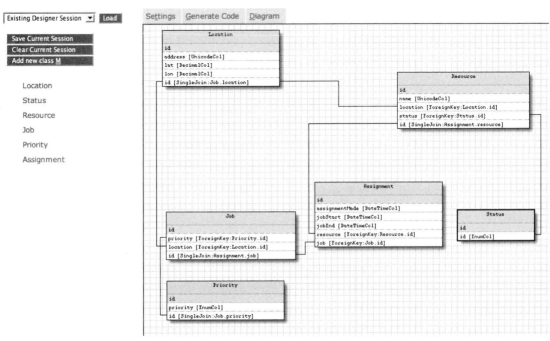

Figure 7-3

You use the Settings tab to design and modify the model using a form-based page, as shown in Figure 7-4.

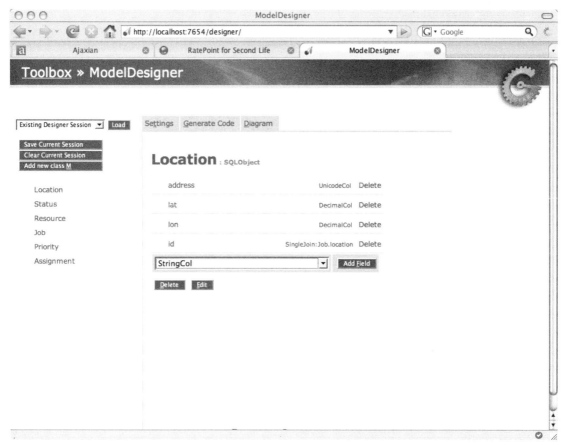

Figure 7-4

When you're satisfied with the model, you use the Generate Code tab to generate the model.py file and create the application tables. The database that is used depends on what you specified in your project's dev.cfg file. If you never change this, it defaults to sqlobject.dburi="sqlite://%(current_dir_uri)s/devdata.sqlite". Figure 7-5 shows a portion of the code for the cable repair assignment application.

Figure 7-5

The model description for your project is saved in a file called `model_designer.tmp` when you select Save Current Session from the interface.

CatWalk

Another tool available from the TurboGears Toolbox (shown previously in Figure 7-2) is a model browser and manipulation tool called CatWalk, shown in Figure 7-6. Although you can use SQL scripts and command-line tools to create and populate a database during development, using a GUI tool such as CatWalk enables you to visualize the elements of a table and prevent annoying syntax errors.

Figure 7-6

The Model

Now that you've seen and perhaps had a chance to play with the TurboGears tools, let's get back to the actual design problem at hand (although playing with new tools is always a worthwhile diversion). Listing 7-1 presents the code for this model in its entirety, followed by a detailed discussion of the model design and how to build this `model.py` code. You can either code this model by hand or construct it via Web-based tools.

Listing 7-1: The TurboGears model.py

```
 1 from turbogears.database import PackageHub
 2 from sqlobject import *
 3 from datetime import datetime
 4
 5 hub = PackageHub("ce")
 6 __connection__ = hub
 7
 8 class Location(SQLObject):
 9   address   = UnicodeCol(notNone=True, length=256)
10   lat  = DecimalCol(size=10, precision=7, default=0.0)
11   lon      = DecimalCol(size=10, precision=7, default=0.0)
12
13 class Job(SQLObject):
```

```
14    location = ForeignKey('Location')
15    priority = ForeignKey('Priority')
16
17 class Resource(SQLObject):
18    name     = UnicodeCol(alternateID=True, notNone=True, length=30)
19    location = ForeignKey('Location')
20    status   = ForeignKey('Status')
21
22 class Assignment(SQLObject):
23    assignmentMade = DateTimeCol(default=datetime.now)
24    jobStart= DateTimeCol(default=datetime.now)
25    jobEnd  = DateTimeCol(default=datetime.now)
26    resource      = ForeignKey('Resource')
27    job       = ForeignKey('Job')
28
29 class Status(SQLObject):
30    status = StringCol(default='AVAIL', length=20)
31
32 class Priority(SQLObject):
33    priority  = StringCol(default='MEDIUM')
34    icon = StringCol()
```

This listing begins by importing the PackageHub class that connects your model code to the underlying data storage, and then brings in the SQLObject package.

Time is an important element in any service call, so it's likely you'll need to create some TIMESTAMP objects (which SQLObject refers to as DateTime objects). In this application, you'll see a quick and easy way to create a TIMESTAMP using the datetime class. Import this class as follows:

```
from turbogears.database import PackageHub
from sqlobject import *
from datetime import datetime
```

In general, TurboGears models are simple to test via the tg-admin shell interface in a terminal window, and that's what will be used as the testing method for validating the model later in this chapter. In general, you should always use test-driven development as well. TurboGears provides a test-model.py file to exercise the model and check for regressions, but again you may also find it useful to simply exercise the model through the interpreter.

Ultimately, it all depends on whether you trust the generated code. In the case of Java Hibernate, for example, where the connection to the underlying data store is delivered through decorators, it is a little harder to exercise the interface interactively, so you may be better off writing a suite of test cases. Here, however, you can get almost instant feedback on the model validity through making a few Python calls in the model.py code.

The Location Class

In this application, it is essential for the operations controller who takes the customer call to get the location for the service outage. Additionally, the repair resources will be at some location in the operations area, so the Location class will do double duty.

Define the `Location` class as follows:

```
class Location(SQLObject):
    address  = UnicodeCol(notNone=True, length=256)
    lat      = DecimalCol(size=10, precision=7, default=0.0)
    lon      = DecimalCol(size=10, precision=7, default=0.0)
```

In this code, you make the address field itself a `UnicodeCol` so that you can represent a wide character set in place names. You also make it an alternate `ID`, because your crew controller is going to want to look places up by something other than the system-generated `ID` field (the default primary key). By specifying `address` as an alternate `ID`, you guarantee the uniqueness of the address string as well.

This example uses the Google Maps API for its map interface, which requires a latitude and longitude for placing a location on the map. You can just use the defaults for now — when the user makes the initial assignment, the API will return the latitude and longitude of the address and you'll update the model with those values. Notice that the `precision` values are fairly large — Google Maps is very precise.

Conversely, notice that the definition of what a location represents has been left pretty loose. If you've filled out a typical web form with multiline address fields, this may surprise you. In this application context, the Google Maps geocoder needs only a loose textual description of an address to make its geocoding decision. Thus, you don't need to overdesign the application logic. Be aware, though, that the geocoder makes a best-effort selection when it has multiple choices, so if this code is the basis for a real application, you need to add some validation logic. The right place to do something like that is in the `addjob` method of `controllers.py`, which you will use to add job and truck resources later in this chapter.

You can validate that the model is working by firing up the interactive shell and creating a new `Location` as follows:

```
>   tg-admin shell
Python 2.4.4 (#1, Oct 18 2006, 10:34:39)
Type "copyright", "credits" or "license" for more information.
In [1]: loc = Location(address='1010 President St.,  Brooklyn, NY')
In [2]: print loc
<Location 2 address="u'1010 President ...'" lat=0.0 lon=0.0>
In [3]: Location.get(2)
Out[3]: <Location 2 address="u'1010 President ...'" lat=0.0 lon=0.0>
In [4]: locs = Location.select()
In [5]: for l in locs: print l.address
   ...:
4 Irving Pl., NY, NY
1010 President St.,  Brooklyn, NY
```

Obviously, the latitudes and longitudes are incorrect (unless someone moved Brooklyn to the west coast of Africa while you were on coffee break), but because the interactive shell uses the Python classes declared in your `model.py`, you can add and select `Location` records from the underlying database. Correct latitude and longitude values are supplied by the Google Maps geocoder interface, which is implemented as a part of the view (discussed in more detail in the section "The View" later in this chapter).

Note that because you didn't do any actual transactions (which would have required you to specify a `hub.begin` before the record and `hub.commit` after it), the bogus record and any other changes that you make to the model will not persist beyond the session. You can see the methods available via the `hub` class in the interactive shell by using the following Python `dir` request:

```
In [7]: dir(hub.hub)
Out[7]:
['__class__',
 ...
 'begin',
 'commit',
 'end',
 'getConnection',
 'params',
 'reset',
 'rollback',
 'supports_transactions',
 'threadConnection',
 'threadingLocal',
 'uri']
```

Following the control flow in an AJAX application is a little like following the bouncing karaoke ball, but as long as you remember that visual elements of the server-based controller can act asynchronously without forcing a page refresh, you don't have to think too hard about the coordination. What you'll see in this application is that as soon as the user types an address and creates a new repair job, the location passes to both the Google server and your own `controllers.py`. This sets off a chain of events that will do the following:

1. Invoke the geocoder API (which resides somewhere on the Internet — where specifically is really unimportant from your standpoint).

2. Use the latitude and longitude returned by the geocoder plus the address typed by the user to invoke your controller so it creates a new `Location` record.

3. Asynchronously refresh the onscreen map and onscreen repair jobs table so that the user gets visual confirmation that the repair job has been recorded.

Model Class: Job

Next you'll create the job model. A simple job model might have a unique identifier, a location, and a priority. The `Location` class you created gives you a way to model locations for a job, so the logical thing to do would be to hold a pointer to an instance of `Location` in your job model. You also want to include some way to assign a priority to a job — perhaps the imaginary cable company will grow quite large and will need to sort out important repairs from *very* important repairs. You could simply add a priority indicator into the `Job` class, but it's better to keep discrete, enumerable values in another part of the model and have the `Job` class point to it. Create the `Job` class as follows:

```
class Job(SQLObject):
    location = ForeignKey('Location')
    priority = ForeignKey('Priority')
```

Notice that the SQLObject notation for saying "point to an instance of . . . " is to use ForeignKey, passing it the name of the other table. Optionally, you can pass a specific column name, but by default the value of the ForeignKey is the unique ID field of the other class. You don't see a declaration of the ID field, because it's both hidden and assumed, but it's there nonetheless. Now, open up the shell again and test out the model as follows:

```
In [1]: l = Location(address="1700 . 17th St., Arlington, VA")
In [2]: p = Priority(priority="HIGH")
In [3]: job = Job(location=1.id, priority=p.id)
In [4]: job.location.address
Out[4]: u'1700 . 17th St., Arlington, VA'
In [5]: job.priority.priority
Out[5]: u'HIGH'
```

The semantic "this table in, that table field out" structure used as in lines 4 and 5 above is quite a common idiom in table joins, and there's a certain beauty, even elegance of expression, in being able to operate the model this way. This is not precisely how you'll create a new job via the controller, shown in Listing 7-3 later in this chapter, but it illustrates the ease of new record construction.

Model Class: Priority

Before leaving the job model altogether, let's take a look at Job's companion, the Priority class. You define this class as follows:

```
class Priority(SQLObject):
  priority  = StringCol(default='MEDIUM')
  icon = StringCol()
```

As mentioned previously, the reason for breaking job priorities out into their own class is that it's an easy way to expand the range of priorities without breaking the job model. Even if all job records with a high priority are cleared, the concept of a high priority itself should survive for use with the next job added by the operations controller. Later, in the controlpanel.kid template and controller code, you'll see how relational integrity (which ensures that only legitimate values are associated with a job) is enforced. Although you could create fields for job priorities in the Job class, that would clearly be wasteful — every job would require a priority column — when all you really need is one instance of each value in the priority and status tables, with many jobs pointing to the various values.

Normally, this would suggest the use of a multijoin field in the Priority class as the "one" side of a one-to-many relationship as well as a foreign key specification. However, for purposes of illustrating distributed value integrity enforcement, this design will serve.

Here's another structure that you will see frequently for value lookup–style tables:

```
class Priority(SQLObject):
    priority  = EnumCol( enumValues=['HIGH', 'MEDIUM', 'LOW', 'FIXED'], ↩
      default='MEDIUM')
```

This works fine if the values are never likely to change. However, the disadvantage of this class design is that any new values added would entail a schema change, with the attendant pains of unloading the data, updating the schema, re-creating the tables, and reloading the data.

Model Class: Resource

The design rationale behind Resource is very similar to that for Job, the only difference being that, to make the search for and retrieval of resources as user-friendly as possible, the Resource class for this model uses a string identifier (name) as an alternate index to reference them. This class also holds pointers to a Location record and a Status record. Therefore, you define the Resource class for this model as follows:

```
class Resource(SQLObject):
  name     = UnicodeCol(alternateID=True, notNone=True, length=30)
  location = ForeignKey('Location')
  status   = ForeignKey('Status')
```

Model Class: Status

The Status class follows a rationale identical to the rationale for the Priority class. You define it as follows:

```
class Status(SQLObject):
  status = StringCol(default='AVAIL', length=20)
```

Now you can test the Job class again, using the interactive shell as follows:

```
tg-admin shell
Python 2.4.4 (#1, Oct 18 2006, 10:34:39)
In [1]: l = Location(address='10 Moulton St., Cambridge, MA')
In [2]: s = Status()
In [3]: r = Resource(name="truck-001", location=l.id, status=s.id)
In [4]: print r.name,"is at", r.location.address,"and is ", r.status.state
truck-001 is at 10 Moulton St., Cambridge, MA and is AVAIL
```

Model Class: Assignment

The last model class in this example is Assignment. This class ensures that a resource's location and a job's location are the same — which is good news for the cable subscriber, because it means that the cable guy has arrived. Here's how to define this class:

```
class Assignment(SQLObject):
  assignmentMade = DateTimeCol(default=datetime.now)
  jobStart= DateTimeCol(default=datetime.now)
  jobEnd  = DateTimeCol(default=datetime.now)
  resource     = ForeignKey('Resource')
  job     = ForeignKey('Job')
```

You test the Assignment class with the same interactive shell as you've been using:

```
In [5]: l2 = Location(address='Fawcett St., Cambridge, MA')
In [6]: p = Priority(priority="HIGH")
In [7]: j = Job(location=l.id, priority=p.id)
In [8]: j = Job(location=l2.id, priority=p.id)
In [9]: a = Assignment(resource=r, job=j)
```

You can even create a statement as wacky as the following:

```
In [10]: print "Job assignment located at", a.job.location.address,"made
at",a. assignmentMade, "to",a.resource.name, "currently located at",
a.resource.location.address
Job assignment located at Fawcett St., Cambridge, MA made at 2007-04-15 23:09:16 to
truck-001 currently located at 10 Moulton St., Cambridge, MA
```

Note that in a fashion similar to the Ruby on Rails design philosophy of convention over configuration, the names for the links to other classes were deliberately chosen. If the names chosen for the `ForeignKey` variables in the `Job`, `Resource`, and `Assignment` classes are not the same as the name of the referenced class, the syntactically elegant drill-down scheme will not work. If, for example, the name for the `ForeignKey` link to the `Resource` class were `'foo'` and not `'resource'`, the `a.foo.location.address` subexpression would fail. TurboGears and SQLObject can orchestrate their referencing magic explicitly because of consistency in naming. You can "pretty-print" the result of the joined object model query as follows:

```
In [9]: print "Job assignment located at",Job.get( a.job).location.address, " made
at", a.assignmentMade,"to", Resource.get(a.resource).name, "currently located at",
Resource.get(a.resource).location.address
```

And the interpreter will output the following:

```
Job assignment located at 10 Fawcett St. Cambridge, MA made at 2007-04-15 22:27:41
to truck-001 currently located at 10 Moulton St., Cambridge, MA
```

Now that you have a reasonable data model in place, you can start concentrating on the controller logic.

The Controller

The controller for this application, like most, fulfills the rather unglamorous role of mediating the `put` and `get` functions from the underlying data model. In the next several sections, you will see the controller elements come together. The controller is shown complete in Listing 7-3.

The Imports Class

The controller begins by importing a number of necessary libraries.

```
from turbogears import controllers, expose, flash, redirect, url
from turbogears.toolbox import catwalk
from model import *
from docutils.core import publish_parts
import logging
log = logging.getLogger("ce.controllers")
import time
```

The first statement brings into scope the necessary TurboGears imports and enables Python to resolve such elements as the `expose` decorator and the `controller` class.

Next, you import the CatWalk controller. This is optional, but as mentioned in Chapter 3 and earlier in this chapter, it's useful to have CatWalk easily available during development. If you need to take a look at the backing store, you can simply invoke it with the following statement:

```
Localhost:8088/catwalk
```

After you bind CatWalk to the `Root` class (which you will do in the next section),you can use it without having to start up the TurboGears Toolbox first.

Next, the import of the model makes the model elements shown previously in Listing 7-1 available to the controller.

You then set up a logger by importing `logging` and constructing a `log` object. Log output will, by default, go to the console and will be labeled with the identity of the issuing controller. Thus, if you invoke the `addjob` method (shown below) with an HTTP GET with the proper elements — for example

```
http://localhost:8080/addjob?address=1010%20President%20St.%2C%20%20Brooklyn%2C%20N
Y&lat=40.668822&lon=-73.958243&priority_id=2
```

— the controller, on successfully creating the record, will report the following in the console window:

```
2007-04-17 00:14:54,002 ce.controllers DEBUG add Job succeeded; 11 1010 President
St., Brooklyn, NY 40.668822 -73.958243 MEDIUM
```

You can tailor the reporting level to be more or less verbose, and redirect the output via the Python logging API.

The Root Class

Here you bind a variable `catwalk` to the TurboGears `Root` class, which is subclassed from a Python class constructed from the methods of the current controller itself. Define the Root class for this model as follows:

```
class Root(controllers.RootController):
    catwalk = catwalk.CatWalk()
    @expose(template="ce.templates.controlpanel")
    def index(self, optmsg=None):
        now=time.ctime()
        content = publish_parts(now, writer_name="html")['html_body']
        root = str(url('/'))
        if (optmsg):
            tg_flash = optmsg
        return dict(tg_flash=optmsg, data=content, priority=Priority.select(),
status=Status.select())
```

The @expose statement in this definition is a *decorator*. Decorators became an intrinsic part of Python in release 2.4. TurboGears uses decorators to determine whether something (typically a method) can be invoked via an HTTP request. When @expose precedes the `index` method definition as it does here, the decorator accepts an optional argument: the template that's completed with the values returned by the method in this case.

Any time you specify a template as an argument to the decorator, a new page is returned to the browser. However, when AJAX calls affect the page from which the method was invoked, the affected portion of the current page is refreshed with new data rather than the server returning a fresh page. Controller methods invariably return an associative array, which is used as a namespace for rendering the Kid template (when one is supplied) into HTML. When a template isn't supplied, it's assumed that you are returning into the calling page. You can specify both an input data format and a data return format.

Returning to the index method defined in this code, the contents of the controlpanel.kid template are published, as are all the Priority codes and Status codes, as follows:

```
return dict(tg_flash=optmsg, data=content, priority=Priority.select(),
status=Status.select())
```

The contents of these unordered arrays are used to populate the combo boxes for priority and status on the page (previously shown in Figure 7-1).

In summary, the expose decorator essentially enables you to make an explicit call, which maps a portion of the URL directly to a method in the controller aggregated under the RootController. For example, if you type http://localhost:8080/catwalk into the address bar, it displays the CatWalk tool page because the controller for CatWalk is contained within the current controller.

The Resourcelist Method

The controller defines a resourcelist method as follows:

```
@expose()
@expose("json")
def resourcelist(self):
    return dict(resources=[[r.id, r.name, r.location.address, r.location.lat,
        r.location.lon] for r in Resource.select(orderBy=Resource.q.name)]
```

This method is similar to the other controller methods in that it returns an entire list of elements from the backing store. The first expose statement makes the method public. It has no template declaration because you're going to be invoking the resourcelist method from Javascript in controlpanel.kid (later in this chapter). The second expose statement tells TurboGears to return the data as JavaScript Object Notation (JSON). JSON is a compact notation immediately useable by a JavaScript function as an associative array.

You can see the effect of returning the data as JSON by invoking a URL such as http://localhost:8080/resourcelist on this controller as the code base. The call is routed to the resourcelist method defined here. Because the return data type is JSON, the result returned to your browser will resemble something like Listing 7-2. (You'll see how the JSON elements returned by the method are used in more detail later in this chapter.)

Listing 7-2: TurboGears JSON

```
{"tg_flash": null,
"resources": [
[1, "TRK-001", "800 President St.,  Brooklyn, NY", 40.674059, -73.976484],
[2, "TRK-006", "1600 President St.,  Brooklyn, NY", 40.667216, -73.934957],
[3, "TRK-007", "1010 President St.,  Brooklyn, NY", 40.668822, -73.958243]
]}
```

The actual mechanism for `resourcelist` is interesting and speaks to the compactness and expressiveness of both Python and TurboGears. The production of the method is (as usual) an associative array, whose value is a mutable list constructed via Python list comprehension. The `Resource.select()` method (`Resource` is the class in this model) chooses an entire set of records from the backing store.

The `for` loop iterates over the collection, choosing specific elements and building the list. Certain elements of the list are themselves composed of joins to other parts of the model. For example, `r.location.address` says "With the current resource row from the backing store, use the foreign key called `location` that points to the `Location` object model, and get the `address` string." It does the same type of thing for the `lat` and `lon` attributes.

> *It may be possible to construct a more succinct expression for doing a compound database fetch and creating an array of the results, but it probably wouldn't be easy.*

You can see a similarly powerful expression in the `assignmentlist` method that gets the list of assignments. In this model, the job assignments associate cable repair trucks and outages. The controller method defines the `assignmentlist` method as follows:

```
@expose()
@expose('json')
def assignmentlist(self):
    return dict(assignments=[[assignment.id, assignment.resource.name,
    assignment.job.location.address, assignment.assignmentMade]
    for assignment in Assignment.select()]
```

Here the expression `assignment.job.location.address` uses double-pointer chaining. It gets an address string by using the `Address` instance's pointer (a foreign key) to the associated `Job` instance and using *its* pointer to get to the associated `Location` instance to get to *its* address attribute.

None of this controller's methods are providing anything in the way of exception handling or validation. In truth, the example has been architected such that few errors are likely to crop up. That's a hallmark of reasonable front-to-back design, and it also makes a statement about the overall robustness of the TurboGears framework. Note though that error handling would be important in most real applications, and because your sense of professionalism is screaming at you to provide error handling robustness anyway, you will probably want to read the section "Controller Error Handling," later in the chapter.

Controller: addjob

Next you need a method that adds a job location and assigns it a priority. To do this, you define the `addjob` controller method as follows:

```
@expose()
@expose('json')
def addjob(self, address, lat,lon, priority_id):
    l = Location(address=address, lat=lat, lon=lon)
    p = Priority.get(priority_id)
    j = Job(location=l.id, priority=p.id)
    log.debug("add Job succeeded; "+str(j.id)+" "+j.location.address+"
"+str(j.location.lat)+
        " "+str(j.location.lon)+" "+j.priority.priority)
    return dict(job=[j.id,j.location.address,j.location.lat, j.location.lon,
j.priority.priority])
```

The `addjob` method gets input via the user interface and creates a new data object in to controller. The controller acts as a translator between the action in the view and the underlying model. The JavaScript in the main page invokes the `addjob` method, passing it an address string (the latitude and longitude) and a job priority.

In the view, the user invokes `addjob` by entering a location and clicking the Add Job button, which places a job marker on the map as shown in Figure 7-7.

`Addjob` demonstrates the affordances offered by the controller as a translator between the action in the view and the underlying model. JavaScript in the main page invokes the `addjob` method, passing it an address string, latitude and longitude and a job priority. In the view, the user invokes `addjob` by entering a location, and pressing the Add Job button. This user action along with the resulting placement of the job marker is shown in Figure 7-7.

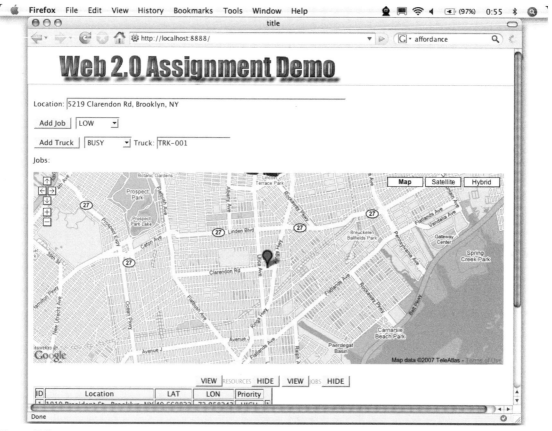

Figure 7-7

From the discussion earlier on mapping URLs to controller methods, you now know that the user action results in an HTTP Get call being passed to the addjob method. If you could look at the call itself for the address shown in Figure 7-7, it would look like this:

```
http://localhost:8888/addjob?address=5219%20Clarendon%20Rd%2C%20Brooklyn%2C%20NY&la
t=40.644569&lon=-73.927437&priority_id=3
```

This call passes the address, lat, lon, and priority values to the method in the format it expects to receive them. Recall from the model (Listing 7-1) that in order to create a new Job object, you need to create a new Location object and associate an existing Priority object with it. The Job object itself merely holds pointers to the Location and Priority.

So this is exactly how you implement addjob. The following line shows the syntax for creating a new Location object:

```
l = Location(address=address, lat=lat, lon=lon)
```

That syntax results in a new record being created in the underlying data store. You use the Location constructor with keyword arguments in whatever order you wish (another of Python's developer-friendly features), and this inserts a record into the database.

You next use p = Priority.get(), passing it the ID from the invoking page. Because the index method used in the initial construction of the page passed the legal values of priorities from the underlying database, you are assured that the value is legitimate. Line 23 creates a new job, which, as you may recall from Listing 7-1 simply holds IDs for the associated Location and Priority object.

Next, as shown in the addjob code snippet shown earlier, you create a job via the following constructor:

```
j = Job(location=l.id, priority=p.id)
```

The log statement on the the line following the constructor for Job is functionally unnecessary but is used in the code snippet above to demonstrate that whenever a new job is added, it logs a line to the console.

The Google Maps geocoder, which is called by JavaScript in the invoking page, assures that the address the end user types will map to a legitimate latitude-longitude pair. If the user enters something totally nonsensical such as **etaoin shrdlu**, the geocoder API's external mapping returns an alert saying the location can't be found. On the other hand, if the user enters anything that's even remotely address-like, he or she *will* receive something from the geocoder in the view, even if it's not the desired address.

You will see the rest of the page-routing JavaScript code — from the request itself being made (the displayJobs method) to the result being posted on the map (the showJobs method) — later in this chapter.

Listing 7-3 shows the entire controllers.py code for this model.

Listing 7-3: The complete controllers.py application controller

```
1  from turbogears import controllers, expose, flash, redirect,url
2  from turbogears.toolbox import catwalk
3  from model import *
4  from docutils.core import publish_parts
5  import logging
6  log = logging.getLogger("ce.controllers")
7  import time
8
9  class Root(controllers.RootController):
10     catwalk = catwalk.CatWalk()
11     @expose(template="ce.templates.controlpanel")
12     def index(self, optmsg=None):
13         now=time.ctime()
14         content = publish_parts(now, writer_name="html")['html_body']
15         root = str(url('/'))
16         if (optmsg):
17           tg_flash = optmsg
18         return dict(tg_flash=optmsg, data=content,
19           priority=Priority.select(), status=Status.select())
20
21     @expose()
22     @expose('json')
23     def addjob(self, address, lat,lon, priority_id):
24       l = Location(address=address, lat=lat, lon=lon)
25       p = Priority.get(priority_id)
26       j = Job(location=l.id, priority=p.id)
27       log.debug("add Job succeeded; "+str(j.id)+" "+j.location.address+
28         " "+str(j.location.lat)+
29         " "+str(j.location.lon)+" "+j.priority.priority)
30       return dict(job=[j.id,j.location.address,j.location.lat,
31         j.location.lon,j.priority.priority])
32
33     @expose()
34     @expose('json')
35     def addresource(self, name, address,lat,lon,status_id):
36       l = Location(address=address, lat=lat, lon=lon)
37       s = Status.get(status_id)
38       r = Resource(name=name, location=l.id, status=s.id)
39       return dict(id=r.id, address=r.location.address,
40                status=r.status.status)
41     @expose()
42     @expose('json')
43     def addassignment(self, resource, joblocation):
44       r = Resource.selectBy(name=resource)
45       l = Location.selectBy(address=joblocation)
46       j = Job.selectBy(location=l[0].id)
47       a = Assignment(resource=r[0].id , job=j[0].id )
48       return dict(id=a.id, resource=a.resource.name,
49         location=a.job.location.address, assignmentMade=a.assignmentMade)
50
51     @expose()
52     @expose("json")
```

```
53      def resourcelist(self):
54        return dict(resources= [[r.id, r.name, r.location.address,
        r.location.lat,
55          r.location.lon]
56        for r in Resource.select(orderBy=Resource.q.name)]])
57
58      @expose()
59      @expose("json")
60      def joblistwithicons(self):
61        return dict(jobs=[[j.id, j.location.address, j.location.lat,
62          j.location.lon, j.priority.priority, j.priority.icon]
63        for j in Job.select(orderBy=Job.q.id)])
64
65      @expose()
66      @expose('json')
67      def assignmentlist(self):
68        return dict(assignments=[[assignment.id, assignment.resource.name,
69          assignment.job.location.address, assignment.assignmentMade]
70        for assignment in Assignment.select()] )
71
72      @expose()
73      def default(self, *args, **kw):
74        return self.index()
```

Controller Error Handling

In order to use relatively compact code, none of the methods you defined in the controller code include anything in the way of error handling, but they really ought to. To add robustness in the face of possible errors, there is a couple of simple, proven approaches.

Consider adding a `truck` method that, given the ID of a truck resource, returns a JSON array containing some relevant data about the truck. Such a method without error handling might look like Listing 7-4.

Listing 7-4: Truck method — version 1

```
@expose('json')
def truck(self, ID):
  truck = Resource.get(ID)
  return dict(name=truck.name, address=truck.location.address,  ⏎
      status=truck.status.status )
```

If you added this to the controller, you would then be able to invoke a URL such as `http://localhost:8888/truck/1`, which is a method mapping style supported by TurboGears. TurboGears is smart enough to translate that syntax into a call to the `truck` method and parse the subsequent slash-delimited data as the arguments to the method. This is similar to the standard URL addressing syntax (such as `http://localhost:8888/truck?ID=1`), except it's more human-readable and easier for your end user to type.

Using either method invocation syntax, your controller will find the truck resource by its ID and return the following:

```
{"status": "AVAIL", "name": "TRK-001", "tg_flash": null, ↩
"address": "5219 Clarendon Rd, Brooklyn, NY"}
```

Because you haven't provided a template for the truck method to complete and return to the browser, the browser will display only the contents of the associative array produced by the method. For example, if you invoke truck with http://localhost:8888/truck/999999999, you'll get a "500 Internal Server Error" message.

There are some things that you can do to improve the feedback you provide to the end user so it's not just a sea of Python stack trace. To take a look at alternatives, create the Truck.kid template shown in Listing 7-5. This will give you a page to render into so that you can look at the effect of adding some error handling.

For the sake of brevity, the surrounding HTML is not included in this listing.

Listing 7-5: Truck.kid

```
<table id="truck-info">
  <tr>
    <td class="fld">Name:</td>
    <td class="val"><span py:replace="name" /></td>
  </tr>
  <tr>
    <td class="fld">Address:</td>
    <td class="val"><span py:replace="address" /></td>
  </tr>
  <tr>
    <td class="fld">Status:</td>
    <td class="val"><span py:replace="status" /></td>
  </tr>
</table>
```

This template will render a truck when you supply the controller with a valid ID, as shown in Figure 7-8.

However, if you supply an index into the backing store, you still get the onerous "500 Internal Server Error" message. To ensure against this, there are some techniques you can try. For one thing, you can surround the get() call with a try/except block to catch any exceptions and return a message to the invoking page. Now your code should resemble Listing 7-6.

Listing 7-6: Truck method — version 2

```
from sqlobject import SQLObjectNotFound
@expose(template="ce.templates.truck")
def truckV2(self, ID):
  try:
    truck = Resource.get(ID)
    return dict(name=truck.name, address=truck.location.address,
        status=truck.status.status )
```

```
    except SQLObjectNotFound:
      tg_flash="NO truck, no way"
      return dict(tg_flash="NO truck, no way", name="", address="", status="")
```

This refactoring now catches the error and supplies an error text. By default, TurboGears returns a null tg_flash element. A tg_flash element, if returned to the page template as non-null, will render as a text message of your choosing. Thus, you can conveniently supply an error string to the user whenever necessary, as shown in Figure 7-9.

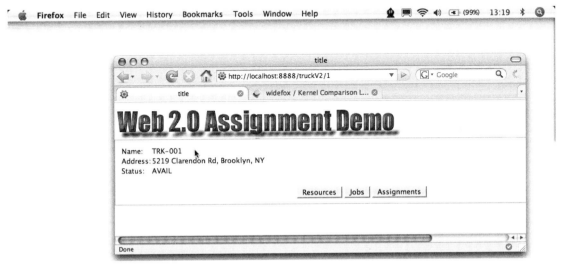

Figure 7-8

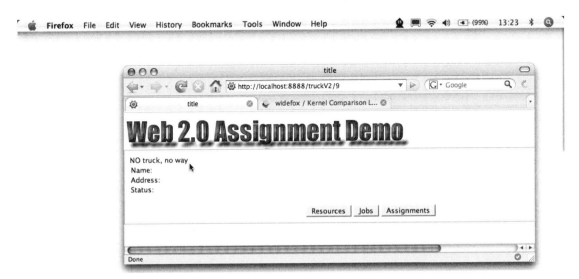

Figure 7-9

That's an improvement. What else? A different approach to the error handling issue would be to just route the error to a 404 ("Not Found") type of exception, as shown in Listing 7-7.

Listing 7-7: Truck method — version 3

```
from sqlobject import SQLObjectNotFound
@expose(template="ce.templates.truck")
def truckV2(self, ID):
  try:
    truck = Resource.get(ID)
    return dict(name=truck.name, address=truck.location.address,
        status=truck.status.status )
  except SQLObjectNotFound:
    tg_flash="NO truck, no way"
    return dict(tg_flash="NO truck, no way", name="", address="", status="")
```

Your user will still get a torrent of traceback, though, so maybe it's not all that much better. A third strategy is to redirect to a page that swallows the errors. This is shown in Listing 7-8, which is another refactoring of the truck method code.

Listing 7-8: Truck method — version 4

```
@expose(template="ce.templates.truck")
def truckV4(self, ID):
  from sqlobject import SQLObjectNotFound
  from turbogears import redirect
  from cherrypy import NotFound
  try:
    truck = Resource.get(ID)
  except SQLObjectNotFound:
    raise redirect("/index?optmsg=NOTFound")
  return dict(name=truck.name, address=truck.location.address, ↵
status=truck.status.status )
```

Add in a little refactoring of the index method to accept the optional message, as shown in Listing 7-9, and now errors route the user back to the base control panel page.

Listing 7-9: Refactored index method

```
@expose(template="ce.templates.controlpanel")
def index(self, optmsg=None):
  now=time.ctime()
  content = publish_parts(now, writer_name="html")['html_body']
  root = str(url('/'))
  if (optmsg):
    tg_flash = optmsg
  return dict(tg_flash=optmsg, data=content,
    priority=Priority.select(),
    status=Status.select()))
```

Now calling a URL with a bad ID would display the message shown in Figure 7-10, which is perhaps the most reasonable of all.

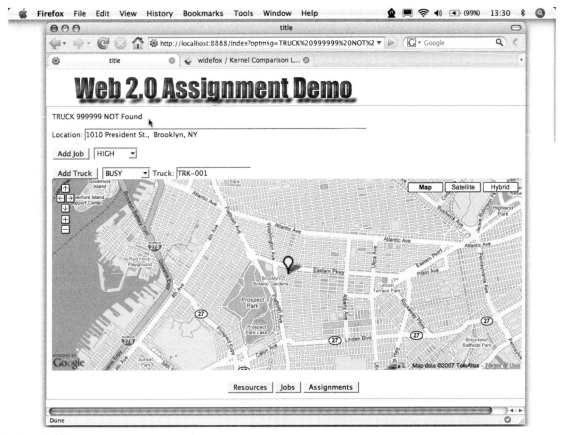

Figure 7-10

The View

You now have much of the application defined, and can turn your attention to the user experience. As stated at the start of the chapter, this model is representative of a real application, similar to one actually working commercially. Much of the code implements the geospatial interface, which is interesting in its own rite but doesn't serve to illustrate crucial points about either TurboGears or MochiKit. Accordingly, much of the code dealing with the map-handling aspects has been left out, but the full application code is available for download at www.wiley.com.

As discussed in Chapter 3, the TurboGears framework supplies a template called master.kid, which contains the elements, JavaScript methods, and styles that are common to all Kid template files. The master.kid in Listing 7-10 is no different with respect to its overall structure.

Listing 7-10: master.kid

```
<!DOCTYPE html PUBLIC "-//W3C//DTD XHTML 1.0 Transitional//EN"
"http://www.w3.org/TR/xhtml1/DTD/xhtml1-transitional.dtd">
<?python import sitetemplate ?>
<html xmlns="http://www.w3.org/1999/xhtml" xmlns:py="http://purl.org/kid/ns#">
<head py:match="item.tag=='{http://www.w3.org/1999/xhtml}head'"
py:attrs="item.items()">
  <meta py:replace="item[:]"/>
  <style type="text/css" media="screen">
  @import "/static/css/style.css";
  </style>
<script src="/static/javascript/MochiKit/MochiKit.js"
type="text/javascript"></script>
 </head>
 <body py:match="item.tag=='{http://www.w3.org/1999/xhtml}body'"
py:attrs="item.items()">
    <div id="header"> </div>
    <div id="main_content">
      <div py:if="tg_flash" class="flash" py:content="tg_flash"></div>
      <div py:replace="[item.text]+item[:]"/>
    </div>
    <div id="footer">
      <button onClick="toggleResourceList()">Resources</button>
      <button onClick="toggleJobList()">Jobs</button>
      <button onClick="toggleAssignmentList()">Assignments</button>
      <div id="resourcelist_results" style="display: none;"></div>
      <div id="joblist_results" style="display: none;"></div>
      <div id="assignmentlist_results" style="display: none;"></div>

    </div>
  </body>
</html>
```

In addition to the usual `match` instructions that enable you to replace whole segments of the body in Kid templates, this one also creates a common footer (`<div id="footer">`) that enable you to populate, show, and hide tables for jobs, truck resources, and job assignments. The footer contains the Resources, Jobs, and Assignment buttons (previously shown in Figure 7-1) that activate callbacks in the `controlpanel.KID` file.

The template also explicitly includes the `MochiKit.js` library. This is necessary only when you want to get visual effects, as you do in this application. As of this book's publication, MochiKit 1.4 is required to get the MochiKit port of the `script.aculo.us` effects libraries but is not the default version directly supported with the download of TurboGears. You can get a current version of MochiKit from `http://mochikit.com`. For development purposes, you should put the JavaScript libraries in your project path at `<install-dir>/<projectname>/static/javascript`.

To assure that you get an overload of newer MochiKit, you will also need to override a stanza generated by default from quickstart generation from quickstart, by removing the following:

```
<!DOCTYPE html PUBLIC "-//W3C//DTD XHTML 1.0 Transitional//EN"
"http://www.w3.org/TR/xhtml1/DTD/xhtml1-transitional.dtd">
<?python import sitetemplate ?>
<html xmlns="http://www.w3.org/1999/xhtml" xmlns:py="http://purl.org/kid/ns#"
py:extends="sitetemplate">
```

and replacing it with

```
<!DOCTYPE html PUBLIC "-//W3C//DTD XHTML 1.0 Transitional//EN"
"http://www.w3.org/TR/xhtml1/DTD/xhtml1-transitional.dtd">
<?python import sitetemplate ?>
<html xmlns="http://www.w3.org/1999/xhtml" xmlns:py="http://purl.org/kid/ns#">
```

as shown in Listing 7-10.

Listing 7-11 shows selected elements of the page implementation previously shown in Figure 7-1.

Listing 7-11: controlpanel.kid page implementation

```
<head>
<script    src="http://maps.google.com/maps?file=api&amp;v=2&amp;key=GMapsAPIKey"
 type="text/javascript"/>
...
function init(){
    setupDBG();
    refresh();
}
function setupDBG() {
  logDebug("Page (re)loaded");
}
function refresh(){ //Load all jobs and resources via the controller
  if (__map == null){ loadMap(); }
...
  displayJobs();
  displayTrucks();
}
function loadMap() {
if (GBrowserIsCompatible()) {
      __map = new GMap2(document.getElementById("map"));
      ...
    }
}
function displayJobs(){
   __jobs = [];
   var deferred = loadJSONDoc("${tg.url('/joblist', tg_format='json')}");
   deferred.addCallback(showJobs);
}
function displayTrucks(){
   __trucks = [];
    var deferred = loadJSONDoc("${tg.url('/resourcelist', tg_format='json')}");
    deferred.addCallback(showTrucks);
}
...
</head>
```

Setting Up and Debugging the View

When the page is loaded, `init()` is called via `<body onload="init()">` (see Listing 7-11). The debugger is loaded, the map is loaded (using the Google Maps API), and the page with the data supporting the tables is loaded. Because you are including MochiKit, setting up a logger and debugger is so easy that it's almost ridiculous not to do so. (No longer will you have to pepper your page code with `alert()` statements to trace program logic.)

The `MochiKit.Logging` package includes several features that enable and enhance logging. A simple example is the `setupDBG` function. If you are using Firefox (recommended) and the Firebug extension (also critical for a developer, and available at `https://addons.mozilla.org/en-US/firefox/addon/1843`), you will see a new panel that can be revealed or hidden as needed. In Listing 7-11, the `init` function fires with the `logDebug("Page (re)loaded")` message from the `setupDBG()` method and the following two JavaScript asynchronous HTTP GET calls to the controller to fetch the `Jobs` and `Resource` lists:

```
GET http://localhost:8888/joblistwithicons?tg_format=json
GET http://localhost:8888/resourcelist?tg_format=json
```

These calls are issued from the logic chain `init` ⇨ `refresh` ⇨ `displayJobs` and `displayTrucks`. Figure 7-11 shows the result.

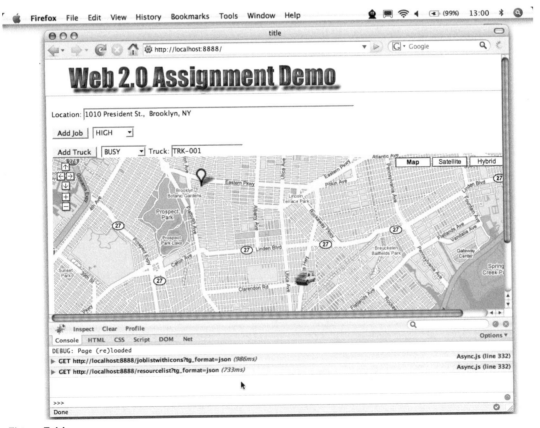

Figure 7-11

The capabilities provided by Firebug are little short of miraculous, giving you a set of tabbed panes for examining console output, stepping through the JavaScript logic, inspecting the Document Object Model (DOM), seeing the application of style sheets, and analyzing the network calls from your page.

Generally, you will see logging outputs to your browser's console. Firefox has this built in, as do Safari on Mac OS/X and Opera. Internet Explorer provides support for this feature via the Microsoft Script Debugger. The easiest way to avoid all cross-browser inconsistencies (actually, Explorer is the only inconsistent one) is to add a call to createLoggingPane(inline=true) in a page you want to debug. This adds a new DOM element at the lowest point in the page and is almost as useful as Firefox.

View: Map Loading

The enabling Google Maps API is loaded with the following script specification (entered after the <head> tag in Listing 7-11):

```
<script    src="http://maps.google.com/maps?file=api&amp;v=2&amp;key=GMapsAPIKey"
   type="text/javascript"/>
```

Note that GMaps API Key in this code is simply a placeholder for an actual valid key. You will have to acquire a good API key from Google (www.google.com/apis/maps/signup.html) in order to include the JavaScript.

After the JavaScipt library is visible to the page, you use the following simple call from loadMap():

```
if (GBrowserIsCompatible()) {
        __map = new GMap2(document.getElementById("map"));
}
```

and replace the map DOM element map (see Listing 7-12) with the actual map.

There are some additional features added to the map in the online version of the code that are not shown here, such as the navigation controls. Now your page has a map, courtesy of init ⇨ refresh ⇨ loadMap. Next, you'll get the Jobs and Truck resources from the controller, and then overlay the map with markers in the correct locations.

View: Getting the Data

The displayTrucks and displayJobs methods are very similar in their construction. They both create an AJAX call, assign it to a deferred object, and then assign a callback to that object. In displayTrucks, the code looks like this:

```
var deferred = loadJSONDoc("${tg.url('/resourcelist', tg_format='json')}");
deferred.addCallback(showTrucks);
```

What happens here is that (in general terms) you don't care precisely when the data result actually comes back from the controller. Therefore, you set a deferred callback for sometime in the (hopefully near) future so that when the event does complete and data are returned, a control thread will ensure transfer to showTrucks. Figure 7-12 (shown later in the chapter) depicts both the outbound calls in the debugger pane and the result overlaid onto the map.

In the asynchronous call to the controller, you are calling loadJSONDoc. A possible alternative form is doSimpleHttpRequest with a URL argument. JSON was specified in the controller as shown in the following code snippet from Listing 7-3:

```
@expose()
@expose("json")
def resourcelist(self):
```

As a result, the following call is constructed and issued by the page:

```
http://localhost:8888/resourcelist?tg_format=json
```

And showTrucks is assured that the return data will be JSON.

View: Displaying the Map Data

Both the showJobs and showTrucks methods shown in Listing 7-12 have similar logic. The method signature expects the argument to be an associative array formatted exactly as shown previously in Listing 7-2. They add truck and job icons to the map in a separate layer above the tiled map background and at the appropriate latitudes and longitudes.

Listing 7-12: The showJobs and showTrucks methods of controlpanel.kid

```
<head>
...

function showJobs(result){
  for (var i = 0; i < result["jobs"].length; i++){
    var jobData = result["jobs"][i];
    var location = jobData[1];
    var latLng = new GLatLng(Number(jobData[2]), Number(jobData[3]));
    var priority = jobData[4];
    var priority_icon = jobData[5];
    var job = new Job(location, latLng, priority);
    __jobs.push(job);
    var marker = hereMarker(latLng,  location, priority, priority_icon);
    __map.addOverlay(marker);
  }
  if (__jobs.length > 0){
    __map.setCenter(__jobs[__jobs.length-1].pointOfJob, 13);
  }
}
```

```
function showTrucks(result){
  for (var i = 0; i < result["resources"].length; i++){
    var truckData = result["resources"][i];
    var name = truckData[1];
    var location = truckData[2];
    var latLng = new GLatLng(Number(truckData[3]), Number(truckData[4]));
    var marker = createTruckMarker(latLng, name);
    var truck = new Truck(location, latLng, name, marker);
    __trucks.push(truck);
    GEvent.addListener(marker, "dragstart", function() {
      __oldTruckLocation = this.getPoint();
      __map.closeInfoWindow();
    });
    // A new event that returns the new latlng when the drag ends
    GEvent.addListener(marker, "dragend", onTruckDrag);
    __map.addOverlay(marker);
  }
}
...
</head>
```

As this listing shows, after the data is returned from the call, you access the contents of the array in a `for` loop. The array of truck data is referenced by `result["resources"]`. This was returned from the following controller method (discussed in detail previously in the section "The Resourcelist Method"):

```
return dict(resources=[[r.id, r.name, r.location.address, r.location.lat,
       r.location.lon] for r in Resource.select(orderBy=Resource.q.name)]
```

So now you can simply pick off the elements from the data. These are used to construct a `Truck` object in JavaScript (not shown here, but available online at www.wrox.com with the complete application) to manage the onscreen user interaction. The front-to-back chaining of the page logic is now complete:

`view:init` ⇨ `view:refresh` ⇨ `view:displayJobs` ⇨ `controller:joblist` ⇨ (Deferred) `view:` `showJobs` and `view:init` ⇨ `view:refresh` ⇨ `view:displayTrucks` ⇨ `controller:resourcelist` ⇨ (Deferred) `view:showTrucks`.

View: Displaying the Table Data

A final task is to show the tabular data on demand. The `master.kid` template creates a button and fires the `toggleResourceList` JavaScript method as follows:

```
<button onClick="toggleResourceList()">Resources</button>
```

Listing 7-13 shows the event chaining that results from a user click.

Listing 7-13: Show and hide effects method in controlpanel.kid

```
function toggleResourceList() {
  if ($('resourcelist_results').style.display == "none") {
    getResourceList();
    appear('resourcelist_results')
  } else {
    dropOut('resourcelist_results')
  }
}
function getResourceList(){
    var d = loadJSONDoc("${tg.url('/resourcelist', tg_format='json')}");
    d.addCallback(buildResourceTBL);
}
function buildResourceTBL(result) {
    var resourceTBL = TABLE({'border': '2px', 'bgcolor':"#eee"},
        THEAD(null,
            tblRow_display(["ID", "Resource", "Location", "LAT", "LON"])),
        TFOOT(null,
            tblRow_display(["ID", "Resource", "Location", "LAT", "LON"])),
        TBODY(null,
            map(tblRow_display, result["resources"]))
        );
    replaceChildNodes("resourcelist_results", resourceTBL);
    var resHeading = H1("Resources");
    insertSiblingNodesBefore(resourceTBL, resHeading);
}
```

The first job of the `toggleResourceList` method is to determine whether the table is visible or not. When the table is not visible, it reloads the table through an AJAX call to the controller, gets the list of truck resources via `getResourceList`, and routes the deferred call to `buildResourceTBL`, which creates the table. Additionally, if the table is not visible, `toggleResourceList` uses the MochiKit `appear` effect to make the table appear; otherwise, it uses the `dropOut` visual effect to make it go away.

The `buildResourceTBL` method uses MochiKit syntax to create the table and display it as shown in Figure 7-12.

The final logic in the `buildResourceTBL` method manipulates the page DOM to replace the `resourcelist_results` <div> with the newly constructed table.

Adding RSS Feed Capability

A final item to be covered is the ease with which TurboGears enables a page to generate a Really Simple Syndication (RSS) feed. The `FeedController` class included with TurboGears makes this downright simple. To take advantage of RSS publishing for your site, just include the following line in your `controllers.py` file:

```
class Root(controllers.RootController):
    ...
    feed = Feed()
    ...
```

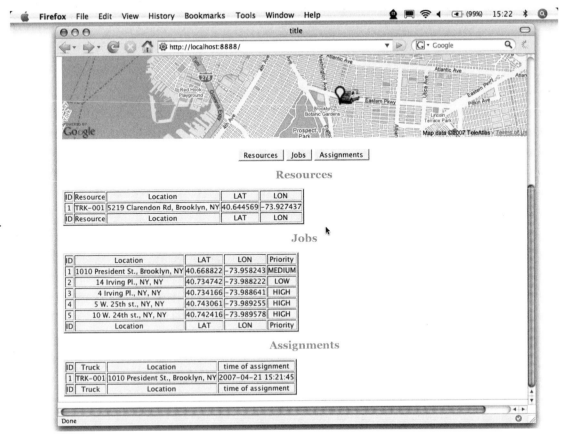

Figure 7-12

Then create a simple `Feed` class as shown in Listing 7-14.

Listing 7-14: Feed.py

```
from turbogears.feed import FeedController
from datetime import datetime
class Feed(FeedController):
  def get_feed_data(self):
    entries = []
    fakeFeed = {}
    fakeFeed["updated"] = datetime.now()
    fakeFeed["title"] = "All your base"
    fakeFeed["published"]=  datetime.now()
    fakeFeed["link"] = "http://127.0.0.1:8888/truckV4/1"
    fakeFeed["author"] = {"name":"dana_virtual", "uri":"bbn.com"}
    fakeFeed["summary"] = "Lorum ipsum"
    entrys.append(fakeFeed)
    return dict(
```

(continued)

Listing 7-14 *(continued)*

```
        title="Controller RSS Feeds",
        link="http://127.0.0.1:8888/truckV4/1",
        author = {"name":"Dana Moore","email":"dana_virtual@yahoo.com"},
        id = "http://127.0.0.1:8888:8888",
        subtitle="Controller alerts",
        entries = entrys
    )
```

Figure 7-13 shows the effects of calling a URL such as `localhost:8080/feed`.

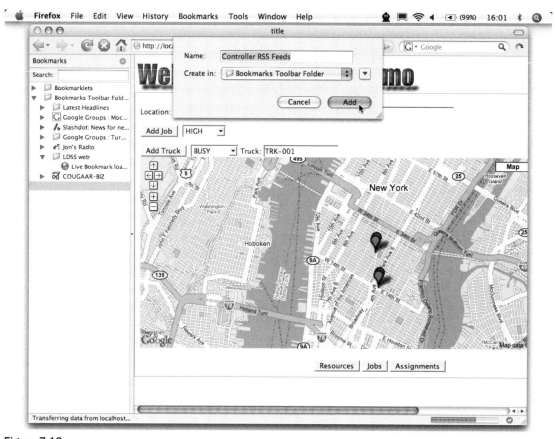

Figure 7-13

In this figure, the RSS feed has been offered, but the Firefox Bookmark sidebar has not yet been populated with the Controller RSS Feeds. When the user clicks Add, the feed is created and added to the Firefox sidebar. Then when the user selects the "All your base" article, the feed contents are displayed as shown in Figure 7-14.

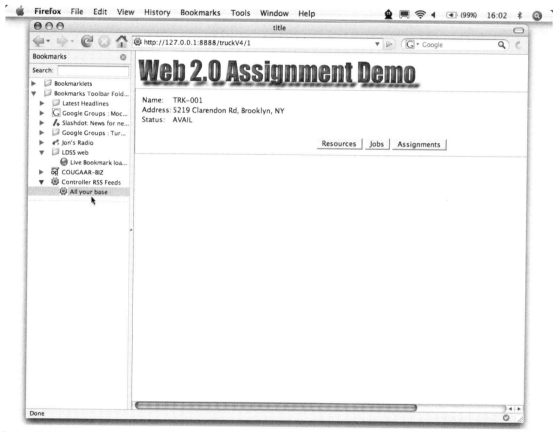

Figure 7-14

Summary

In this chapter you took apart and reassembled a fairly complex real-life application and peered deeply into the inner mechanisms of TurboGears. As stated early in the chapter, it's not always easy to understand the flow control of a framework-generated and -hosted Rich Internet Application (RIA). Although the effort may have seemed tortuous, you now have a much deeper understanding of how TurboGears applications work, and where to begin looking when things don't work as you expected them to. That inevitably turns out to be well worth the effort you expend. Chapter 8, "Dblog: A Blog Implemented in Django," begins coverage of Django, a framework more attuned to building user portal and content management systems. Django uses a very different but no less effective programming model. Grab your favorite beverage and buckle up for the ride.

Part III
Django

Dblog: A Blog Implemented in Django

Look with favor upon a bold beginning

—**Virgil** in *The Georgics*

Django is a high-level Python web framework that supports rapid development and elegant design. In this chapter you'll see how Django works to automate production of common web-development tasks so that the developer can concentrate on higher-level application issues instead of low-level data handling. You'll see how Django supports the model-view-controller (MVC) separation of concerns in a way that makes development easier and more productive.

Django Design Philosophies

The developers of Django call it "The Web framework for perfectionists with deadlines." We take this to mean that clean design and adherence to some standard practices are not the enemy of rapid development, but are required for it. With Django, as with most frameworks, you can follow its model of how to design and structure your code and reap the benefits of the framework, or you can fight with the framework and take your chances. So it's worthwhile to examine some of the Django design philosophies.

The components that come in the Django stack have been designed with specific software best practices in mind. Most of these are of the motherhood and apple pie variety, but explicitly stating them helps clarify the design. You examine the following important Django design philosophies in this section (for the full set of Django design philosophies, consult the Django web site at http://www.djangoproject.com/documentation/design_philosophies/):

❑ **Loose coupling:** Django aims to make each element of its stack independent of the others. For example, there should be no references or dependencies between the template processor and the URL redirector; and the data model classes shouldn't need to know about HTML. A design like this enables you to swap out parts of the stack if you choose without requiring a big rewrite of the other pieces. Even if you plan to use the standard Django stack, loose coupling makes learning the stack easier because you can learn each element in isolation. More importantly, loose coupling makes the code easier to maintain. The more loosely the stack components are coupled, the less likely a change to one will break another in unforeseen ways.

❑ **Less code:** It stands to reason that the less code you have to write, the faster you can write it, and Django is very much about rapid development. It's also true that the less code you have to write, the fewer bugs you'll write. Because Django is implemented in Python, it can take full advantage of Python's ability to pack a lot of functionality into a few lines of code. Django also tries to minimize the amount of boilerplate code that has to be written by providing code and template inheritance for common functions.

❑ **Quick development:** The developers of Django built it to support a news website that has rapid and frequent changes. "The Web framework for perfectionists with deadlines" implies that every design decision should support rapid and robust development.

❑ **Don't Repeat Yourself (DRY):** Every concept should be expressed in exactly one place. We're all familiar with systems that require you to make consistent changes in multiple places, and those changes are prone to error. If you find yourself typing the same thing in two different places, there's probably a better way to do it.

❑ **Explicit is better than implicit:** The framework shouldn't do too much magic. That is, the code should be compact, but not depend on obscure tricks that may make it difficult to read and maintain by developers who aren't seasoned veterans.

❑ **Consistency:** A consistent framework is one that operates as expected at all levels. If you know how to operate one aspect of the framework, learning another aspect is easy when they both use consistent concepts.

An Example: A Simple Blog Site

As you saw in Chapter 3, the best way to learn a framework is to put it to use, so in this section you develop a simple blogging website. This site will do the following:

❑ Show a list of all blog entries

❑ Allow an author to submit a new entry

❑ Allow readers to comment on each entry

Initializing the Project

Once you've installed Django (see the appendix for details), it's easy to set up a new project. Just use the `django-admin.py` command to make an empty project skeleton. Pick a place on the file system for the code to live. Note that the code doesn't need to be in your web server's document root, and probably shouldn't be there to avoid any security issues. You sure don't want a server misconfiguration to result in your source code being sent to web browsers.

Run this command at a shell to create a new project called `simpleblog`:

```
django-admin.py startproject simpleblog
```

If successful, this command prints no output, but creates a subdirectory called `simpleblog` with four little files in it. These files are described in the following table.

File	Description
__init__.py	This is an empty file that identifies this directory as a Python package.
manage.py	You run this file from the command line to administer the project. It actually just calls `django-admin.py` after initializing some project-specific configuration.
settings.py	This file contains configuration information about things like database connections and file locations.
urls.py	Django uses this file to map the URL of web requests to specific Python methods.

Django comes with a built-in web server that is very convenient for development. Just to see that everything is working, try running the empty project using the `runserver` command of `manage.py`. Change to the `simpleblog` directory and run the command like this:

```
C:\simpleblog>python manage.py runserver
Validating models...
0 errors found.
Django version 0.95.1, using settings 'simpleblog.settings'
Development server is running at http://127.0.0.1:8000/
Quit the server with CTRL-BREAK.
```

Now that the development server is running, load that URL into a browser and you'll see something like Figure 8-1. (Note that the default port for the development server is 8000, not 80).

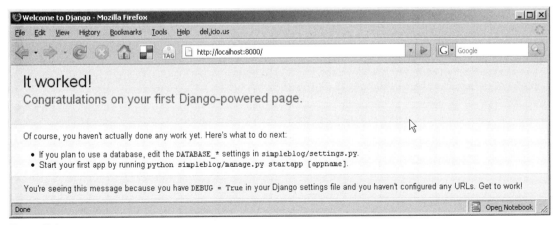

Figure 8-1

For this example, configure the database to use a SQLite database file by editing the `settings.py` file in the `simpleblog` directory. There are only two settings required to use SQLite, so find the section of `settings.py` that defines the database connection and set DATABASE_ENGINE and DATABASE_NAME to look like this:

```
MANAGERS = ADMINS
DATABASE_ENGINE = 'sqlite3'      # 'postgresql', 'mysql', 'sqlite3' or 'ado_mssql'.
DATABASE_NAME = r'databasefile'  # Or path to database file if using sqlite3.
DATABASE_USER = ''               # Not used with sqlite3.
DATABASE_PASSWORD = ''           # Not used with sqlite3.
DATABASE_HOST = ''               # Not used with sqlite3.
DATABASE_PORT = ''               # Not used with sqlite3.
```

This tells Django to use a `sqlite3` database stored in a file called `databasefile`.

Next, initialize the database with the `manage.py syncdb` command. If this is the first time you've run `syncdb`, it will create the database tables used by Django and ask you to create a superuser. Create one and remember the password for later. Here's an example of what you'll see when you initialize the Django database:

```
C:\simpleblog>python manage.py syncdb
Creating table auth_message
Creating table auth_group
Creating table auth_user
Creating table auth_permission
Creating many-to-many tables for Group model
Creating many-to-many tables for User model
Creating table django_content_type
Creating table django_session
Creating table django_site
You just installed Django's auth system, which means you
    don't have any superusers defined.
Would you like to create one now? (yes/no): yes
Username: root
E-mail address: root@root.com
Password:
Password (again):
Superuser created successfully.
Adding permission 'message | Can add message'
Adding permission 'message | Can change message'
Adding permission 'message | Can delete message'
Adding permission 'group | Can add group'
Adding permission 'group | Can change group'
Adding permission 'group | Can delete group'
Adding permission 'user | Can add user'
Adding permission 'user | Can change user'
Adding permission 'user | Can delete user'
Adding permission 'permission | Can add permission'
Adding permission 'permission | Can change permission'
Adding permission 'permission | Can delete permission'
Adding permission 'content type | Can add content type'
Adding permission 'content type | Can change content type'
```

```
Adding permission 'content type | Can delete content type'
Adding permission 'session | Can add session'
Adding permission 'session | Can change session'
Adding permission 'session | Can delete session'
Creating example.com Site object
Adding permission 'site | Can add site'
Adding permission 'site | Can change site'
Adding permission 'site | Can delete site'
C:\simpleblog>
```

Initializing the Application

Like the default page in Figure 8-1 says, you haven't really done any work yet. You'll start by defining the database properties in the settings.py file and then creating an application and the model classes to go with it.

First create the application called dblog (which stands for *Django blog*) by running the following command in the simpleblog directory.

```
python manage.py startapp dblog
```

The startapp command produces no output, but creates a subdirectory named dblog containing the three files described in the following table.

File	Description
__init__.py	As with the project, this is an empty file that identifies this directory as a Python package.
models.py	This is the file in which you'll code your model classes.
views.py	This is the file in which you'll code your views.

Next you need to add your new application to the Django project by adding it to INSTALLED_APPS in the settings.py file. Toward the bottom of the settings.py file, change INSTALLED_APPS to look like this:

```
INSTALLED_APPS = (
    'django.contrib.auth',
    'django.contrib.contenttypes',
    'django.contrib.sessions',
    'django.contrib.sites',
    'django.contrib.admin',
    'simpleblog.dblog',
)
```

Note that you're also adding the Django admin interface as you did in Chapter 3.

Creating the Model

The class structure for the model is shown in Figure 8-2.

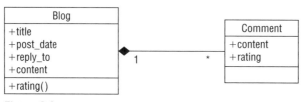

Figure 8-2

This model contains just the following two simple classes:

❑ **Blog:** Represents an entry blog site and contains the four attributes described in the following table.

Attribute	Description
title	The title of the entry
post_date	The datetime at which the entry was created
reply_to	The e-mail address of the posting author
content	The text of the blog entry

The Blog class also includes a rating() operation, which computes the average of the ratings in the comments list from 1 (bad) to 5 (good). You'll often find it handy to have operations in your model classes to compute values based on the model's attributes.

❑ **Comment:** Represents the comments made on a blog entry by visitors to the site. It contains the two attributes described in the following table.

Attribute	Description
content	The text of the comment.
rating	The rating given to the blog entry by the commenting visitor. This can range from 1 to 5.

To create this Django model, enter the Python code shown in Listing 8-1.

Listing 8-1: Dblog model classes

```
1    """Django model classes for a simple Blog site
2
3        This example shows a one-to-many relationship
         between aBlog and its Comments and various
4        computed fields.
5    """
6
7    from django.db import models
8
9    class Blog(models.Model):
10       """The class representing an entry in the blog"""
11
12       """The title or subject of the blog entry"""
13       title = models.CharField(maxlength=128)
14
15       """The date that the post was created"""
16       post_date = models.DateTimeField('date posted')
17
18       """The email address of the posting author"""
19       reply_to = models.EmailField()
20
21       """The actual text content of the posting"""
22       content = models.TextField()
23
24       def rating(self):
25           """Compute the average rating based
                on the comments received"""
26           comments = self.comment_set.all()
27
28           # Don't divide by zero
29           if len(comments) == 0:
30               return "(unrated)"
31
32           sum = 0.0
33           for c in comments:
34               sum = sum + c.rating
35           average = float(sum)/len(comments)
36           return "%.2f"%average
37
38       """The possible ratings for each blog entry"""
39       RATING_CHOICES = (
40                   (1 , 'Lame'),
41                   (2 , 'Weak'),
42                   (3 , 'OK'),
43                   (4 , 'Nice'),
44                   (5 , 'Rocks'),
45                   )
46       """Empty class enables the Django
             admin web interface"""
```

(continued)

Listing 8-1 *(continued)*

```
47        class Admin:
48          pass
49
50        """String representation is used by the
              Django admin interface"""
51        def __str__(self):
52            return "Blog(title = '%s')"%(self.title)
53
54    class Comment(models.Model):
55
56        in_reference_to = models.ForeignKey(Blog)
57        content = models.TextField(maxlength=256)
58        rating = models.IntegerField(choices=Blog.RATING_CHOICES)
59
60
61        def ratingText(self):
62            """Return this comment's rating as a text
63                string rather than an integer"""
64          return Blog.RATING_CHOICES[self.rating-1][1]
65
66        """Empty class enables the Django admin
              web interface"""
67        class Admin:
68          pass
69
70        def __str__(self):
71            """String representation is used by the
                Django admin interface"""
72            return "Comment(content = '%s', rating = ←
                    %s)"% \
73                    (self.content, str(self.rating))
```

This listing defines the two classes that make up the model: Blog (lines 9 through 52) and Comment (lines 54 through 73). The model's Blog class is defined as follows:

❑ Line 7 imports the django.db.models package, which includes the models.Model superclass that is required for Django models.

❑ Line 9 starts the definition of the Blog class and declares it a subclass of models.Model.

❑ Line 13 defines the first attribute of the Blog object: title. This is defined as a character field with a maximum length (maxlength) of 128 characters. maxlength will be used to create the SQL statement necessary to create the data column in the database defined in the settings.py file (which is sqlite3 in this case).

❑ Line 16 defines the post_data attribute as a DateTime object. The 'date posted' string is a human-readable name that will be used in the Django admin interface instead of the field's identifier name.

❑ The e-mail address of the poster is stored in the reply_to attribute (line 19), and the free-form text of the blog entry is stored in the content attribute (line 22). The Django object-relational mapping (ORM) code maps all of the Blog class's attributes directly into columns in a database table.

- ❑ The `rating()` method starts at line 24, loops through all of the attached comments (`self.comment_set.all()`), and computes the average rating.

- ❑ `RATING_CHOICES` (lines 39 through 45) defines the set of ratings that commenters can assign to the blog entry. This list is used by the view methods to build the appropriate HTML `<select>` input.

- ❑ Lines 47 and 48 define an inner `Admin` class that tells the code that generates the Django `admin` web interface that the Blog class should be represented on the `admin` interface.

- ❑ Lines 51 and 52 define the Python-standard __str__ method that is used to get a human-readable string representation of this object.

The `Comment` class is similar to the `Blog` class, but here are a few differences worth pointing out:

- ❑ Line 56 uses the `models.ForeignKey` class to identify the many-to-one relationship between this class and the `Blog` class. Django will automatically create the columns and constraints necessary to implement this in the database.

- ❑ At line 58, you define an attribute to hold the rating associated with this comment as an `Integer` field. Because this field is constrained to the values 1 through 5, you use the optional `choices` argument to provide a list of legal values for the integer. Later in this chapter, you'll see how this list is used by the `admin` interface and your own views.

- ❑ Lines 61 through 64 define a convenience method that you can use however you want. The model is just Python code, so you're free to add whatever makes life easier.

Now that you've coded the model classes, you need to load them into the database. Run the `manage.py syncdb` command again to synchronize the database with the model classes. This creates the database tables for your two new classes. If you're curious about what SQL commands were run to make the tables, you can use the `manage.py sql` command to show the table creation commands as follows:

```
C:\simpleblog>python manage.py sql dblog
BEGIN;
CREATE TABLE "dblog_blog" (
    "id" integer NOT NULL PRIMARY KEY,
    "title" varchar(128) NOT NULL,
    "post_date" datetime NOT NULL,
    "reply_to" varchar(75) NOT NULL,
    "content" text NOT NULL
);
CREATE TABLE "dblog_comment" (
    "id" integer NOT NULL PRIMARY KEY,
    "in_reference_to_id" integer NOT NULL REFERENCES "dblog_blog" ("id"),
    "content" text NOT NULL,
    "rating" integer NOT NULL
);
COMMIT;
```

The `django.db.models` package includes several field classes that you'll find useful for creating your data models. The following table briefly describes the most common classes. Consult the online Django documentation at `www.djangoproject.com/documentation/model_api/` for more details.

Field Class	Description
AutoField	An integer auto-increment field as supported by most databases. You probably won't need to use this because Django automatically creates a primary key field unless you tell it not to. The id fields in the two tables created in the previous SQL are examples of this type of field.
BooleanField	A field that takes a value of True or False, just like you'd expect.
CharField	A string of some maximum length. For a large amount of text, use a TextField instead. A maxlength argument is required.
DateField	A field for a date. Two optional arguments, auto_now and auto_now_add, cause the field to be set to the current time when the object is modified or created, respectively.
DateTimeField	A field that holds the date and the time. It has the same optional arguments as DateField.
EmailField	A CharField that is constrained to be a valid e-mail address. The maximum length is fixed at 75 characters.
FloatField	This class represents a floating-point number.
IntegerField	This class represents an integer number.
PhoneNumberField	A CharField that is constrained to be in the format of a valid U.S. phone number.
TextField	A large text field of indeterminate length.
TimeField	A field that holds the time of day. It has the same optional arguments as DateField.
URLField	A field for a URL. If the optional argument verify_exists is True, URLField will try to verify that the URL exists.
XMLField	A TextField that verifies that its contents make a valid XML document.
ForeignKey	Defines a many-to-one relationship between two model classes. You saw an example of this in the Comment class in Listing 8-1.
ManyToManyField	Defines a many-to-many relationship between two model classes.
OneToOneField	Defines a one-to-one relationship between two model classes. The Django developers discourage the use of the OneToOneField, because it's expected to change soon.

In addition to the options listed in this table, all Field classes share a common set of options that you may find useful. For all field types except the relationship fields, the first optional argument is a positional argument that defines a human-readable name. You saw examples of a few options in Listing 8-1, and the following table describes the important ones. Again, for the complete list, consult the online Django documentation at www.djangoproject.com/documentation/model_api/.

Field Class	Description
null	If True, allow null values in the database for this field.
blank	If True, allow this field to be empty.
choices	A list or tuple of allowed values for this field. You saw an example of this in the rating field of the Comment class in Listing 8-1.
db_column	The name of the database column used for this field. The default is the same as the field name.
unique	If True, Django ensures that this field's value is unique among all instances of the class.
unique_for_date	If True, Django ensures that this field's value is unique among all instances of the class that share the same date value for the referenced field. For example, if you added unique_for_date="post_date" as an argument to the reply_to field, no more than one entry by that author could be entered per day.
unique_for_month	Similar to unique_for_date, this allows no more than one common value of the field per month. If you added unique_for_month="post_date" as an argument to the reply_to field, no more than one entry by that author could be entered per month.
unique_for_year	Similar to unique_for_date and unique_for_month this allows no more than one common value of the field per month. If you added unique_for_year="post_date" as an argument to the reply_to field, no more than one entry by that author could be entered per year.

Exploring the Model with Django's Admin Interface

Now that you've created the model, you can use Django's built-in admin interface to view and edit the model. Run the development server using the manage.py runserver command like this.

```
python manage.py runserver
```

Then open a web browser, navigate to http://localhost:8000/admin, and log in using the username and password you configured earlier. This should display the page shown in Figure 8-3.

Notice at the bottom that Blogs and Comments are now available for administration. This means you can use the Django admin interface to create, edit, and delete blog entries and comments. Try adding a blog and some comments to see how it works.

First, click the Add link next to Blogs to add a new entry. The Django admin interface creates a form based on the data types of the Blog fields, as shown in Figure 8-4.

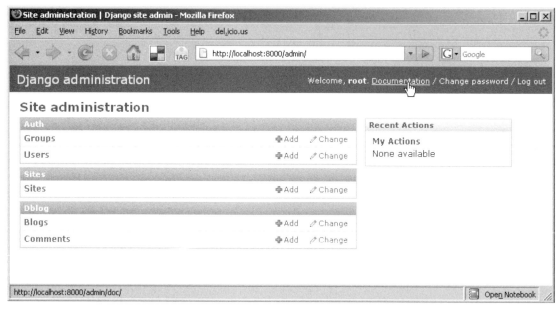

Figure 8-3

Figure 8-4

The Blog class doesn't allow any of the fields to be null (by setting the optional null argument to True), so fill in something for each of the fields and click Save. You should see a page that shows the blog successfully saved, similar to Figure 8-5.

Notice that the admin interface used the Blog class's __str__ method to display the edit link for the new entry. If you click that link, you'll get the same edit form shown in Figure 8-5, with an additional option to delete the Blog.

Figure 8-5

Now navigate back to the top-level administration page at http://localhost:8000/admin and try adding some comments. This time, click the Add link next to Comments to add some comments. You should see a form for editing a comment, as shown in Figure 8-6.

Notice how Django recognized that the In Reference To field is a foreign key reference to a Blog, so it uses a <select> input populated with Blog objects. It also recognizes the choices option to the rating field and uses a <select> there as well. Click Save and Add Another to commit the changes, and then add another comment the same way. You should see a page like Figure 8-7.

So you can create, edit, and delete Blog and Comment objects from the Django admin interface, which is pretty cool functionality "for free," but now it's time to add some custom views.

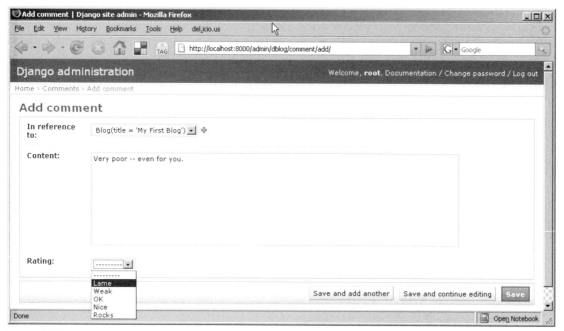

Figure 8-6

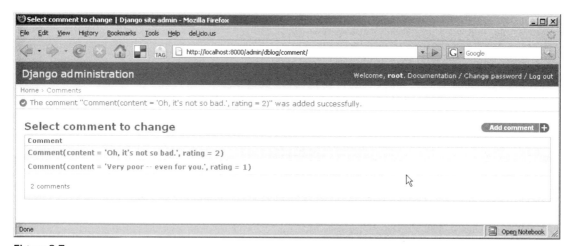

Figure 8-7

Creating the Views

As mentioned in Chapter 3, Django *views* are similar to what other MVC frameworks might call *controllers* but, setting aside semantics, how they work is what's important. Django views are Python methods that usually work with a template to generate an HTML page. In this section, you'll build Django views that enable the user to display, add, and edit blog entries and comments.

Adding the index view method

Earlier in this chapter, the `manage.py startapp` command created an empty file named `views.py` to contain the view methods. Now you need to add the index method in Listing 8-2 to `views.py` as the default blog entry list view.

Listing 8-2: The index view method

```
def index(request):
    """Generate the context for the main summary page"""
    latest_blog_list = Blog.objects.all().order_by('-post_date')[:3]
    return render_to_response('templates/index.html',
                    {'latest_blog_list': latest_blog_list})
```

This two-line method first uses `Blog.objects.all()` to retrieve a list of `Blog` objects. Then it uses `order_by()` to sort the list, passing the `'-post_date'` argument to tell `order_by()` to order the `Blog` objects in descending order using the `post_date` field. The Python list-slicing operation `[:3]` yields a list containing only the three most recent blog entries.

Next, this method uses the Django `render_to_response` function to populate a template from a dictionary. In this case, the template is called `templates/index.html`, and the dictionary contains one entry, `latest_blog_list`, for use by the template. That's all there is to the view method.

Your index template, shown in Listing 8-3, is a little more interesting. Enter this code into the `index.html` template.

Listing 8-3: The index template

```
1   <!DOCTYPE html PUBLIC "-//W3C//DTD XHTML 1.0 Strict//EN"
2       "http://www.w3.org/TR/xhtml1/DTD/xhtml1-strict.dtd">
3   <html xmlns="http://www.w3.org/1999/xhtml"
4       xmlns:v="urn:schemas-microsoft-com:vml">
5
6       <head>
7       <meta http-equiv="Content-Type" content="text/html; charset=utf-8"/>
8
9       <title>Simple Django Blog</title>
10
11      <!-- Load our color and font preferences -->
12      <link rel=StyleSheet href="/scripts/style.css" TYPE="text/css">
13      </head>
14
15      <body>
```

(continued)

Listing 8-3 *(continued)*

```
16    <h1> Simple Django Blog </h1>
17    <hr>
18    <div class="bloglist">
19    {% if latest_blog_list %}
20      <ul>
21      {% for blog in latest_blog_list %}
22        <li> <a href="blog/{{blog.id}}/">{{ blog.title }}</a>
23              Posted on
24              {{ blog.post_date|date:"F j, Y" }}
25              by {{blog.reply_to}}
26        </li>
27
28      {% endfor %}
29      </ul>
30    {% else %}
31      <p>No blogs are available.</p>
32    {% endif %}
33    <p/>
34    </div>
35    <hr>
36    <div class="footerlink">
37    <a href="writeBlog">Add new entry</a>
38    </div>
39
40    </body>
41 </html>
```

The template is an XHTML document with some Django template tags embedded between `{%` and `%}` or between `{{` and `}}`. Lines 1 through 18 are just regular XHTML with no Django template tags. The template processor just passes this text through, unmodified, to the requesting client. The following table lists the most common built-in Django template tags. For the complete reference, consult `www.djangoproject.com/documentation/templates/`.

Template Tag	Description
Block	This tag defines a block that can be overridden by derived templates. You'll learn more about template inheritance in the next chapter.
Comment	Defines a comment. The terminator tag is `{% endcomment %}`.
Debug	This tag causes the template processor to print some debugging information.
extends	Defines the current template as a subclass of another template. You'll learn more about template inheritance in the next chapter.
filter	Passes the variable through a filter. This is similar in function and semantics to Unix pipes.
for	Your basic `for` loop. The terminating tag is `{% endfor %}`.

Template Tag	Description
if	Your basic conditional statement. It supports an optional {% else %} tag. The terminating tag is {% endif %}.
include	Loads and interprets another template in the current context. This is similar to a C #include statement.
load	Loads a set of custom template tags.
now	Displays the current datetime. It can be formatted using the same specifiers as the PHP date() functions.
templatetag	Used to output the text of a template tag, such as {% or }}.

Line 19 in Listing 8-3 is the first line that requires interpretation by the template processor. This is a conditional if statement, so lines 20 through 29 will be processed if the template context latest_blog_list is not None, and line 31 will be processed if latest_blog_list is None.

The blog entries are presented as a bulleted HTML list starting at line 20. Line 21 starts a loop through the blogs in the list. Notice that the loop terminator is the endfor tag at line 28. Each <li> element of the list includes its title as a hypertext link to a detail page, the date of its posting, and the poster's e-mail address.

First look at the link to the detail page:

```
<a href="blog/{{blog.id}}/">{{ blog.title }}</a>
```

The text {{blog.id}} is replaced with the automatically generated private key of the current blog entry, and {{blog.title}} is replaced with the title of the current entry.

Next, line 24 passes the post_date field of the current blog entry through the date template filter to convert it to the desired text format, as follows:

```
{{ blog.post_date|date:"F j, Y" }}
```

The F is replaced by the month name, the j is replaced by the day of the month, and the Y is replaced by the four-digit year. The other options to the date filter are the same as the PHP date() function and can be found at http://php.net/date. The following table lists some of the common Django filters. Consult www.djangoproject.com/documentation/templates/ for the complete list and details.

Template Filter	Description
add	Arithmetic addition.
center	Centers text in a field.
cut	Removes all occurrences of one string from another string.
date	Formats a date using PHP's format specifiers.
dictsort	Sorts a list based on the property given as an argument.
escape	Converts < to &lt, > to &gt, and so on.
first	Takes only the first element in a list.
floatformat	Formats a floating-point number.
length	Returns the length of a list.
lower	Returns a lowercase version of the string
pluralize	Returns the plural suffix if the piped value is not 1. The default is s.
slice	Extracts a sublist from a list the same way Python list slicing does.
stringformat	Formats a string the same way Python string formatting does.
time	Formats the time of day using PHP's format specifiers.
timesince	Calculates and returns a string representation of the difference between now (or any other datetime) and a time in the past.
timeuntil	Calculates and returns a string representation of the difference between now (or any other datetime) and a time in the future.
truncatewords	Returns the first few words of a string.
upper	Returns an uppercase version of the string.
wordcount	Returns the number of words in the piped string.

The last section of the template file (lines 34 through 41 in Listing 8-3) is just plain HTML that makes a link to a page for authoring new blog entries.

Before you can admire your new view into a browser, you still need to configure its URL and tell Django where to find the template. Because the template references a CSS file (line 12 of Listing 8-3), you need to configure the development server to serve static pages as well as Django views. Fortunately, there is a built-in view that serves static files for development. To configure the URLs, edit the `urls.py` file to add a line for the new page and an entry for the static file server like this:

```
from django.conf.urls.defaults import *
urlpatterns = patterns('',
    (r'^simpleblog/$', 'simpleblog.dblog.views.index'),
    (r'^scripts/(?P<path>.*)$',
    'django.views.static.serve',
                        {'document_root': './scripts'}),
    (r'^admin/', include('django.contrib.admin.urls')),
)
```

Next, configure the `settings.py` file to include the new template file in the `TEMPLATE_DIRS` as follows.

```
TEMPLATE_DIRS = (
    # Put strings here, like "/home/html/django_templates".
    # Always use forward slashes, even on Windows.
    '/some/path/here'
)
```

Now load `http://localhost:8000/simpleblog` into a browser to see the blog that you added with the `admin` interface. It should look like Figure 8-8.

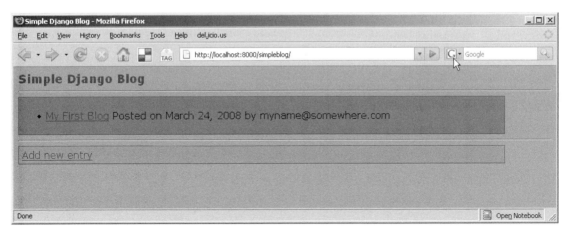

Figure 8-8

That was easy. Notice that My First Blog and Add New Entry are hypertext links. Next you'll code the pages to which these link.

URL Mapping

The link behind My First Blog (the `blog.title`) was generated by line 22 in Listing 8-3, repeated here for ease of reference:

```
22 <li> <a href="blog/{{blog.id}}/">{{ blog.title }}</a>
```

As a result, the link generated for a `blog` with an `id` of 1, for example, would be the URL `http://localhost:8000/simpleblog/blog/1`. Django maps URLs to views using the `urlpatterns` variable defined in `urls.py`. You added a few entries by rote in the examples so far, but it's time to dig into how it works.

The `urlpatterns` variable contains a list of string pairs. The first string in the pair is a Python regular expression that is matched against the requested URL (not including a `protocol://host:port/` specifier such as `http://localhost:8000/`). The second string is the name of the view method that is invoked if the regular expression matches the URL. The regular expressions are tried in the order they appear in the list, so be careful that a pattern early in the list doesn't shadow a pattern later in the list.

Look again at the following pattern, which you used for the blog summary page:

```
(r'^simpleblog/$', 'simpleblog.dblog.views.index'),
```

When the regular expression `"^simpleblog/$"` matches a requested URL, the `simpleblog.dblog.views.index` method is invoked to generate the response. The `^` and `$` are *metacharacters* that match the beginning and end of the URL, respectively, so this pattern will match only a URL of exactly `simpleblog/` and nothing else. The following table lists several metacharacters that you may find useful for URL pattern matching.

Metacharacter	Description
`^` (caret)	Matches the beginning of the string.
`$`	Matches the end of the string.
`.` (period)	Matches any single character.
`*`	Matches zero or more instances of the previous character (or other regular expression).
`?`	Matches one or more instances of the previous character (or other regular expression).
`+`	Matches zero or one instances of the previous character (or other regular expression).
`\d`	Matches a decimal digit.
`\D`	Matches any character except a decimal digit.
`\w`	Matches any alphanumeric character.
`\W`	Matches any character except an alphanumeric character.

Metacharacter	Description
\	Used to escape any metacharacter. For example the regular expression \. would match the string '.'.
(regex)	Anything that matches the regular expression between the parentheses is captured as a group. You use this to extract pieces of the matched string and refer to them by position.
(?P<name>regex)	Anything that matches the regular expression between the parentheses is captured as a group and given the name specified between < and >. You use this to extract pieces of the matched string and refer to them by name.

Regular expressions are a very powerful tool for text processing and should be in every programmer's tool-box. For more information on Python regular expressions, consult www.python.org/doc/howto/.

Next, add a line for the blog detail view page as follows:

```
urlpatterns = patterns('',
    (r'^simpleblog/$', 'simpleblog.dblog.views.index'),
    (r'^simpleblog/blog/(?P<blog_id>\d+)/$', 'simpleblog.dblog.views.readBlog'),
    (r'^scripts/(?P<path>.*)$', 'django.views.static.serve',
                        {'document_root': './scripts'}),
    (r'^admin/', include('django.contrib.admin.urls')),
)
```

Now any URL request that matches the pattern ^simpleblog/blog/(?P<blog_id>\d+)/$ will be routed to the simpleblog.dblog.views.readBlog method (which you haven't written yet). There are three things to note about this regular expression:

❑   The caret at the beginning means that this URL path must start with simpleblog/blog/.

❑   The expression (?P<blog_id>\d+) will match one or more decimal digits (that's the \d+ metacharacter expression) and assign it the name blog_id.

❑   The $ at the end means that there must be nothing else following the blog_id number.

As a result, the readBlog method is called with a named argument blog_id set to the primary key of the blog to be displayed.

Now look at the readBlog view method in Listing 8-4, which you should add to the views.py file.

Listing 8-4: The readBlog view method

```
def readBlog(request, blog_id):
    """Generate the context for the page that displays a
        single blog entry"""
    blog = get_object_or_404(Blog, pk=blog_id)
    return render_to_response('templates/readBlog.html', {'blog': blog})
```

Unlike the previous view method, this method accepts two parameters: the `request` object and the `blog_id`. The `blog_id` is the number extracted from the URL by the regular expression. For example, if the following URL is requested, the `readBlog` method is called with `blog_id=100`:

```
http://localhost:8000/simpleblog/blog/100
```

There are only two lines of code in `readBlog`. The first one uses the Django `get_object_or_404` convenience method, which queries the database for an object by type and query field. It returns the object if it's found; otherwise it throws an exception that causes an HTTP 404 error (Not Found) to be returned to the requestor.

In this case, you're looking up a `Blog` object by primary key (`pk=blog_id`) as follows:

```
blog = get_object_or_404(Blog, pk=blog_id)
```

When the object is retrieved, the method passes it to a template to be rendered and returned to the requestor, like this:

```
return render_to_response('templates/readBlog.html', {'blog': blog})
```

Now you need to write the `readBlog.html` template referenced by that `render_to_response` call. Listing 8-5 shows an example you can use.

Listing 8-5: The blog detail template

```
1   <!DOCTYPE html PUBLIC "-//W3C//DTD XHTML 1.0 Strict//EN"
2       "http://www.w3.org/TR/xhtml1/DTD/xhtml1-strict.dtd">
3   <html xmlns="http://www.w3.org/1999/xhtml"
4       xmlns:v="urn:schemas-microsoft-com:vml">
5
6     <head>
7       <meta http-equiv="Content-Type" content="text/html; charset=utf-8"/>
8
9       <title>Simple Django Blog</title>
10
11      <!-- Load our color and font preferences -->
12      <link rel=StyleSheet href="/scripts/style.css" TYPE="text/css">
13    </head>
14
15    <body>
16
17    <h1>{{ blog.title }}</h1>
18
19    <p>Published on {{blog.post_date|date:"F j, Y"}}</p>
20    <p>Posted by {{blog.reply_to}}</p>
21    <p>Current rating is {{blog.rating}} out of 5</p>
22
23
24    <div class="blogtext">
25
26    {{blog.content}}
27
28    </div>
29    <hr/>
```

```
30    <div class="footerlink">
31      View <a href="comment">{{blog.comment_set.count}}
32        comment{{blog.comment_set.count|pluralize}}</a><br/>
33      Return to <a href="/simpleblog">Top</a><br/>
34
35    </div>
36    </body>
37 </html>
```

Note the following in this listing:

❑   The first 16 lines of this template define the HTML header and are exactly the same as the previous template you saw. Of course, this violates Django's DRY (Don't Repeat Yourself) guidance. You'll see how to avoid this repetition in the next chapter, when you learn about template inheritance.

❑   Lines 17 through 21 pull out several of the Blog fields and insert them into the HTML that the template generates. Line 19 runs the Blog object's post_date field through a date filter in the same way the previous template did. Line 21 calls the Blog object's rating method, which computes the average of all this Blog's comment ratings.

❑   The actual content text of the blog entry is inserted into a <div> at lines 24 through 28.

❑   The template includes a footer (lines 31 through 33) with a couple of links. The link generated by lines 31 and 32 points to a page to view comments. This link uses the pluralize filter to add the plural suffix to the word comment if there are zero comments or more than one comment. The link generated by line 33 just points back to the index page. Figure 8-9 shows what this page looks like rendered in a browser.

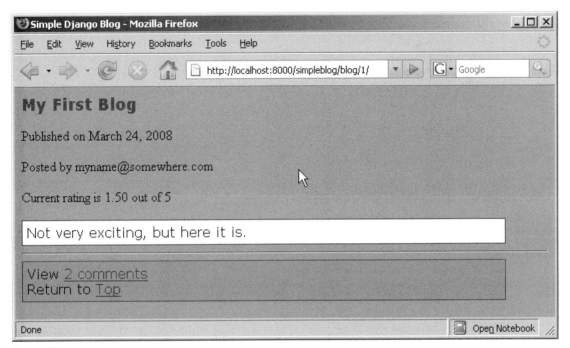

Figure 8-9

The URL in Figure 8-9 ends with /1/, so you know this blog entry has primary key 1. Also notice that the current rating displayed is 1.50, which is the average of the two comment ratings you entered previously (1 and 2).

The two links in the footer area were rendered correctly, too. If you click the Return to Top link, the index page is displayed. However, the View 2 Comments link won't work, because you haven't written that page yet. That's next.

Drilling Down on the Blog Object

As previously mentioned, lines 31 and 32 in Listing 8-5 generate the link for the comment view page. This is relative to `simpleblog/blog/1/`, so the full URL for this blog entry is as follows:

```
http://localhost:8000/simpleblog/blog/1/comment/
```

Add an entry to `urlpatterns` in `urls.py` to match this URL. Remember that you need to extract the blog primary key from the middle of the URL. Here's an example that works:

```
(r'^simpleblog/blog/(?P<blog_id>\d+)/comment/$', 'simpleblog.dblog.views.comment'),
```

This is like the URL pattern you added for the `Blog` detail page with the addition of the `/comment/` string after the `blog_id`.

These URLs Look Funny

You might be wondering why these URLs look different than most — they don't use URL query parameters. Here is one common way to encode the blog ID in a request:

```
http://localhost:8000/simpleblog/blog?id=100
```

URL parameters are ignored by the `urlpatterns` regular expression processing and are not often used in Django applications. You can extract the query parameters from the request object passed to the view method, but it's usually easier to have the regular expression extract parameters from the URL itself.

Next, write the `simpleblog.dblog.views.comment` method invoked by this URL pattern, as shown in Listing 8-6.

Listing 8-6: The comment list view method

```
def comment(request, blog_id):
    """Generate the context for the page that displays the
       comments for a particular blog entry"""
    blog = get_object_or_404(Blog, pk=blog_id)
    return render_to_response('templates/comment.html',
                    {'comments': blog.comment_set.all(),
                     'blog': blog})
```

This method looks a lot like the `readBlog` method you saw in Listing 8-4. It uses the `get_object_or_404` method to find the requested `Blog` object, and then calls `render_to_response` to render the template. The context for this template contains two objects: the `Blog` object (called `blog`) and the list of comments on that `Blog` (called `comments`). This view method looks so much like the others that it seems to violate the DRY principle again. In the next chapter you'll see how Django's generic views can help in these cases.

Enter the `comment.html` template as shown in Listing 8-7.

Listing 8-7: The comment template

```
1   <!DOCTYPE html PUBLIC "-//W3C//DTD XHTML 1.0 Strict//EN"
2       "http://www.w3.org/TR/xhtml1/DTD/xhtml1-strict.dtd">
3   <html xmlns="http://www.w3.org/1999/xhtml"
4       xmlns:v="urn:schemas-microsoft-com:vml">
5
6     <head>
7       <meta http-equiv="Content-Type" content="text/html; charset=utf-8"/>
8
9       <title>Simple Django Blog</title>
10
11      <!-- Load our color and font preferences -->
12      <link rel=StyleSheet href="/scripts/style.css" TYPE="text/css">
13    </head>
14
15    <body>
16      <h1> Comments on "{{blog.title}}" </h1>
17      <hr>
18      <div class="commentlist">
19
20        {% if comments %}
21          <ul>
22          {% for comment in comments %}
23            <li>
24              [{{comment.ratingText}}] --
25              {{ comment.content }}
26
27            </li>
28
29          {% endfor %}
30          </ul>
31        {% else %}
32            <p>No comments on this entry.</p>
33        {% endif %}
34      </div>
35      <hr/>
36      <div class="footerlink">
37
38        Add a <a href="add">comment</a> <br/>
39        Return to <a href="..">{{blog.title}} </a> <br/>
40        Return to <a href="/simpleblog">Top</a> <br/>
41
42      </div>
43    </body>
44  </html>
```

The first 13 lines of this template define the HTML header. The first template operation is at line 16, where the title of the `Blog` is printed in an `<H1>` heading. Line 20 tests to see if there are any comments. If there are no comments, the `else` clause (which starts at line 31) prints "No comments on this entry." Otherwise, the loop (which starts at line 22) cycles through all of the `Comment` objects and prints their rating text and contents as list elements.

This page's footer (lines 36 through 42) contains three links. The first one links to a page in which the user can add a comment. It is a relative URL `add` link, so the full URL from this position for blog_id `100` would be as follows:

```
http://localhost:8000/simpleblog/blog/100/comment/add
```

The next link is a link back to the main `Blog` view, using the title of the `Blog` as the link text. The third link in the footer links back to the `Blog` summary list page. Figure 8-10 shows the comment view page for this example.

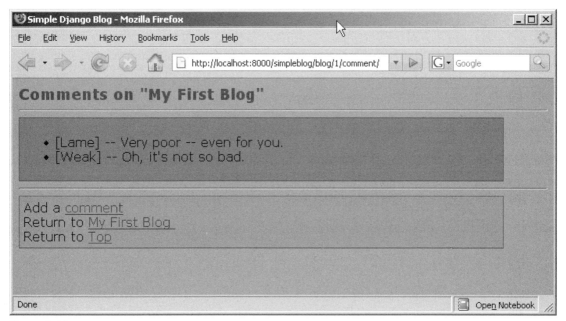

Figure 8-10

Form Processing

Now that you've written the pages to view the blogs and comments, you'll need to write some pages for composing those blogs and comments. Starting with the `Blog` summary page previously shown in Figure 8-8, notice that "Add a New Entry" is a hypertext link. In the `index.html` template, you defined this link to point to `http://localhost:8000/simpleblog/writeBlog`, so now you need to define a `urlpattern`, view method, and template file for that page.

Because the page doesn't reference any particular data, the `urlpattern` entry is a simple regular expression. Add the following line to `urlpatterns` in `urls.py`:

```
(r'^simpleblog/writeBlog/$', 'simpleblog.dblog.views.writeBlog'),
```

This should look familiar by now. A URL request of `http://localhost:8000/simpleblog/writeBlog/` will get routed to the view method `simpleblog.dblog.views.writeBlog`. The regular expression captures no parameters, so `writeBlog` will only need to accept the request parameter.

Enter the `writeBlog` view as shown in Listing 8-8.

Listing 8-8: The blog entry view method

```
def writeBlog(request):
    """No context for this page.
       Just render the template"""
    return render_to_response('templates/blogEntry.html')
```

This template has no context to render, so this could even be a static page rather than a template. Listing 8-9 shows the `blogEntry.html` file that you can use.

Listing 8-9: The blog entry template

```
1  <!DOCTYPE html PUBLIC "-//W3C//DTD XHTML 1.0 Strict//EN"
2      "http://www.w3.org/TR/xhtml1/DTD/xhtml1-strict.dtd">
3  <html xmlns="http://www.w3.org/1999/xhtml"
4      xmlns:v="urn:schemas-microsoft-com:vml">
5
6    <head>
7      <meta http-equiv="Content-Type" content="text/html; charset=utf-8"/>
8
9      <title>Simple Django Blog</title>
10
11     <!-- Load our color and font preferences -->
12     <link rel=StyleSheet href="/scripts/style.css" TYPE="text/css">
13   </head>
14
15   <body>
16
17     <h1>Post new blog entry</h1>
18
19     <form action="/simpleblog/blog/postEntry/" method="post">
20       Title:
21       <input type="text" name="title"> <br/>
22       Author's email address:
23       <input type="text" name="reply_to"> <br/>
24       <textarea rows="30" cols="80" name="content"></textarea>
25       <p/>
26       <input type="submit" value="Post" />
27     </form>
28   </body>
29 </html>
```

The interesting part of this template starts at line 19 with the form that the blog author will use to create the blog entry. The `action` attribute at line 19 means that, when submitted, this form is sent to the URL `/simpleblog/blog/postEntry` (another view method that needs to be written). Lines 20 and 21 define a text box for the blog title. Lines 22 and 23 define another text box for the author's e-mail address. Line 24 defines a `textarea` for the `Blog` content text and line 26 adds the `submit` button. The view method at `/simpleblog/blog/postEntry` will use the contents of the text fields to create a new `Blog` object.

Figure 8-11 shows how the blog entry form looks in a browser.

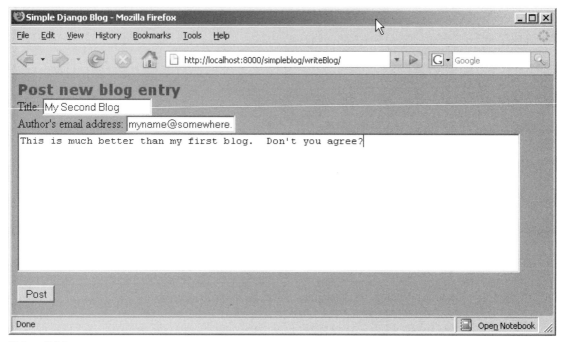

Figure 8-11

When the user clicks the Post button, the form is submitted to the view at `/simpleblog/blog/postEntry`, so create that view next. Add the following `urlpattern` to `urls.py`:

```
(r'^simpleblog/blog/postEntry/$', 'simpleblog.dblog.views.postEntry'),
```

Just like the `Blog` entry form, this view needs no URL parameters. The browser sends the form contents as HTTP `POST` data to the `postEntry` view method. Listing 8-10 shows the `postEntry` method you can enter.

Listing 8-10: The blog submission view

```
 1 def postEntry(request):
 2     """Accepts the HTTP POST data of a new blog entry and
 3       updates the database accordingly"""
 4     b = Blog()
 5     b.title = request.POST['title']
 6     b.reply_to = request.POST['reply_to']
 7     b.content = request.POST['content']
 8     b.post_date = datetime.now()
 9     b.save()
10     return HttpResponseRedirect('/simpleblog/blog/%s/' % b.id)
```

Line 4 of this `postEntry` method creates a new (empty) `Blog` object. Then lines 5 through 7 set the fields in the new `Blog` object from the `POST` data in the request. The request object includes a dictionary called `POST` that contains the HTTP `POST` data. The string indexes in the square brackets (`[ ]`) correspond to the input names in the HTML form that you entered in Listing 8-9. The `Blog` object's `post_date` field is set to the current time using the standard Python `datetime.now()` method in line 8. Line 9 commits the new `Blog` object to the database. The last line of `postEntry` redirects the requestor to the `Blog` view that you wrote earlier, using the newly generated `Blog` primary key to format the correct URL. It's a good idea to redirect after a `POST` so the user doesn't accidentally `POST` the same data twice by clicking the browser's Back button.

Entering Blog Comments

The last page you need to create enables visitors to enter comments on a blog entry. The comment includes some text and also a rating. The URL for the addcomment page is generated by the template code in Listing 8-7, line 38. That URL is of the following form:

```
http://localhost:8000/simpleblog/blog/<blog_id>/comment/add
```

So you need a URL pattern that captures the `Blog` primary key. This will do the trick:

```
(r'^simpleblog/blog/(?P<blog_id>\d+)/comment/add/$',
             'simpleblog.dblog.views.addComment'),
```

This URL pattern routes matching requests to the `addComment` view method, which is shown in Listing 8-11.

Listing 8-11: The comment entry view method

```
def addComment(request, blog_id):
    """Generate the context for the form in which new
       comments are entered"""
    blog = get_object_or_404(Blog, pk=blog_id)
    return render_to_response('templates/addComment.html', {'blog': blog})
```

The `addComment` method follows the familiar pattern for views. First it looks up a `Blog` object using `get_object_or_404`, and then it uses `render_to_response` to render a template.

Create the addComment.html template file shown in Listing 8-12, which contains an HTML form for entering the Comment data.

Listing 8-12: The addComment template

```
1   <!DOCTYPE html PUBLIC "-//W3C//DTD XHTML 1.0 Strict//EN"
2       "http://www.w3.org/TR/xhtml1/DTD/xhtml1-strict.dtd">
3   <html xmlns="http://www.w3.org/1999/xhtml"
4       xmlns:v="urn:schemas-microsoft-com:vml">
5
6   <head>
7       <meta http-equiv="Content-Type" content="text/html; charset=utf-8"/>
8
9       <title>Simple Django Blog</title>
10
11      <!-- Load our color and font preferences -->
12      <link rel=StyleSheet href="/scripts/style.css" TYPE="text/css">
13  </head>
14
15  <body>
16
17      <h1>Comment on {{ blog.title }}</h1>
18
19      <form action="/simpleblog/blog/{{ blog.id }}/postComment/"
20          method="post">
21          <textarea rows="10" cols="30" name="content"></textarea>
22          <p/>
23          How do you rate this entry:
24          <select name="rating">
25            {% for r in blog.RATING_CHOICES %}
26              <!-- Use the template system to treat '.'
                     as '[]' r[0] is the rating number, r[1]
27                   is the rating text -->
28              <option value="{{r.0}}">{{r.1}}</option>
29            {% endfor %}
30          </select>
31          <p/>
32          <input type="submit" value="Post" /7>
33      </form>
34  </body>
35 </html>
```

Line 17 prints the title of the Blog for this comment. When this form is submitted, it is POSTed to the URL configured at line 19. This URL includes the primary key of the Blog object so the view method can update the correct Blog object. The form includes a textarea for the comment text (line 21) and a select element for the rating (lines 24 through 30). The choices in the select are extracted from the

`Blog` model's `RATING_CHOICES` field. Recall from Listing 8-1 that the `RATING_CHOICES` attribute was defined as a tuple of tuples, like this:

```
RATING_CHOICES = (
                (1 , 'Lame'),
                (2 , 'Weak'),
                (3 , 'OK'),
                (4 , 'Nice'),
                (5 , 'Rocks'), )
```

The first element of each two-tuple is the numeric rating value, and the second element is the human-readable version. At line 28, the template populates the `option value` field with the number and displays the text in a drop-down box.

Notice how the template processor requires `r.0` and `r.1` rather than `r[0]` and `r[1]` as you might expect. When processing a dot operator, the template engine tries several approaches to convert the template expression to Python code. If it finds a conversion that works, the template engine inserts the resulting string into the output stream. It tries these approaches in the following order:

1. **Dictionary lookup:** In this case, `r.0` would translate to the Python code `r['0']` (no match).

2. **Attribute lookup:** In this case, `r.0` would translate to the Python code `r.0` (no match).

3. **Method call:** In this case, `r.0` would translate to the Python code `r.0()` (no match).

4. **List-index lookup:** In this case, `r.0` would translate to the Python code `r[0]`. This one works.

Figure 8-12 shows what the comment entry form looks like in the browser.

Figure 8-12

When the form on this page is submitted, the contents are posted to the view mapped to `/simpleblog/`
`blog/{{ blog.id }}/postComment/` as defined on line 19 of Listing 8-12. Add the following line to
`urlpatterns` in `urls.py` to create the mapping:

```
(r'^simpleblog/blog/(?P<blog_id>\d+)/postComment/$',
    'simpleblog.dblog.views.postComment'),
```

As you saw with the other form submission, the HTTP POST parameters are passed to the `postComment`
method attached to the `request` parameter. Listing 8-13 shows the `postComment` view method you
can create.

Listing 8-13: The postComment view method

```
1 def postComment(request, blog_id):
2     """Accepts the HTTP POST data of a new blog comment
3         and updates the database accordingly"""
4     blog = get_object_or_404(Blog, pk=blog_id)
5     comment = blog.comment_set.create(content=request.POST['content'],
6         rating=request.POST['rating'])
7     comment.save()
8     return HttpResponseRedirect('/simpleblog/blog/%s/comment' % blog.id)
```

At line 4, this method fetches the appropriate `Blog` object using `get_object_or_404` as you've seen
before. Then, on lines 5 and 6, it creates a new `Comment` object associated with the `Blog` object using a
method that Django generated for the `Blog` model called `comment_set_create()`. This method initializes the new `Comment` object using the named parameters, which were extracted from the HTTP POST
data as you saw in the previous form example. Line 7 commits the new `Comment` object to the database,
and line 8 redirects the requestor to the comment list page for this `Blog` so the commenter can see his or
her comment along with the others. Figure 8-13 shows how the comment list page looks in a browser.

Figure 8-13

You now have a simple blogging website, as promised in the beginning of this chapter. You've built two model classes, seven views, and five templates to implement a simple but complete application.

Summary

In this chapter you saw the details of writing a simple Django application, including the following:

❑ Initializing the project and application

❑ Configuring the database and template search path

❑ Writing the model classes and using them to configure the database tables

❑ Using the Django `admin` interface to view and edit the model data

❑ Creating web pages by editing `urlpatterns`, writing view methods, and making template files

These are the core skills you need to build Django applications. In the next two chapters, you'll build on these skills as you develop applications that use some of the more advanced Django features.

Django Views and Users

I don't want someone shoving his views down my throat, unless they're covered in a crunchy candy shell.

—**Stephen Colbert**

In the previous chapter you saw some of the great features that make getting started with Django easy. Django's support for model-view-controller (MVC) web applications, automatic object-relational mapping (ORM), and powerful template processor make setting up simple web applications a snap. In this chapter you'll learn about additional Django features that address some of the issues affecting large-scale web applications. You'll see examples of how to reduce duplicated code through template reuse, how to use Django's generic views to avoid writing boilerplate view methods, and how to use Django's built-in capability for user authentication and authorization to manage user accounts and permissions.

Although the simple blog application presented in the previous chapter worked, there are some parts of its design that are less than ideal. For example, all of the templates contain text that is exactly the same for all pages. This makes maintenance more difficult than necessary because any change to that common text will have to be propagated correctly to all of the other copies. This is a very error-prone and labor-intensive process. Django's template inheritance enables you to put that common text in one template file and reference it from other template files.

Similarly, many of the view methods were very simple, consisting of the following two steps:

1. Populate a context from the database.
2. Render a template using that context.

Django includes a set of generic views that can perform these two steps and don't require you to write and maintain any view methods.

Finally, the blog application you created in the previous chapter would allow anyone who wanders in off the Internet to make blog entries and comments. In this chapter you see how to use Django's built-in authentication and authorization framework to control access permissions.

Template Inheritance

You surely noticed in the previous chapter that much of the template code was the same (or very similar) in every page. This violates one of the core principles of Django design: Don't Repeat Yourself (DRY). Most of the pages were structured to contain the following elements:

- ❑ **XHTML header:** This sets up the start of the document, brings in the CSS file, and so on. It is identical in every page.

- ❑ **Title:** The contents of this section vary, but the structure is always the same. It's just a phrase between <H1> tags.

- ❑ **Main content:** This part is the meat of each page and varies quite a bit between pages.

- ❑ **Footer:** This part of the page includes a few links that vary a little depending on the context.

Ideally, you'd like to write the XHTML header section only once and have it included in every page. Using Django's template inheritance, you can make a single page that implements this structure and includes all of the boilerplate and default contents.

The DRY Problem

To review, Listing 9-1 shows the main blog entry list page from the previous chapter.

Listing 9-1: Master list template without inheritance

```
1    <!DOCTYPE html PUBLIC "-//W3C//DTD XHTML 1.0 Strict//EN"
2    "http://www.w3.org/TR/xhtml1/DTD/xhtml1-strict.dtd">
3      <head>
4        <meta http-equiv="Content-Type"
5             content="text/html; charset=utf-8"/>
6
7        <title>Simple Django Blog</title>
8
9        <!-- Load our color and font preferences -->
10       <link rel=StyleSheet href="/scripts/style.css"
                  TYPE="text/css">
11     </head>
12
13     <body>
14     <h1> Simple Django Blog </h1>
15     <hr>
16     <div class="bloglist">
17     {% if latest_blog_list %}
18       <ul>
19       {% for blog in latest_blog_list %}
```

```
20          <li> <a href="blog/{{blog.id}}/">{{ blog.title }}</a>
21              Posted on
22              {{ blog.post_date|date:"F j, Y" }}
23              by {{blog.reply_to}}
24          </li>
25
26      {% endfor %}
27      </ul>
28    {% else %}
29      <p>No blogs are available.</p>
30    {% endif %}
31    <p/>
32    </div>
33    <hr>
34    <div class="footerlink">
35    <a href="writeBlog">Add new entry</a>
36    </div>
37
38    </body>
39 </html>
```

Here's a basic breakdown of this listing:

❑   Lines 1 through 13 contain the boilerplate header text that is identical for each page you wrote in the previous chapter. This text will go in the base template so it is inherited by all pages in the application.

❑   Lines 14 and 15 contain the inline title for the page. Each page has this section, but the text between the `<h1>` and `</h1>` tags is different for each page. The base template will include this section, but each inheriting template will override that text.

❑   Lines 16 through 32 contain the main content of the page. Each page has this section, but its contents vary widely. Some pages have forms to fill out, some have lists, and some have single text fields. The base template will include this as a blank section for the inheriting template to fill out.

❑   Lines 33 through 39 contain the footer text. Each page has a footer, and the contents are similar on each one, so the base template will define a footer that is appropriate for most pages. The pages that require a different footer can override or add to the default.

Defining a Base Template

A base template looks the same as the templates that you wrote in the previous chapter, with one exception. A base template defines some named blocks using the `{% block %}` and `{% endblock %}` directives. Inheriting templates have the option of replacing the content between these directives by defining their own blocks by the same name. They can also retain the contents of the base template's block by not overriding the named block.

Listing 9-2 shows a base template that implements the structure and content described previously. Create a template file called `baseTemplate.html` that contains the code in Listing 9-2.

Listing 9-2: Base template

```
1  <!DOCTYPE html PUBLIC "-//W3C//DTD XHTML 1.0 Strict//EN"
2      "http://www.w3.org/TR/xhtml1/DTD/xhtml1-strict.dtd">
3  <html>
4    <head>
5      <meta http-equiv="Content-Type"
6                content="text/html; charset=utf-8"/>
7
8      <title>Simple Django Blog</title>
9
10     <!-- Load our color and font preferences -->
11     <link rel=StyleSheet href="/scripts/style.css"
             TYPE="text/css">
12   </head>
13
14   <body>
15
16     <h1>
17       <div class="title">
18          {% block title %}{% endblock %}
19       </div>
20     </h1>
21     <hr>
22
23     <div class="content">
24          {% block content %}{% endblock %}
25     </div>
26
27     <hr>
28     <div class="footer">
29       {% block footer %}
30         Return to <a href="/simpleblog">Top</a><br/>
31       {% endblock %}
32     </div>
33   </body>
34 </html>
```

Here's what's going on in this template:

❑   Lines 1 through 17 are the XHTML header section. Because these lines are not in a `{% block %}` / `{% endblock %}` pair, they will be included verbatim in any page that inherits from this template.

❑   Line 18 defines an empty block called `title` that inheriting templates can fill in with their specific title phrase.

❑   Lines 19 through 23 contain common structure code that will be in every page that inherits from this template.

❑ Line 24 is another empty block called `content` that the inheriting template will fill in with the main content of the page.

❑ Lines 29 through 31 define a block called `footer` that inheriting templates can replace with their own content, or they can use the default content provided in the base template.

Using the {% extends %} Directive

Now that you've written a base template, you need to modify the other templates to inherit it, starting with the blog subject list page that is the top-level entry into the blog application. Figure 9-1 is a reminder of how this page appears in a browser.

Figure 9-1

This page has three sections separated by horizontal lines (HTML `<hr>` tags), which correspond to the three sections that can be overridden in the base template. The top section is the `title` block, the middle section is the `content` block, and the bottom section is the `footer` block.

In this page, the inheriting template overrides all three sections. The `title` block gets the text "Simple Django Blog," the `content` block gets the list of blogs, and the `footer` block gets a link to the blog entry page. The footer in the base template (previously shown on line 30 of Listing 9-2) just points to this page, so it needs to be overridden anyway. Listing 9-3 shows how the template for this page is implemented. This will be your new `index.html`.

Listing 9-3: Master list template with inheritance

```
1  {% extends "dblog/baseTemplate.html" %}
2  {% block title %} Simple Django Blog {% endblock %}
3  {% block content %}
4    <div class="bloglist">
5    {% if object_list %}
6      <ul>
7      {% for blog in latest_blog_list %}
8          <li> <a href="blog/{{blog.id}}/">
              {{ blog.title }}</a>
9              Posted on
10             {{ blog.post_date|date:"F j, Y" }}
11             by {{blog.reply_to}}
12         </li>
13
14      {% endfor %}
15      </ul>
16    {% else %}
17      <p>No blogs are available.</p>
18    {% endif %}
19    <p/>
20    </div>
21 {% endblock %}
22 {% block footer %}
23    <div class="footerlink">
24    <a href="writeBlog">Add new entry</a>
25    </div>
26 {% endblock %}
```

Line 1 of this listing declares that this template extends the base template shown in Listing 9-2. Line 2 uses the {% block %} and {% endblock %} directives to override the title section of the base template. The meat of this page is the content block on lines 3 through 21, which are the same as lines 16 through 30 of the original, noninheriting template shown previously in Listing 9-1.

You can follow a similar strategy for the blog detail page. Modify the blog detail page to extend the base template and place the content that is specific to this page in the three blocks. Your template will then look something like Listing 9-4. This will be your new readBlog.html file.

Listing 9-4: Blog detail with inheritance

```
1  {% extends "dblog/baseTemplate.html" %}
2
3  {% block title %}
4  {{ blog.title }}
5  {% endblock %}
6
7  {% block content %}
8
9  <p>Published on {{blog.post_date|date:"F j, Y"}}</p>
10 <p>Posted by {{blog.reply_to}}</p>
11 <p>Current rating is {{blog.rating}} out of 5</p>
12
```

```
13 <div class="blogtext">
14   {{blog.content}}
15 </div>
16
17 {% endblock %}
18
19 {% block footer %}
20   View <a href="comment">{{blog.comment_set.count}}
21     comment{{blog.comment_set.count|pluralize}}</a><br/>
22   {{ block.super }}
23
24 {% endblock %}
```

This template extends the same base template as the master blog list page, so it will automatically get all of the same style sheet and header information. The template uses the attributes of the Blog object to fill in the title block (lines 3 through 5), the content block (lines 7 through 17), and the footer block (lines 19 through 24).

Notice that the {{ block.super }} directive on line 22 pulls in the contents of the base template's footer section. You can use this technique to add to a template block rather than replace it completely.

The end result, shown in Figure 9-2, looks exactly the same as the non-inheriting version, but has much less code to write and maintain.

Figure 9-2

All of the other templates from the previous chapter will benefit similarly from extending the base template. You can replace the template blocks with any content, so you can fill them in with forms, images, or anything else you can imagine.

The template inheritance hierarchy can be arbitrarily deep, so a template that extends another template can itself be extended by a different one. Including this flexibility in your initial design can make your site much easier to implement and maintain.

Generic Views

Now that you've eliminated (or at least minimized) the offensive duplicate code in the templates, turn your attention to the unnecessary view methods. Most of the view methods that you wrote for the previous chapter look similar to the example in Listing 9-5.

Listing 9-5: Blog detail view

```
def readBlog(request, blog_id):
    """Generate the context for the page that
        displays a single blog entry"""
    blog = get_object_or_404(Blog, pk=blog_id)
    return render_to_response('templates/readBlog.html',
                              {'blog': blog})
```

These view methods just read some stuff from the database using `get_object_or_404()` and send it to the template processor using `render_to_reponse()`. Django's generic view methods can do these operations for you, reducing the amount of code you have to write and maintain.

List-Detail Generic Views

You still write the template when using a generic view, so you still control how the object or objects are displayed, but you don't have to handle querying the database and rendering the template yourself. The following Django generic views are specially designed for rendering the type of list/detail pages used in the blog application:

- ❑ `django.views.generic.list_detail.object_list`: Renders a summary list of objects.
- ❑ `django.views.generic.list_detail.object_detail`: Renders details about a specific object.

Try replacing the main blog summary list view with a `django.views.generic.list_detail` `.object_list` view as follows:

1. Find the following line in the `urls.py` file:

```
(r'^simpleblog/$', 'simpleblog.dblog.views.index'),
```

And replace it with this:

```
(r'^simpleblog/$', 'django.views.generic.list_detail.object_list', blog_set),
```

Now when a browser requests the `/simpleblog/` URL, it will be serviced by the `object_list` generic view rather than your custom view.

2. Generic views require a set of objects to collect and pass to the template, so add the following code before the `urlpatterns` in `urls.py` to define that set:

```
blog_set = {
  'queryset': Blog.objects.all(),
}
```

The 'queryset' element of this dictionary is the set of `Blog` objects to be rendered by the template. You could filter this set by date or author or whatever, but this example includes all `Blog` objects.

3. The `object_list` view fetches the objects from the database and populates a template context with those objects. The template you wrote earlier expected the list of `Blog` objects to be named `latest_blog_list`. However, the `object_list` view calls the list of objects to be displayed `object_list`, so you need to update the template, changing `latest_blog_list` references ""
to `object_list`.

4. By default, the `object_list` generic view looks for a template called <app_label>/<model_name>_list.html, so rename `index.html` to `dblog/blog_list.html`.

5. Edit `settings.py` to make sure that the renamed template is available from the TEMPLATE_DIRS list.

6. Load the `/simpleblog/` page in a browser. The page should look exactly the same as before, but now you're using the generic view to handle the request. You can delete the custom view method `index()` from the `views.py` file now. It's no longer referenced.

7. Convert a detail page to use the `django.views.generic.list_detail.object_detail` generic view. Find the following custom view line in `urls.py`:

```
(r'^simpleblog/blog/(?P<blog_id>\d+)/$', 'simpleblog.dblog.views.readBlog'),
```

And replace it with the following generic view lines:

```
(r'^simpleblog/blog/(?P<object_id>\d+)/$',
    'django.views.generic.list_detail.object_detail', blog_set),
```

8. The `object_detail` generic view can use the same `blog_set` that you used previously for the `object_list` view, so there's no need to add it again. The `object_detail` generic view will select the requested object from the set using the `object_id` captured from the regular expression in the URL. The previous version of this view called it `blog_id`, so you'll have to change `(?P<blog_id>\d+)` to `(?P<object_id>\d+)` in the `urlpatterns` list.

9. By default, the `object_detail` generic view looks for a template called <app_label>/<model_name>_detail.html, so rename `readBlog.html` to `dblog/blog_list.html`. Then load one of the blog detail views to see the results. Again, this page should look the same as the nongeneric view you saw before, and you can delete the custom view `readBlog()`, which is no longer used.

10. You can use the `object_detail` generic view for the comment view page, too. Find the following custom view lines in `urls.py`:

```
(r'^simpleblog/blog/(?P<blog_id>\d+)/comment/$', 'simpleblog.dblog.views.comment'),
```

And replace them with these generic view lines:

```
(r'^simpleblog/blog/(?P<object_id>\d+)/comment/$',
        'django.views.generic.list_detail.object_detail',
        dict(blog_set, template_name='dblog/comment.html')),
```

11. Notice that you have to change the regular expression capture name from `blog_id` to `object_id` as you did in the previous view because the generic view looks for the specific object instance id using that name. Also, recall that the `object_detail` generic view renders a template called `<app_label>/<model_name>_detail.html`, which in this case would be `dblog/blog_list.html`. You used that template name already, so you need to override the default by adding `template_name` to the dictionary passed as the third element of the URL pattern. The Python function `dict()` returns a dictionary that includes all of the items of the dictionary in its first argument plus the item that follows as an additional mapping.

Other Generic Views

Django includes several other types of generic views that you may find useful. It provides the following simple generic views for situations that don't require access to the data model:

❑ `django.views.generic.simple.direct_to_template`: Renders a template passing a dictionary called `params`, which contains only the parameters captured in the URL.

❑ `django.views.generic.simple.redirect_to`: Redirects the requestor to a different URL.

Django includes generic views that make it easy to organize objects by their date of creation. Django was developed to support an online news operation, and these views are especially useful for that kind of time-sensitive data. They include the following:

❑ `django.views.generic.date_based.archive_index`: Shows the most recent objects in the `queryset`.

❑ `django.views.generic.date_based.archive_year`: Shows the available months in the year.

❑ `django.views.generic.date_based.archive_month`: Shows the objects with dates within the selected month.

❑ `django.views.generic.date_based.archive_week`: Shows the objects with dates within the selected week.

❑ `django.views.generic.date_based.archive_day`: Shows the objects with `datetime` values that fall within the selected day. There is a special version of this view, called `archive_today`, which automatically selects the current date as the one to display.

❑ `django.views.generic.date_based.object_detail`: Shows a detailed view of an individual object by date and ID.

Generic views for creating, updating, and deleting individual objects are also available. They use the Django forms framework, which makes creating, validating, and processing HTML forms easier. These generic views include the following:

- ❑ `django.views.generic.create_update.create_object`: Presents a form that can be used to create a new instance of an object, validate the form, and store the new object.

- ❑ `django.views.generic.create_update.update_object`: Presents a form that can be used to edit an existing instance of an object, validate the form, and store the updated object.

- ❑ `django.views.generic.create_update.delete_object`: Displays a confirmation page before an existing object is deleted.

Django Forms Library

At the time of this writing, the forms library is undergoing a major overhaul. The old method has been deprecated, and the API for the new method is not finalized yet. For that reason, we're not going to discuss the forms library any further, but if you use a lot of forms, you might want to check out the Django documentation page at `www.djangoproject.com/documentation/` for the latest status.

The additional generic views discussed in this section are similar in operation to the `object_list` and `object_detail` generic views that you tried in the previous examples. Detailed documentation for Django generic views is at `www.djangoproject.com/documentation/generic_views/`.

User Authentication and Authorization

Most interactive websites include some kind of user management to control and track who accesses and updates the content on the site. Django provides a mechanism for user management that is integrated with the model classes, making it easy to control which users have access to which objects. In this section you learn how the Django `auth` framework enables user *authentication* (logging in known users) and user *authorization* (controlling which users have access to which functions).

Installing User Management

If you used the `django-admin.py startproject` command to initialize your project, you've already installed the components required for user management. If you didn't, adding them later just involves a few edits to the `settings.py` file.

The `django.contrib.auth` Django application implements the user management functions. To enable this application, edit your `settings.py` file and look for the `INSTALLED_APPS` setting. Add the `django.contrib.auth` application to it as follows:

```
INSTALLED_APPS = (
    'django.contrib.auth',
    'django.contrib.contenttypes',
    'django.contrib.sessions',
    'django.contrib.sites',
    'django.contrib.admin',
    'simpleblog.dblog',
)
```

After you change `INSTALLED_APPS`, you need to synchronize the database tables. To do this, run the following command:

```
python manage.py syncdb
```

This command creates any tables that the application models require and prompts you to create a super-user account if one does not already exist. You don't need to be concerned about whether you should run the `syncdb` command. It creates tables only if it needs to. It doesn't delete any tables or data, so if in doubt, run it.

Next, add the middleware components necessary for Django to hook the user objects into the web request objects. Find the `MIDDLWARE_CLASSES` in `settings.py`, and add the `django.contrib.sessions.middlware.SessionMiddlware` and `django.contrib.auth.middlware.AuthenticationMiddleware` classes as follows:

```
MIDDLEWARE_CLASSES = (
  'django.middleware.common.CommonMiddleware',
  'django.contrib.sessions.middleware.SessionMiddleware',
  'django.contrib.auth.middleware.AuthenticationMiddleware',
  'django.middleware.doc.XViewMiddleware',
)
```

Now you're all set to try out some user accounts.

The User Model

Django users, groups, and permissions are implemented as Django model classes, so you can treat them in the same way as the `Blog` or `Comment` objects. The fields of the `User` model are listed in the following table. Only the `username` and `password` fields are required.

Field	Description
Username	A CharField of maximum length 30. This field is required and must be unique.
first_name	A CharField of maximum length 30.
last_name	A CharField of maximum length 30.
Email	An EmailField
Password	A hash of the user's password, stored as a CharField. To set the user's password, use the User.set_password method.
is_staff	If True, the user can access the Django admin pages.
is_active	If True, the user can log in. Set this to False to disable an account.
last_login	The DateTime at which the user last logged in.
date_joined	The DateTime at which the User object was created.
Groups	A ManyToManyField of groups to which this user belongs.
user_permissions	A ManyToManyField of permissions granted to this user.
is_superuser	If True, the user has all permissions. Otherwise, only the permissions enumerated in user_permissions are granted.

Authenticating a User

The django.contrib.auth application includes view methods to handle user login and logout actions. You can use these like you used the generic views earlier in this chapter to avoid writing custom views. All you need to write is a template and a URL pattern. To add the login and logout views, add the following two entries to the urlpatterns in urls.py:

```
(r'^accounts/login/$', 'django.contrib.auth.views.login',
                {'template_name': 'dblog/login.html'}),
(r'^accounts/logout/$', 'django.contrib.auth.views.logout',
                {'template_name': 'dblog/logout.html'}),
```

The login.html template extends the same base template as the other pages. This gives the login page the same look and feel as the other pages in the application. Listing 9-6 shows the template. You should enter this code as a file named login.html in your templates directory.

Listing 9-6: User login template

```
1  {% extends "dblog/baseTemplate.html" %}
2  {% block title %}
3    Login to DBlog
4  {% endblock %}
5
6  {% block content %}
7
8  {% if form.has_errors %}
9    <p>Login Failed. Please try again.</p>
10 {% endif %}
11
12 <form method="post" action=".">
13   <h2>Login existing user</h2>
14   <table>
15     <tr>
16       <td><label for="id_username">Username:</label></td>
17       <td>{{ form.username }}</td>
18       <td><label for="id_password">Password:</label></td>
19       <td>{{ form.password }}</td>
20     </tr>
21   </table>
22
23   <input type="submit" value="Login" />
24   <input type="hidden" name="next" value="{{ next }}" />
25 </form>
26
27 {% endblock %}
```

Line 1 declares that this template extends the base template that you wrote earlier in this chapter. Recall that the base template handles all of the HTML boilerplate and CSS references, and also defines three sections that deriving templates can override if they choose. Lines 2 through 4 override the base template's `title` block with a descriptive title for this page. Lines 6 through 27 override the content block with the username and password entry form. This template does not override the `footer` block, so the `footer` from the base template will appear at the bottom of this page.

The `django.contrib.auth.login` view uses Django's form validation to check that all of the fields contain data and that the username and password are valid. If the form has been submitted before but contained errors, lines 8 through 10 will display an error message on the page. Lines 12 through 25 are the form in which the user can enter his or her username and password. This form contains a text box for the username and one for the password. The Django forms library renders the directive `{{ form.username }}` as the appropriate HTML input type (a string, in this case) with constraints from the model (length, required, and so on) enforced by the form where possible.

Line 24 of the listing defines a hidden field called `"next"`. If the user successfully logs in using the login form, he or she will be redirected to the URL referenced by this field. Often, a user who hasn't logged in yet will navigate the pages that don't require a login for awhile before clicking a link that redirects him or her to a login. The `"next"` field holds the desired link so the user can be redirected to that page after a successful login.

If you load this page in a browser, you'll see the new login page shown in Figure 9-3.

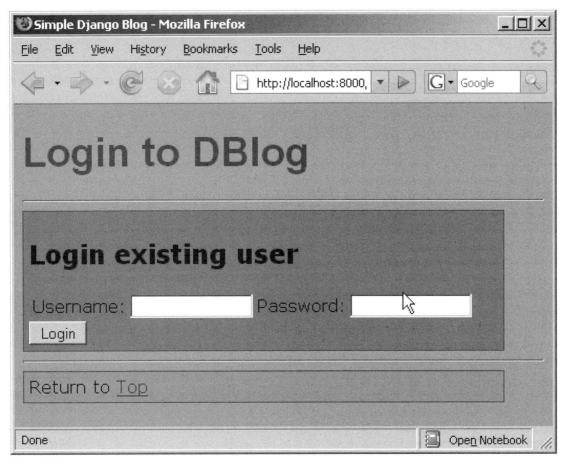

Figure 9-3

If the user enters a valid username-password combination, he or she is logged in and redirected to the next link (if the form includes a value for next). If the login fails, the error message in lines 8 and 9 is displayed, and the user can try again.

If the "next" value is empty, the user is redirected to the default user profile page accounts/profile/, so you need to write that view next. Add the following line to urlpatterns in urls.py:

```
(r'^accounts/profile/$', 'simpleblog.dblog.views.viewProfile'),
```

The viewProfile view in Listing 9-7 is very simple, but adds one wrinkle that you haven't seen yet. Add this method to views.py.

Listing 9-7: User profile view

```
1 def viewProfile(request):
2   return render_to_response('dblog/user_profile.html', {},
3         RequestContext(request))
```

The template `user_profile.html` requires access to the `User` object to display its fields, but the currently logged-in user is associated with the HTTP request, not an object ID extracted from the URL as you've seen before. The `RequestContext()` method (line 3 of Listing 9-7) makes a template context from a request object, making the request data available to the template.

In the template, the current user is called `user` and can be referenced as shown in Listing 9-8. Enter this template code in a file called `user_profile.html`.

Listing 9-8: User profile template

```
1   {% extends "dblog/baseTemplate.html" %}
2
3   {% block title %}
4   Account for
5   {{ user.first_name }}
6   {{ user.last_name }}
7   {% endblock %}
8
9   {% block content %}
10
11 <p>Username: {{user.username}}</p>
12 <p>Email Address: {{user.email}}</p>
13 {% endblock %}
```

The template in Listing 9-8 extends the same base template as the other templates (line 1), so it will inherit the same look and feel as the other pages. It overrides the `title` block with the user's `first_name` and `last_name` at lines 3 through 7. It overrides the `content` block with the user's username and e-mail address on lines 9 through 13. The `footer` block is not overridden, so the default `footer` will appear on this page.

Figure 9-4 shows the account summary page for a user named `some_user`.

Enhancing the Base Template

Now that you have the login, logout, and account profile pages, you need to link to them from existing pages on the site. You could edit every template to add links to the login and logout pages, but that would be a bad idea (remember DRY).

A better solution is to add the `login` and `logout` functions to the base template. That way, it automatically appears on every page. Try adding the following capabilities to the base template:

❑   If the user is logged in, present a link to the logout page.

❑   If the user is not logged in, present a link to the login page and a link to the page that handles creating new user accounts, which you'll build later in this chapter.

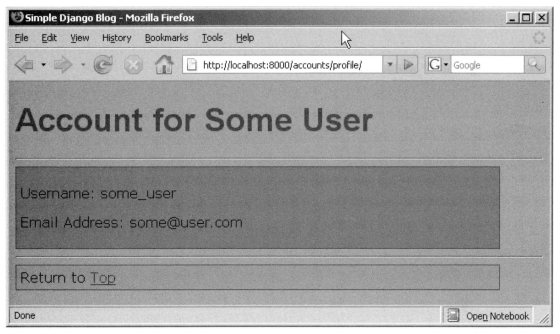

Figure 9-4

The highlighted code in Listing 9-9 shows one way to include these links.

Listing 9-9: Base template with login and logout functions

```
1   <!DOCTYPE html PUBLIC "-//W3C//DTD XHTML 1.0 Strict//EN"
2       "http://www.w3.org/TR/xhtml1/DTD/xhtml1-strict.dtd">
3
4   <head>
5     <meta http-equiv="Content-Type" content="text/html;
              charset=utf-8"/>
6
7     <title>Simple Django Blog</title>
8
9     <!-- Load our color and font preferences -->
10    <link rel=StyleSheet href="/scripts/style.css"
              TYPE="text/css">
11  </head>
12
13  <body>
14
15    <h1>
16      <div class="title">
17            {% block title %}{% endblock %}
18      </div>
19    </h1>
```

(continued)

Listing 9-9 *(continued)*

```
20    <hr>
21
22    <div class="content">
23      {% block content %}{% endblock %}
24    </div>
25
26    <hr>
27    <div class="footer">
28      {% block footer %}
29        Return to <a href="/simpleblog">Top</a><br/>
30      {% endblock %}
31
32      {% if user.is_authenticated %}
33        <p><a href="/accounts/logout">Logout
             {{user.username }}.</a></p>
34      {% else %}
35        <p><a href="/accounts/login">Login </a>here</p>
36        <p><a href="/accounts/newUser">
             Create new account </a>here</p>
37      {% endif %}
38    </div>
39  </body>
40 </html>
```

Figure 9-5

Lines 32 through 37 add the login and logout links. Line 32 tests whether the user has successfully authenticated (logged in) yet. If so, a link to the logout page is emitted by line 33; if not, lines 35 and 36 print a link to the login page and a link to the page used to create new user accounts.

Notice that this listing places the login and logout links in the footer <div> but not within the footer template block. This way, the links will get the same CSS settings as the footer, and they will appear on every page, even if templates override the footer block. Of course, you may choose to place them elsewhere in your application.

Figure 9-5 shows how the main blog summary page looks with these changes. As you can see at the bottom of the page, the two links show that this user is not authenticated yet.

User Permissions

The main reason to create user accounts is to control access to some part of the web application. For this blog application, say you want to enforce these restrictions:

- ❑ Only authenticated users can enter comments.
- ❑ Only authenticated users with specific permission can make blog entries.

You can enforce these restrictions by limiting access to specific views based on the attributes of the user attempting to access them. To limit the comment entry function to authenticated users, you need to redirect unauthenticated users to the login page when they try to access a view that requires authentication.

Try it first with the page that presents the comment entry form. Unfortunately, you can't use a generic view directly when you're requiring authentication, but you can write a one-liner view method that calls only the generic view. Update the comment/add URL pattern in urls.py to reference that view method as follows:

```
(r'^simpleblog/blog/(?P<object_id>\d+)/comment/add/$',
                'simpleblog.dblog.views.addComment',
                dict(blog_set, template_name='dblog/addComment.html')),
```

Now you need to add an addComment view to the views.py file; that view does two things:

1. It ensures that the user is authenticated.

2. If the user is authenticated, it renders the generic view.

Django provides a convenient decorator to accomplish step 1. You just add the @login_required decorator to any view method that you want to restrict to authenticated users. If the user is logged in, the decorator does nothing and access is allowed. If the user is not logged in, he or she is redirected to the accounts/login page and "next" is filled in with the URL that the user originally requested. If the user successfully logs in, he or she is redirected back to this view and @login_required will pass.

Listing 9-10 shows this view method. Add it to `views.py`.

Listing 9-10: View with login required

```
@login_required
def addComment(*args, **kwargs):
    return django.views.generic.list_detail.object_detail(*args, **kwargs)
```

The first line is the decorator that ensures the user is logged in. If the user is logged in, the last line renders the generic `object_detail` template.

Now you've restricted access to the comment entry form so unauthenticated users cannot enter comments using that form. However, a determined, nefarious individual could still hand-craft a POST request to the `postComment()` view method, which is the method that actually commits the comment to the database. Be sure to add the `@login_required` decorator to that view, too.

User permissions are defined in the Django data model classes. For every class in the data model, Django automatically creates three permissions that correspond to the canonical `create`, `update`, and `delete` operations. These permissions are called add_*<name>*, change_*<name>*, and delete_*<name>* where *<name>* is the class name of the object being modified.

It's important to note that these permissions are just names — Django doesn't enforce permissions on your model objects unless you enforce them in your views.

You can also create custom permissions by adding them to your model's `Meta` nested class. The `Blog` model class in Listing 9-11 shows the syntax for creating a custom permission.

Listing 9-11: Blog model with a custom permission

```
1    class Blog(models.Model):
2      """The class representing an entry in the blog"""
3
4      """The title or subject of the blog entry"""
5      title = models.CharField(maxlength=128)
6
7      """The date that the post was created"""
8      post_date = models.DateTimeField('date posted')
9
10     """The email address of the posting author"""
11     reply_to = models.EmailField()
12
13     """The actual text content of the posting"""
14     content = models.TextField()
15
16       def rating(self):
17           """Compute the average rating based on the comments received"""
18           comments = self.comment_set.all()
19
20           # Don't divide by zero
21           if len(comments) == 0:
22               return "(unrated)"
23
24           sum = 0.0
```

```
25              for c in comments:
26                  sum = sum + c.rating
27              average = float(sum)/len(comments)
28              return "%.2f"%average
29
30      """The possible ratings for each blog entry"""
31      RATING_CHOICES = (
32                      (1 , 'Lame'),
33                      (2 , 'Weak'),
34                      (3 , 'OK'),
35                      (4 , 'Nice'),
36                      (5 , 'Rocks'),
37                  )
38      """Empty class enables the Django admin web interface"""
39      class Admin:
40        pass
41
42      """This custom permission is required to create a new Blog entry"""
43      class Meta:
44        permissions = (
45          ("may_create_blogs", "May Create Blogs"),
46        )
47
48      """String representation is used by the Django admin interface"""
49      def __str__(self):
50              return "Blog(title = '%s')"%(self.title)
```

Add lines 42 through 46 to your copy of models.py. Line 45 defines a new permission called "may_create_blogs" with the friendly name "May Create Blogs" that you will require before you allow a user to create a new blog entry. Obviously, you could just use the automatic permission add_blog for this purpose, but a custom permission gives you more flexibility.

After you add the Meta nested class to the Blog class, rerun manage.py as follows to create the new permission:

```
python manage.py syncdb
```

Now you need to modify the blog entry views to require this permission. First add the @login_required decorator to the view that renders the blog entry form (addEntry) and the view that accepts the completed submission form (postEntry) so that unauthenticated users will be redirected to the login page. Then add a line that checks for the specific permission in the addEntry view method. Listing 9-12 shows how the updated view should look after you're done.

Listing 9-12: View requiring a custom permission

```
1 @login_required
2 def addEntry(request, *args, **kwargs):
3     if not (request.user.has_perm("dblog.may_create_blogs")):
4         return HttpResponse("Permission Denied")
5     else:
6         return django.views.generic.simple.direct_to_template(request,
7             *args, **kwargs)
```

The decorator at line 1 ensures that the user is logged in. Line 3 checks that the requesting user possesses the custom permission, `"dblog.may_create_blogs"` (notice that Django requires the module name `dblog` as prefix to the name of the custom permission). If the permission check fails, an error page is returned at line 4. Otherwise, the blog entry form is rendered using the `direct_to_template` generic view at lines 6 and 7. Figure 9-6 shows the really cool error page.

Figure 9-6

Don't forget to add the same permission check to the `postEntry` view method as shown in Listing 9-13.

Listing 9-13: Checking permissions on submitted data

```
1  @login_required
2  def postEntry(request):
3      """Accepts the HTTP POST data of a new blog entry and
4         updates the database accordingly"""
5      if not (request.user.has_perm("dblog.may_create_blogs")):
6          return HttpResponse("Permission Denied")
7      b = Blog()
8      b.title = request.POST['title']
9      b.reply_to = request.POST['reply_to']
10     b.content = request.POST['content']
11     b.post_date = datetime.now()
12     b.save()
13     return HttpResponseRedirect('/simpleblog/blog/%s/' % b.id)
```

This view checks for the required permission at line 5 and returns the "Permission Denied" message if the check fails. Otherwise, it proceeds to create and store the new `Blog` object.

You can grant users the `may_create_blogs` permission through the Django `admin` site. Log in to the `admin` site as the root user, click Users, and then click a username to edit. Scroll down to the User permissions section, and you should see `blog` ⇨ `May Create Blogs` as one of the available user permissions. Select it and click the right arrow between the boxes to add it to the list of chosen user permissions. The screen should now look like Figure 9-7.

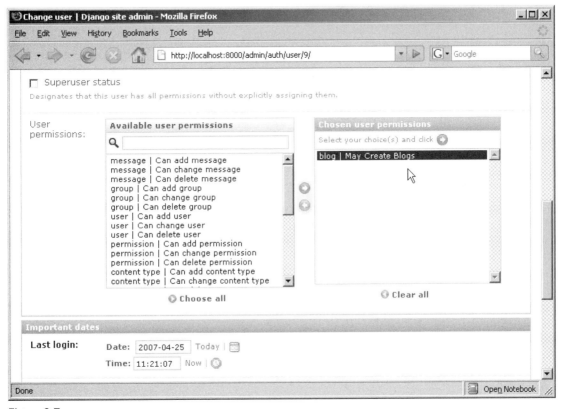

Figure 9-7

Scroll down further, and click Save. The user now has permission to make new blog entries.

Creating a User

You can create users through the `admin` interface or through your own views. Figure 9-8 shows the top-level Django admin screen in which you can see Groups and Users available for editing.

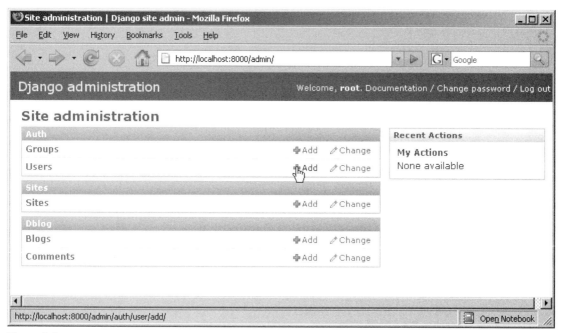

Figure 9-8

Click the Add link for Auth Users (under the pointer in Figure 9-8) to display the first of two forms for entering new users in the `admin` application. This form is used to enter the two required data fields: `username` and `password`. Fill it out as shown in Figure 9-9, and then click the Save and Continue Editing button.

The next form that is displayed provides entry fields for the optional components of the `User` object, including the username, e-mail address, permissions, and group memberships. Fill in whatever you like on this form, and then click the Save button to update the `User` object. The new user can now log in and request the views that require authentication.

Using the `admin` site to create a user account is part of the basic Django functionality, but it is probably not the right solution for most sites. Many sites allow users to create their own accounts, but you wouldn't want to give everyone access to the `admin` site. The solution is to write your own view that creates a new user account.

By now you know that to add a view you edit the `urls.py` file. Add the following custom view pattern to the `urlpatterns` list:

```
(r'^accounts/newUser/$', 'simpleblog.dblog.views.newUser'),
```

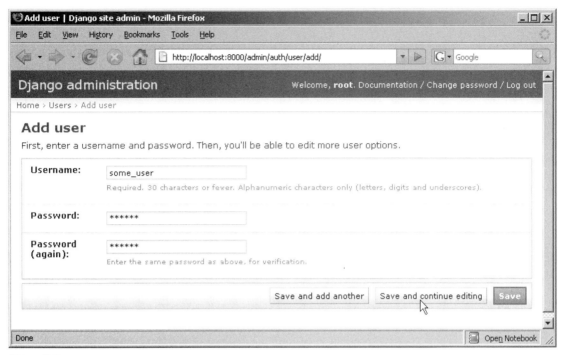

Figure 9-9

Notice that the URL starts with `accounts`, rather than `simpleblog` as all of the previous views did. These accounts are global to the whole site, not just the `simpleblog` application, so it's appropriate to use a different URL prefix. As you'll see later, many of Django's account management functions assume a default URL prefix of `accounts`, so this is a convenient choice.

On an HTTP GET request to the `accounts/newUser` URL, respond with the form to be filled in with user account data. This form will POST back to the same URL, so you need only one view method, but it will handle GET and POST requests differently. Edit `views.py` to add the view method shown in Listing 9-14.

Listing 9-14: A view that adds a user account

```
 1 def newUser(request):
 2   """Creates a new user with comment-only permissions"""
 3   if request.POST:
 4     try:
 5       username = request.POST['username']
 6       password = request.POST['password']
 7       email = request.POST['email']
 8       firstname = request.POST['firstname']
 9       lastname = request.POST['lastname']
10       if (len(username) == 0 or
11           len(password) == 0 or
12           len(email) == 0 or
```

(continued)

Listing 9-14 *(continued)*

```
13              len(firstname) == 0 or
14              len(lastname) == 0):
15          return render_to_response('dblog/newUser.html',
16              {'username':username,
17               'email':email,
18               'firstname':firstname,
19               'lastname':lastname,
20               'msg':'All fields are required. Please resubmit.'})
21      user = User.objects.create_user(username, email, password)
22      user.first_name = firstname
23      user.last_name = lastname
24      user.save()
25      # Log the user in here
26      # This should be successful because we just created the user
27      # with that password
28      newuser = authenticate(username=username, password=password)
29      login(request, newuser)
30      return HttpResponseRedirect('/accounts/profile/')
31  except:
32      import sys,traceback
33      traceback.print_exc()
34      print sys.exc_info()
35
36      # If the username is already in use, a constraint error is thrown.
37      # The type of exception thrown depends on the database backend in use
38      # so here we assume that any exception is a
39      # "username already in use" error
40      return render_to_response('dblog/newUser.html',
41          {'email':email,
42           'firstname': firstname,
43           'lastname': lastname,
44           'msg':'Username "%s" is in use. Please choose another.'%
45           username})
46 #    else:
47    return render_to_response('dblog/newUser.html', {})
```

Line 3 checks to see if this is a POST request. If it's not, the view responds with the empty form template at line 47. Lines 5 through 9 read the five fields of the form from the request object, and lines 10 through 14 check to make sure a value was entered for each field. If any of the fields are blank, the render_to_response call at line 15 sends the form back to the user so he or she can try again. Lines 16 through 20 fill in template context with whatever values were entered, which the template uses to pre-populate the input boxes for the next submission. This way the user only has to enter the missing fields, not reenter all of the fields.

Line 21 attempts to create the new user object with the requested username, password, and e-mail address. If the user cannot be created, create_user() throws an exception, which is caught at line 31. If the user is successfully created, lines 22 and 23 initialize the remaining two fields and line 24 commits the new User object to the database.

At line 24, the new user is created, but he or she is not yet logged in. Line 28 calls the `authenticate()` method, which checks a username and password against the database and, if they are valid, returns the associated `User` object. If the username and password are invalid, `authenticate()` returns `None`. Because you just created the user using this username and password pair, `authenticate()` should return successfully. The `login()` method at line 28 associates the authenticated user with the current session, and line 29 redirects the browser to the account profile page.

Line 32 starts the exception-handling block that is invoked if the `create_user()` method at line 21 fails. The specific type of exception thrown depends on the database backend, so lines 32 through 34 print the exception to the text output of the Django development server just in case anyone's interested. For example, the exception thrown by the SQLite backend is `pysqlite2.dbapi2.IntegrityError`. Line 40 sends the browser back to the user entry form with appropriate fields pre-populated as in the other error case at line 15.

The template associated with the `newUser` view is a simple form, as you'd expect. Enter the code shown in Listing 9-15 into the file `newUser.html`.

Listing 9-15: New user entry form template

```
 1 {% extends "dblog/baseTemplate.html" %}
 2 {% block title %}
 3 Create New User
 4 {% endblock %}
 5
 6 {% block content %}
 7
 8 {% if msg %}
 9 <p>{{ msg }}</p>
10 {% endif %}
11
12 <form method="post" action=".">
13
14 <p>Username: <input type="text" name="username"
15     maxlength="30" value="{{username}}"/></p>
16
17 <p>Password: <input type="text" name="password"
18     maxlength="30"/></p>
19
20 <p>Firstname:<input type="text" name="firstname"
21     maxlength="30" value="{{firstname}}"/></p>
22
23 <p>Lastname: <input type="text" name="lastname"
24     maxlength="30" value="{{lastname}}"/></p>
25
26 <p>Email:    <input type="text" name="email"
27     value="{{email}}"/></p>
28
29 <input type="submit" value="Submit" />
30 </form>
31
32 {% endblock %}
```

This template, like all the others, extends the base template using the {% extends %} directive at line 1. It overrides the title block at lines 2 through 4 and the content block at lines 6 through 32. It does not override the footer block. Any error message passed in the template context is displayed at the top of the form by lines 8 through 10. Lines 12 through 30 define the five input fields and the submit button that make up this form. The value of each of the input elements can be filled in from the template context, or they will be left empty if the template context doesn't contain that element.

Figure 9-10 shows how the new user input form looks in a browser.

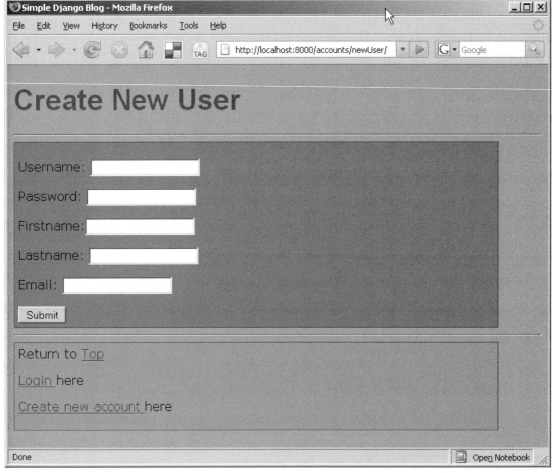

Figure 9-10

As you can see, the form picked up the colors and fonts from the base template, so it looks the same as the rest of the site.

Summary

In this chapter you saw some Django features that help maximize developer productivity for real-world websites. You learned how:

- ❑ Template inheritance can reduce the amount of boilerplate template code you have to write.

- ❑ Generic views can reduce the amount of boilerplate Python code you have to write.

- ❑ Django's user authentication and authorization package provides a convenient way to manage user accounts and permissions on your site.

In the next chapter you'll see even more Django features that you can use to make professional-quality, Rich Internet Applications.

10

Advanced Django Topics: AJAX, RSS, and More

The future is here. It's just not widely distributed yet.

—**William Gibson**

Now that you've seen some of the basics of how to use Django and some of the ways it can make your life easier, it's time to turn to the more advanced features of Django. Not that these things are hard to do (they're not), but they're the kind of features that separate the amateur home page from the professional web application.

Asynchronous JavaScript and XML (AJAX) is all the rage lately as a technique for building dynamic web pages that can be updated without a full page refresh, which traditional web usage requires. The essence of AJAX is JavaScript on the web page that makes requests for data from the server and updates Document Object Model (DOM) elements on the page while the user is viewing and interacting with the page. In this chapter, you learn how to use Django to handle those back-end requests.

When you're deciding which, if any, framework to adopt for your project, it's important to consider the availability of add-on modules that may not be part of the core code base, but can be leveraged when you develop your site. This chapter provides an overview of some add-on modules available for Django and discusses the Really Simple Syndication (RSS) module in detail.

You'll also see some options for deploying Django with the popular Apache web server. Apache is a great choice for deploying Django applications because it's free, it's good, and the `mod_python` Apache module makes integration simple.

AJAX and Django

You've seen a few examples of AJAX already in this book so you know it's not rocket science. It's just some code in the browser talking to some code on the server. But if you've done much JavaScript programming, you know that it can be a royal pain. So, the browser-side code in this chapter uses the MochiKit library, which its creators claim "makes JavaScript suck less."

Unlike TurboGears, which includes the MochiKit JavaScript library, Django ships without a JavaScript library, leaving the decision about which library to use up to the developer. The philosophy is that many sites won't need any JavaScript library, and those that do will have the flexibility to select the one that best meets their needs. As you'll see, incorporating a JavaScript library is not difficult.

Django does provide the mechanism to support AJAX on the server site. Specifically, it provides an easy way to serialize model objects into JavaScript Object Notation (JSON), YAML Ain't Markup Language (YAML), or Extensible Markup Language (XML) in response to asynchronous requests.

MochiKit

The MochiKit JavaScript library that you'll use with Django is the same one that is included with TurboGears, so the learning curve is not steep. It's generally considered a *Pythonic* JavaScript library, so we Python programmers tend to prefer it to other similar libraries. Its creators say MochiKit improves programmers' JavaScript experience by providing some high-level operations that are needed by most AJAX applications, including:

- ❑ Managing asynchronous tasks
- ❑ Functional programming and comparisons
- ❑ DOM manipulation
- ❑ Drag-and-drop management
- ❑ Color handling
- ❑ Date and time handling
- ❑ String formatting
- ❑ Iterators and sorting
- ❑ Logging and debugging
- ❑ Cascading Style Sheets (CSS) manipulation
- ❑ Event handling
- ❑ Visual effects

To enable MochiKit in your Django application using the development server, you just need to unpack the MochiKit .js files into a directory, make that directory available using the `django.views.static.serve` view, and link it in to the appropriate pages. For example, you might unpack the MochiKit code into the same `/scripts/` URL that you used for the CSS files. Then the same URL pattern that serves the CSS file will also serve the MochiKit code automatically. Here's that URL pattern as a reminder:

```
(r'^scripts/(?P<path>.*)$', 'django.views.static.serve',
                        {'document_root': './scripts'}),
```

This URL pattern serves up all files at or below the level of the `document_root` value. Note that you may have to change the `document_root` value if you put the CSS and JavaScript files somewhere else.

To link MochiKit into your pages, just include the following line in the template:

```
<script type="text/javascript" src="/scripts/MochiKit/MochiKit.js"></script>
```

If you use MochiKit throughout your site, you might want to put it in your base template so it gets inherited by all other templates. That's all there is to integrating MochiKit with Django.

Django Serialization for AJAX

To transmit objects between the server-side Python code and the browser-side JavaScript code, they need to be encoded, or *serialized*, into a form that can be transmitted over HTTP and interpreted by both languages. Here are a few of the most common serialization formats included with Django:

❑ **XML:** Good old XML put the *X* in AJAX.

❑ **JSON:** Trivial to parse into JavaScript and Python.

❑ **YAML:** A format intended to be both easy to parse and human-readable.

Classes in the `django.core.serializers` package implement these serialization formats, so to use these features in your view methods you need to import them with a line like this:

```
from django.core import serializers
```

Then you can serialize a list of objects as shown in the following table.

Format	Serialization Code Example
XML	`xmltext = serializers.serialize("xml", [someObject])`
JSON	`jsontext = serializers.serialize("json", [someObject])`
YAML	`yamltext = serializers.serialize("yaml", [someObject])`

So you can see what this looks like, Listing 10-1 shows the `Blog` and `Comment` model objects as you defined them in the previous chapters.

Listing 10-1: models.py

```
1     """Django model classes for a simple Blog site
2
3        This example shows a one-to-many relationship
4          between a Blog and its Comments and various
             computed fields.
5     """
6
7     from django.db import models
8
9     class Blog(models.Model):
10      """The class representing an entry in the blog"""
11
12      """The title or subject of the blog entry"""
13      title = models.CharField(maxlength=128)
14
15      """The date that the post was created"""
16      post_date = models.DateTimeField('date posted')
17
18      """The email address of the posting author"""
19      reply_to = models.EmailField()
20
21      """The actual text content of the posting"""
22      content = models.TextField()
23
24      def rating(self):
25          """Compute the average rating based on the
                 comments received"""
26          comments = self.comment_set.all()
27
28          # Don't divide by zero
29          if len(comments) == 0:
30              return "(unrated)"
31
32          sum = 0.0
33          for c in comments:
34              sum = sum + c.rating
35          average = float(sum)/len(comments)
36          return "%.2f"%average
37
38      """The possible ratings for each blog entry"""
39      RATING_CHOICES = (
40                      (1 , 'Lame'),
41                      (2 , 'Weak'),
42                      (3 , 'OK'),
43                      (4 , 'Nice'),
44                      (5 , 'Rocks'),
45                      )
46      """Empty class enables the Django admin web
             interface"""
47      class Admin:
48        pass
49
```

```
50          """This custom permission is required to create a
                new Blog entry"""
51          class Meta:
52              permissions = (
53                  ("may_create_blogs", "May Create Blogs"),
54              )
55
56          """String representation is used by the Django
                admin interface"""
57          def __str__(self):
58              return "Blog(title = '%s')"%(self.title)
59
60      class Comment(models.Model):
61
62          in_reference_to = models.ForeignKey(Blog)
63          content = models.TextField(maxlength=256)
64          rating = models.IntegerField(choices=Blog.RATING_CHOICES)
65
66          def ratingText(self):
67              """Return this comment's rating as a text
                    string rather than an integer"""
68
69              return Blog.RATING_CHOICES[self.rating-1][1]
70
71          """Empty class enables the Django admin web
                interface"""
72          class Admin:
73              pass
74
75          def __str__(self):
76              """String representation is used by the
                    Django admin interface"""
77              return "Comment(content = '%s', rating = %s)"% \
78                          (self.content, str(self.rating))
```

This listing shows the model objects in Python, but to transmit an instance of an object, Django must convert it to a language-independent form (XML, JSON, or YAML). In the abstract, the `Blog` object is made up of these fields:

- title
- post_date
- reply_to
- content
- A list of comments, each of which contains the following:
  - content
  - rating

Serializing into XML

Listing 10-2 shows how Django serializes a Blog object into XML.

Listing 10-2: XML blog object

```
1   <?xml version="1.0" encoding="utf-8"?>
2   <django-objects version="1.0">
3     <object pk="3" model="dblog.blog">
4       <field type="CharField" name="title">This is the blog title</field>
5       <field type="DateTimeField" name="post_date">2007- 05-26 13:48:36</field>
6       <field type="CharField" name="reply_to">myaddress@email.com</field>
7       <field type="TextField" name="content">
8         This is the blog text. There's not much to it, is there?
9       </field>
10    </object>
11  </django-objects>
```

Notice the following about this XML:

❑   The fields of the model object are in lines 4 through 9. The field names are encoded in the name XML attribute, and the value of the field is between the opening and closing tags.

❑   The XML includes several pieces of metadata that might be useful in certain circumstances. The primary key and class name of the model object are included as attributes of the <object> at line 3. These might be useful if you need to construct a URL in the JavaScript code. The type of each field is also provided as an attribute of the <field> tag.

❑   Notice that the serializer did not serialize the related comment objects. If the serializer followed references, it might get into circular relationships that would never end, so if you need to serialize related objects, you'll have to do it explicitly.

Serializing into JSON

Listing 10-3 shows how Django serializes a Blog object into JSON:

Listing 10-3: JSON blog object

```
1  [{"pk": "3",
2    "model": "dblog.blog",
3    "fields": {
4      "post_date": "2007-05-26 13:48:36",
5      "reply_to": "myaddress@email.com",
6      "content": "This is the blog text. There's not much to it, is there?",
7      "title": "This is the blog title"}
8  }
```

In this listing, the four data fields are in lines 4 through 7 as elements in a dictionary. The JSON serializer includes a little less metadata than the XML serializer, but the important parts are still there. The primary key is in line 1, and the class name of the model object is in line 2.

Serializing into YAML

If you want to use the YAML serailizer, you'll have to download PyYAML from `http://pyyaml.org/` and follow the instructions to install it. Listing 10-4 shows how Django serializes a `Blog` object into YAML.

Listing 10-4: YAML blog object

```
1 - fields: {content: 'This is the blog text. There''s not much to it, is there?',
2       post_date: !!timestamp '2007-05-26 13:48:36.343000',
3       reply_to: myaddress@email.com,
4       title: This is the blog title}
5   model: dblog.blog
6   pk: '3
```

The YAML in this listing contains the same information as the JSON in Listing 10-3. The four fields are in lines 1 through 4, the model class name is at line 5, and the object's primary key is at line 6.

Choosing a Serializer

All three serializers emit the same information, so your choice of which to use depends mostly on how well it integrates with other parts of the application. JSON is trivial to parse in JavaScript, so it's becoming a popular serialization format for AJAX applications. XML is interoperable with many other systems, so it may be a better choice for other applications.

AJAX-ified Blog Example

With MochiKit on the browser and Django serialization on the server, you have the pieces you need to update your blog application with some AJAX effects. The implementation from the previous chapter used separate pages to view blog entries and comments. How could you change the blog view page to show comments when requested? Figure 10-1 is a reminder of what the blog view page you created in the previous chapter looks like.

Notice the View 2 Comments link in the bottom box. This links to the comment view page. It is just a relative URL generated by this section of the `blog_detail.html` template.

```
View <a href="comment">{{object.comment_set.count}}
  comment{{object.comment_set.count|pluralize}}</a><br/>
```

When clicked, this link takes the user to the comment view specified by this URL pattern in `urls.py`:

```
(r'^simpleblog/blog/(?P<object_id>\d+)/comment/$',
    'django.views.generic.list_detail.object_detail',
    dict(blog_set, template_name='dblog/comment.html')),
```

This loads a whole new page into the browser.

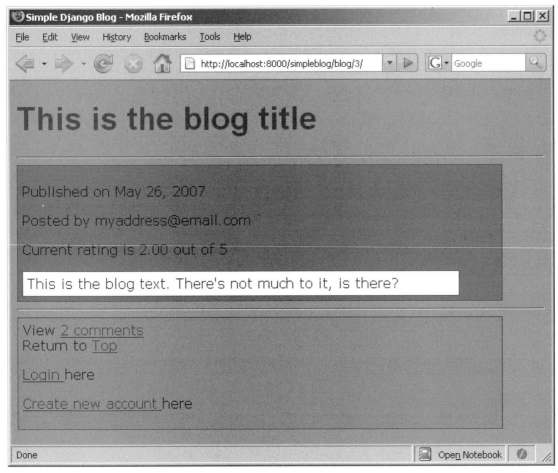

Figure 10-1

It works fine, but the approach is a little dated. If, instead, you want to dynamically update the `blog_detail` page and replace the link with the list of comments, you need to write some JavaScript to do these things when the link is clicked:

❑   Start an asynchronous request for the comment model data.

❑   Replace the DOM element containing the link with some indication that the data is being requested.

❑   When the comment model data arrive, replace the indicator DOM element with the comments themselves.

Rewriting the blog_detail.html Template

First, you need to rewrite the `blog_detail.html` template to link in MochiKit and your own JavaScript. If you're AJAX-ifying your whole application, you might want to update your base templates, but for clarity Listing 10-5 shows a `blog_detail.html` template that doesn't use Django's template inheritance. The shaded sections show the additions that you'll need to add to support the AJAX functions you'll add later in this chapter.

Listing 10-5: AJAX-ready blog_detail.html

```
 1  <!DOCTYPE html PUBLIC "-//W3C//DTD XHTML 1.0 Strict//EN"
 2      "http://www.w3.org/TR/xhtml1/DTD/xhtml1-strict.dtd">
 3  <html>
 4    <head>
 5      <meta http-equiv="Content-Type" content="text/html; charset=utf-8"/>
 6      <title>Simple Django Blog</title>
 7
 8      <!-- Load our color and font preferences -->
 9      <link rel=StyleSheet href="/scripts/style.css" TYPE="text/css">
10
11      <!-- Load MochiKit and our own JavaScript -->
12      <script type="text/javascript" src="/scripts/MochiKit/MochiKit.js">
13      </script>
14      <script type="text/javascript" src="/scripts/dblog.js">
15      </script>
16    </head>
17
18    <body>
19      <h1>
20        <div class="title">
21          {{ object.title }}
22        </div>
23      </h1>
24      <hr>
25      <div class="content">
26        <p>Published on {{object.post_date|date:"F j, Y"}}</p>
27        <p>Posted by {{object.reply_to}}</p>
28        <p>Current rating is {{object.rating}} out of 5</p>
29        <div class="blogtext">
31          {{object.content}}
32        </div>
33      </div>
34
35      <hr>
36      <div class="footer">
37        <div id="comment_view_area">
38          View <a href="javascript:viewComments({{object.id}})">
39          {{object.comment_set.count}}
40          comment{{object.comment_set.count|pluralize}}</a><br/>
41        </div>
42        Return to <a href="/simpleblog">Top</a><br/>
43
```

(continued)

Listing 10-5 *(continued)*

```
44        <script type="text/javascript">
45          var rating_choices = Array({{object.RATING_CHOICES|length}} + 1)
46          {% for r in object.RATING_CHOICES %}
47            rating_choices[{{r.0}}] = "{{r.1}}";
48          {% endfor %}
49        </script>
50        {% if user.is_authenticated %}
51          <script type="text/javascript">var is_authenticated = 1;</script>
52          <p><a href="/accounts/logout">Logout {{user.username }}.</a></p>
53        {% else %}
54          <script type="text/javascript">var is_authenticated = 0;</script>
55          <p><a href="/accounts/login">Login </a>here</p>
56          <p><a href="/accounts/newUser">Create new account </a>here</p>
57        {% endif %}
58      </div>
59    </body>
60  </html>
```

Notice the following about this listing:

❑   Lines 11 through 15 link in the MochiKit library and your own JavaScript file, `dblog.js`, which you'll write soon. Linking in these JavaScript files makes all of the functions and data in those two files available in this page.

❑   Lines 37 through 41 replace the simple relative URL link with a call to the JavaScript function `viewComments`. Notice how the template variable for the blog's `{{object.id}}` primary key fills in the parameter to `viewComments`. The `viewComments` function will need that primary key to construct the URL to which it will make its asynchronous data request. Lines 37 and 41 wrap this little section in a named `<DIV>` to make it easier to find and replace in the DOM when the time comes.

❑   Recall that the comment ratings are stored in the model as integers, but displayed as text strings (with the options defined previously in lines 39 through 44 of Listing 10-1). Lines 45 through 48 of this listing create a JavaScript array that you can use to map the numbers to their corresponding strings using the model's `RATING_CHOICES` field. Of course, you could just explicitly define the array here by copying and pasting the code, but that would violate the DRY principle, which could create maintenance problems later on.

❑   Lines 50 through 57 fill out the footer with the `login` and `create new account` links if the user is not already logged in or the `logout` link if the user is currently logged in. Notice especially lines 51 and 54. They define a JavaScript variable called `is_authenticated`, which the code will use in `dblog.js` to make similar decisions.

Writing the JavaScript Functions in dblog.js

Next, write the JavaScript functions in `dblog.js` as shown in Listing 10-6. These functions will use the MochiKit library to make the asynchronous requests and handle updating the page's DOM.

Listing 10-6: dblog.js

```
 1
 2 /* Keeps track of the DOM element currently displayed */
 3 var currentElement;
 4
 5 /* Holds the DIV from the original HTML in case we
 6    want to swap it back in */
 7 var view_area;
 8
 9 /* The MochiKit asynchronous request object */
10 var thisRequest;
11
12 /* A couple shorthand CSS elements */
13 var headerClass = {'class': 'commentheader'};
14 var dataClass = {'class': 'commentdata'};
15
16 /*
17  * Called when the user clicks on the "View Comments"
18  * link. id = the primary key of the blog
19  */
20 function viewComments(id) {
21   currentElement = DIV(null, "Fetching...")
22   view_area = getElement("comment_view_area");
23   swapDOM(view_area, currentElement);
24   thisRequest = loadJSONDoc("/simpleblog/getComments/"+id);
25   thisRequest.addCallbacks(commentsReady, commentsError);
26 }
27
28 /*
29  * Called when the user clicks on the "Hide Comments"
30  * link. It swaps the original DIV in place of the
     * comment list.
31  */
32 function hideComments() {
33   swapDOM(currentElement, view_area);
34   currentElement = view_area;
35 }
36
37 /*
38  * This function formats a single row of the comment
     * display table
39  */
40 row_display = function (row) {
41   var d = rating_choices;
42   return TR(dataClass,
43     TD(dataClass, row.fields.content),
44     TD(dataClass, rating_choices[row.fields.rating]));
45 }
46
47 /*
48  * Called when the comment model objects are received
49  * from the server.
50  */
```

(continued)

Listing 10-6 *(continued)*

```
51 var commentsReady = function (meta) {
52    var commentList = evalJSONRequest(thisRequest.results[0]);
53
54    var newTable = TABLE({'class': 'commenttable'},
55        THEAD(headerClass, TD(headerClass, "Comment"),
56                          TD(headerClass, "Rating")),
57        TBODY(null, map(row_display, commentList))
58    );
59
60    var hide = P(null, 'Hide ',
61        A({'href': 'javascript:hideComments()'}, 'comments'));
62    if (is_authenticated) {
63        var a = P(null, 'Enter new ',
64                    A({'href': 'comment/add/'}, 'comment'));
65        var newDiv = DIV({'class': 'footer'}, hide, newTable, a);
66    } else {
67        var newDiv = DIV({'class': 'footer'}, hide, newTable);
68    }
69    swapDOM(currentElement, newDiv);
70    currentElement = newDiv;
71 }
72
73 /*
74  * Error function called if an error occurs while
75  * fetching the async data
76  */
77 var commentsError = function (err) {
78    alert("commentsError");
79 }
```

The first few lines of this file define some data elements that the functions that follow will use. The functions in this file will be swapping DOM elements in and out, so line 3 defines a variable used to keep track of the currently active DOM element. When the link is first clicked, the original `"comment_view_area"` DOM element (the simple link and comment count) is replaced by some text that shows that the data fetch is in progress. The `view_area` variable at line 7 holds that original element so it can be reused if needed. Line 10 defines a variable that holds the MochiKit asynchronous request object used to fetch the comment data. The last data items (lines 13 and 14) create two variables that you can use as shorthand for specifying CSS attributes.

The `viewComments` function (lines 20 through 26) is invoked when the user clicks the link previously defined in lines 27 through 41 of Listing 10-5. Its argument is the primary key of the blog being viewed. Line 21 makes a new <DIV> DOM fragment using the MochiKit `DIV()` function that gives the user some feedback that the comment fetch operation is in progress. MochiKit includes similar functions for most common tags. These functions can really reduce the amount of ugly HTML you have to write, but you can always create these tags manually if you prefer. Line 22 searches the DOM to find the DIV that you're going to replace, and line 23 uses the handy MochiKit `swapDOM()` to replace it with the `"Fetching..."` DIV. (`swapDOM()` just replaces one DOM element with another.)

Now that the user has been told that his request is in progress, it's time to actually make the request. Line 24 uses the MochiKit `loadJSONDoc` function to start an asynchronous request for data in JSON format. Be aware that this is an asynchronous request, so the `thisRequest` object returned from `loadJSONDoc` is not the data itself, but rather a handle to the request. Line 25 connects two functions to the request: `commentsReady` is called when the request completes successfully, and `commentsError` is called if the request fails for some reason. Notice also how the argument in line 24 is constructed using the primary key of the blog object. Your Django view uses this to fill in the response data.

Figure 10-2 shows what the page looks like while the request is being processed.

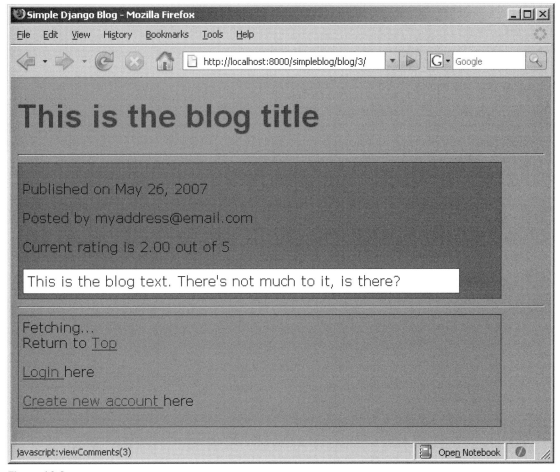

Figure 10-2

It looks the same as before the request except the View 2 Comments link has been replaced with a Fetching . . . message.

When the comment data return successfully from the server, the `commentsReady` callback (lines 51 through 71) is invoked. The first thing this function does is extract the JSON object from the asynchronous request object using MochiKit's `evalJSONRequest` function at line 52. This object is created from JSON data similar to Listing 10-7.

Listing 10-7: JSON comment data

```
[
{"pk": "6",
 "model":
 "dblog.comment",
 "fields": {
    "content": "This is a comment on your blog",
    "rating": 1,
    "in_reference_to": 3}
},
{"pk": "7",
 "model": "dblog.comment",
 "fields": {
    "content": "This is another comment on the blog",
    "rating": 3,
    "in_reference_to": 3}
}
]
```

In this instance, the blog has two comments that are returned as a list, and all of the comment fields include primary keys. For example, the `"in_reference_to"` field is the primary key of associated the `Blog` object. You can use this primary key to construct URLs for the object if necessary.

Returning to Listing 10-6, lines 54 through 58 create an HTML table using MochiKit's DOM fragment creation functions. Each row of the table is populated by the `row_display` function (lines 40 through 45). The two <TD> elements are filled in with the content of the comment (line 43) and the rating of the comment (line 44). Notice how line 44 uses the `rating_choices` array defined in the Django template (lines 45 through 48 of Listing 10-5).

That completes the table of comments, but it would be nice to be able to hide the comments, too. Lines 60 and 61 of Listing 10-6 create a <P> element that that contains an <A> element that, when clicked, invokes the `hideComments()` function. That function is defined on lines 32 through 35 and simply replaces the element currently displayed with the original element.

Also, it would be nice to insert a link to the Add a Comment page, but that page is available only to registered users. Recall that the Django template for this page (lines 51 and 54 in Listing 10-5) created a JavaScript variable called `is_authenticated` that is 1 (true) if the user is authenticated and 0 (false) otherwise. If the user is authenticated, lines 63 and 64 in Listing 10-6 create a hypertext link to the comment entry page, and line 65 creates a new DIV that includes this link and the other new DOM elements. If the user is not authenticated, line 67 creates a new DIV without the link to the comment entry page.

Finally, line 69 swaps in the new DIV, and line 70 remembers it in case it needs to be swapped out again.

Writing the Django View and getComments Function

Ugh. That's quite enough JavaScript for now — it's time to get back to Python. The only piece left to write is the Django view that serves up the JSON comment objects. As usual, you have to add a URL pattern to `urls.py`. Recall that the JavaScript will request `/simpleblog/getComments/<blog_id>`, so this pattern needs to capture it and route it to the `getComments` Python function. To do this, add the following lines to `urls.py`:

```
(r'^simpleblog/getComments/(?P<blog_id>\d+)/$',
        'simpleblog.dblog.views.getComments'),
```

Next, write the `getComments` function in views.py. Like most Django views, it's pretty simple.

```
1 def getComments(request, blog_id):
2   b = get_object_or_404(Blog, pk=blog_id)
3   jsontext = serializers.serialize("json", b.comment_set.all())
4   time.sleep(2)
5   return HttpResponse(jsontext, "application/json")
```

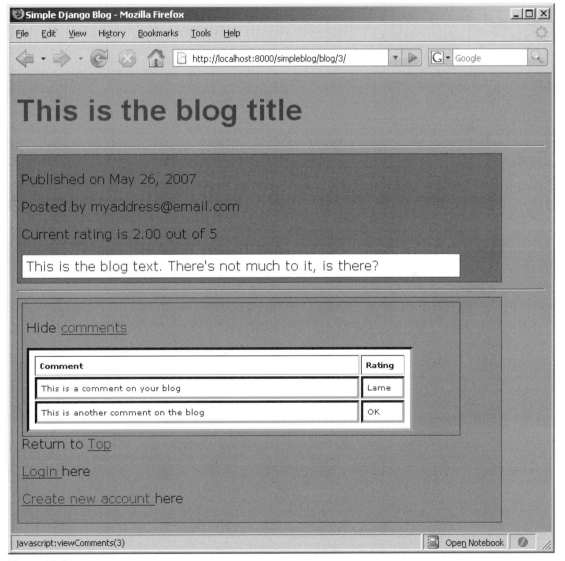

Figure 10-3

Line 2 fetches the `Blog` object from the database by primary key. Line 3 serializes its comment list to JSON format, and line 5 returns it as the HTTP response. Line 4 is just a little delay to give the user a chance to enjoy the Fetching . . . message.

Figure 10-3 shows the updated comment page after comments have been received and the DOM is updated.

That's the pattern for adding some dynamic AJAX to your application. It wasn't trivial, but without tools like Django and MochiKit, it would be a massive effort.

Django Add-Ons

Like most open source frameworks, Django has inspired several add-on packages that extend the capabilities provided by the core distribution. The official Django distribution comes with a few useful add-ons in the `django.contrib` package, and there are plenty more on source code repository sites like SourceForge (`http://sourceforge.net`) and Google Code (`http://code.google.com`).

django.contrib Add-Ons

There are a few Django applications that come bundled with the Django core distribution. These add-ons tend to be generally useful for web development, so they're maintained and supported just like the core. You've already seen a couple of the more useful `contrib` packages: `django.contrib.admin`, which generates the administration site, and `django.contrib.auth`, which handles user authentication. Here are some of the other Django `contrib` packages:

❑   `django.contrib.comments`: A framework for enabling visitors to your site to leave their comments about the content. It has facilities for accepting comments from registered users or from anonymous unregistered users. A commenter can do things like provide ratings, attach images, and acquire a good (or bad) reputation over time. There is even a way for the administrator to moderate the comments to keep out offensive posts.

❑   `django.contrib.databrowse`: Introspects Django models and generates a website for browsing them. Unfortunately, this package is not available on the 0.96 version of Django, so you'll have to upgrade to a later version to get it.

❑   `django.contrib.flatpages`: Serves HTML content from a database and enables you to manage it from the Django `admin` interface. It also includes an API that you can use from any Python code to access that content. You might use `flatpages` if you find it convenient to store simple, static content in a database.

❑   `django.contrib.redirects`: Enables you to store and manage URL redirect information in the database. It intercepts any 404 (Not Found) errors raised by a Django application and looks in the database to see if that resource has moved. If so, the requestor is redirected to the new location; if not, the 404 is processed as usual. You might find this application useful if you need to move content around and change URLs frequently.

❑ `django.contrib.sites`: Enables you to handle multiple websites from a single Django installation. It is especially useful if your sites share some content because you don't have to maintain multiple copies of the content — just share it between multiple sites. The sites also share the Django `admin` interface, which makes it easier for one person to manage multiple sites. Several of the other `contrib` add-ons make use of the `sites` framework when generating their content.

❑ `django.contrib.sitemap`: Automates the generation of `sitemap` XML files, which search engines use to index your site and to keep track of content changes and the relative importance of the pages. This framework enables you to express the contents of `sitemap` files in Python code rather than XML.

❑ `django.contrib.syndication`: Enables you to generate RSS and Atom feeds from your site. Users of your site can use RSS or Atom syndication to get automatic notification of content updates. Later in this chapter, you'll see a detailed RSS example that uses this add-on.

Other Add-Ons

Several people have built add-ons for Django that could be useful in particular situations, but aren't general enough or aren't mature enough to be included in the `django.contrib` distribution. Browse through the following list to see if there's something you can use (and for even more add-ons, visit `http://code.djangoproject.com/wiki/DjangoResources`):

❑ `django-registration`: This is a simple user-registration application that implements a typical self-registration model. The user requests an account and is e-mailed a registration link that, when clicked, activates the account. The code and details for this application are at `http://code.google.com/p/django-registration/`.

❑ `django-databasetemplateloader`: This is a custom template loader engine that gets its templates from a database rather than the file system. You can get details and code at `http://code.google.com/p/django-databasetemplateloader/`.

❑ `django-tagging`: This Django application manages the association and retrieval of tags with model objects. You could use it to implement a social tagging site like `http://del.icio.us`. You can get details and source code at `http://code.google.com/p/django-tagging/`.

❑ `django-xmlrpc`: This application provides a way to make your views available as XML-RPC interfaces. XML-RPC is a simple protocol for web services that lets you enable other applications to use your Django application. You can get the code at `http://code.google.com/p/django-xmlrpc/`.

RSS in Detail

In this section you'll see how to add RSS to the example blog application using the `django.contrib.syndication` framework. You'll see how easy it is to add RSS feeds that can alert your viewers to new blog posts.

Syndication feeds are just small XML documents that contain a few standard fields. These fields describe the feed, the current items in the feed, and URLs for each item. RSS and Atom are two similar means of accomplishing syndication, and Django supports both of them directly. This example focuses on generating an RSS version 2.0 feed, but Atom works the same way. Listing 10-8 shows an example RSS version 2.0 document that describes a blog feed with three current entries.

Listing 10-8: An RSS feed

```
1  <?xml version="1.0" encoding="utf-8"?>
2  <rss version="2.0">
3    <channel>
4      <title>Latest blog entries</title>
5      <link>http://localhost:8000/feeds/latest</link>
6      <description>The most recent blog
                    entries</description>
7      <language>en-us</language>
8      <item>
9        <title>My First Blog</title>
10       <link>http://localhost:8000/simpleblog/blog/1/
         </link>
11       <description>Not very exciting, but here it is.
         </description>
12       <guid>http://localhost:8000/simpleblog/blog/1/
         </guid>
13     </item>
14     <item>
15       <title>This is the blog title</title>
16       <link>http://localhost:8000/simpleblog/blog/3/
         </link>
17       <description>This is the blog text. There's...
         </description>
18       <guid>http://localhost:8000/simpleblog/blog/3/
         </guid>
19     </item>
20     <item>
21       <title>My Second Blog</title>
22       <link>http://localhost:8000/simpleblog/blog/2/
         </link>
23       <description>Here we go again....</description>
24       <guid>http://localhost:8000/simpleblog/blog/2/
         </guid>
25     </item>
26   </channel>
27 </rss>
```

There are two main items of interest in this listing:

❑   The feed channel itself is described in lines 4 through 7. The `<link>` is the URL from which this document is available.

❑   Each of the `<item>` elements (lines 8–13, 14–19, and 20–26) describes one of the blogs being syndicated by this feed. They contain the same type of information as the channel itself, including a URL for each item. You can see in the `<link>` lines (line 10, for example) that the URL is just the absolute URL for each blog entry's `blog_detail` page.

Creating the RSS Feed

It would be completely straightforward to write the Django template and the view method that generate this document, but the `django.contrib.syndication` framework makes it dead easy. To create an RSS feed for your site, you need to create a URL for it. Add the following expression to `urlpatterns` in `urls.py`:

```
(r'^feeds/(?P<url>.*)/$', 'django.contrib.syndication.views.feed',
    {'feed_dict': feeds}),
```

This pattern associates the Django syndication view (`django.contrib.syndication.views.feed`) with URLs that include `/feeds/url`. The `feed_dict` argument to the URL pattern is a dictionary that maps from feed name (the `url`) to the class that generates the feed content. Although you could make lots of feeds, you'll just make one feed for this example, so add the following dictionary to `urls.py`:

```
from simpleblog.dblog.feeds import LatestEntries
feeds = {
  'latest': LatestEntries,
}
```

This dictionary associates the `/feeds/latest` URL with the `LatestEntries` feed class. The next step is to write that class.

Writing the LatestEntries Feed Class

The `LatestEntries` class must be a subclass of the `django.contrib.syndication.feeds.Feed` class, which defines the methods required for the syndication framework. You can put the `LatestEntries` class anywhere you want, but it's convenient to put it in its own file, called `feeds.py`, in the same folder with `models.py` and `views.py`. Listing 10-9 shows a simple `feeds.py` that syndicates the three newest blog entries.

Listing 10-9: RSS feed class

```
1  from django.contrib.syndication.feeds import Feed
2  from simpleblog.dblog.models import Blog
3
4  class LatestEntries(Feed):
5      title = "Latest blog entries"
6      link = "/feeds/latest"
7      description="The most recent blog entries"
8
9      def items(self):
10         return Blog.objects.order_by('-post_date')[:3]
11
12     def item_link(self, blog):
13         return "/simpleblog/blog/%d/"%blog.id
```

Lines 5, 6, and 7 of this listing fill in the `title`, `link`, and `description` elements of the RSS XML document (as previously shown on lines 4, 5, and 6 in Listing 10-8). On lines 9 and 10, the `items()` method returns a list of `Blog` objects retrieved using the Django model. The `'-post_date'` retrieves the list sorted by date in descending order, and the `[:3]` selects the most recent three entries from that list.

Each subelement of the <item> element is filled in using information from the Blog object. The title element and the description element are filled in using two templates. By default, the templates are named <url_prefix>_title.html and <url_prefix>_description.html, where <url_prefix> is feeds/latest in this case. These templates receive two context variables: obj is an object from the list returned from items(), and site is an object from the Django sites framework.

These two templates won't be elaborate. They just need to return a small piece of text, so they are both one-liners. For the feeds/latest_title.html template, you just need to return the Blog title like this:

```
{{ obj.title }}
```

Figure 10-4

For the `feeds/latest_description.html`, you can use the `truncatewords` template filter to return the first 10 words of the blog entry content like this:

```
{{obj.content|truncatewords:10}}
```

There are two ways to specify the `link` subelement of the `<item>` element. You can define a `get_absolute_url()` method on the item returned in the `items()` list, or you can define an `item_link()` method in the feed class that, given an object, returns the URL to that object. Listing 10-9 defines an `item_link()` method (lines 12 and 13) that returns the URL using the `Blog` object's primary key.

Accessing the RSS Feed

Now that all the pieces are in place, you can access the new RSS feed. Figure 10-4 shows how Firefox displays the `/feeds/latest` URL.

The three latest blog entries are shown, along with the titles and descriptions you just implemented. At the top, Firefox gives some options for subscribing to the feed.

Be aware that the syndication framework generates absolute URLs for the feed links by adding the `sites` framework's notion of the site domain before the URLs that you provide (such as `/feeds/latest`). If you haven't configured the domain of your site using the Django `admin` interface, you'll see links like `http://example.com/feeds/latest`, which won't work unless you happen to be building a site for example.com Inc.

Follow these steps to change the site domain:

1. Log in to the `admin` site and click the Change link for Sites, as shown in Figure 10-5.

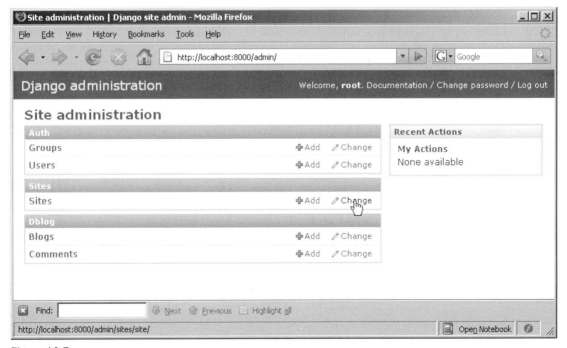

Figure 10-5

2. Select the `example.com` domain name, as shown in Figure 10-6.

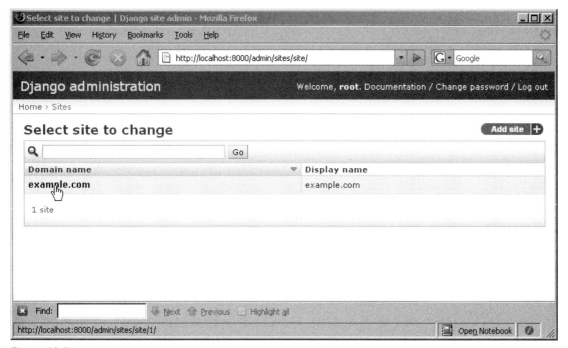

Figure 10-6

3. Change `example.com` to a domain name that will work for your installation. You can specify `localhost:8000` if you're using the development server on the same machine as your browser; otherwise, you need to use a real domain name. Figure 10-7 shows how to configure the development server for local access.

4. Enter a display name that matches the domain name you entered in step 3 and click Save to commit your changes. Now any absolute URLs should have the correct domain name, and all your feeds will work from any location.

5. Provide a link so that readers can find your RSS feed. For example, add the following line to the `footer` section of the base template to have that link show up on every page:

```
Subscribe to <a href="/feeds/latest/">rss</a><br/>
```

Now users can find and subscribe to your RSS feeds.

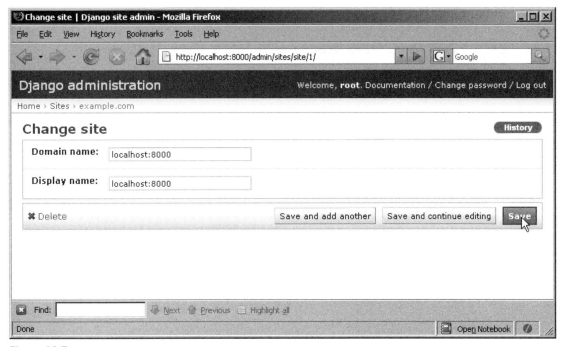

Figure 10-7

Deploying Django with Apache HTTPD

The Django development server is great for developing your code and some light testing, but when it's time to go live, you need a production-quality server. The Django folks recommend the Apache HTTP Server with the mod_python extension, so that's what you learn about in this section. Other deployment options are similar and are documented at www.djangoproject.com/documentation/.

Installing and Configuring Apache

Follow these steps to configure the Apache HTTP Server:

1. If you haven't already installed Apache, consult the appendix for instructions.

2. Download the latest version of mod_python from www.modpython.org/. (The examples in this section were developed using version 3.3.1, but another version greater than 3 will probably work for you too.)

   ❑ For UNIX, download and build the source according to the instructions on the modpython site.

   ❑ For Windows, you can download one of the Win32 binaries, but make sure you get the binary that matches your Python version (2.3, 2.4, or 2.5) *and* your Apache version (2.0 or 2.2) or you'll be hating life. The Win32 binary is an installer package that finds your Apache installation and installs into it automatically.

3. Configure the Apache server to load the `mod_python` module. Edit your `httpd.conf` file and find the section with the `LoadModule` statements. Add the following line to that section:

```
LoadModule python_module modules/mod_python.so
```

4. If you'd like to test your `mod_python` installation, follow the instructions at www.modpython.org/live/current/doc-html/inst-testing.html.

5. Add the section shown in Listing 10-10 to the end of `httpd.conf` to tell Apache how to find your Django application.

Listing 10-10: mod_python apache configuration

```
1 <LocationMatch "/(simpleblog|admin|accounts|feeds)">
2     SetHandler python-program
3     PythonHandler django.core.handlers.modpython
4     SetEnv DJANGO_SETTINGS_MODULE simpleblog.settings
5     PythonDebug On
6     PythonPath "['C:\some\path\here\dblog']+sys.path"
7 </LocationMatch>
```

If you examine the URL patterns in `urls.py`, you'll see that there are four top-level URLs in the `simpleblog` application:

❑ `/simpleblog`: The main application

❑ `/admin`: The Django administration interface

❑ `/accounts`: The user account management pages

❑ `/feeds`: The RSS syndication feeds

In Listing 10-10, the `<LocationMatch>` directive configures all four of these locations. Line 2 tells Apache that these URLs should be handled by the `mod_python` module rather than just being read as files from the file system. Line 3 tells the `mod_python` module that the requests will be handled by the Django `modpython` request handler.

Line 4 configures an environment variable that Django relies upon to find the `settings.py` file. Recall that `settings.py` contains the database connection information and other important configuration data. Line 5 turns on some debugging output, just in case something goes wrong. You'll want to turn debugging off on a production server so you don't accidentally disclose sensitive information to a web client. Line 6 adds the location of the `simpleblog` source code to the Python search path. You'll have to edit this example to reflect where you put your code.

Configuring Other Items

Now Apache knows how to find and run the code, but there are still a couple of pieces missing. Recall that the development server served static data (CSS files, JavaScript, and so on) using the `django.views.static.serve` view. You now need to configure Apache to serve those files. You can either add some `<Directory>` directives to `httpd.conf` or just copy the directories that contain those files to Apache's `htdocs` directory. Here are the directories that need to be copied:

❑   `scripts/`: Contains the `simpleblog` JavaScript and CSS files. Copy this directory to `htdocs/scripts`.

❑   `django/contrib/admin/media`: Contains the static files for the Django `admin` interface. You'll find this in your Python `site-packages` directory. Copy it to `htdocs/media`.

That takes care of the static files, but there are still a few more configuration items to check. If you've been using relative paths to your database file and template directory in `settings.py`, you need to change them to absolute paths. Apache doesn't run in the same directory as the development server, so relative paths won't work. Make this change by editing your `settings.py` file and make sure that `DATABASE_NAME` is the fully qualified absolute path to the SQLite database file. Also make sure that the directory in `TEMPLATE_DIRS` is the absolute path to the root of the directory containing the template files (the directory that contains the `dblog/` and `feeds/` subdirectories).

Finally, fire up the Django `admin` site and check the `site` configuration as you did previously in Figures 10-5, 10-6, and 10-7. The absolute URL to the `simpleblog` application probably changed when you moved from the development server to Apache.

That's it. Now your Django application is up and running on a production-ready server. As you've seen, there are a few configuration items to consider, but it's easy to switch back and forth after they're both set up.

Summary

This concludes our whirlwind tour of Django. In this chapter, you saw some ways to use Django for sophisticated web applications. It's easy to add MochiKit or any other JavaScript library to your Django application, and Django's support for different serialization formats makes communicating data between the browser and the server easy.

You saw some of the add-on applications that are available with the Django distribution or through other sources. Some of these add-ons, such as the authentication framework, are useful for most websites. Others, such as the syndication framework, can make the difference between a good site and a great one in special situations.

Finally, you saw how easy it is to take a Django application constructed using the built-in development server and deploy it to the Apache HTTP Server. This production-ready server is the recommended deployment platform for Django applications.

That concludes Part III of this book. We hope we've given you a flavor for what you can do with Django. For more details and up-to-date changes, be sure to consult the Django documentation site at `http://www.djangoproject.com/documentation/`. In Part IV you'll see some exciting tools and techniques for enhancing the client side of your Rich Internet Applications.

A Conversation with Django's Adrian Holovaty

Adrian Holovaty led the initial development and implementation of Django as lead developer for the World Online web department at the World Company news organization located in Lawrence, Kansas. He now develops websites for the Washington Post Company, but he continues to oversee Django development. He spoke with us about software development in general and Django in particular in May 2007.

Q: *What motivated Django and how did it come about?*

Adrian Holovaty: I was working for a small web-development team at a small newspaper in Lawrence, Kansas, and in a newspaper environment, the deadlines are pretty stringent. For example, our boss, the top editor would say, "Oh, there's a big news event that's happened, and we've got a bunch of data that we need to publish online" or "A presidential debate is happening tonight and we'd like our readers to be able to interact with each other on the website and discuss the debate after it happens and can you please build that in two hours?" That's the really rapid deadline environment.

We originally used PHP to get that stuff done, but it became unmaintainable and not very fun, so we developed Django. We really didn't set about to create a framework in the first place; it just sort of grew out of the conventions that we had written over time.

Q: *What do you consider Django's primary value to developers?*

AH: It's the fact that they don't have to reinvent all sorts of web development tools. So the classic web developer's path (at least the one that I took and that a lot of my friends have taken) is that you create a website from scratch, you create website number two from scratch, you realize what the two sites have in common, and you somehow extract common code — the commonalities. Then you build website number three and you see, "Oh, it has this other thing; if only I could tweak it and remove some redundancy, and I'll create another abstraction . . ." and before you know it you've invented this framework. So, what Django developers avoid primarily is going through those steps. Also, because there are thousands or tens of thousands of people using it around the world, you have this shared community and the shared knowledge of the "best-practices" way of solving problems.

Q: *How do you compare Django to something that gets more buzzword press like Ruby on Rails?*

AH: I've never actually used Rails. I've had no reason to use it. I've got Django. People tend to not do very much research and to assume that Django is a response to it, that it's a sort of a "me too" framework. But actually, almost four years ago was when we started to piece it together. Rails was open-sourced first, while Django was still a proprietary project. I remember the day that Ruby on Rails was released we saw the announcement and went to the website. The other Django developers and I said to ourselves, "Wow, this is a lot like Django but they do all this stuff really differently and it's kind of crappy . . . we'll stick with Python and Django."

Also, we've deliberately not done much marketing because we're not yet at version 1.0 and we have some backwards-incompatible changes to make. But once we hit version 1.0, we're going to definitely do a screencast and some pretty exciting things in the marketing arena.

Q: *What kind of things do you do to generate the kind of buzz that Rails has?*

AH: They've had a lot of success with dissing the big boys, particularly Java. What I think they were really successful in doing was introducing not just Rails and Ruby but the concept of a high-level dynamic language. Java people, who are used to the compilation stage and a lot of configuration and XML all over the place, saw Ruby on Rails and they thought, "Oh, wow, what a breath of fresh air." So I think that the Java people who adopt Ruby on Rails aren't necessarily into Ruby on Rails, they're just new to this concept of high-level languages. Ruby on Rails was a confirmation that this was actually usable in a production setting. So I think that the fact that it was Ruby on Rails doesn't really matter; it was more that it was some high-level language.

Q: *Do you think that there's any chance that languages like Ruby will drag the Java camp into lightweight languages?*

AH: Oh, yeah. A rising tide lifts all ships. I consider myself friends with David Hansson of Rails. We both live in Chicago. I had him over to play the Wii the other day. We may publicly tease each other's frameworks, but really, we're on the same team. He put it very well one time; he said that we really shouldn't be fighting over a tiny piece of the pie, which is the dynamic language piece of the pie. We should, instead, be trying to expand the pie and get users of legacy — I don't want to use the term "legacy" because that carries too much baggage — but environments like Java, C++, and PHP, especially, and Perl. So if people migrate from those technologies to something like Ruby on Rails, I'm a happy camper. If they migrate from something like that to Python, I'm also a happy camper.

Q: *How many people are on the development team? How is the team structured and what is the development process?*

AH: We have seven or eight committers spread across the world. I'm in Chicago, with people in Lawrence, Kansas, where Django was created, and in the U.K., Australia, New Zealand, and Germany. Many of those people I've never actually met in person. I still get a kick, to this day, out of the fact that there are people whom I haven't met in person who contribute brilliant code. It's just astounding.

We keep the number of committers deliberately small. The reason is we prefer quality over quantity when it comes to getting committers and also making changes to the code base. Although we do make changes on an almost daily basis to the Django trunk, to the subversion repository, it's not an overwhelming amount. We're trying to hit the sweet spot in terms of making smart improvements and not making too many.

The process is pretty standard when it comes to open source projects. We've got a bug-tracking system that anyone can use. Anyone can submit a bug or a patch or a feature request. As soon as that gets logged in there, we have a team of ticket triage people, not included in the seven or eight committers, who are a second rung of people who look at every single change that comes in, every request that comes in, every ticket. First of all, they verify that it's a problem or whether it's a good idea. In some cases, they're not qualified to make the decision, so they say "design decision needed," and that flags it for some of the committers on the mailing list to discuss. Then it gets shot over to the committers, and we take care of it.

Patches work the same way. People can submit a patch and that triage team will take a look at it and make sure that it applies cleanly, make sure the code matches our standards, and make sure that it actually fixes the problem without breaking any other stuff. That triage level was something that we implemented maybe two months ago, and it's just revolutionized development and streamlined it in so many good ways. Before then, the committers would haphazardly choose random tickets in the ticket system whenever we had free time, so it's a lot more efficient now.

Q: *You mentioned that you're coming up on a version 1.0 release. What drives your product vision? How do you decide on priorities and releases?*

AH: The main criterion that we always have in the back of our heads is, whatever proposed change is being talked about, does that actually help in the real world? That philosophy stems from the fact that this was a proprietary project for two years back when I was working for the team in Kansas. It wasn't until two years after we first conceived the framework that it was open source. Because of that, we have very focused design decisions. Because it was two or three people working on this full-time for a couple years, it didn't have the "design-by-committee" feel that some open source projects have.

Because of that history, we are very oriented toward, "Does this proposed change fit in with our philosophy? Does it fit in with our look and feel? Does it actually help people in the real world?"

Q: *Why did you decide to take Django from proprietary to open source?*

AH: That's a really good question. It's for a number of reasons. One, we wanted to give something back to the open source community. That web operation used open source for everything from Apache and PostgreSQL, sendmail . . . The company also owned an ISP, which could pretty much thank open source for being profitable in the first place. If it weren't for open source technologies, it would have to be paying all these license fees and it probably wouldn't be in the black. So, there's that feel-good reason for wanting to give something back.

Another reason was we were releasing a commercial content-management system for newspapers called Ellington, named after Duke Ellington. Ellington was built on Django, so in order to get the word out about it, we figured that if we open-sourced the underlying framework, that would at least give some buzz to Ellington. And indeed it has. Ellington has been tremendously successful.

Another thing was, hiring people. As a small web-development shop in the middle of Kansas, you don't really get top-notch job applicants. Sometimes you do, but it's hard to convince people to move to a small town in Kansas. So we figured, if we open-sourced this and it gains traction, that community of people using it will be very ripe to hire people from. Not only would the Kansas operation have an easy way to find people who know the technology, but these people would have no need for training. Before we had an open source Django, we would hire a Python programmer, and that Python programmer would require some training in the framework that we developed because it was this proprietary thing. By open-sourcing it, they removed that. Since we open-sourced Django almost two years ago, that web-development team in Kansas has hired at least three, maybe four, people from the community who are just top-notch developers.

Another thing: open-sourcing the framework encourages contributions from people all over the globe. That's obvious. That's a no-brainer. We figured that if we open-sourced Django, we would get all sorts of contributions from people who were using it in a variety of ways that we never even thought of. One of the first big contributions after we open-sourced it was the internationalization framework. There's no way a tiny newspaper in the middle of Kansas would have ever needed internationalization, but we got it for free because we open-sourced it and a fellow in Germany worked with a group of other Django developers and put that together. So now, because Django now has internationalization, Ellington, the commercial product that the operation is selling, now has that functionality.

Q: *Unlike some of the other open source frameworks, you don't include a bunch of other open source tools bundled in with Django. Why did you decide to structure it that way?*

AH: That's an artifact of how we started almost four years ago. We did look for existing Python frameworks and tools that we could somehow build on top of, but that long ago there really wasn't anything that great. We looked at the Cheetah templating system, the CherryPy, and they were okay, but Simon Willison and I, the people who were originally building this, were and still are very picky web developers. So the stuff that was already out there just wasn't up to snuff.

Since we've open-sourced it, obviously there are all sorts of other Python libraries available now. And some of them are actually pretty good, but we're pretty committed to being the one, very, very easy-to-use, full-stack framework. There are a number of benefits in being full-stack rather than being a collection of disparate pieces, such as, there's only one place to go for documentation. You don't have "for the database layer, you go over here" and maybe it's not really written that well, and "for the template language, you go over here" and the pieces don't really know about each other so there's no cohesive documentation about how to use the pieces together — let alone the differences in styles and quality of the documentation.

Documentation is something we take very seriously. I'm a journalist by training. I've always worked at newspaper websites. We have pretty stringent guidelines on our documentation in terms of the quality, the style, the grammar, and just the coverage, the breadth of the documentation. That's an obvious benefit.

There's a pretty obvious benefit in the fact that it all just works. You don't have to worry about this obscure error message in this layer versus this other layer that doesn't interact with it that well.

With that said, the various bits of Django are pretty loosely coupled, so just because it comes in one package doesn't mean that it is all this amalgam of spaghetti code. You can just use the Django template system, or just use the database layer, or use another template system with Django.

Q: *We read that you're working for* The Washington Post *now. Coming there as a new person, how do you go about evangelizing tools like Django and Python in an organization that may have its own way of doing things?*

AH: I kind of lucked out because, how can I put this, the newspaper industry is really backward when it comes to the Internet, and there aren't a lot of people who know how to use technology well in a journalism setting. Because I had that experience and they were pretty keen on hiring me, I essentially was given carte blanche in deciding which technology to use. So it was easy for me. I just said, "I'm not going to work here unless it's Python," and they said, "Okay." Another thing is journalists don't know about technology, so they're willing to defer to you. It was really easy.

Part IV
Advanced Client-Side Topics

Chapter 11: MochiKit—Pythonic JavaScripting

Chapter 12: Flash-Based Interfaces and TurboGears

11

MochiKit — Pythonic JavaScripting

Once in seven years I burn all my sermons; for it is a shame if I cannot write better sermons now than I did seven years ago.

—John Wesley

Rather like the prescription to start fresh periodically offered by the founder of Methodism, JavaScript (in the opinion of many frustrated web developers) should have taken a trip back to the drawing board at least a couple of times for a complete rewrite. Since its inception and deployment in Netscape 2 in 1995, JavaScript (now officially referred to as ECMAScript), has undergone a number of ad hoc repairs, but it's still the same basic language: syntactically similar to languages like Java and C, but with semantics that are utterly different and an object model unrelated to and largely incompatible with Java or Python.

Small wonder that as the need for a robust in-browser language has grown from nice-to-have to absolutely critical, a number of generally similar JavaScript library collections have appeared in the open source community. Perhaps unsurprisingly, Django and TurboGears are the epitome of tough employers when it comes to libraries and frameworks. Although they are both quite capable of working with a number of underlying frameworks, they will toss the current choice aside when something better comes along. TurboGears, for example is being re-based to move to Genji and SQLAlchemy. In the case of the preferred JavaScript library, though, it's unlikely that either Django developers or TurboGears developers will want to move away from MochiKit — it's quite simply the best of its ilk. Not only that; its design center makes it something that most definitely appeals to Pythonists.

Why MochiKit?

Why should you even bother with a JavaScript library at all? If you are doing something very simple, with perhaps one or two method calls, no AJAX handling, no manipulation of page elements, you may not even need JavaScript (or even need to read this book, for that matter). On the other hand, if you are developing Rich Internet Applications (RIAs) of even moderate complexity, you are probably writing lots of JavaScript — which is not likely to be a joyful experience. MochiKit's avowed aim is to make this side of RIA development less painful, or in the words of MochiKit's creator, Bob Ippolito, "MochiKit makes JavaScript suck less."

JavaScript is often considered a rather chaotic language — strangely familiar in some ways (at least if you are a C or Java programmer), but curiously unlike C-based languages in other ways. In the early Web era, JavaScript was used primarily to handle fairly simple on-page tasks; thus, it really didn't need to be a hugely capable language. Because JavaScript usually didn't have to do anything beyond the occasional page animation, there was little compromise in user experience regardless of whether the JavaScript in a page actually worked or not.

In truth, because the page could work quite well with or without JavaScript, developers didn't work exceptionally hard to assure that a particular piece of scripting worked in multiple browsers or in multiple versions of the same browser. In the early days, JavaScript developers almost always tossed in a coding convention that effectively exempted the browser from the responsibility of either interpreting or supporting JavaScript code. It essentially said, "Feel free to ignore the JavaScript altogether." You've seen the following type of convention used in the code examples in this book, or perhaps used it in your own code development:

```
<script type="text/javascript">
//<![CDATA[>
... JavaScript methods here ...
//]]>
</script>
```

This is a kind of throwback to a simpler time when JavaScript was very much an afterthought — a vestigial part of the browser's implementation. Now however, pages and applications are far more interactive, and the RIA model levies a much higher performance and capability requirement on any in-browser language. Thus, the importance of JavaScript working correctly across browsers and browser versions as a modern object-based language has grown more critical. Although it was considered broken as a language by many developers, and vilified by many more, JavaScript has become a better language over time (see Figure 11-1). ActionScript (discussed in detail in Chapter 12, "Flash-Based Interfaces and TurboGears,") is used as the implementation language for Adobe Flex in an effort to create a more robust, rigorously specified form of JavaScript, but the bottom line is that most developers have to learn to work with basic JavaScript. Nothing better is going to suddenly and magically emerge. However, the MochiKit library can make JavaScript more tractable, generally easier to work with, almost as exciting, and more *Pythonic*.

A most important, even critical, event occurs early on in the timeline shown in Figure 11-1: the appearance and support for *XMLHttpRequest* (*XHR*) in Internet Explorer 5. Because of XHR, communications with server-side functionality was revolutionized, and static web pages suddenly came alive with content asynchronously contributed after page load. Amongst all the other capabilities enabled by modern JavaScript, this one is the critical differentiator.

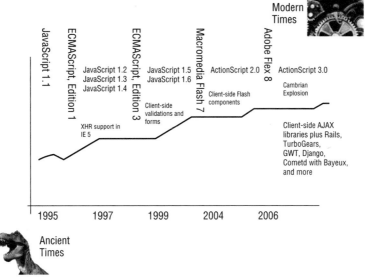

Figure 11-1

Although it's clearly visible, XHR almost seems to be a footnote in history. It was lurking in the background, seemingly unnoticed, until Google made a huge splash with it by basing all their features, from Google Maps to GMail, on it.

To better understand the need for a unifying JavaScript library, consider the requirements of implementing and handling an XHR. You have probably written a wiring diagram like Listing 11-1 many times in creating responsive, server-backed RIAs. This example is excerpted from a companion book in this series, *Professional Rich Internet Applications: AJAX and Beyond* (Wiley Publishing, 2007).

Listing 11-1: XMLQueryExample.html (excerpt)

```
<script type="text/javascript">
var xmlhttp = false;
  function onLoad() {
   if (window.XMLHttpRequest) {
    xmlhttp = new XMLHttpRequest();
    xmlhttp.overrideMimeType('text/xml');
   } else if (window.ActiveXObject) {
    xmlhttp = new ActiveXObject("Microsoft.XMLHTTP");
   }
  }
...
  function queryHandler(url) {
    try {
      netscape.security.PrivilegeManager.enablePrivilege ↩
    ("UniversalBrowserRead");
    } catch (e) {
    }
```

(continued)

Listing 11-1 *(continued)*

```
      if(url !== ""){
        xmlhttp.open('GET', url, true);
        xmlhttp.onreadystatechange = function() {
          if(xmlhttp.readyState == 4 && xmlhttp.status == 200) {
            // update the document DOM
          } else {
            // do something else
          }
        };
        xmlhttp.send(null);
      }
  }
  ...
    function doQuery() {
      var uri = ↩
          "http://api.search.yahoo.com/ImageSearchService/V1/ ↩
          imageSearch?appid=YahooDemo&query=orange ↩
          +&results=1&output=xml";
    queryHandler(uri);
    }
  </script>
  <button onClick="doQuery()">Do Something</button>
```

Without diverting your attention with a lengthy explanation of what's going on in this listing, the following brief walkthrough is provided to illustrate that this is a fairly standard (and tedious) stanza of code that you don't want to have to write every time the code in your web pages talks with a server, nor do you want to have to look it at every time you debug your code.

What happens in the code is typical of the wiring you must create to effect communications with a back-end service. You declare a variable (xmlhttp) that will, depending on the browser running this code, create either a new ActiveXObject (if the browser is Internet Explorer), or an XMLHttpRequest object (for everyone else). That's the first point of pain you would like to avoid — browser testing. Next, notice that the first thing you do in handling the query is another browser-specific check (netscape.security .PrivilegeManager.enablePrivilege) — another point of pain. Then there's remembering to specify a callback handler in doQuery, and handling the results in the callback (queryHandler) itself. Could this last item — having to test completion states and mining the results of the xmlhttp object — be any more of a pain?

Clearly, it would be better to create abstractions for all this manipulation, and this is only one aspect of a modern RIA. Consider all the repetitive code you find yourself writing to perform the simplest of tasks, like analyzing or manipulating the document's DOM.

What to do? Well, of course you can do what we developers always do, which is to create another level of abstraction. In fact, as JavaScript became more critical to RIAs, this is exactly what the open source community did. The community started sharing snippets of commonly required JavaScript in places such as SourceForge. However, as often happens with this approach, many code collections had no quality control, and worse yet, little or no functional coherence. Individual library efforts varied vastly in terms of how well they were written, how well they worked, how well-supported they were (especially over the long haul), and how easy they were to use. Another issue was that they usually defined global functions or variables that frequently conflicted when integrating with other scripts.

Over time, though, a few winners began to emerge. One of the biggest winners in terms of its Pythonic point of view is Bob Ippolito's MochiKit.

What Is MochiKit?

MochiKit is a library implemented in JavaScript, but it sometimes resembles Python in its design approach. It's available at www.mochikit.com. MochiKit is medium-sized library that focuses on simplifying JavaScript and provides extensible enhancements such as a framework for defining and handling events. MochiKit is included in the TurboGears web application framework. MochiKit is said to be *Pythonic*, because many of its method calls emulate a Python coding style, and because its creator, Bob Ippolito, comes from a Python development background.

MochiKit is medium-sized in comparison to certain other JavaScript libraries such as Dojo Toolkit and Yahoo! UI Library (YUI), because it has a running size of around 300KB (with a base script size of a little over 100K on load) as compared with Dojo's and YUI's over-3.5MB running size. Even so, MochiKit has complete functionality with affordances for DOM manipulation, browser-independent logging, AJAX and callback handling, special effects (ported over from the popular script.aculo.us library,) and a host of other handy usability features.

Bob Ippolito initially released the MochiKit library in July of 2005. His primary goal at that time was to provide a well-documented and tested library that didn't interfere with normal JavaScript. Python, which heavily influences the library, adds functional programming capabilities to JavaScript and incorporates many ideas from Twisted and other Python-related frameworks and libraries. MochiKit currently comes bundled with TurboGears.

What's Inside MochiKit?

MochiKit packages all of its included subpackages in such a way that you can invoke any MochiKit functionality simply by including MochiKit.js in a single <src/> tag in your HTML (or template file), like this:

```
<script src="/static/javascript/MochiKit/MochiKit.js"
type="text/javascript"></script>
```

MochiKit is lazily loaded though (an advantage of good namespace packaging and separation), so not all of the various library pieces are loaded initially. The base load is under 200KB, which is well within the range of most end users' network capacity.

As is common with Python and other languages, you can use just the capabilities that you need in an application. Thus, you can source the DOM manipulation library by including only MochiKit.Dom, or the AJAX library with MochiKit.Async. The following table describes MochiKit's modules and their capabilities.

Module	Functionality
Async	Responsible for wiring up outbound AJAX calls and handling the asynchronous results of the call.
Base	Makes certain things in JavaScript behave rationally, such as comparisons between objects and array operations.
Color	Provides convenience and conversion functions for dealing with the differing representations of color on the Web.
DOM	Well-formed HTML conforms to an XML document object model (DOM). The DOM functions enable you to manipulate (add, replace, and delete) a document's tagged elements from inside the document.
DateTime	Date and time convenience functions.
DragAndDrop	Adds visual drag-and-drop capabilities to a page. This was added to MochiKit prior to the introduction of the MochiKit.Visual library, so it is not implemented as a `script.acluo.us` port.
Format	Includes useful precision string formatting functions.
Iter	Implements a very Pythonic iteration syntax.
Logging	A browser-agnostic solution for logging. (As `Mochikit.org` points out, "We're all tired of `alert()`.")
LoggingPane	Works across browsers. (As opposed to Firebug, which is fabulous and a developer must-have, but is a Firefox-only solution.)
Signal	Provides generic event-handling capabilities.
Sortable	Unusual library that enables you to drag and drop DOM elements on a structured basis.
Style	Cascading Style Sheets (CSS) helper functions.
Visual	A special visual effects library.

The following sections describe some of MochiKit's parts individually, beginning with the AJAX-handling abstractions. Rather than offering an exhaustively long discussion of each of MochiKit's sublibraries, the focus is on some of the best features. For more detailed information, consult the online reference documentation at www.mochikit.com.

MochiKit.Async

The inspiration for MochiKit's AJAX support was the Twisted event-driven networking framework in Python. The core of this implementation is the concept of a `Deferred` object as an abstraction for any asynchronous operation in JavaScript. You can create deferred objects that correspond to asynchronous requests, and assign a collection of callback functions to be executed on successful or failed execution. It also provides a useful `loadJSONDoc` function that enables you to make an `XMLHttpRequest` and get the response as a JSON document.

As suggested in the previous section, creating an asynchronous request and setting up functions to handle the successful and unsuccessful return could be made simpler, given a higher level of abstraction. That's exactly the point of the MochiKit.Async package. The Deferred object is created as a result of making an outbound XMLHttpRequest. An easy way to explore this (and the other concepts in this chapter) is to use the interactive interpreter at http://mochikit.com/examples/interpreter/index.html. You can use this handy tool in much the same way as you would the Python command-line interpreter. Figure 11-2 shows an example of using the interactive interpreter.

Figure 11-2

Follow these steps to use the interpreter as shown in the figure:

1. Create a simple function that does something with the result from the XMLHttpRequest call. In the figure, this function is as follows:

```
showResult = function(xmlhttp){ alert(xmlhttp.responseText); }
```

2. Create another function to handle any errors that might occur:

```
showErr = function(err){alert(err.text);)
```

3. Make the call itself:

```
d = doSimpleXMLHttpRequest("http://mochikit.com/examples/interpreter/index.html");
```

4. Add callbacks for both result types, and link them to the deferred object:

```
d.addCallbacks(showResult, showErr);
```

In Figure 11-2, the JavaScript functions have been entered and evaluated at runtime via the web-based interpreter. As soon as the callbacks are added (shown at the bottom of the figure), they are invoked and an alert box is displayed that contains the contents of the page returned in the XMLHttpRequest's response text (see Figure 11-3).

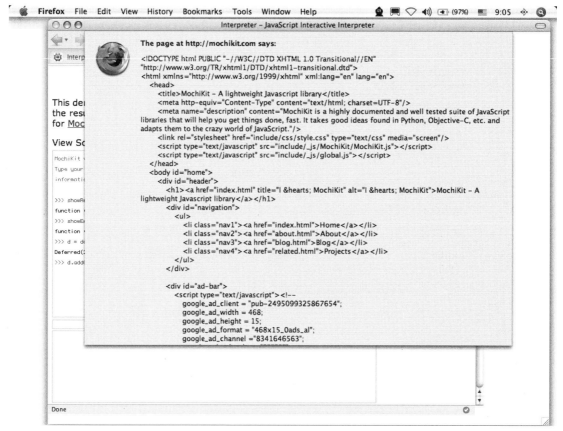

Figure 11-3

That's really all there is to making a call. The following table shows additional method signatures on the Deferred object through which you can vary the handling of the result.

Method Signature	Description
d.addCallback(method_name)	Adds a callback for the success case only
d.addErrback(method_name)	Adds a callback for the error case only
d.addCallbacks(success_method_name, error_method_name)	Adds both method callbacks
d.addBoth(method_name)	Adds a single callback to handle both conditions

The following table describes the methods for creating Deferred objects from XMLHttpRequest calls.

Method	Description
doSimpleXMLHttpRequest(url)	Creates a Deferred object from an XMLHttpRequest using GET. The returned data are contained within an XML stanza that must be parsed by the callback method to be useful.
loadJSONDoc(url)	Creates a Deferred object from an XMLHttpRequest. When the callback is triggered by successful completion, the result can be loaded directly into a JavaScript object without additional XML processing.
sendMXLHttpRequest(request, data)	Creates a Deferred object from an asynchronous XMLHttpRequest.

You saw some additional MochiKit.Async functionality in Chapter 7, "Advanced TurboGears Topics," where Listing 7-11 showed another variant of making an XMLHttpRequest and attaching a callback method to the Deferred object. Here's a stanza of code from controlpanel.kid:

```
function displayTrucks(){
  __trucks = [];
    var d = loadJSONDoc("${tg.url('/resourcelist', tg_format='json')}");
  d.addCallback(showTrucks);
}
```

In this instance, the loadJSONDoc method was used because the contract with the controller logic was guaranteed to return JSON. Here's the correlated method signature from controllers.py:

```
@expose()
@expose("json")
def resourcelist(self):
    ...
```

Call Restrictions

An astute observer will note that the outbound XMLHttpRequest shown in Figure 11-2 made a call to the same site that served up the interpreter web page (mochikit.com). If the call had been made to some other site (such as google.com as shown in the first figure here), the call would have failed and an error callback would have been fired (as shown in the second figure here).

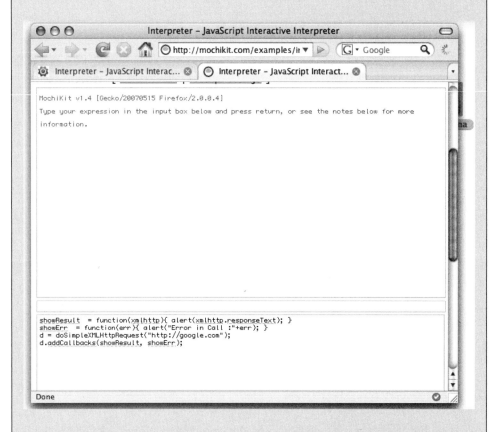

Although this is not a MochiKit issue *per se*, it's worth a minor diversion. The explanation for why modern browsers restrict the call shown in Figure 11-2 is rooted in concerns over desktop security that have arisen as a result of the clever misuse of browsers to deliver nefarious code to unsuspecting end users.

Originally browsers were equivalent to printing presses in that the user instantiated a browser and typed in a URL, resulting in the end-to-end connection shown here:

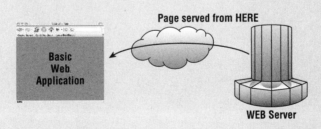

You could even serve out web pages from your own host to test your HTML or your server logic. Typically, in the Web 1.0 era, you could create this type of one-line browser in Python:

```
python -m SimpleHTTPServer 8080 # for Python 2.4
```

(continued)

Call Restrictions *(continued)*

Or you could do this:

```
python -c "from SimpleHTTPServer import test; test()" # Python 2.3,
2.2
```

You then executed the file from the command line and served out the pages from the folder for which the web server was started by accessing `localhost:8080`, as depicted here:

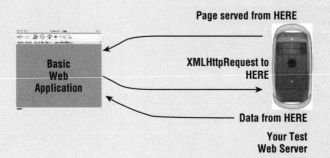

What you could not do is what you see in the next image — that is, route a request to the web server that is serving up the page, pass the request to some other web server, and have *that* web server return the page. Most browsers simply do not let the HTML page served from one domain open a network connection of any kind to domains other than the one that served up the HTML page.

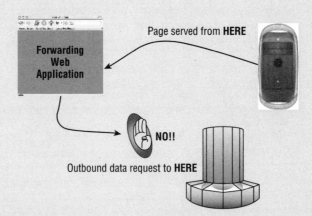

The reason for this is that modern browsers prohibit cross-domain calls. The process by which your page loads a request that originates from your browser and terminates at `http://mochikit.com/examples/interpreter/index.html` cannot hopscotch across to another site, fetch its content, and return that to your browser.

> Working around this sort of restriction is beyond the scope of this MochiKit
> discussion, and is even beyond the scope of this book, but a complete discussion of
> the issue and workarounds can be found in the companion book in this series,
> *Professional Rich Internet Applications: AJAX and Beyond* (Wiley Publishing, 2007).

MochiKit.Base

JavaScript is indisputably flawed as a language. Simple concepts such as object comparison just do not
work. Further, working with collection classes in general is nontrivial in the way that we Python developers have come to expect, and although the default collection class in JavaScript is a very nice and
Pythonic dictionary, even this does not work as expected (by a Python user) because JavaScript promotes
keys to `String` (although values may be any legal object). `MochiKit.Base` helps you cope with all
these annoyances and anomalies, as shown in the following examples.

Object Comparisons

JavaScript may appear insane in very basic ways to a Python programmer. For example, take a look at
this Python code:

```
$ python
Python 2.4.4 (#1, Oct 18 2006, 10:34:39)
[GCC 4.0.1 (Apple Computer, Inc. build 5341)] on darwin
>>> a = [1,2,3]
>>> b = [1,2,3]
>>> a == b
True
```

You would expect the `True` result, because Python's comparison inspects the content of the arrays
deeply rather than asking whether the memory addresses are the same. This is what a rational developer
hopes for, and Python delivers it. But what happens if you try the same thing in JavaScript?

Using MochiKit's interactive interpreter, you could do the following:

```
>>> a = [1,2,3];
[1, 2, 3]
>>> b = [1,2,3];
[1, 2, 3]
>>> a == b
false
```

But this time the result is `false`. You would never want this result, and yet that's what JavaScript gives
you. This is a simple demonstration of JavaScript insanity.

The `MochiKit.Base` library fixes this. If you use the `compare` function, you get the following result:

```
>>> compare(a,b);
0
```

This result follows the well known C/C++/Java convention that when the two objects being compared are equivalent, 0 is returned; when the first is smaller than the second, -1 is returned, and when the first is larger, 1 is returned as shown in the following code snippet:

```
>>> c = [4,5,6];
[4, 5, 6]
>>> compare(a,c)
-1
>>> compare (c,a);
1
```

MochiKit.Base also has a convenience function called objEqual, which you can use like this:

```
>>>> objEqual(a,b);
true
>>> objEqual(a,c);
false
```

Again you get just what you might hope for — reasonable and consistent results.

So MochiKit fixes JavaScript cmparison brokenness. What else?

Associative Arrays

Both Python and JavaScript have the notion of associative arrays or dictionaries. The traditional and sane Python method is to create a Python dictionary and populate it like this:

```
$ python
>>> gamma = {}
>>> gamma["life"] = 1
>>> gamma["universe"] = 2
>>> gamma['everything'] = 42
```

There's also another way in Python to get dictionary-like behaviors. You could create an empty class and just add attributes to it like this:

```
$ python
>>> class Alpha: pass
...
>>> alpha = Alpha()
>>> alpha.life = 1
>>> alpha.universe = 2
>>> alpha.everything = 42
```

Then you could reference the object instance's attributes. This is an example of an unusual method for creating a static (but not easily iterable) property and value pair, where the property name may be thought of as a key.

JavaScript attributes are rather like the second method. Again using the interactive JavaScript interpreter, you could do the following:

```
(on mochikit.com/examples/interpreter/index.html):
>>> alpha = new Object();
alpha.life = 1;
alpha.universe = 2;
alpha.everything=42;
42
>>> alpha["life"]
1
```

One painful reality is that all keys are coerced to a string type, which may or may not make you happy. Associated values retain their object type identity.

MochiKit provides both `keys` and `items` methods, but not an elegant way of navigating key-value pairs, as you can see here:

```
>>> keys(alpha);
["life", "universe", "everything"]
>>> items(alpha)
[["life", 1], ["universe", 2], ["everything", 42]]
```

To move through key-value pairs (rather inelegantly compared to Python), you can do this:

```
>>> key = keys(alpha)
>>> for (i in key) alert ("KEY>>>"+key[i]+" VALUE >>>"+alpha[key[i]]);
```

The more you work with `MochiKit.Base`, the more you will grow to appreciate the way it provides a myriad of JavaScript usability enhancements. This library contains several methods that range from affordances for object creation and comparison, to better dictionary usability, manipulating dates and times, improved array operations and iteration mechanisms, and a variety of string formatting and manipulation functions.

MochiKit.DOM

MochiKit includes a large set of functions for DOM manipulation, including functions for adding, replacing, and swapping out DOM nodes, elements, and attributes. Similar to `script.aculo.us`, MochiKit uses `$()` as a concise and useful encapsulation of the `getElementById` function. It also takes a functional approach to the construction of documents that is quite powerful. But MochiKit's real strength is its ability to create, replace, and destroy DOM elements on the fly. The `createDOM` method makes a new page DOM element according to the type specification provided as the method arguments. The following table describes the three DOM manipulations possible:

Method	Description
appendChildNodes(parent, children...)	Adds nodes via createDom and adds them to the parent
replaceChildNodes(parent, children...)	Removes all subordinate nodes to the parent and then appends children
swapDOM(dest, src)	Replaces dest with src, or nulls dest out if src is null

MochiKit also supports aliases for HTML tag elements. Thus, as Figure 11-4 shows, the two expressions of DOM creation will write identical DOM elements to the document (shown via the interactive JavaScript interpreter). In the first instance, the slightly more verbose createDOM notation is used. In the second instance, the UL and LI synonyms are used.

Interpreter - JavaScript Interactive Interpreter

This demo is a JavaScript interpreter. Type some code into the text input and press enter to see the results. It uses MochiKit's MochiKit.DOM to manipulate the display. It also supports waiting for MochiKit.Async Deferreds via blockOn(aDeferred).

View Source: [index.html | interpreter.js]

```
>>> writeln(createDOM('ul', null, createDOM('li', null, 'alpha'), createDOM('li', null, 'beta')));
    • alpha
    • beta

>>> writeln(UL(null, LI('alpha'), LI('beta')));
    • alpha
    • beta
```

Figure 11-4

MochiKit.Logging

MochiKit has an excellent browser-agnostic logging capability that includes several useful features. You can write a message to the log at a specified level (such as debug or warn). This log can be captured in the browser's native JavaScript console (depending on the browser version), in a MochiKit console at the bottom of the browser window, or in a MochiKit console in a separate window. The MochiKit console also allows you to filter by log level or regular expression. When you want an independent logging and debug window, you can simply add createLoggingPane() to create one. When you want a DIV at the bottom of your browser window, use the alternate createLoggingPane(true). Figure 11-5 shows an example of the logging pane in use, with logging statements written to it.

MochiKit.Signal

MochiKit provides a powerful event handling system. This includes a replacement for the base event API to handle events like onmouseover and onkeypress. It also enables you to define and broadcast custom events. Even though all modern browsers (thankfully) implement in-page event handling, the handling is frequently problematic, often for unseen reasons such as memory leaks in Internet Explorer. MochiKit.Signal gives you a easy-to-use model with a single, easy-to-remember API and consistently working library. This in itself is a worthwhile reason for adoption.

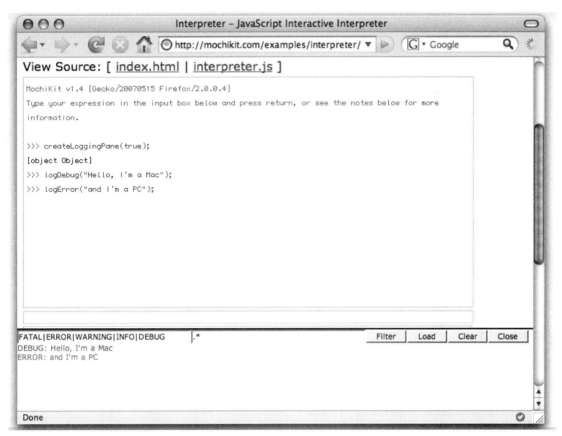

Figure 11-5

Figure 11-6 shows an interactive visualizer session in which MochiKit.DOM is used as an alias for createDOM. In this session, a button is created with the ID MKBUTTON, and a callback function is allocated to the button by the connect signal specification.

The basic syntax for connecting a source, which can be either a string identifying the DOM element or a JavaScript object, is simple and uniform:

```
Connect(source_id_asString, signal_id_asString, method));
```

Or

```
Connect(source_object, signal_id_asString, method));
```

An alternative signature is only slightly more complex:

```
Connect(source_id_asString, signal_id_asString, dest, method);
```

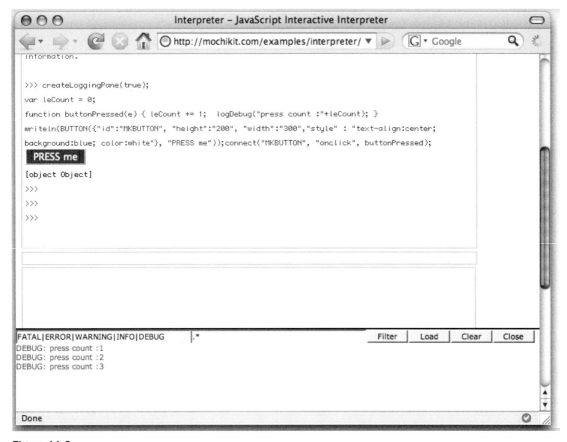

Figure 11-6

Or

```
Connect(source_object, signal_id_asString, dest, method);
```

In this form, the destination specifier is a JavaScript object or a method. If a non-null method is specified, then it is applied to the object bound to `dest`.

Additionally, note that the result returned by the `Connect` method is a unique identifier (a UID) for the connection. If (similar to the toy code shown in Figure 11-6 showing input typed into the interactive MochiKit interpreter), you had done

```
var thisConnection = connect("MKBUTTON", "onclick", buttonPressed);
```

the variable `thisConnection` would actually be a UID.

Should you decide at some later point in the code to sever the connection, you could use the following `disconnect` method to do so:

```
disconnect(thisConnection);
```

And, as you might guess, there is a `disconnectAll` method as well, which severs all connections.

MochiKit.Visual

As this book is being written, MochiKit's visual effect capability is the newest and possibly most exciting of the library features. With `MochiKit.Visual` plus `MochiKit.DragAndDrop`, you can add significant user appeal to your RIA. (Of course, if visual effects are overused, you can also add unneeded eye candy and user annoyance.)

You can include significant visual user aids with MochiKit. The demonstration web page at `http://mochikit.com/demos.html` has a comprehensive set of examples, and Chapter 6, "Widgets," showed toggling visual elements (tables) in the mashup application. For your amusement and to give you just a small sample of what `MochiKit.Visual` can do, this section gives you some examples that you can try out in the interactive interpreter.

Enter the following stanza in the interpreter:

```
writeln(DIV({"class": "presto-1", "style" : "text-align:center; background:black;
color:white"}, "Square"));
writeln(DIV({"class": "presto-2", "style" : "text-align:center; background:black;
color:white"}, "ROUND"));
```

You'll see two DIVs appear, both with square corners. Now type in the following method call:

```
roundClass("div", "presto-2");
```

The result should look like Figure 11-7, where the corners of the specified DOM elements are now rounded all over.

Here's another more dramatic effect you can try:

```
writeln(DIV({"id": "ghostly", "class":"pooka", "style" : "text-align:center;
background:black; color:white"}, "BOO!"));
roundClass("pooka");
hideElement("ghostly");
```

This creates a `DIV` and immediately hides it from view. Make it appear using one of the MochiKit.Visual methods, such as the following:

```
grow("ghostly");
```

The `DIV` element will now appear to grow from the page.

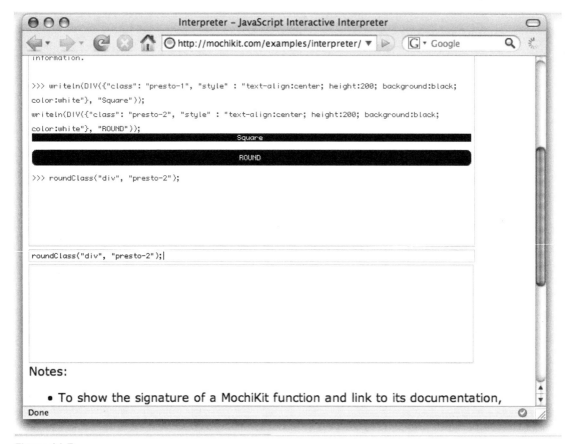

Figure 11-7

You can create a toggle effect by using the following `toggle` method:

```
toggle(element [, effect, options]);
```

In this method, `element` is an existing DOM element and `effect` specifies one of a set of paired effects. Currently the visual effect pairs you can specify in the effects argument are `slide`, `blind`, `appear`, and `size`. The MochiKit documentation at `http://mochikit.com/doc/html/MochiKit/Visual.html` contains a complete listing of visual effects and options for timing, opacity, and other fine-tuning specifications.

MochiKit Miscellany

MochiKit is the default JavaScript library that is shipped with TurboGears (and the one used in the Django examples in this book), and it offers a first-rate collection of capabilities, providing a highly reusable and extensible set of components. In addition to the library packages discussed previously, here are some other great capabilities that MochiKit provides:

❑   **Namespace support:** MochiKit takes a unique and effective approach to namespace support. All components are defined in the MochiKit namespace, but the inclusion of the MochiKit namespace is optional. If the following script is specified before including the MochiKit script in your page, you can turn compatibility mode on:

```
<script type="text/javascript">MochiKit = {__compat__: true};</script>
```

❑   When compatibility mode is on, you are required to use the fully qualified name for any MochiKit function. For example, the `compare` function is executed with `MochiKit.Base` `.compare(x, y)`. When compatibility mode is turned off, you aren't required to include the namespace, so the `compare` function is simplified to `compare(x, y)`.

❑   **Element style manipulation:** MochiKit includes a small set of functions that allow you to analyze and modify an element's style. For example, you can reposition, show, or hide elements. It also provides a set of functions for creating and manipulating colors. This includes mechanisms to translate colors to and from a variety of formats (such as RGB or HSL), analyze a document to ascertain its colors, and retrieve standard colors.

❑   **Java-style number and currency formatting:** MochiKit provides an extensible number-formatting capability, patterned on regular expression syntax lifted from Java.

Summary

In this chapter, you experienced some of MochiKit's extensive support for better JavaScript coding and design. MochiKit is open source, is well supported, and has a lively developer community (make sure you check out the Google groups for MochiKit questions, answers, bugs, tips, and tricks). Additionally, the documentation at www.mochikit.com is extensive and easy to navigate. MochiKit's creative team has done an especially good job of documentation and unit testing, and the result is a fast, compact, and robust language API for JavaScript. The design philosophy makes it easier to pick up MochiKit idioms and coding style. Additionally, MochiKit is a good citizen when used in conjunction with other JavaScript in the same RIA. Because you can turn namespace support on or off, you're not required to use namespaces but can benefit from them when needed.

The MochiKit design focus on component extensibility ensures that the library is reusable and adaptable to a particular web application. It was designed with the intent that web developers would extend the base objects with their own behaviors.

12

Flash-Based Interfaces and TurboGears

You don't understand! I coulda had class. I coulda been a contender. I could've been somebody.

— **Marlon Brando in** *On the Waterfront*

Thus far in this book, you've seen the user interface or *view* portion of Rich Internet Applications (RIAs) either hand-crafted in HTML and Cascading Style Sheets (CSS), or constructed dynamically on the server using a templating system such as Kid. This chapter covers the union of Flex with Python frameworks — and make no mistake, this combination absolutely *does* have class, it *is* a contender, and it's destined to be a *somebody*.

The Flex Difference

The major difference between previous models and the Flex coding paradigm covered in this chapter involves how the initial and subsequent pages are generated. In hand-coded Python, browsing to a URL reference produces an initial page that is often static HTML, perhaps with embedded JavaScript calling a Python service-side script via an XMLHttpRequest (XHR). This is illustrated in Figure 12-1.

In using frameworks like Django, and TurboGears in particular, when the user browses to a URL, the web server redirects the call, and pages spring into existence as a result of Python-based controller code transforming a template into an HTML page and serving it up to the browser. An illustration of this model is shown in Figure 12-2.

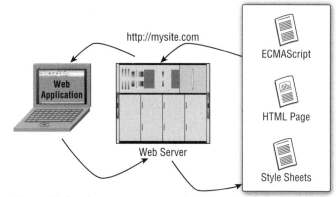

Figure 12-1

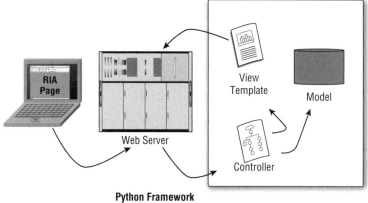

Figure 12-2

In this chapter you'll learn a third paradigm (illustrated in Figure 12-3) in which a separate build step compiles source files into a binary form that is then loaded by the web server as part of the page load. This may seem to run counter to major themes in this book, which advocate frameworks that implement dynamic RIA construction. However, after reading this chapter, using Adobe's Flex software development kit (SDK) alone, and using it in conjunction with Python Web 2.0 frameworks, you may decide that there are significant deployment flexibility advantages to this hybrid approach.

In addition to introducing a third way of generating an RIA, this chapter also introduces the concept of domain-specific languages (DSLs). Adobe's Flex API is a DSL that is focused entirely on the creation of user interfaces which are both visually stunning and potentially very feature-laden.

What's Flex and Why Should I Use It?

Many of us can still remember back to a time when the Web was young and web page developers used to decorate their sites with animations developed and implemented using a technology called *Flash*. The idea behind Flash was that, using an animation toolkit, you could compile a sequence of images into

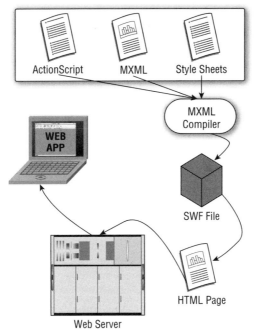

Figure 12-3

object code, which could then be embedded into HTML. Provided the user downloaded a browser extension, page content would spring to life, changing flat, primarily textual sites into something extraordinary (if not in the eyes of the end user, then at least in the opinion of the site creator). In the infancy of the Web, Flash overuse was akin to the "font abuse" (the inclusion of multiple fonts in a document just because it was possible) that was seen in the infancy of the even-earlier desktop publishing era.

After the novelty wore off however, much of the Flash content was replaced by an animated Graphic Interchange Format (GIF) for the simple reasons that the effect was roughly equivalent to Flash animations and creating an animated GIF arguably took less skill (or at least less developer skill). The timeline-style tools seemed more suited to moviemakers than to software developers. Over the course of the Web's evolution, however, something rather strange and wonderful happened. Macromedia (the original developers of Flash) added a library of beautifully rendered and completely functional desktop widgets to the collection of developer tools.

As a result, a new meme began to emerge. Developers began to tumble to the notion that by using the Flex widget set and embedding complex application controls into a browser that hosts a uniformly implemented execution engine (the Flash plug-in), it would be possible to both create RIAs and generally stop worrying about the underlying platform dependencies altogether. This realization by and large mirrored the same kind of "Aha!" moment that developers experienced when they discovered AJAX. Accordingly, the authors of this book are giving Flex and Flash-based RIA tools and techniques specific coverage because they may be less familiar to you than HTML, JavaScript, and CSS. Initially a few stand-alone code examples are shown, and then one example illustrates the power of Flex and TurboGears working together.

Getting and Installing the Flex SDK

One of the many great features of Flex is that the toolkit is freely available from its provider, Adobe. You can download it from `www.adobe.com/products/flex/sdk/`. Installing it is the usual one-step operation. Just make certain that the Flex compiler is in your execution path somewhere — perhaps in `C:\Program Files` on a Windows system, or in the default `/Applications/Flex2` install location on Mac OS X systems. Flex libraries themselves can be located in a convenient folder. Because Flex libraries are compiled into a deployable object, relative location doesn't have the same significance as it does for other elements in a framework-based deployment.

Creating Basic Flex Applications

It's entirely possible to create basic applications using just the Flex toolkit, stand-alone and without a framework such as TurboGears backing it. This chapter first shows you the three basic varieties of how the Flex SDK is commonly used to create applications that can exist either on the desktop or in a browser. Then you learn some methods for incorporating TurboGears into a Flex-based application.

This book is not intended to discuss Flex in great depth. What you can hope to pick up from this chapter is a good, basic understanding of at least a few methods for creating applications using Flex.

Flex Features

As you saw in preceding chapters, modern development practices commonly use a combination of a templating language and logic in an agile language, such as Python, to create distributed applications that adhere to the model-view-controller (MVC) design paradigm. Flex is notionally similar but with a bit of a twist: although it's a DSL whose specific purpose is page layout and rendering (referred to as the *view*), Flex itself is a micro-MVC. The visual components can be described in an XML dialect called MXML (for Macromedia XML) and collected in a Document Object Model (DOM) that is bound by a pair of `Application` tags and expresses the look and feel of the application. However, the logic for dealing with user interaction is always coded in ActionScript (a strongly typed variant of ECMAScript and JavaScript).

There's no one recipe for how much of the look and feel you might decide to code in MXML versus ActionScript. The same results can generally be achieved with various approaches. The layout can be expressed completely in MXML, or in a combination of MXML for logic plus additional external ActionScript compile units that implement the logic of the view. Or it can be mostly ActionScript for both layout and logic, with a thin MXML wrapper for declaring the outermost containment layer of the application. Examples of these three options will be shown later in this chapter, while serving to remind you that there is not necessarily a best-design strategy for Flex application development.

Listings 12-2, 12-6, and 12-8 show examples of these three variations on a theme while serving to remind that there is not necessarily a "best" design strategy for Flex application development. Depending on your facility and comfort with writing straight XML as opposed to code (ActionScript), you will probably lean in one direction or another. If you enjoy writing raw HTML, then you may well prefer to create your visual objects in MXML. Bear in mind, though, that because MXML is XML-based, it will not tolerate the ambiguity of unbalanced tags in the same way that HTML might.

Flex User Interface Controls

Rather than the standard set of text markup tags that are included with HTML, MXML has a large set of rich components that can be used to create complex visual fixtures with a high level of event-driven functionality. The following list shows the basic controls. Because MXML-defined widgets are rendered by the Flash Player plug-in in the browser, or by the stand-alone player (often used for debugging rather than deployment), they provide a more desktop-type experience both visually and functionally than traditional HTML tagged widgets. Bear in mind that the objects in the list are extensible — because they represent rich classes of user elements, you can tailor them by modifying their properties, or use them as a superclass for your own custom-created widgets.

Alert	HRule	ProgressBar	TextInput
Button	HScrollBar	ProgressBar-Direction	TileList
ButtonBar	HSlider		ToggleButtonBar
ButtonLabel-Placement	Image	ProgressBarLabel-Placement	ToolTip
	Label	ProgressBarMode	Tree
CheckBox	LinkBar	RadioButton	VideoDisplay
ComboBase	LinkButton	RadioButton-Group	VRule
ComboBox	List	RichTextEditor	VScrollBar
Color-Picker	Menu	Spacer	VSlider
DataGrid	MenuBar	SWFLoader	
DateChooser	NavBar	TabBar	
DateField	NumericStepper	Text	
FormItem-Label	PopUpButton	TextArea	
HorizontalList	PopUpMenuButton		

As this list shows, Flex supports a set of user interface components, such as developers used to find only in proprietary foundation frameworks for the desktop. In addition to traditional data input controls — such as TextInput for single-line inputs; TextArea for free-form multi-line inputs; and CheckBox, RadioButton, and ComboBox for indicating user choices — MXML includes advanced components to model structured data (the Tree component) and support for tabular data (the DataGrid component). Flex also provides navigation components to hide and reveal pieces of the application. These can be seen in the TabNavigator, ViewStack, and Accordion components, which act like smart panels.

In addition to basic widget functionality, MXML components, being Flash-based, also support features such as alpha transparency, animations, gradients, fades, and resizes that maintain the essential visual characteristics of the application.

Flex User Interface Containers

A complaint that most developers have when creating RIAs using straight HTML components is that layout and containment can sometimes go a bit haywire in different browser or on resize. Java and Python wxWidgets developers will find much to be happy with in the Flex containment model, where there are real panels, real layout managers, and real spacing elements. Using Flash-based containers (shown in the following list) will give your RIAs the professional feel that cannot easily be matched using HTML and CSS alone. Layout management and positioning in a Flex RIA can be either relative or absolute, and as you'll see in this chapter's example code, the syntax and usage will be familiar to those of you with experience in creating desktop applications.

Accordion	FormHeading	Panel
ApplicationControlBar	FormItem	TabNavigator
Box	FormItemDirection	Tile
BoxDirection	Grid	TileDirection
Canvas	GridItem	TitleWindow
ControlBar	GridRow	VBox
DividedBox	HBox	VDividedBox
Form	HDividedBox	ViewStack

To allow accurate positioning of controls in the user interface, these Flex containers give you precise and absolute layout management policies (when you want them) as well as a looser "relative" positioning. To use the grid container, for example, you specify a cell in the grid as row and column coordinates an element should occupy. Any grid cell can itself contain a grid and therefore, you can get decently fine-grained positioning control.

HBoxes and VBoxes are examples of looser positioning rules. An HBox merely lays out the components horizontally, in the order in which they are declared. In a similar fashion, a VBox lays out its contained components vertically. The Canvas, which you'll see used in the examples, doesn't define any layout management policy. Within a Canvas, you can use absolute positioning by providing x and y coordinates. This can be very handy, but it can also take some iterating to get perfect.

Flex User Interface Control Logic

Visual element creation using a markup language is only part of the Flex story. XML is a declarative language, and it's just not sufficiently complete to express the complexity of programmatic interaction between the user and the screen. In Flex, you do this by using ActionScript to create event handlers. To be quite precise about the compilation process, even when you code user interface (UI) elements in MXML, they are actually converted into ActionScript and *then* used to generate the resulting binary SWF file.

You have already used ECMAScript and JavaScript in the examples in this book to control interaction with the in-browser widgets, navigation of the screen real estate, appearance and hiding of elements, and communications with the server-side logic and data model. With Flex-based RIAs, you're doing essentially the same things as before, except you're using ActionScript.

ActionScript is based on the ECMA-262 standard. It is an optionally strongly typed object-oriented language, and it will certainly feel familiar to those of you who have coded in languages that use semicolons and curly braces such as Java or C#. Static typing is *not* mandatory for the use of ActionScript, but because it's incorporated, you may want to use this capability, especially if you're a Java fan. If you don't use strong typing, you'll get annoying warnings in the compile process.

Listing 12-1 illustrates the similarities and differences in plain ECMAScript and the more strictly specified ActionScript. ActionScript usages are shown in bold.

Listing 12-1: Similarities and differences between ECMAScript and ActionScript

```
// semi-colons -- use 'em please in both ActionScript and ECMAScript
var foo: Number = getFoo(); // ActionScript
var foo = getFoo(); // ECMAscript
// object attributes and function: Use dot notation in both
someObject.someFunction();
someObject.someAttribute;
// typical function call, first in ActionScript and then in ECMAScript
private function setHourRange(min: Number, max: Number):void{} // ActionScript
function setHourRange(min, max){}//ECMAScript
// both primitives and objects a la Java
var foo: Number = getFoo(); // --> ActionScript syntax
var fooint = 42; // --> ECMAScript syntax
// lazy string declaration
var stringyThing = "Hello, I'm a Mac!"'// ECMAScript syntax
var achyBrakeyString: String = "A formal \ //ActionScript
string \
says what?";
// ActionScript formal String object creation syntax
var aFormalString: String = new String("Hello, I'm a Mac!");
// Note that ActionScript works just the way us Java folks like it!
// --> [H,e,l,l,o, ,I,',m, , a, ,M,a,c,!]
var aNumber = 42; // lazy number declaration --> 42
var numberToo: Number = new Number (42); // --> 42 too; the ActionScript way
//Regular expressions are happily identical (and better than Java) in both,
// and have flexbile expression. Note the following two examples
// ECMAScript declaration
var stringyThing = "Hello, I'm a Mac!";
stringyThing.replace(/Mac/, "PC");// --> Hello, I'm a PC! In either
// ActionScript formal declaration/instantiation
var stringyThing: String = new String("Hello, I'm a Mac!");
// ActionScript Java-like replacement syntax
stringyThing.replace(new RegExp( "Mac"), 'PC'); // --> Hello, I'm a PC!
```

As you can see in this listing, the syntactic differences between regular ECMAScript and ActionScript are fairly pronounced. At first glance, ActionScript would seem syntactically at least somewhat like Java or C#. Many constructs are similar — for example, when a variable is declared, its type is a part of the declaration. Strong typing may be unfamiliar to a Python and even an ECMAScript developer, but it's common in certain languages. At the same time, the declaration syntax, both for variables and for method signatures, is unusual even for Java developers — the variable's type is listed *after* the variable's name and after a mandatory colon as well, such as in the following declaration:

```
var actionscriptString: String;
```

ActionScript functions have protection qualifiers and should specify a return type as well, as in this example:

```
private function setHourRange(min: Number, max: Number):void{}
```

The `private` qualifier prevents the function `setHourRange` from being called outside the class to which it belongs, and the return type of `void` signifies a null return. Mixing in protection and other qualifiers can become downright headspinning, as in the following example:

```
private static const RIGHT:Number = 0x0100;
```

In ActionScript as well as in ECMAScript and other C-like languages, don't forget to separate statements with a semicolon. Forgetting to do this religiously is almost always an invitation to grief and much head-scratching over scripts that fail mysteriously.

In summary, writing a Flex application normally involves using a combination of MXML to capture the declarative set up of the user interface (primarily) and ActionScript to provide the logic for responding to user interactions. After you have assembled MXML, ActionScript, and CSS files, you compile them using the `mxmlc` compiler into a form that can be embedded in a normal web page.

Although the SDK is free for development purposes and the object code is free from licensing or other encumbrances, Adobe needs to realize revenue somehow. That *somehow* is the Flex Builder IDE that plugs into Eclipse. Adobe sells a plug-in that has many niceties, such as code completion and a visual layout editor. This chapter's examples are simple enough to code by hand, however, so unless you are flush with coin, you can simply download the SDK and fire up your favorite text editor or IDE.

Simple Tester Version 1 — All Logic in MXML

Listing 12-2 shows a simple example of Flex code. If you have downloaded the Flex 2 SDK, you can test the next several applications by entering the code with your favorite IDE or text editor as usual, and then compiling the parts using the `mxmlc` compiler. The resulting main application file is an SWF file with the same name as the MXML file that defines the application. You can double-click the SWF file, provided you have associated the file type with the desktop Flash Player, and test the application out. Listing 12-3 shows an example of a simple build script for a UNIX–like system (such as Linux and Mac OS X).

Listing 12-2: Main.mxml

```
1  <?xml version="1.0"?>
2
3  <mx:Application xmlns:mx="http://www.adobe.com/2006/mxml">
4      <mx:Script><![CDATA[
5          import flash.events.Event;
6          // Event handler function to print a message
7          // describing the selected Button control.
8          private function printMessage(event:Event):void  {
9            message.text += event.target.label + " pressed";
10           }
11     ]]></mx:Script>
12
```

```
13      <mx:Button id="MyButton" label="Click Me"
            click="printMessage(event);" />
14      <mx:TextArea id="message" text="" editable="false" height="100%"
            width="100%" color="#0000FF"/>
15 </mx:Application>
```

Listing 12-3: build.sh

```
#!/bin/sh
OPTS=-use-network=false
cssFiles=`find . -name '*.css' -print`
for css in ${csslFiles}; do
        echo "building $css"
        (${FLEX_HOME}/bin/mxmlc $OPTS ${css})
done
mxmlFiles=`find . -name '*.mxml' -print`
for mxml in ${mxmlFiles}; do
        echo "building $mxml"
        (${FLEX_HOME}/bin/mxmlc $OPTS ${mxml})
done
```

What gets sent to the compiler and compiled into one or more SWF files is any MXML files plus any CSS files. ActionScript files are not compiled into SWF files, except when they are completely defined within the MXML file. When you web-deploy, you need to assure that any ActionScript files in separate compilation units are visible to the browser. The code supplied via the MXML files and CSS files will not be exposed in the browser. Only the ActionScript will normally be viewable by a user inspecting the RIA page source. Some developers have pointed out that not having your code open for the world to inspect is not necessarily a bad thing. If you intend to web-deploy your Flex-based RIA, you need to set the environmental variable as follows before compiling:

```
OPTS=-use-network=true
```

Otherwise the application will terminate with a network security violation. The general rule is that when you want to build and test on `localhost`, the `use-network` option should be `false`; when you want to web-deploy, the `use-network` option should be `true`.

Returning to the Flex code in Listing 12-2, notice that the file declares its conformance to the XML 1.0 standard. Accordingly, the elements of the application defined must be contained by an appropriate tag pair. In MXML, an application must conform to the nomenclature of the particular XML dialect, which is defined in the `xmlns` specification. Multiple namespaces can be included in the `Application` tag as a way to use multiple libraries and still maintain namespace coherence.

Figure 12-4 is a screenshot of an application run on the desktop by Adobe Flash Player. Because every element must be bound by an `Application` tag pair, the visual button and text area are subnodes in the application's XML DOM. The `Application`, `Button`, and `TextArea` tags have a namespace qualifier of `mx`. When this qualifier is encountered in the `mxml` file that defines the application, the `mxmlc` compiler knows that the tag definitions can be found at `www.adobe.com/devnet/flex/mxml_as.html`, so it brings them into the compilation process, much as an `import` statement does in normal Python.

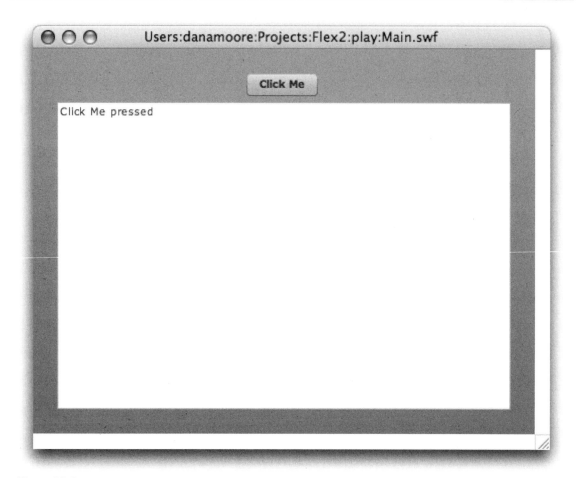

Figure 12-4

A button is implemented in the DOM element as follows:

```
<mx:Button id="MyButton" label="Click Me" click="printMessage(event);" />
```

A tag can contain a variety of optional clauses that customize behavior and specify event handling. You may be familiar with the same concept from HTML. This tag style is sometimes called a partial form of declarative programming, where logic and control flow is implied by the tag content describing what something is like, rather than how to create it. Flex as a DSL exhibits these characteristics in part, at least. This differs from an imperative programming language such as Python, which requires explicit explanation of the implementation algorithm. The declarative model falls apart slightly because the implementation of click handling (as specified by the click clause) is delegated to an ActionScript function contained within the <mx:Script> tag.

The ActionScript function ties the `Button` to the `TextArea` (which is also created in the MXML) as follows:

```
private function printMessage(event:Event):void  {
  message.text += event.target.label + " pressed";
}
```

The message variable in this `printMessage` function refers to the `TextArea` instance via the `id="message"` clause in the `TextArea`'s declaration. The mechanics of implementing the button click (noticing that a button has been clicked, transferring of control to the callback, and actually writing the message to the `TextArea`) are deep within the Flash Player's code, and the developer can just assume they work. The product of compilation is a file called `Main.swf` that, as mentioned previously, can be exercised directly with the Flash Player supplied with the SDK. Alternatively, you can embed the SWF in an HTML page as illustrated in Listing 12-4.

Listing 12-4: Main.html (embedded in HTML)

```
 1 <html lang="en">
 2 <head>
 3 <meta http-equiv="Content-Type" content="text/html; charset=utf-8" />
 4 <title>Main</title>
 5 <style>
 6 body { margin: 0px; overflow:hidden }
 7 </style>
 8 </head>
 9
10 <body scroll='no'>
11         <object classid="clsid:D27CDB6E-AE6D-11cf-96B8-444553540000"
12                       id="Main" width="100%" height="100%"
13                       codebase="http://fpdownload.macromedia.com ↵
        /get/flashplayer/current/swflash.cab">
14                <param name="movie" value="Main.swf" />
15                <param name="quality" value="high" />
16                <param name="bgcolor" value="#869ca7" />
17
18                <param name="allowScriptAccess" value="sameDomain" />
19                <embed src="Main.swf" quality="high" bgcolor="#869ca7"
20                    width="100%" height="100%" name="Demo" align="middle"
21                    play="true"
22                    loop="false"
23                    quality="high"
24                    allowScriptAccess="sameDomain"
25                    type="application/x-shockwave-flash"
26                    pluginspage="http://www.adobe.com/go/getflashplayer">
27                </embed>
28         </object>
29 </body>
30 </html>
```

In this listing, the SWF object is embedded in an HTML file. The file is pretty simple because the CSS and JavaScript code referenced in the XML file are both a part of the compiled object and are hidden from casual inspection. To deploy this version (to your ISP-hosted site, for example), you need only upload the `Main.html` and `Main.swf` files. Even when there are ActionScript and CSS files incorporated, these are fully contained within the embedded SWF file.

The resulting Flex2 interface is shown in running in a browser in Figure 12-5. At a minimum, your HTML file should specify an `<object>` DOM element, and within that an `<embed>` tag should specify the name of the SWF file.

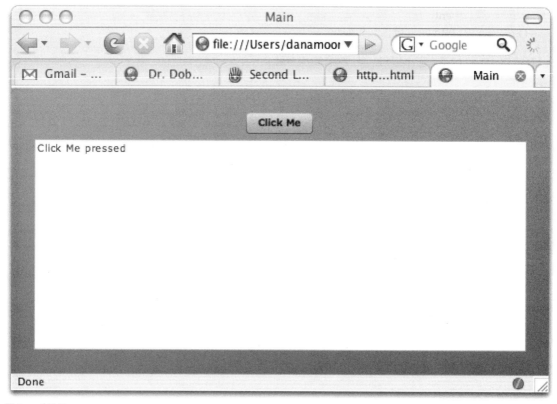

Figure 12-5

Adding CSS

In addition to using declarations in MXML to create and shape widgets, you can also avail yourself of a traditional method for tailoring the look and feel of your page's DOM elements: the well-known and sometimes hated CSS. What's different in this case is that in contrast to having to web-publish the style sheets (and any external ActionScript files), they are published as a part of the binary SWF file. Another great feature is that any fonts you define for your application will always be available — font definitions are also embedded in the byte code of your SWF file. This ensures that fonts are rendered correctly even if they're not available on the end user's machine.

As of this writing, you don't have to write style by hand. You can browse to a sample application at `http://examples.adobe.com/flex2/consulting/styleexplorer/Flex2StyleExplorer.html` and use the excellent design aids there. This RIA is an interactive designer and CSS code generator. You can simply take the style sheet that is generated and compile it into your MXML code, and from there, into your SWF. Listing 12-5 shows a style sheet generated by this tool. (Of course, there's never a problem with generating style sheets by hand, but this technique seems irresistibly attractive.)

Listing 12-5: Main.css

```
Application {
    backgroundGradientColors: #006699, #0033cc;
    themeColor: #0000ff;
    color: #0000ff;
}
Button {
    cornerRadius: 14;
    textIndent: 0;
    letterSpacing: 0;
    highlightAlphas: 0.17, 0.84;
    fillColors: #ffffff, #a10d0d, #cf9d1c, #eeeeee;
}
TextArea {
    fontFamily: Monaco;
    fontSize: 16;
    color: #0000ff;
    backgroundAlpha: 0.39;
    backgroundColor: #ffff00;
    borderColor: #003399;
    borderThickness: 6;
    cornerRadius: 11;
    dropShadowEnabled: true;
    shadowDirection: right;
    shadowDistance: 7;
}
```

Although this is a pretty simple application, the CSS file demonstrates the richness of style specification possible with MXML.

Add the external style to the `Main.MXML` file as follows:

```
<?xml version="1.0"?>
<!-- logging/ButtonLifeCycle.mxml -->
<mx:Application xmlns:mx="http://www.adobe.com/2006/mxml">
<mx:Style source="Main.css"/>
    <mx:Script><![CDATA[
        import flash.events.Event;
                    // Event handler function to print a message
                    // describing the selected Button control.
                    private function printMessage(event:Event):void  {
                       message.text += event.target.label + " pressed" + "\n";
                    }
    ]]></mx:Script>
    <mx:Button id="MyButton" label="Click Me" click="printMessage(event);" />
    <mx:TextArea id="message" text="" editable="false" height="100%" width="100%"
color="#0000FF"/>
</mx:Application>
```

The resulting page is stylistically transformed by the declarative language of the CSS inclusion in the MXML, as shown in Figure 12-6.

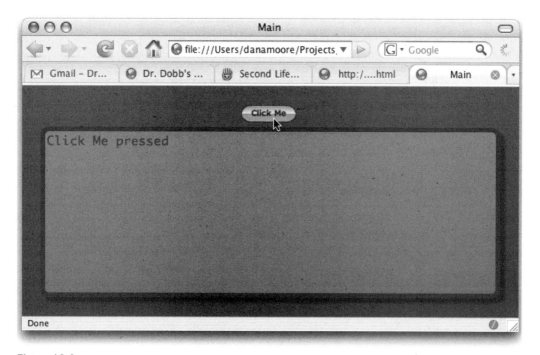

Figure 12-6

Simple Tester Version 2 — Logic Moved to ActionScript

As you saw previously in Listing 12-3, the MXML `Button` tag incorporates the event handler as an attribute appropriate to the widget's type, which in this case is the `click="printMessage(event)"` handler that responds to a user click. In the case of other elements, such as text input fields or combo boxes, it's important to react to any change in the content of the component — thus their event handlers are appropriate to recognizing and responding to change.

Flex is clearly event-driven, and for simple interactions, such as shown in Listing 12-3, coding the logic inline (also shown in Listing 12-3) is a reasonable approach. However, RIAs are rarely that simple. When the logic is more complex, you would do well to modularize the problem by putting the functional logic into a separate ActionScript file and calling that function from the component event handler tag attribute. Using separate compilation units, you could rewrite `Main.MXML` as shown in Listing 12-6.

Listing 12-6: AnotherMain.MXML — Main.mxml refactored into separate compile units

```
<?xml version="1.0" encoding="utf-8"?>
<mx:Application xmlns:mx="http://www.adobe.com/2006/mxml" xmlns:local="*" >
 <local:MainClass/>
</mx:Application>
```

Now there's no ActionScript within the MXML file at all — there's simply a containment statement. Where did all the objects go? And the code logic? Notice that there is a single object declaration:

```
<local:MainClass/>
```

Everything went in the `Application` tag of this `MainClass`. The object declaration and instantiations, the visual control logic, everything except style tailoring is now in an ActionScript module. Would you want to program the application this way? Perhaps so. To some degree, it depends on where you come from as a software developer. Coding only in MXML has a decidedly web developer feel to it, much like coding in HTML, only much less tolerant of sloppy coding (missing end tags especially). Without a design tool and IDE, such as the Flex IDE plug-in for Eclipse, large application design and coding could become burdensome.

Working primarily in ActionScript, on the other hand, has a cleaner feel to it than MXML, especially if you're a Python developer used to working in environments such as WxPython or PythonCard. Listing 12-7 shows an example of code where everything is happening in the ActionScript.

Listing 12-7: MainClass.as

```
1 package {
2
3  import flash.display.*;
4  import flash.events.*;
5  import mx.containers.*;
6  import mx.controls.*;
7
8  public class MainClass extends Canvas
9  {
```

(continued)

Listing 12-7 *(continued)*

```
10    private var a:Button = new Button();
11    private var b:ComboBox = new ComboBox();
12    private var c:TextInput = new TextInput();
13
14    public function MainClass(){
15    a.label = "Click Me!";
16    a.addEventListener(MouseEvent.CLICK, printMessage, false, 0, true);
17    a.y = 10;
18    addChild( a );
19
20    b.dataProvider = ["one", "two", "three"];
21    b.y = 40;
22    addChild( b );
23
24    c.y = 70;
25    addChild(c);
26    }
27    public function printMessage(event:Event):void  {
28        c.text += event.target.label + " pressed" + "\n";
29    }
30  } // end public class TestMainClass
31 } // end package
```

The `package` statement is a namespace qualifier. As you saw previously in Listing 12-6, the XML namespace attribute of the `Application` tag (`xmlns:local="*"`) assigns the name to a wildcard character to specify that `mxmlc` should regard every compilation module without a specific package name as belonging to the `local` namespace. When the `mxmlc` compiler looks for elements to satisfy references to `local:MainClass`, it finds the `MainClass.as` defined in Listing 12-7 in the same folder as `Main.MXML`. In the MXML file, it seems that whatever is within the application will be in `MainClass.as`.

Remember that the way the `mxmlc` compiler works is that it converts MXML into ActionScript anyway, so there should be no surprise that this coding style works well. The first order of business in `MainClass.as` is to import all the `flash` and `mx` packages needed in the class.

As you can see from the declaration of `MainClass.as`, the MXML main application uses only publicly visible classes. The `private` attribute may be used only on class property definitions, and as you can see from the declarations of the `Button`, `ComboBox`, and `TextInput` components, these should (in true fashion for this mutant branch of the Java family tree) be declared `private`, because (in theory at least) they should remain immune from external manipulation outside the boundaries of the class itself.

Listing 12-7 compiles into the SWF file and the resulting application shown in Figure 12-7 Although the figure doesn't show it, you could as easily apply the styles from Listing 12-5 here as well. The ActionScript version is not as compact as the MXML version. You can see that each attribute is specified on a separate line of code, and the arguments to the event handler are perhaps more verbose. Other than these details, the functionality is essentially the same. One difference is that you must explicitly add a component to the container through `addChild()` in order for it to become visible and operable. In this case, `MainClass` extends the `Canvas` container, which is a weak layout manager, and the `Canvas` and all its contained items are contained by the `Application` itself.

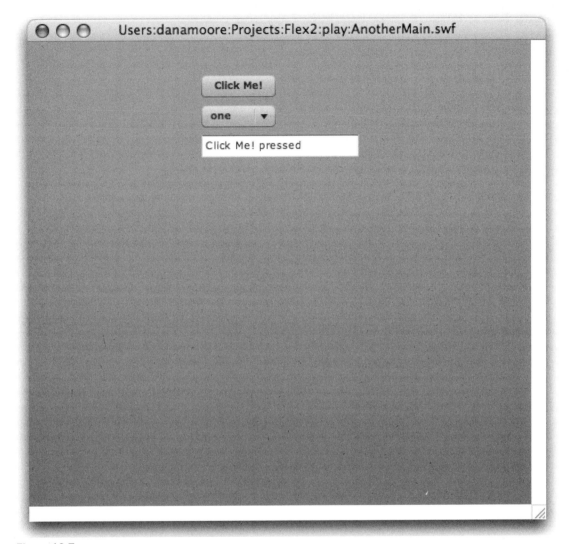

Figure 12-7

In Listing 12-7, a ComboBox was added to illustrate the use of a data provider. You haven't seen this implementation yet, but it will be a significant part of the Flex and TurboGears shown as the application example for this chapter. A component can have a data provider, which in this case is just an array of strings. More usefully, an external (URL-style) data provider can support and update a component. Knowing this, you might already be assuming that controllers.py would make a pretty fine data provider; and you would be correct in your assumptions, as you'll soon see.

Simple Tester Version 3 — Attribute Customization

The point of this example is to illustrate that in addition to (or in place of) CSS, you can very specifically manipulate the attributes of a component, and in particular its visual attributes. You do this with an MXML specification like Listing 12-8.

Listing 12-8: ThirdAndMain.mxml

```
<?xml version="1.0"?>
<mx:Application xmlns:mx="http://www.adobe.com/2006/mxml">
    <mx:Script>
        <![CDATA[

            import flash.events.Event;
            private function printMessage(event:Event):void {
              message.text += event.target.id + " pressed" + "\n";
            }
        ]]>
    </mx:Script>
    <mx:Panel title="Button Control Example"
        height="75%" width="75%" layout="horizontal"
        paddingTop="10" paddingBottom="10" paddingLeft="10" paddingRight="10">
        <mx:VBox>
            <mx:Label width="100%" color="blue" text="Select a Button control."/>
            <!-- The button can contain an image -->
            <mx:Button id="iconButton" icon="@Embed('assets/bbn_logo.gif')"
                label="iconic"
                color="#993300" click="printMessage(event);"/>

            <mx:Button label="Custom Button" id="Custom" color="#993300"
                toggle="true" selected="true"
                textAlign="left" fontStyle="italic" fontSize="13"
                width="{iconButton.width}"
                click="printMessage(event);"/>
            <!-- The look and feel of the customized button is
                similar to the Default Button.  -->
            <mx:Button label="Default Button" id="Default"
click="printMessage(event);"/>
        </mx:VBox>
        <mx:TextArea id="message" text="" editable="false" height="100%"
width="100%"
                color="#0000FF"/>
    </mx:Panel>
</mx:Application>
```

As you see in Figure 12-8, the look and feel of the application is quite detailed and exhibits per-component tailoring.

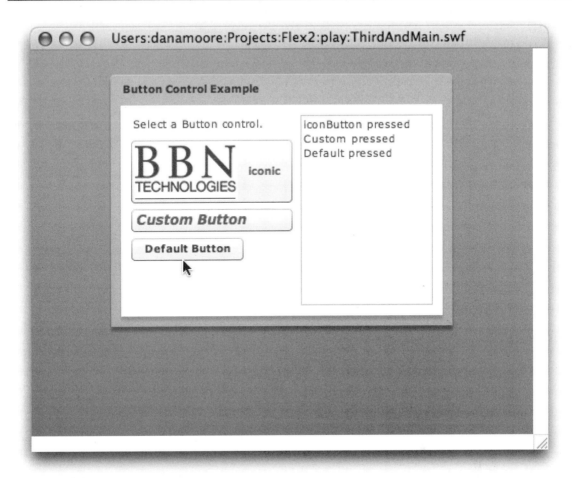

Figure 12-8

Adding Effects

RIAs should provide the same level of user experience as Rich Client Platform (RCP) applications, and increasingly, they do. A hallmark of RIAs is their apparent ease of use when compared to RCPs. Some have argued that RCPs are intended to be used by highly trained employees in the enterprise, whereas RIAs must rely on appealing to a wider audience. RIAs have to deliver a better end-user experience rather than relying on organizational mandates to force usage. RIA UIs that are not self-evident or that are unintuitive will not survive long.

In this regard, effects are not simply eye candy or an attempt to cover up bad design (although they have served both purposes from time to time). Effects, when applied correctly, provide users with cues about the current context of the application. With MXML, you declaratively set up effects, often as an attribute of a component, and then satisfy the logic of the effects.

Listing 12-9 illustrates an effect from the Flex library of behaviors. This example applies the Move effect to move a graphic to the focus of the mouse click on the background canvas. As with previous examples in the chapter, you can compile this with mxmlc and run it directly with a double-click of the SWF file. In the next mini-project (FBlog) you will need to embed the compiled SWF into an HTML file for reasons that will be explained in greater detail then.

Listing 12-9: EffectsSample.mxml

```xml
<?xml version="1.0"?>
<mx:Application xmlns:mx="http://www.adobe.com/2006/mxml">
    <mx:Script>
        <![CDATA[
            private function moveImage():void {
                myMove.end();
                myMove.xTo=mouseX-60;
                myMove.play();
            }
        ]]>
    </mx:Script>
    <mx:Move id="myMove" target="{img}"/>
    <mx:Panel title="Move Effect Example" width="95%" height="95%"
        paddingTop="5" paddingLeft="10" paddingRight="10" paddingBottom="5">
        <mx:Text width="100%" color="blue"
            text="Click anywhere on the canvas to move the image horizontally to ⤴
that position"/>
            <mx:Canvas id="canvas" width="100%" height="100% "mouseDown="moveImage();">
                <mx:Image id="img" source="@Embed(source='assets/bbn_logo.png')"/>
            </mx:Canvas>
    </mx:Panel>
</mx:Application>
```

This listing sets up a Canvas element that is sensitive to mouse clicks ("mouseDown="moveImage();"). It embeds an image, giving it an id of img, so that the ActionScript logic has a handle to the image. The user of the @Embed directive (a feature you're seeing for the first time) assures that the image will be compiled into the resulting SWF file so it is available to the Flex application regardless of which website it's deployed from. ActionScript is invoked on mouseDown, and the logic of the move is provided by the moveImage method. The Move tag is one of the effects available in the Flex 2 library of effects elements. Its target attribute instructs the player on the item to be moved. Note the succinctness of this tag. Once again, it's a declaration of what you want to have happen, but not how to do it — a hallmark of a DSL. A screen shot of the resulting application is shown in Figure 12-9.

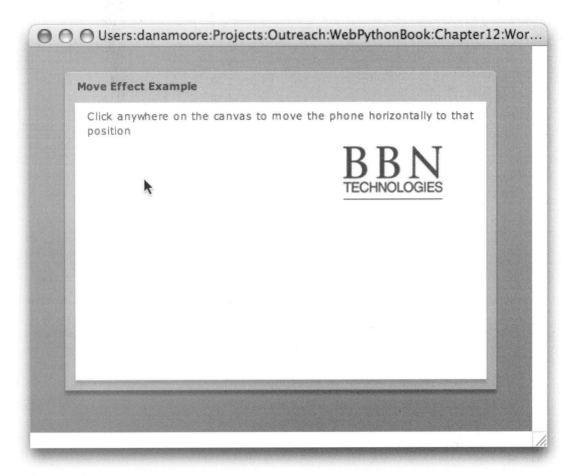

Figure 12-9

For additional exploration of effects (as well as containers and components), the samples folder included with the Flex2 SDK is an excellent place to begin. Try invoking the ~/samples/explorer/ explorer.html file and looking at the examples (each of which has been generated from an MXML file, exactly as you're doing in this chapter).

Figure 12-10 shows a screen shot with the index tree of potential choices, plus a mini-application that uses the effect and the MXML source code for the application with the embedded effect below it.

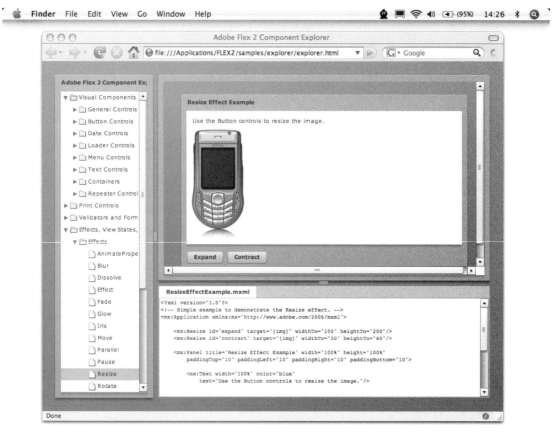

Figure 12-10

A Flex2-Based Blog

This chapter concludes with an application type that has become a venerable tradition — another blog. Blogs have been big in this book. You've created two blogs so far — one in TurboGear and one in Django. Why not a third? Only this time, you'll use your newly gained and freshly practiced skills with Flash to flex your Flex.

This blog application is illustrated in Figure 12-11. Initially only a list of blog subjects is shown. When a list item is clicked (Lorem Ipsum in this case) a window slides right and the blog entry surfaces, available for viewing and editing as shown in Figure 12-12. If the end user clicks the Save button, the content is written back to the data model. If the user clicks the New button, whatever subject and detail have been entered are saved as a new record.

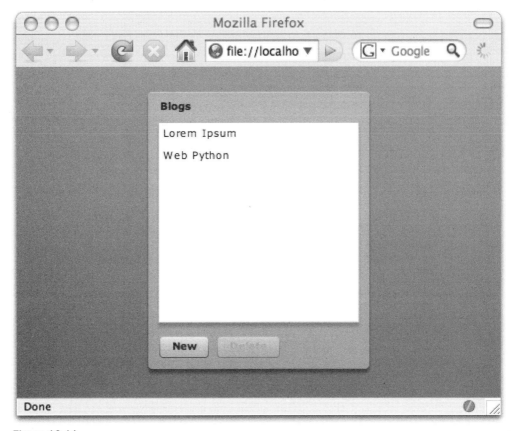

Figure 12-11

The Supporting Model

As always in TurboGear, you begin by using `tg-admin quickstart` to create the project. Call this one FBlog (for Flex Blog). This will create the `fblog` folder and contents and, as usual, stub versions of model and controllers. The model will be trivially simple, containing just a subject and the text of the entry. Because it's neat to be able to support rich text in a blog, FBlog uses a `RichTextEditor` component; thus the model will use SQLite, which supports the Unicode type natively (MySQL doesn't).

That's really all the object support you'll need for this application. The model is shown in Listing 12-10.

Listing 12-10: model.py for FBlog

```
from turbogears.database import PackageHub
from sqlobject import *
hub = PackageHub("fblog")
__connection__ = hub
class FBlog(SQLObject):
    subject = UnicodeCol()
    entry = UnicodeCol()
```

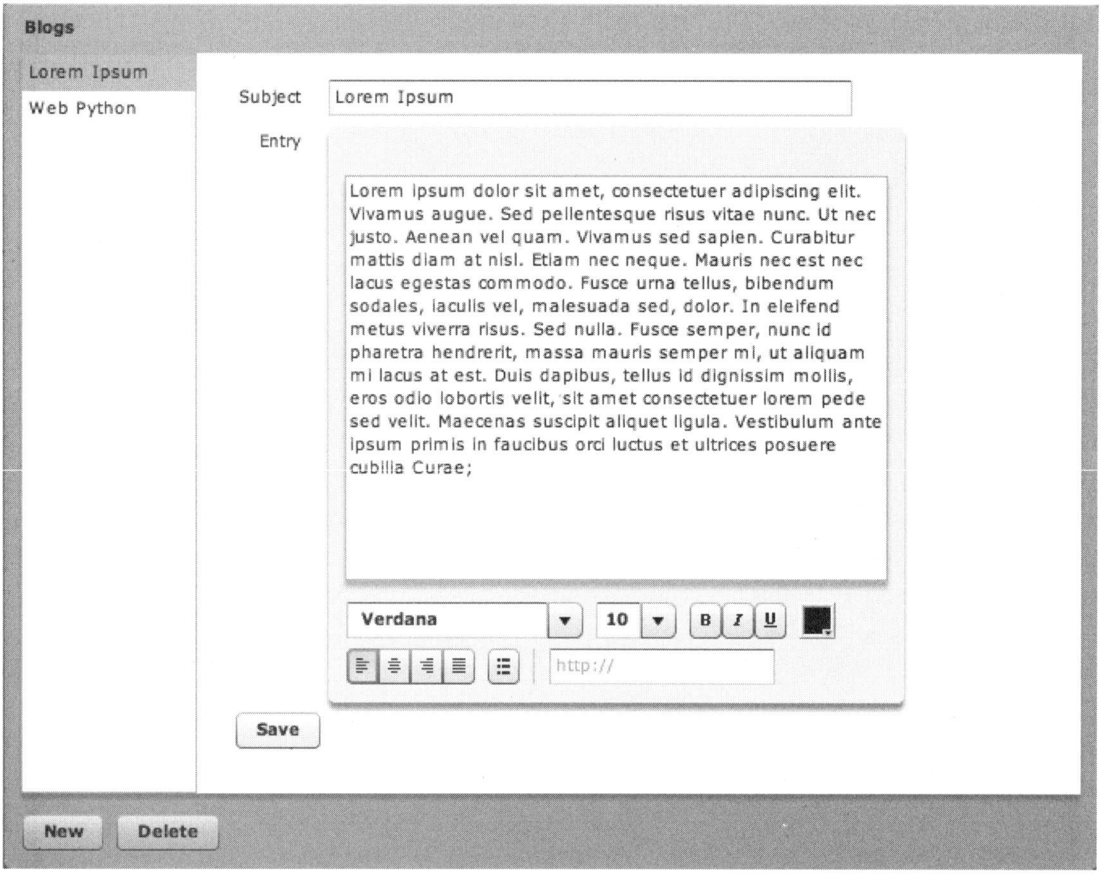

Figure 12-12

The Application Controller

The interactive model for FBlog will support `add`, `change`, and `delete` blog entries as dictated by user interaction with the Flex components. You won't be using any of the templates in this application, so the controller decorators don't reference them. The `controllers.py` file shown in Listing 12-11 provides the interface between the model and the visual interface.

Listing 12-11: controllers.py for FBlog

```
1 from turbogears import controllers, expose, flash, redirect,url
2 from turbogears.toolbox import catwalk
3 from model import *
4 import logging, time
5 from docutils.core import publish_parts
6
7 from fblog import json
8 log = logging.getLogger("fblog.controllers")
9 class Root(controllers.RootController):
10     catwalk = catwalk.CatWalk()
11     @expose()
12     @expose("json")
13     def index(self):
14        fblog = FBlog.select()
15        return dict(fblog=fblog)
16
17     @expose()
18     def save(self, id=None, subject="", entry=""):
19         if not id:
20             blog = FBlog(subject=subject, entry=entry)
21         else:
22             blog = FBlog.get(id)
23             blog.subject = subject
24             blog.entry = entry
25         return dict()
26
27     @expose()
28     def delete(self, id):
29         blog = FBlog.get(id)
30         blog.destroySelf()   # yet another marvelous method on SQLObject
31         return dict()
```

On lines 11, 17, and 27 of this listing, the simple @expose statements merely make the methods available to the web server. The expose decorator at line 12 tells the index method to output the response as JSON.

The index method will be called on to populate the list of subjects of the blog entries whenever a screen refresh is needed. Because the select statement (line 14) is unqualified, it selects and returns all FBlog records (line 15).

The save method (line 18) enables the user to both modify current records and save new records. This method uses a trivial differentiator to decide whether it's being handed a new record or a modification to a current one: The default value for the record ID is None. As defined on line 13, the index method returns all existing FBlog records. The entire record is returned (including its id) and used to populate a list of blog entries. Thus, if an object is handed back to the save method without the optional id argument (line 19), it's assumed to be a new record and a new FBlog entry is constructed (line 20). Otherwise, the existing record is fetched, and the subject and entry fields are updated (lines 21 through 24). Because the method must return a dictionary by convention, it returns an empty one (line 25).

The delete method (lines 28 through 30) will expect the ID of an existing record, fetch it, and use the destroySelf method to delete it from the backing store.

Three fairly simple methods should be kept in mind in the design of the front-end, the next stop on the tour.

The Flex Front-End

The first three Flex examples in this chapter were pretty simple, but they illustrated the spectrum of expression you can achieve when you use a combination of MXML and ActionScript. This example extends your Flex vocabulary by showing visual effects, state transitions, variables binding, and communications with a TurboGears back-end.

If you choose to download and plug in the free trial version of the Flex IDE for Eclipse, create a new Flex project and call it FBlog. Figure 12-13 shows the code view. You can switch between this view and the visual design view shown in Figure 12-14, and the code and design will remain synchronized.

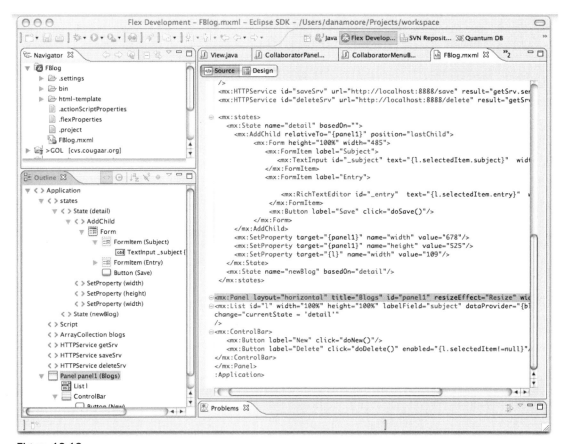

Figure 12-13

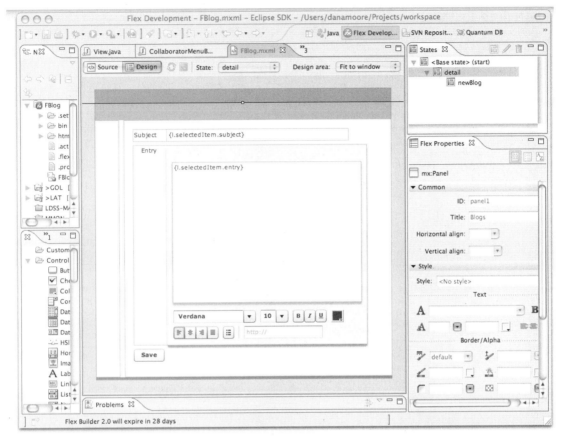

Figure 12-14

FBlog's MXML Implementation

The design view in Figure 12-14 shows the visual elements of the application as well as a property editor. For example, the major elements of the application are shown in a visual designer panel in the middle of the figure. In addition to containers (`Panel`) and components (`Buttons`, `TextInputs`, and `RichTextEditors`), the view in the right-side panel also displays other items called *states*. These are interesting nonvisual elements of the design, and are discussed in more detail in the next section.

Listing 12-12 shows the MXML code for the FBlog application in its entirety, and then critical sections are discussed in the sections that follow the listing.

Listing 12-12: FBlog.mxml

```
 1 <?xml version="1.0"?> 1 <?xml version="1.0"?>
 2 <!--
 3 in order to avoid security complaints, this MXML file
 4 should be run in an HTML file called with local file URL semantics:
 5 for example: file://localhost/Users/Projects/FBlog/bin/FBlog.html
 6 This will permit it to make the localhost:8888 calls specified
 7 in the HTTPService tags.
 8 -->
 9 <mx:Application xmlns:mx="http://www.adobe.com/2006/mxml"
       layout="vertical" creationComplete="getSrv.send()">
10     <mx:Script><![CDATA[
11         import flash.system.Security;
12          Security.allowDomain("127.0.0.1");
13         import com.adobe.serialization.json.JSON;
14         private function handleGetResult():void {
15             var decoded:Object=JSON.decode(getSrv.lastResult.toString());
16             blogs=new ArrayCollection(decoded.fblog);
17         }
18         private function doSave():void {
19             var newBlogItem:Object = new Object();
20             if (currentState=='detail'){
21                 newBlogItem.id = l.selectedItem.id;
22             }
23             newBlogItem.subject = _subject.text;
24             newBlogItem.entry = _entry.text;
25             saveSrv.send(newBlogItem);
26             currentState = "";
27         }
28         private function doNew():void{
29             currentState = 'newBlog' ;
30             l.selectedIndex = -1;
31         }
32         private function doDelete():void{
33             deleteSrv.send({id: l.selectedItem.id});
34             currentState = '';
35         }
36     ]]></mx:Script>
37
38     <mx:ArrayCollection id="blogs"/>
39     <mx:HTTPService id="getSrv"
40         url="http://localhost:8888/?tg_format=json"
41         resultFormat="text" result="handleGetResult()"
42     />
43     <mx:HTTPService id="saveSrv"
        url="http://localhost:8888/save" result="getSrv.send()" />
44     <mx:HTTPService id="deleteSrv"
        url="http://localhost:8888/delete" result="getSrv.send()" />
45
```

```
46      <mx:states>
47        <mx:State name="detail" basedOn="">
48          <mx:AddChild relativeTo="{panel1}" position="lastChild">
49              <mx:Form height="100%">
50                  <mx:FormItem label="Subject">
51                      <mx:TextInput id="_subject"
                            text="{l.selectedItem.subject}" />
52                  </mx:FormItem>
53                  <mx:FormItem label="Entry">
54                      <mx:TextArea id="_entry"
                            text="{l.selectedItem.entry}" />
55                  </mx:FormItem>
56                  <mx:Button label="Save" click="doSave()"/>
57              </mx:Form>
58          </mx:AddChild>
59        </mx:State>
60        <mx:State name="newBlog" basedOn="detail"/>
61      </mx:states>
62
63      <mx:Panel layout="horizontal" title="Blogs" id="panel1"
        resizeEffect="Resize">
64      <mx:List id="l" width="100%" height="100%" labelField="subject"
         dataProvider="{blogs}"
65      change="currentState = 'detail'"
66      />
67      <mx:ControlBar>
68          <mx:Button label="New" click="doNew()"/>
69          <mx:Button label="Delete" click="doDelete()"
                enabled="{l.selectedItem!=null}"/>
70      </mx:ControlBar>
71      </mx:Panel>
72 </mx:Application>
```

Deconstructing FBlog

As you have seen in the chapter's previous examples, the application must be the XML DOM parent of all contained objects. Some of these objects are typically visual, and others are not. For example, there are State tags (lines 46 through 61 of Listing 12-12) that declare a certain visual context. If the currentState global variable is set to a different state, that part of the GUI is surfaced and focused. You might think of this mechanism as implementing a finite state machine in a (mostly) declarative fashion, where the state transitions are managed not by you directly but by the underlying Flash platform.

The Application tag has the equivalent of an OnLoad attribute on an HTML <body> tag. It instructs the Flash player to call getsrv.send() when the load of the SWF file into the browser is complete. Getsrv is an HTTPService (declared on line 39).

There are three HTTPService declarative tags in this application. There are also three URL destinations (index, save, and delete) in the controller (as shown previously in Listing 12-11). Not surprisingly, each declarative tags shown in Listing 12-12 maps to one of the controller methods.

At line 13, the `Application` mixes in a little secret sauce:

```
import com.adobe.serialization.json.JSON;
```

To manipulate (both read and write) JSON directly from the `index` method in `controller.py`, you need to download a library called `corelib.swc` from the Flex developer's site (which you can find at `http://as3corelib.googlecode.com/files/corelib-.90.zip` as well as other mirror sites). In the Flex world, SWF libraries are called `.swc` files. To install these files in your development path, unzip the `corelib.zip` to a location in your hard disk.

Using the Flex Eclipse Plug-In

If you are using the Eclipse Flex IDE plug-in, go to the Navigator view in the Flex Development Perspective, and then create a new folder named `lib` by right-clicking the project folder. Copy the `corelib.swc` file from the `bin` folder of the unzipped `corelib` folder, and paste it in the newly created `lib` folder of the project.

Flex Builder still needs to know that `corelib` is associated with this project, so you need to specify it as an external library in the Flex build path. If you're following along and building everything by hand, just include the library in the compilation of the MXML file into an SWF file with a compile line option. For example, a simple build file for Linux and Mac OS X systems would modify Listing 12-3 to include the following optional libraries:

```
(${FLEX_HOME}/bin/mxmlc $OPTS -library_path+=<thePlaceWhereYouPutCoreLib> ${mxml})
```

FBlog Event Handlers

The `handleGetResult` function is implemented starting at line 13 in Listing 12-12, and it has the optional (and verbose for any Python programmer) return specified as `void`. This function responds asynchronously to the `HTTPService` tag (lines 39 through 42). The URL is specified as `http://localhost:8888/?tg_format=json`. Thus, the function will return its data as JSON, as indicated by the `tg_format=json` parameter passed to the HTTP GET Request URL, and it will expect its data to be returned this way. You can prove this yourself by simply invoking the index page using the same URL the application will use. Remember from Listing 12-11 that there's no template for the index page and that the Python `index` method returns a dictionary. The following is a sample of what the blog entries would look like (a form you saw in Chapter 6, "Widgets," and elsewhere in this book):

```
{"tg_flash": null,
 "fblog": [{"entry":
              "id": 1,
              "Lorem ipsum dolor sit amet, consectetuer adipiscing elit. ",
              "subject": "Lorem Ipsum"}
          ]}
```

Because the callback handler in the FBlog application also expects to work with dictionaries, this turns out to be a very happy conjunction of programming paradigms, as you can see here:

```
private function handleGetResult():void {
        var decoded:Object= JSON.decode(getSrv.lastResult.toString());
        blogs = new ArrayCollection(decoded.fblog);
}
```

The `handleGetResult` method creates an `Object` from the JSON dictionary. The `blogs` variable is an `ArrayCollection`, which is an ActionScript addition to the basic JavaScript `Collection` class. `ArrayCollection` is an associative array structured just like a Python dictionary. `"blogs"` is declared as an `ArrayCollection` on line 38 of Listing 12-12, giving it global scope in the `Application` DOM. Note that the `id` attribute gives a name to the `blogs` variable, thereby making it available for reference (as on line 15).

The `doSave` method constructs an object on the fly based on bits and pieces from the list and from the detail containers, as follows:

```
private function doSave():void {
        var newBlogItem:Object = new Object();
        if (currentState=='detail'){
           newBlogItem.id = l.selectedItem.id;
        }
        newBlogItem.subject = _subject.text;
        newBlogItem.entry = _entry.text;
        saveSrv.send(newBlogItem);
        currentState = "";
    }
```

Creating States

There are three states (roughly corresponding to TurboGears views) in FBlog. You can see the declaration of two named states, `detail` and `newBlog`, on lines 47 and 60. A third state is the basic (or default) state, which is unnamed. Whenever the global variable `currentState` is modified, its value (which must be `State`) is entered. When the basic state is entered, the list of blog topics is shown. In order for the detail state to become active, an item must be selected from the list. This action is implemented within the `List` tag at line 64 of Listing 12-12. (This tag will be explored more fully in short order.)

The `doNew` method is both succinct and elegantly expressive, as shown in the following code snippet from Listing 12-12 (lines 28–31):

```
private function doNew():void{
    currentState = 'newBlog' ;
    l.selectedIndex = -1;
}
```

Because the purpose of `doNew` is to record a new blog entry, you want to assure two things: that the `newBlog` state becomes current, and that the list is deselected. Because `newBlog` is derived from the `detail` state, it shares `detail`'s visual elements.

The `doDelete` method is equally elegant code, as shown in the following code snippet from Listing 12-12 (lines 32–35):

```
private function doDelete():void{
    deleteSrv.send({id: l.selectedItem.id});
    currentState = '';
}
```

This method takes the ID of the selected item and constructs an anonymous dictionary that will be passed as a part of the HTTP request (line 44 of Listing 12-12). Remember from Listing 12-11 (`controllers.py`) that the `delete` method accepts the system-generated ID of the record to be deleted. Right after the asynchronous call is made, `currentState` is assigned the default string. The detail panel slides shut, and FBlog shifts back to the simple list view.

You might be wondering how you assure that there's a good selected item in the list. The `doDelete` method is activated via the Delete button shown previously in Figure 12-11. Notice that the Delete button is disabled in that figure. A final detail in the Delete button's declaration takes care of assuring that a valid item has been selected for deletion before the button is activated. This declaration is as follows:

```
<mx:Button label="Delete" click="doDelete()" enabled="{l.selectedItem!=null}"/>
```

In ActionScript, an attribute's value may be set to the result of a computational expression, which you indicate within curly braces as shown here (the same convention is used on lines 51 and 54 of Listing 12-12). The ActionScript name for this capability is *binding expression*. The tag's `enabled` attribute uses the value of the binding expression to enable and disable the button. Thus, the end user can't delete a record unless one is selected.

Connecting to TurboGears

Lines 38 through 44 of Listing 12-12 are declarations of the connections to the TurboGear controller. The following code snippet shows these declarations again for quick reference:

```
<mx:ArrayCollection id="blogs"/>
    <mx:HTTPService id="getSrv"
        url="http://localhost:8888/?tg_format=json"
        resultFormat="text" result="handleGetResult()"
    />
    <mx:HTTPService id="saveSrv" url="http://localhost:8888/save"
     result="getSrv.send()" />
    <mx:HTTPService id="deleteSrv" url="http://localhost:8888/delete"
     result="getSrv.send()" />
```

Whenever a record is being saved (either as a new record or as an update of a current one), or when one is deleted, the list is always completely refreshed. This is implemented again by a `tag` attribute. The `result` attribute can be set to a function, either within FBlog or via a URL reference. In both cases, the trick is that you always invoke the `send` method of the `getSrv` request in `HTTPService`. In turn, `GetSrv` always transfers flow control to the `handleGetResult` method (line 14 of Listing 12-12). As explained previously, its job is simply to refresh the list.

More FBlog Flow Control

Lines 46 through 61 of Listing 12-12 are the declarations for the various states. The `addChild` DOM element functions just like an `addChild` method in ActionScript, and there's a corresponding `removeChild` tag as well. Through the use of these `add` and `remove` tags, you can dynamically control the inclusion and exclusion of elements from the `Application` DOM. The existence of such tags should not be surprising — as mentioned earlier, MXML is turned into ActionScript prior to compilation.

Form Handling

In the following `Form` construction (excerpted from Listing 12-12, lines 49–57), the values of the Subject and Entry fields are supplied by the `List` object:

```
<mx:states>
        <mx:State name="detail" basedOn="">
          <mx:AddChild relativeTo="{panel1}" position="lastChild">
              <mx:Form height="100%">
                  <mx:FormItem label="Subject">
                      <mx:TextInput id="_subject" text="{l.selectedItem.subject}" />
                  </mx:FormItem>
                  <mx:FormItem label="Entry">
                      <mx:TextArea id="_entry" text="{l.selectedItem.entry}" />
                   </mx:FormItem>
                   <mx:Button label="Save" click="doSave()"/>
              </mx:Form>
          </mx:AddChild>
        </mx:State>
        <mx:State name="newBlog" basedOn="detail"/>
      </mx:states>
```

Just as a reminder, even though the blog's `ArrayCollection` constructed from the controller shows only the topic in the `List` state, it contains the entire content of the set of records, so when program flow is transferred to the `detail` state the selected item's parts are available through simple dot notation (such as `l.selectedItem.subject`) to populate the form.

As may be discerned from Figures 12-11 and 12-12, there is a `ControlBar` containing a pair of simple buttons. These are wired to the `doNew` and `doDelete` methods (discussed previously) as follows:

```
<mx:ControlBar>
    <mx:Button label="New" click="doNew()"/>
    <mx:Button label="Delete" click="doDelete()"
     enabled="{l.selectedItem!=null}"/>
</mx:ControlBar>
```

Deploying FBlog

There you have it. A complete and pretty useful application in fewer than 200 lines of code. In order to access the previous applications in this chapter, you used the Flash Player included with the Flex2 SDK. You got away with this because there are no outbound `HTTPService` requests being made. In the FBlog application, however, you access the model through calls to the controller. The Flex sandbox model won't allow the application to operate by making HTTP requests in this way.

This necessitates that the FBlog SWF be contained by an HTML page, and preferably one in the same domain as the controller. Otherwise, you will be making a so-called *cross-domain* call, which is forbidden in modern browsers. You may be familiar with ways around this limitation, the most common being a `crossdomain.xml` file installed at the root of the web server that serves up the page. That's out of the scope of this chapter, though. However, take a quick look at Listing 12-13, which shows a typical HTML file in the context of the FBlog.

Listing 12-13: FBlog.html

```
 1 <html lang="en">
 2 <head>
 3 <meta http-equiv="Content-Type" content="text/html; charset=utf-8" />
 4 <title>FBlog</title>
 5 <style>
 6 body { margin: 0px; overflow:hidden }
 7 </style>
 8 </head>
 9
10 <body scroll='no'>
11 <object classid="clsid:D27CDB6E-AE6D-11cf-96B8-444553540000"
12    id="FBlog" width="100%" height="100%"
13                        codebase= ↵
"http://fpdownload.macromedia.com/get/flashplayer/current/swflash.cab">
14    <param name="movie" value="FBlog.swf" />
15    <param name="quality" value="high" />
16    <param name="bgcolor" value="#869ca7" />
17
18    <param name="allowScriptAccess" value="sameDomain" />
19    <embed src="FBlog.swf" quality="high" bgcolor="#869ca7"
20     width="100%" height="100%" name="FBlog" align="middle"
21    play="true"
22    loop="false"
23    quality="high"
24    allowScriptAccess="sameDomain"
25    type="application/x-shockwave-flash"
26    pluginspage="http://www.adobe.com/go/getflashplayer">
27          </embed>
28          </object>
29 </body>
30 </html>
```

For the purposes of illustration, much of this HTML file is boilerplate code. One thing you should note, however, is that you must embed the name of the Flex SWF file into the HTML page, as shown on line 19. You almost always want to make the SWF occupy all of the available browser screen real estate as specified on line 20. Additionally, you want to allow script access to the same domain while in testing and development, as line 18 and 24 indicate.

Don't forget that to test FBlog, you will need to first start your CherryPy server and then bring up FBlog.html.

Summary

This chapter presented an alternative method for developing RIAs in conjunction with a Python web framework. A prominent feature of Flex is that it's a domain-specific language (DSL) and thus it relies on code generation to reduce the amount of code a developer has to write by hand. Its succinctness is something all Python programmers will appreciate.

Using the open source Flex DSL, you can create a complete user experience and be assured of cross-browser compatibility. Flex has evolved from its roots in Flash, and it is several huge steps beyond the original creators' intent of developing a tool to make movie-like web pages. Now it's become an exciting new way to develop RIAs using a mixture of a declarative XML-based language for laying out UIs and ActionScript for providing custom logic in the UI. ActionScript is a next-generation ECMAScript with extra features like optional static type checking.

Flex and ActionScript can be considered a language that works across all platforms, as a plug-in to all popular browsers. MXML components are actually written in ActionScript, and you can write additional components in ActionScript or add capabilities to existing ones. Flex applications compile directly into SWFs (Flash binaries), which are then just-in-time (JIT) compilations provided by the Flash runtime for extra speed. For example, SWF binaries are very compact compared to Java applets.

As this book is being published, Flex is in the process of becoming open source software (OSS) licensed. You can already develop and deploy Flex-based RIAs without cost, but OSS means more than that. Here are some of the benefits that Flex evangelist James Ward says may result from this bold step by Adobe:

❑   There will be a formal process for contributing to Flex.

❑   You won't be locked into a single vendor's monetization strategy. Flex becomes part of the *Open Web*.

❑   You have more rapid innovation. Although Adobe has some really smart people, when they team up with many other really smart and passionate OSS developers, they may come up with a Flex version that's a tipping point in application design and development.

❑   Flex is bigger than Adobe. Watch for many big organizations to further invest in Flex.

❑   Open source Flex will further stimulate the already-booming Flex ecosystem.

Tools Used

This appendix includes all the information you need to know to get up and running with the tools used in this book. All of the tools that have been used in this book are free or open source software, so it's not a matter of expense to buy the software, but sometimes it can be quite a chore to scour the Internet looking for tools, and it can be equally difficult to get them to all work together after you've found them. Hopefully, this appendix can help ease some of that pain.

OS Versions Used

There are three sections in this appendix, one for each of the three operating systems that we think are most common: Windows XP, Mac OS X, and Linux. Each section covers the tools used in the book. The versions of software that the authors used to develop the examples in the book are listed in the following table. That's not to say that you can't use other versions, but your mileage may vary, as they say.

Software Package	Version
Microsoft Windows	XP Service Pack 2
Apple Mac OS	OS X 10.4
Linux	Fedora Core 5
TurboGears	1.0.1
Django	0.96
Python	2.4.4
Apache HTTP Server	2.2.4
SQLite	2.3.3
Firefox	2.0.0.3
pysqlite	2.3.2

Installing Tools in Windows

Installation of the tools under Windows XP is straightforward, but it does require some big downloads. Some of the installations are online installations that download and install packages as needed from the Internet. Obviously, you need to be connected to the Internet to download these packages.

Python

Although the 2.5 version of Python has been available for some time, as of this writing many of the other tools we use don't support it yet. So we'll stick with version 2.4. Download the Windows installer from `www.python.org/download/releases/2.4.4/`. There are separate versions for x86 and Win64-Itanium processors. We used the x86 version for this book, but you should get the version that's appropriate for your setup. Python is distributed as Microsoft Installer (MSI) files, so all you have to do is download `python-2.4.4.msi` and run it, and it will walk you through the rest.

After the installation has completed, add Python to your path so you can run it from the command line. Here are the steps:

1. Right-click My Computer and select Properties.

2. Click the Advanced tab, and then click Environment Variables.

3. Edit the PATH variable to include `C:\Python24;C:\Python24\Scripts`. You will have to change these paths if you installed Python somewhere besides the default location.

TurboGears

The TurboGears `easy_install` tool makes installing TurboGears a snap. First, make sure you have Python 2.4 installed, and then go to `www.turbogears.org/` and click the Download Now link. Follow the instructions to download the `tgsetup.py` script, and run it from a command-line prompt. You'll see it chug away and download a couple dozen egg files.

After `easy_install` finishes, run the following `tg-admin` command to make sure everything is set up correctly:

```
G:\temp>tg-admin info
TurboGears Complete Version Information
TurboGears requires:
* turbogears 1.0.1
* configobj 4.3.2
* ruledispatch 0.5a0.dev-r2115
* setuptools 0.6c3
* formencode 0.6
* celementtree 1.0.5-20051216
* pastescript 1.1
* elementtree 1.2.6-20050316
* simplejson 1.5
* cherrypy 2.2.1
* turbokid 0.9.9
* turbocheetah 0.9.5
* turbojson 1.0
```

```
* pyprotocols 1.0a0dev-r2082
* cheetah 2.0rc7
* pastedeploy 1.1
* paste 1.1.1
* kid 0.9.5
* cheetah 2.0rc7
Identity Providers
* sqlobject (turbogears 1.0.1)
* sqlalchemy (turbogears 1.0.1)
tg-admin Commands
* info (turbogears 1.0.1)
* shell (turbogears 1.0.1)
* quickstart (turbogears 1.0.1)
* update (turbogears 1.0.1)
* sql (turbogears 1.0.1)
* i18n (turbogears 1.0.1)
* toolbox (turbogears 1.0.1)
Visit Managers
* sqlobject (turbogears 1.0.1)
* sqlalchemy (turbogears 1.0.1)
Template Engines
* kid (turbokid 0.9.9)
* cheetah (turbocheetah 0.9.5)
* json (turbojson 1.0)
Widget Packages

TurboGears Extensions
* visit (turbogears 1.0.1)
* identity (turbogears 1.0.1)
```

We have never had any trouble with a Windows TurboGears installation, but there are some helpful troubleshooting tips at www.turbogears.org/download/ should you need them.

SQLite

We used SQLite for the example databases in this book because it is very simple and easy to configure. For production systems, you'll probably want to use something more robust like MySQL or PostreSQL (or even proprietary databases like Microsoft SQL Server or Oracle). The official command-line client, sqlite.exe, is available from www.sqlite.org/download.html as a precompiled binary and is handy to have around for quick database operations.

For those times when a GUI database browser is useful, a simple GUI client is available on SourceForge at http://sqlitebrowser.sourceforge.net/. Like most SQLite tools, this tool is a single executable file with no dependencies or installation requirements, so it's very simple to run.

pysqlite

The Python bindings for SQLite are available from www.initd.org/tracker/pysqlite. Download the Windows binary for Python 2.4 and run it. The installer will detect the location of your Python installation and install into site-packages there.

If you've already installed TurboGears, then you can try using the `easy_install` tool to grab a version that is compatible with your TurboGears install. Just type this command:

```
G:\ easy_install pysqlite
```

On some systems, this command fails with errors about mismatched versions of Visual Studio. The installer from `www.initd.org/tracker/pysqlite` seems to work more reliably.

Apache HTTP Server

The Apache HTTP Server (often just called Apache) is the most common web server on the Internet. It is very scalable and powerful, but it is not too difficult to set up for development use. To get started, download version 2.2.4 from a mirror listed at `http://httpd.apache.org/download.cgi`. Like Python, Apache comes as an MSI file, so installation is pretty simple. Just download and run `apache_2.2.4-win32-x86-no_ssl.msi`. The installation will ask you for your network domain, server name, and administrator e-mail address — these are not important for development use, so enter whatever you like. You can install the Apache HTTP Server as a Windows service running on the default HTTP port 80, but for development, we prefer to install it to run manually on port 8080. Select a Typical installation and install to the default directory in `C:\Program Files\Apache Software Foundation\Apache2.2`.

The main Apache configuration file is in `C:\Program Files\Apache Software Foundation\Apache2.2\conf\httpd.conf`. To run the CGI programs included with some of the chapters, you'll have to edit the `httpd.conf` file to tell Apache that it should execute the programs as scripts rather than just return them as text. Find the section of `httpd.conf` that starts with this token:

```
<IfModule alias_module>
```

and add a line like this:

```
ScriptAlias /ch4/cgi-bin/ "C:/Program Files/Apache Software Foundation/Apache2.2/
htdocs/ch4/cgi-bin/"
```

Of course, you should substitute the correct directory if you installed the code somewhere else.

Django

Django is built with few dependencies, so installing it is pretty easy. First, make sure you have Python 2.4 installed and download the Django code from `www.djangoproject.com/download/`. We used a release tarball for the examples in this book, but you may choose to use the development code from Subversion if you like to live on the bleeding edge. The tarball comes as a gzipped tar file, so you'll need a tool like WinZip (`www.winzip.com`) or Cygwin (`www.cygwin.com`) to unpack it. Unpack the tarball and run the standard Python `install` command as shown here:

```
G:\ tar xzf Django-0.96.tar.gz
G:\ cd Django-0.96
G:\ python setup.py install
```

`setup.py` will install the Django code in your Python `site-packages` directory. That's all there is to it.

Installing Tools on Mac OS X

Although Python comes pre-installed on Mac OS X, it's often behind the Python release cycle. You'll commonly find Python 2.3 is the rule rather than the exception, even on the newer Intel-based Macs. You really need Python 2.4, especially for TurboGears (which at the time of this writing explicitly requires Python 2.4). If you simply run the latest installer from Python.org (www.python.org/download/mac/), you should be up and running in short order. Do this before installing either Django or TurboGears to ensure the libraries are loaded in the right place relative to the upgraded Python installation.

If you already have Python 2.5 installed, or want to ensure that you're pointing to the correct Python version, you should explicitly correct your path. By default, the stock install point for Python is /System/Library/Frameworks/Python.framework/Versions/2.3/bin/python, and a symbolic link is created for it to /usr/bin/python. You want to ensure that your upgraded install point is listed somewhere *before* /usr/bin in your PATH variable, an example of which is shown here:

```
/usr/local/bin:/usr/local/sbin:/usr/local/mysql/bin:/Library/Frameworks/Python
.framework/Versions/Current/bin:/bin:/sbin:/usr/bin:/usr/sbin
```

You can ensure that you always set a correct path by editing either your .bash_login or .bash_profile file in your login folder. Typically, your .bash_profile is executed after your .bash_login when you bring up your system, so .bash_profile is a good place to tuck the following couple of lines:

```
export
PATH="/Library/Frameworks/Python.framework/Versions/Current/bin:${PATH}"
```

Beyond this, simply follow the Linux install directions listed for either Django or TurboGears.

Installing Tools in Linux

The following sections describe how you install Linux tools in Python, TurboGears, SQLite, pysqlite, Apache HTTP Server, and Django.

Python

Although the 2.5 version of Python has been available for some time, as of this writing many of the other tools we use don't support it yet. So you'll need to stick with Python 2.4. Most Linux distributions come with Python as part of the default installation, so you probably are already set up. If, for some reason, your distribution doesn't include Python, first check to see if there is an add-on package that includes it (for example, an RPM file for Red Hat's Fedora Project or a DEB file for Debian Linux). If all else fails, download the source code from www.python.org/download/releases/2.4.4/. If you download the gzipped file, unpack it with a command like this:

```
tar xzvf Python-2.4.4.tgz
```

If you download the bzip2-compressed file, unpack it like this:

```
bunzip2 -c Python-2.5.5.tar.bz2 | tar xvf -
```

Change directory into the new `Python-2.4.4` directory and type this:

```
./configure
```

This command determines your system's configuration and sets up the compile appropriately.

When the compile setup finishes, you can do the actual compile by typing:

```
make
```

After the compile finishes, install the completed products by changing to the `root` user and running this command:

```
make install
```

This installs the new Python interpreter in `/usr/local/bin`. Add this directory to your system execution path.

TurboGears

The TurboGears `easy_install` tool makes installing TurboGears a snap. Just follow these steps:

1. Make sure you have Python 2.4 installed.

2. Go to `www.turbogears.org/` and click the Download Now link.

3. Follow the instructions to download the `tgsetup.py` script. The `tgsetup.py` script will install into your Python `site-packages` directory, so you'll probably have to run it as `root` from a command-line prompt. You'll see it chug away and download a couple dozen egg files.

After `easy_install` finishes, change back to your non-root user and run the following `tg-admin` command to make sure everything is set up correctly. You may have to add `/usr/local/bin` to your `$PATH` if it isn't already there.

```
G:\temp>tg-admin info
TurboGears Complete Version Information
TurboGears requires:
* turbogears 1.0.1
* configobj 4.3.2
* ruledispatch 0.5a0.dev-r2115
* setuptools 0.6c3
* formencode 0.6
* celementtree 1.0.5-20051216
* pastescript 1.1
* elementtree 1.2.6-20050316
* simplejson 1.5
* cherrypy 2.2.1
* turbokid 0.9.9
* turbocheetah 0.9.5
* turbojson 1.0
* pyprotocols 1.0a0dev-r2082
* cheetah 2.0rc7
```

```
* pastedeploy 1.1
* paste 1.1.1
* kid 0.9.5
* cheetah 2.0rc7
Identity Providers
* sqlobject (turbogears 1.0.1)
* sqlalchemy (turbogears 1.0.1)
tg-admin Commands
* info (turbogears 1.0.1)
* shell (turbogears 1.0.1)
* quickstart (turbogears 1.0.1)
* update (turbogears 1.0.1)
* sql (turbogears 1.0.1)
* i18n (turbogears 1.0.1)
* toolbox (turbogears 1.0.1)
Visit Managers
* sqlobject (turbogears 1.0.1)
* sqlalchemy (turbogears 1.0.1)
Template Engines
* kid (turbokid 0.9.9)
* cheetah (turbocheetah 0.9.5)
* json (turbojson 1.0)
Widget Packages

TurboGears Extensions
* visit (turbogears 1.0.1)
* identity (turbogears 1.0.1)
```

`tgsetup.py` downloads the latest version of each of these tools, so your version numbers might be different. If you have trouble installing TurboGears, you might find some helpful troubleshooting tips at `www.turbogears.org/download/`.

SQLite

We used SQLite for the database examples in this book because it is very simple and easy to configure. For production systems, you'll probably want to use something more robust like MySQL or PostrgeSQL (or even proprietary databases like Microsoft SQL Server or Oracle). The official command-line client, `sqlite<version>.bin`, is available from `www.sqlite.org/download.html` as a precompiled binary and is handy to have around for quick database operations.

For those times when a GUI database browser is useful, a simple GUI client is available on SourceForge at `http://sqlitebrowser.sourceforge.net/`. Like most SQLite tools, this tool is a single executable file with no dependencies or installation requirements, so it's very simple to run.

pysqlite

The Python bindings for SQLite are available from `www.initd.org/tracker/pysqlite`. Download the Windows binary for Python 2.4 and run it. The installer will detect the location of your Python installation and install into `site-packages` there.

If you've already installed TurboGears, then you can try using the `easy_install` tool to grab a version that is compatible with your TurboGears installation. Just switch to the `root` user and type the following command:

```
# easy_install pysqlite
```

`easy_install` downloads and installs the latest pysqlite version into your `site_packages` directory.

Apache HTTP Server

The Apache HTTP server (often just called Apache) is the most common web server on the Internet. It is very scalable and powerful, but it is not too difficult to set up for development use. To get started, download version 2.2.4 from a mirror site listed at `http://httpd.apache.org/download.cgi`.

If you're using a mainstream Linux distribution like Fedora, Red Hat, or Ubuntu, you may want to just get the precompiled binary installer package that goes with your distribution. If you want to build and install it from source code, download the UNIX source and un-tar it into a directory. Then type the following command:

```
$ ./configure
```

You'll see a bunch of messages as the `configure` script determines the capabilities of your system.

After `configure` finishes, you can do the compiling by just running this command:

```
$ make
```

After the `make` process finishes, switch to the `root` user and run the following command to install the server:

```
# make install
```

This installs your server in `/usr/local/apache2`.

Start the server by running this command (also as `root`):

```
# /usr/local/apache2/bin/apachectl start
```

The main Apache configuration file is in `/usr/local/apache2/conf/httpd.conf`. To run the CGI programs included with some of the chapters, you'll have to edit the `httpd.conf` file to tell Apache that it should execute the programs as scripts rather than just return them as text. Find the section of `httpd.conf` that starts with this token:

```
<IfModule alias_module>
```

and add a line like this:

```
ScriptAlias /ch4/cgi-bin/ "/usr/local/apache2/htdocs/ch4/cgi-bin/"
```

Of course, you should substitute the correct directory if you installed the code somewhere else.

Django

Django is built with few dependencies, so installing it is pretty easy. Just follow these steps:

1. Make sure you have Python 2.4 installed, and download the Django code from www.djangoproject.com/download/. We used a release tarball for the examples in this book, but you may choose to use the development code from Subversion if you like to live on the bleeding edge.

2. The tarball comes as a gzipped tar file, so you need a tool like WinZip (www.winzip.com) or Cygwin (www.cygwin.com) to unpack it.

3. Unpack the tarball and run the standard Python install command like this:

```
$ tar xzf Django-0.96.tar.gz
$ cd Django-0.96
# python setup.py install
```

Note that you'll probably have to run the last command as root because setup.py installs the Django code in your Python site-packages directory. That's all there is to it.

Index

W